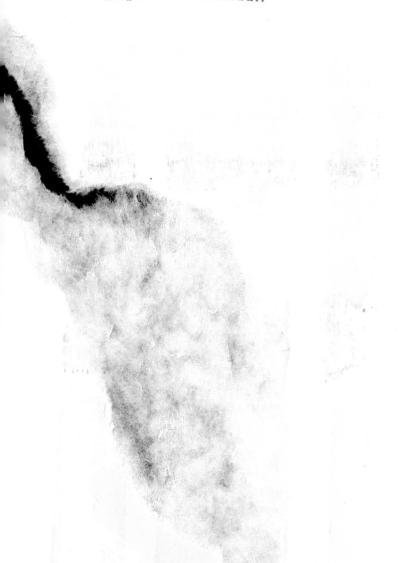

PENGUIN BOOKS

WEST OF EDEN

Frank Rose was born and raised in Virginia and educated at Washington and Lee University. For the past fifteen years he has worked as a journalist in New York City, reporting on technology, the arts, and popular culture for a variety of publications, including *Esquire, Vanity Fair, The New York Times Magazine,* and *The Nation.* He has written extensively about California lifestyles, from the Christian surfers of Los Angeles to the New Age technophiles of Santa Cruz. His previous book, *Into the Heart of the Mind,* described the groundbreaking efforts of a group of artificial-intelligence researchers at Berkeley to give a computer common sense.

FRANK ROSE

# of Eden

The End of Innocence
at Apple Computer

PENGUIN BOOKS

For Ed and Ruth

PENGUIN BOOKS
Published by the Penguin Group
Viking Penguin, a division of Penguin Books USA Inc.,
375 Hudson Street, New York, New York 10014, U.S.A.
Penguin Books Ltd, 27 Wrights Lane, London W8 5TZ, England
Penguin Books Australia Ltd, Ringwood, Victoria, Australia
Penguin Books Canada Ltd, 10 Alcorn Avenue, Suite 300,
Toronto, Ontario, Canada M4V 3B2
Penguin Books (N.Z.) Ltd, 182–190 Wairau Road,
Auckland 10, New Zealand

Penguin Books Ltd, Registered Offices:
Harmondsworth, Middlesex, England

First published in the United States of America by Viking Penguin,
a division of Penguin Books USA Inc., 1989
Published in Penguin Books 1990

10 9 8 7 6 5 4 3 2

Grateful acknowledgment is made for permission to reprint
an excerpt from "The Times They Are A'Changin' " by Bob Dylan.
© 1963 Warner Bros. Inc. All rights reserved.
Used by permission.

LIBRARY OF CONGRESS CATALOGING IN PUBLICATION DATA
Rose, Frank.
West of Eden: the end of innocence at Apple Computer / Frank
Rose.
p. cm.
Reprint. Originally published: New York, N.Y., U.S.A.: Viking,
1989.
ISBN 0 14 00.9372 9
1. Apple Computer, Inc.—History.   2. Computer industry—United
States—History.   I. Title.
[HD9696.C64A867   1990]
338.7'61004'0973—dc20   89–39516

Printed in the United States of America
Set in Sabon
Designed by Francesca Belanger

For Ed and Ruth

CONTENTS

And Cain went out from the presence of the Lord,
and dwelt in the land of Nod, on the east of Eden.

—Genesis 4:16

PROLOGUE

The Art of Corporate Self-actualization

Reinventing the corporation: *That's* what John Sculley had been doing these past few months. It was three years since he'd first flirted with the idea of coming to Apple Computer, and now, with the man who'd lured him there expelled from the company, the time had come to talk about his own plans, his own blueprints, his own vision. It was January 1986. Apple was on the rebound after the most disastrous year in its history, and Sculley's job was to get that across while simultaneously promoting the idea that the company's vision—its most important product, in a way—had not merely survived the messy and unpleasant departure of Steven Jobs, its founder and chairman, but had in fact been transmuted into this new and improved vision that he, John Sculley, would now articulate. As a package-goods guy, as the marketing man behind the "Pepsi Generation," he knew about communicating intangibles. What he had to do now was make the leap from intangible benefit to intangible product. He had to talk about the Apple vision.

They were at the climax of a three-day conference in San Francisco, an electronic wonderland and corporate showcase called Apple-World. Two thousand people—retailers, suppliers, important customers—had come to town for this, all of them wanting to be reassured that Apple was not going to go the way of a half-dozen other personal-computer companies they could name. Nothing had taken place in the past year to encourage them. Sales were down, market share was dropping, the stock had plummeted. There'd been plant closings, employee layoffs, takeover rumors, a highly publicized lawsuit, and red ink. Both of the famous co-founders had walked—first Steve Wozniak, the engineer whose inventions had launched the company, and then Steve Jobs, the entrepreneur whose vision had helped transform it into a Fortune 500 corporation. The feud between Jobs and Sculley had transfixed the business press since June. And now, after twelve months of uninterrupted bad news, John Sculley had to convince these people that things were going to be okay.

The day before AppleWorld began, Apple issued an upbeat financial report—earnings up, costs and inventory down. On the second day, Sculley made some important new product announcements—nothing really whiz-bang, but some significant improvements to existing products. That night there was a speech by Alvin Toffler, America's premier guru of the future. The next morning it was Lester Thurow, the MIT economist and columnist for *Time*. That afternoon it would be Toffler's business clone, John Naisbitt, whose new book, *Re-inventing the Corporation,* promoted the fashionable idea that tired, dowdy corporations could be transformed with a skillful nip-and-tuck and sent back out to the dance floor for a new fling with that old swain profits. But first, before Naisbitt could dazzle the audience with his fast-food infobabble, here was John Sculley himself, onstage at San Francisco's sleek new symphony hall.

Actually, there were two John Sculleys in the hall. One was a pleasant-looking man in a blue pin-striped suit, looking small and a little lost as he sat in a chair in the middle of the stage; but looming overhead was an enormous, two-dimensional, electronic image on a giant television screen. Next to the real John Sculley was an agreeably earnest-looking young man who looked like he'd just walked off the set of "Magnum, P.I." He was a vice-president of Decker Communications, the consulting firm that did speech coaching for Apple's top executives, and he was there to interview Sculley, onstage, about "the new Apple," the one that had been created after Jobs's departure. He and Sculley sat side by side in little armchairs. The first thing he wanted to know was if, now that Apple was in a "change mode," its vision was going to change too.

Judged by his appearance, Sculley seemed an unlikely man to be talking about vision. He had the cautious manner of someone who was more comfortable gazing at the bottom line than at distant horizons. Of course, only recently a healthy bottom line had seemed like the most distant horizon of all, so maybe that was the vision he had in mind. But no, what he said was that although there'd been a major reorganization—that was the euphemism he used for everything the company had been through—the vision was one thing that didn't have to change. Apple's central vision, as he'd reminded everyone in his speech the day before, was "One person—one computer," a democratization of computer technology that carried all the fervor of a populist movement. The only adjustment they had to make to the vision, he went on, was to *expand* it to include the idea that computers should connect with the rest of the world.

The man from "Magnum, P.I." remarked that Apple had always done things a little bit differently. Was that, he wondered, a sign of a "new corporation"? Sculley crossed his legs and adjusted his tie and observed that Apple, with its roots in Silicon Valley and its affinity with schools and universities, really had no historical relationship with corporate America. He had come from corporate America, and the distance was a lot greater than three thousand miles. But the remarkable thing about Apple, he went on, was its focus on people. He told the story—and it was a story that had brought tears to the eyes of Apple's executives when they'd heard it—of the layoffs in Carrollton, Texas, when Apple had closed the factory where the Apple II had been made for years, and how the vice-president of manufacturing had gone down there to do the deed and all the workers had shown up wearing APPLE II FOREVER T-shirts and one of them had stood up to say they weren't mad to be losing their jobs, just thankful they'd had them, because manufacturing the Apple II had been the most wonderful experience of their lives. Apple, he explained, was a company with a soul. And when the man from "Magnum, P.I." asked what message Sculley had for other newly emerging companies, he said it was to "dream the impossible dreams."

Then the man asked what it would take to make Apple a force in the corporate world. Sculley pointed out that Apple was still growing up, and that part of growing up means recognizing that it takes more than hot technology to sell computers: It also takes an appreciation of what people are going to do with them, and a realization that they have to connect to other computers, and a few other things like follow-through and accountability. It had been easy for Apple to build computers for enthusiasts, because so many Apple people were enthusiasts themselves; and it had been easy to build computers for education, because so many Apple people had just gotten out of school. It hadn't been easy to sell computers to corporate America, because most people at Apple had never worked in any other corporation. They didn't understand how business worked. But Sculley had worked in business, and he had a couple of other people who'd worked in business too, and they were listening. In fact, his goal for 1986 was to demonstrate that Apple could be trusted by business people just as it was trusted by educators and computer enthusiasts.

Ah, yes. But what about the future? What did Sculley see ten, fifteen years down the line for Apple?

"My goal is to have Apple be the most exciting corporation in the world," Sculley declared. "Why is 'exciting' so important? It's important because the things that Apple wants to do require passion— not just someone to come in and get a paycheck and perform forty hours of work. It requires a genuine passion to want to change the world."

For the casual observer, for the volume customer, for the beleaguered computer analyst, this was all extremely reassuring. Here was a handsome and polished man who looked very much the CEO and could point to numbers that were marching in the right direction and yet said things like "want to change the world." And just as that phrase was obviously meant to carry forward the Steve Jobs legacy, others seemed intended to send a message that parts of the legacy were no longer operative. "Growing up" . . . "more than hot technology" . . . "connect to other computers" . . . "follow-through and accountability": all these phrases made reference to what were commonly viewed as the failings of Steve Jobs—and that was doubly reassuring. From now on, Sculley was saying, Apple would behave like an adult and listen to the customer and not be so brash. It would ship its visions on schedule.

Finally, the man wanted to know what role, if any, the founders of Apple, Steve Jobs and Steve Wozniak, would be playing. Now, *that* was a loaded question. In the mythology of Apple Computer, Steve Jobs was sort of like George Washington and Abraham Lincoln rolled into one. He'd founded the company; he'd freed the information slaves from the tyranny of IBM. And yet the previous May, after a bitter confrontation in the boardroom, Sculley had fired him from his position as manager of the Macintosh division and from any other position he might occupy save the empty one of chairman; and in September, when Jobs finally left to start a new company, Apple—*Jobs's* Apple, with Sculley at the helm—had sued him for breaching his duties as chairman and for stealing trade secrets. The lawsuit was being settled even as Sculley spoke, but they couldn't make the announcement yet because Jobs wasn't scheduled to sign the papers until late that afternoon. So Sculley tried to duck the issue by pointing out that Woz had become very much involved. When the interviewer pressed him further, Sculley expressed a hope that Jobs would have a role again too. It was Steve Jobs who'd recruited him to Apple, after all, and he hadn't come here to take the man's company away. He hoped that someday all these issues could be resolved and both founders could feel that they had a legacy at Apple, a legacy that was appreciated.

This remark was greeted with applause, and after it died down, John Naisbitt came out to talk about how Sculley was reinventing the corporation. His speech was a marvel of packaging. Ideas slid forth like burgers from a chute: the manager as facilitator for personal growth, the demise of the hierarchical pyramid, *bam, bam, bam,* until you end up with all the attributes of the "Fortunate 500" companies that will dominate in the emerging information economy. But there was something faintly odd in the suggestion that Apple needed reinventing. Apple wasn't some dinosaur from the Rust Belt, staggering under competition from the Japanese and the Koreans. It was still young. It had always been touted as the very model of the new corporation. Reinventing it just didn't seem to make sense.

And yet, in a curious way, it did. Apple wasn't trying to rejuvenate itself; it was trying to grow up. This wasn't a case of geriatric face lift but of adolescent rebellion, a teenager rejecting the ways of its parents and striking out to seek its own identity—what a Maslovian management consultant might call corporate self-actualization. If the whole process seemed backwards, that was because the company's parents—Jobs and Wozniak—had never really grown up themselves. Adolescent rebellion naturally involved some reverse maneuvers when it was played out against child-parents. But this was California at the beginning of 1986. Child-parents were everywhere, and it was only a couple of months before high-school kids started turning them in for smoking dope. Reverse maneuvers were the order of the day.

1.
Being
a Pirate

January–December 1983

□□ **1** □□

Lifestyle

Like David Bowie and several of the other more discerning stars, Steve Jobs liked to stay at the Carlyle when he came to New York. It had large suites, stunning views, plenty of cachet, and a lingering Café Society ambience that recalled the era of big-band jazz and transatlantic crossings. It was particularly nice for press tours—a little out-of-the-way for the journalists, perhaps, but unusual enough to make them take note. Besides, no one would mind going twenty or thirty blocks uptown for a private preview of Lisa, Apple's exciting new business computer. The official unveiling wouldn't take place until the 1983 annual meeting on January 19, which was still two weeks away; and yet Jobs and his entourage—three vice-presidents, a public-relations woman, and some technicians—had flown out from California to demonstrate it in person to a few select members of the press. Andrew Pollack of *The New York Times*. Richard Shaffer of *The Wall Street Journal*. *Forbes*. *Fortune*. *Business Week*. *Time*. *Newsweek*. A handful of influential newsletters that covered the personal-computer industry for the Wall Street investment community. And when these favored reporters arrived—one at a time, at one-to-two-hour intervals—they were ushered into a tower suite high above the city, a secluded aerie overflowing with cut flowers and strawberries, where they found an incredibly buoyant-looking Steve Jobs and, in front of a window overlooking Central Park, his newest machine, the one that would revolutionize the American office.

It looked quite dramatic, this Lisa: tan, sleek, and sexy, its screen cantilevered out over the keyboard and aglow with pictures—file folders, a clipboard, a calculator, a wastebasket. A thin cord led across the tabletop to a palm-sized "mouse" that controlled an arrow onscreen, the arrow and the mouse moving in one-to-one correspondence like partners in some electronic tango. The overhanging screen gave it a powerful forward thrust; the pictures and the mouse made it seem as playful and full of pizzazz as a video game. This was no stodgy number-cruncher, no clunky contrivance devised for anonymous functionaries in the back office. No, Lisa was everything the name implied: pert, vivacious, friendly. And sitting on that table above Manhattan, with the vast sweep of parkland below and the Ramapo Hills of New Jersey on the horizon and the cold January skies above, it looked as if it could soar.

Jobs and his three vice-presidents had been thoroughly rehearsed before they came to New York. The people at Regis McKenna, Apple's public-relations agency, had fed them every embarrassing question they could think of. Why is Lisa so late? (It had been in development for four years.) Is Lisa really ready to be introduced now? Won't Lisa compete with Apple's other products? Regis McKenna was the hottest public-relations and marketing operation in Silicon Valley, headed by a fleshy, red-haired man whose business cards read "Regis McKenna himself" and staffed with uniformly attractive young women who were known around Apple as the Regettes. Jobs had come to Regis an anemic-looking kid in cut-off jeans, his sallow face framed by limp hanks of hair; now he was chairman of the board of Regis's biggest success story. He'd also become an extraordinarily polished young man, having recently discovered double-breasted Italian suits, which made a nice counterpoint to his more typical blue jeans and pressed white shirt. And while he was physically slight—short and thin, with tight, pursed lips and a somewhat high-pitched voice—he resonated with kinetic energy. Blessed with the piercing eyes and magnetic enthusiasm of a born pitchman, he'd been groomed to make the consummate pitch.

And this was the moment for it. A year and a half earlier, when IBM had entered the personal-computer field, Apple had responded with ads that read "Welcome, IBM. Seriously." Now Apple, which had been beating out less formidable competitors like Radio Shack and Commodore, was running afoul of the IBM juggernaut. It wasn't IBM's technology that made the PC sell—the technology, to anyone serious about computers, was almost ridiculous. It was the name. In a world of fly-by-night start-ups pushing gadgets most people were still afraid of, IBM was a name that seemed carved in stone. Apple was six years old and still riding on the success of a single product, the Apple II—an obsolete machine whose appeal seemed likely to dissipate at any moment. The astonishing thing was that this one machine had given Apple a quarter of the personal-computer market and an ever-increasing spiral of sales that in 1982 had hit $600 million. But the company's only follow-up, the Apple III, had fizzled on introduction, with technical problems so severe that the first fourteen thousand had to be recalled and replaced. Any hope of beating IBM seemed to rest with Lisa.

It was hardly surprising that Apple's success should have attracted the notice of the biggest computer company in the world, the $40-billion behemoth that to California's antiestablishment techies had always represented evil incarnate. But the IBM PC, introduced in August 1981, had both "legitimized" the personal computer and changed the course of the revolution it was supposed to engender. "One person—one computer" was Apple's motto, a phrase born of Jobs's conviction that the democratization of computer power would alter the balance between the individual and the institution. But on Wall Street, two things were now becoming apparent: first, that the real usefulness of these machines was not in the home but in the office; and second, that their ultimate effect might be not to liberate the individual but to tie him all the more closely to his fellow workers and perhaps to the mainframe as well. Wall Street's role was to weigh the players and call the odds; and as these realizations began to dawn, the odds were shifting in IBM's favor.

From Apple's perspective, however, things didn't look that way at all. From Apple's perspective, they were on a roll. The Apple II was the most successful personal computer ever sold. The Apple III was a freak, embarrassing yet hardly fatal. And Lisa was going to astound the world. Jobs wasn't worried about Lisa. What he was upset about now was *Time* magazine.

A week earlier, in its final issue of the year, *Time* had named the computer its "Machine of the Year" for 1982. At one point *Time*'s editors had been thinking seriously of naming Steve Jobs Man of the Year; but that fall, as the IBM PC became more and more a success, they'd decided it would be hard to justify putting Jobs on the cover. As the publisher observed in his letter on the contents page, none of the human candidates they might have picked would be viewed by history as more significant than the computer itself. So Jobs had been bounced by the machine on whose behalf he'd been proselytizing, and the extensive profile that would have accompanied his selection had been boiled down to a mere three pages. In those three pages, however, *Time* had managed to telegraph a great deal of embarrassing information—most notably that Jobs, the twenty-seven-year-old entrepreneur with a net worth of some $210 million, was under a court order to pay $385 a month in child support to the mother of a little girl named Lisa.

The name Lisa had been one of the more controversial issues of the new computer's development. For a while Apple's executives had thought of calling it something more professional-sounding, something like the Apple IV or the Apple 400. But Lisa was above all a *friendly* computer, and they wanted a friendly name for it. They thought of other names too, like Applause or Esprit; but Applause didn't stick, and Esprit was already taken. So finally they'd gone back to Lisa, which had been the code name all along. Lisa was the name of the original chief hardware engineer's daughter (that was back in 1980, several chief hardware engineers previously), and he'd started a tradition of code-naming computers that Apple engineers were still following. Lisa was also the name of the little girl who'd been born in the summer of 1978 to the woman Jobs had lived with a few months before. Not many people knew about this Lisa's existence, and Jobs had long contested his paternity; but in going with Lisa for the machine, they'd decided to chance the story's coming out.

The *Time* article had been off the stands only a few days when Jobs and his vice-presidents arrived at the Carlyle; he was still smarting from the treatment. An orphan himself, adopted in infancy, he was now in the awkward position of having publicly disavowed a baby girl whose mother said she was his. And he hadn't done it any too nicely, either: "Twenty-eight percent of the male population of the United States could be the father" was what he was quoted as saying. But it wasn't remorse at what he'd said that Jobs felt; it was outrage at what *Time* had done to him. More than anything else, he felt violated.

But the reporters who came to the Carlyle were more interested in Lisa the computer than in Lisa the child—not surprising for an industry that was more entranced by circuitry than by personalities.

There'd been rumors about Apple's new machine for months. *The Wall Street Journal* had reported its existence more than a year before; *Business Week* had quoted a stock analyst who called it "the next quantum jump in technology." The reporters all knew that Lisa would be much bigger and much more expensive than anything Apple had made previously—as much as $10,000 per machine, compared with $1,500 for the Apple II—and that it represented a development effort that, by Apple's standards at least, seemed almost superhuman. As they marveled at its sophisticated graphics and grappled with its unfamiliar mouse, John Couch, the vice-president who headed the division that built it, told them proudly that the development costs had come to more than $50 million—$20 million of it in software alone.

What Apple had come up with was an office computer that worked in ways most computer users hadn't even dreamed of. The most obvious innovation was the mouse—the palm-sized device you rolled across a desktop to point to a spot onscreen. But that was just emblematic of the deeper changes that had been made. Every other personal computer was controlled by "text-oriented" commands: if you wanted it to do something—say, move a paragraph around—you had to type in some mumbo-jumbo code that you'd either laboriously memorized or just spent half an hour looking up. Lisa used visual commands: if you wanted it to move a paragraph, you used the mouse to shade the paragraph and point to the spot where it was supposed to go; then you clicked the button on the mouse's back and watched as the paragraph magically reappeared where you wanted it. If you wanted to throw the whole letter away, you used the mouse to drag a picture of a letter to a picture of a trashcan and deposit it there. What was great about Lisa, Couch told one reporter after another, was that it was intuitive. You didn't have to spend a month just learning how to use it; as the brochures said, "It works the way you do."

Like Jobs, Couch was young and energetic, with a high-pitched voice and a passion for his work. A computer scientist whose specialty was software, he was emblematic of the new breed of professionals Apple had started hiring in 1978. He'd been brought in to function simultaneously as Jobs's mentor and his sidekick, and it was as a team that they'd discovered the features that made Lisa so special— a fact that had only increased Jobs's anger when Apple's president set up a separate product division for Lisa and picked Couch to head it. Jobs wanted to run Lisa himself; when told he couldn't, he'd taken over an experimental project called Macintosh—five people in an annex who were building a low-cost "people's computer." Couch got the future of the company, and Jobs made do with five people in an annex. They had a $5,000 bet on which of them would come out first.

The same people who were speculating about Lisa right now were also speculating about Macintosh. Esther Dyson, whose industry newsletter was beginning to earn her a reputation as the Rona Barrett of personal computers (she knew the inside story of every piece of circuitry in the business), had just told *The Wall Street Journal* that Macintosh was what's "really exciting," because it had most of Lisa's features at a cheaper price. That was something you heard a lot. But Dyson had also noted another new machine, the Apple IIe, which she'd astutely predicted would be "the breadwinner of the year." The IIe was this year's Apple II, a re-engineered version of the old standby, updated for the consumer's benefit and at the same time cost-reduced for Apple's. The theme of the upcoming product introduction was "evolution/revolution"—a play on the Beatles song— and if Lisa was the "revolution," the IIe was "evolution." It was represented at the Carlyle by another vice-president, Paul Dali, an older and rather distinguished-looking man who was co-manager of the division that was responsible for the II and for its ill-starred successor, the Apple III.

The final vice-president in the room was E. Floyd Kvamme, who'd just been hired to run Apple's sales and marketing. Kvamme (the name is Finnish and, since the *v* is pronounced like a *w*, has a soft, melodious sound) had until November been president of National Advanced Systems, a subsidiary of National Semiconductor which built IBM-compatible mainframe computers. He was generally re-garded as one of the best marketing men in the Valley, and one of the few of whom it could be said that polyester never touched his wrists. His quietly authoritative manner made an effective counter-point to the boisterous behavior of Jobs and Couch. Throughout the day, as the two boy wizards bounced off walls in their eagerness to display each new wonder to the visiting reporters, Kvamme stood in the background, his calm presence providing a reassuring suggestion of corporate stability.

Late in the afternoon, after the last reporter had gone, a final visitor arrived: John Sculley, the president of Pepsi-Cola. Jobs introduced him as a good friend who was thinking of buying Lisas for his company. In fact, he was the man Jobs wanted to run Apple. The current president, Mike Markkula, was a semiconductor millionaire who'd bankrolled the company when Jobs and Steve Wozniak were still running it out of Jobs's parents' garage. He'd been chairman until 1981, when the first president—Mike Scott, an old buddy from his days in the semiconductor industry—was fired for shaking up the company too drastically after the Apple III fiasco. Markkula had stepped in to fill Scotty's role, and Jobs had been named chairman. But Markkula didn't fancy himself a CEO, and it was no secret that he wanted to be replaced. The man most people at Apple thought would replace him was Floyd Kvamme.

Kvamme, however, knew better. Another of Markkula's pals from the semiconductor industry, he'd come to Apple only a couple of weeks before this trip to New York. Before he took the job, he'd asked Markkula if he was going to stay, and Markkula had told him that Apple was looking for a new president. They wanted somebody with experience in consumer marketing, he explained—Kvamme's expertise, like Markkula's, was in marketing to engineers—and they had a candidate who was seriously considering the position. Kvamme got the impression that they were having trouble landing their candidate, and he was secretly hoping that Markkula would stay on a while longer so he could learn the ropes himself. But when Sculley walked into the suite at the Carlyle, Kvamme knew right away that this was their man.

So there they were, Jobs, Couch, Kvamme, Dali, and the chief Regette, all greeting the president of Pepsi-Cola, a trim, self-assured, and very corporate-looking individual whom Jobs was introducing as his good friend from New York. It was obvious to all of them that Jobs liked this person a great deal. Jobs and Couch demonstrated Lisa for him, and like everyone else he marveled at the sheer gee-whizziness of its technology—at the mouse you could roll across the desktop, at the little pictures ("icons," they were called) you could point to when you wanted it to do something new, at the overlapping "windows" which allowed you to flip back and forth from one document to another with ease. But he didn't take to it wholeheartedly. He was cautious. He had reservations. He wasn't sure that this new technology, dazzling as it was, would have much impact at a big corporation like Pepsi, because it didn't carry the IBM logo. Nobody ever got fired, the saying went, for choosing IBM.

After an hour or so they went downstairs, where Sculley's limousine was waiting to take them to the Four Seasons for dinner. It was a car that seemed as big as an airplane, with a bar and a TV and a driver named Fred, all on call twenty-four hours a day. In Silicon Valley the status cars were Porsches, high-powered German driving machines engineered for maximum performance on twisting mountain roads. Status had a different dimension here—it was less egalitarian, more dependent on contrast. In the most crowded city in America, to glide effortlessly through the streets in a long, black limousine while pedestrians elbowed each other furiously for walking space and the homeless slept on cardboard on the sidewalks—that was what success bought you here.

They swept down Park to Fifty-second, turned left at the austere bronze-and-glass facade of the Seagram Building, and pulled up at the discreetly canopied entrance to the Four Seasons. Sculley led them into the travertine anteroom, up the stairway to the reservations desk, past the enormous Picasso stage curtain, and into the stark opulence of the Pool Room—a temple of modernism, three stories high, with rubber trees surrounding a golden pool and enormous plate-glass windows hung with rippling aluminum chains. To enter the Pool Room was to feel the cold, hard edge of executive power. In the evening it was actually more likely to be full of out-of-towners than corporate overlords; but the Apple executives, being out-of-towners themselves, were too awestruck to notice.

Over dinner the unlikely chemistry between Jobs and Sculley became readily apparent. Despite their obvious differences in age and background—Sculley was strictly Ivy League and corporate, having graduated from Brown University and the Wharton School and spent most of his professional life at Pepsi, while Jobs, seventeen years his junior, had dropped out of Oregon's funky little Reed College during his freshman year—they somehow clicked. It was almost as if each tapped something unrealized in the other. There was a cool, crisp professionalism to Sculley that Jobs respected, a utopian fervor to Jobs that Sculley found intriguing. Sculley was a man who knew how to run a multibillion-dollar enterprise. Jobs was a kid who'd proved he could change the world. Put them together . . .

Couch and Kvamme and Dali all went into sell mode. Wall Street might be hedging its bets, but they weren't. They were on the ride of their lives, from zero to $600 million in six short years; and with Lisa coming out, that was just the start. They told Sculley how *exciting* it all was—Apple, Lisa, the chance to build a new company and develop a new technology and pioneer a new industry all at the same time. He responded with question after question.

Then the talk turned to consumer marketing, and at that point it was Sculley's turn to hold forth. Before he'd become president of Pepsi-Cola—the domestic soft-drink subsidiary of PepsiCo, Inc., a multinational conglomerate that also included Frito-Lay, Pizza Hut, and Taco Bell—Sculley had been its vice-president of marketing. He'd moved into the position in 1970, when he was thirty years old and the company had just revived a long-discontinued ad campaign that had become part of advertising history: the "Pepsi Generation." The original campaign was the first example of what later came to be called "lifestyle" advertising, in which the idea is not to sell the consumer on the virtues of the product but to *position* the product so that it gains an aura the consumer wants to share. The new "Pepsi Generation" ads were lavishly produced, sixty-second TV spots aimed squarely at the kids who made up the Baby Boom, and they worked not by touting any taste-test results of Pepsi over Coke but by showing energetic young people guzzling Pepsi during the course of their fun-filled lives. "You've got a lot to live," the ads declared, "and Pepsi's got a lot to give!" It became the longest-running ad campaign in television history, and it was one reason Jobs was so excited about getting Sculley to head his company.

As they sat in the Pool Room, with the city lights sparkling in the winter night outside, Sculley told them how his "Pepsi Generation" campaign had been tailored to appeal to a new cross-section of people who were young and upwardly mobile and had discretionary income in their pockets. When Pepsi showed a bunch of kids in swimsuits sailing a Hobie Cat and drinking soda, Sculley told them, it not only sent Pepsi sales into the stratosphere, it did the same for Hobie Cat. Jobs grew increasingly excited. If there could be a Pepsi Generation in the seventies, why not an Apple Generation in the eighties? Why not sell computers as part of a lifestyle? As far as he was concerned, and the others quickly agreed, Lisa and Macintosh were *exciting*, and the people who'd use them were not today's top executives but their sons and daughters, highly motivated young people who'd just gotten out of Harvard or Stanford or Berkeley and were going into business not to make money but because that's where the action was—the same people who sailed Hobie Cats.

It was after twelve when they left the restaurant; the place was almost deserted. Sculley dropped the others off at the Carlyle and rode on to his home in Greenwich, in the Connecticut suburbs. Jobs and Couch stayed up for hours, excitedly discussing the possibilities. Could you really sell computers that way? No one had ever tried, but that had never stopped Apple before.

2

Reality-Distortion Field

Cupertino, California, is the kind of place where anything electronic seems possible. Situated on the western side of the Santa Clara Valley, between the southern reaches of San Francisco Bay and the redwood forests of the Santa Cruz Mountains, it is a town with no visible past or center, a flat, suburban landscape of tract houses, shopping centers, and office parks, bracketed by freeways and laced with a network of high-tension wires that sets the streets abuzz. In its banality it seems somehow unreal, cut loose from the normal coordinates of space and time. Driving down its preternaturally verdant streets, one could almost think the whole place was computer-generated—which, in a sense, it is.

Although it lacks a downtown, Cupertino does have a center: the intersection of two six-lane boulevards, Stevens Creek and De Anza. Parallel to De Anza and one block west is a short street, only half a mile long, called Bandley Drive. At the beginning of 1983, six years after its inception, Apple occupied six buildings along Bandley Drive—beige structures, one or two stories high, that aspired to a suburbanized Spanish mission style but failed to achieve it. Within Apple they were known as Bandley 1 through 6, according to the order in which they'd been occupied—which was how Bandley 2, for example, came to be between Bandley 4 and Bandley 5. There were also a couple of buildings on the side streets between Bandley Drive and De Anza Boulevard, scattered amidst such other businesses as a ski shop and a nursery. A strikingly contemporary headquarters building was under construction on De Anza itself, next to a car wash that sold Shell. It would be ready by summer, in time for Apple's new president to move in.

The current headquarters was Bandley 6, a two-story brown brick building with a wood shingle roof. It could have been the organic food pavilion at a 1975 state fair. Jobs had his office there, as did Mike Markkula and Floyd Kvamme. Next door were two beige stucco buildings, one of which housed the Lisa division, and next to that was the smaller stucco building the Macintosh group had just moved into. Everything was painted in oddly synthetic-looking earth tones—beige walls, brown roofs, chocolate doors, the hues of Silicon Valley, nature colors for engineers who liked the idea of nature but weren't too sure what it was supposed to look like.

Near Bandley's northern end, on Valley Green Drive, was a tiny shopping center with hexagonal buildings, one of which housed a bar where a lot of Apple people hung out—engineers, technicians, office workers. It was called Eli McFly, after a mythical Victorian inventor whose exploits were celebrated within, and it was decked out with cast-iron fittings and lights that gave off electrical sparks. A travel poster advertised Professor McFly's Temporal Displacement Excursions ("Be There Yesterday"), with destinations like the Isle of Lesbos in 645 B.C. and Alpha Centauri in 2090. A portrait on another wall showed a wild-looking old gentleman wearing rose-colored spectacles, a collarless shirt, and basketball sneakers. He looked like a cartoon version of Nikola Tesla, the renegade inventor whose unorthodox theories of electricity challenged Thomas Edison's a hundred years ago—appropriate, since one of the bar's owners was Rod Holt, Apple's chief engineer in the early years, a man whose interests and Tesla's sometimes converged.

People who drove down Bandley in the other direction, toward Stevens Creek Boulevard, found themselves in a jumble of parking lots, fast-food restaurants, and discount stores—a Sizzler, a Big Boy, a GemCo. It was a landscape that existed solely in the present—no hint of where it had come from, no suggestion of where it was going, only an all-pervasive *now* of asphalt and auto exhaust. The center of town was only a dozen yards away, but it was just an intersection with gas stations. Only the street names could provide a link with the past—and who knew what they meant? Locked within them, however, was the story of how everything had come to be this way.

■ ■ ■

Juan Bautista de Anza was the latter-day conquistador who set off from Monterey in 1776 to explore the San Francisco Peninsula, which at that point was inhabited only by Indians. Local historians, tracing his route with the aid of modern landmarks, have concluded that he and his men rode through San Jose's Almaden Fashion Plaza, around the Westgate Shopping Center, across Interstate 280, and through the links of the Los Altos Country Club. Along the way, they camped at the edge of the mountains beside a creek they named the Arroyo de San José Cupertino, after an obscure Italian saint. Three months later they established the presidio at San Francisco.

It was some seventy-five years after the de Anza expedition that the same creekside attracted the area's first American settler, one Elisha Stevens, a frontiersman who not too many years before had led the first wagon train across the Sierra Nevada. San Francisco, forty miles up the peninsula, had by this time become the "Queen City of the West," transformed by the Gold Rush into a booming Yankee metropolis whose financiers and speculators capitalized the mining operations in the mountains and beyond. Stevens, who looked like a prototype of Uncle Sam with his high cheekbones and full, white beard, was one of the trailblazers who'd made it possible. It was after him that the creek became known as Stevens Creek, and the road that ran from its banks straight across the valley floor to San Jose as Stevens Creek Road. But Stevens, like most pioneers, wasn't too fond of settlements, and in 1864, having decided that this place was "too durn civilized," he sold his land and moved on.

Between de Anza's time and Stevens's, the Santa Clara Valley—initially known as the Llano de los Robles, after the carpet of oaks de Anza found there—had been divided into a vast patchwork of land-grant ranchos whose mellifluous names seemed to embody the romance of the Spanish Southwest. The one that would eventually prove most significant was the Rancho San Francisquito. A 1,500-acre tract—tiny by the standards of the time—it was claimed by some twenty people in the protracted legal battles that were fought after the Americans took over in 1846. Eventually it was acquired by California's Civil War governor, Leland Stanford, the onetime Sacramento grocer who'd made a fortune selling food to hungry miners during the Gold Rush and parlayed that into an even bigger fortune as one of the "Big Four" who bankrolled the transcontinental railroad. Stanford—a hulking, vulpine figure who lived in a garish Nob

Hill mansion and, along with his partners, controlled California's entire transportation network—combined the old rancho with several other properties to form his Palo Alto Horse Farm, named after the giant redwood tree that dominated the surrounding countryside. He raised thoroughbreds there and lived the life of a Spanish don as reinterpreted by an American robber baron. In 1884, when their fifteen-year-old son died in Europe of typhoid fever, he and his wife resolved in their grief to turn the estate into a memorial—the Leland Stanford, Jr., University. Over the next few years they did so, and in the process the bonanza mentality of the Gold Rush years was transmuted into a visionary idealism that focused on practical education—Stanford himself, a self-made man, had never graduated from college—and the potential of the individual.

What is now called Cupertino sprang up several miles to the south when squatters settled on the Rancho Quito, a 13,000-acre Mexican land grant whose owners were unable to chase them off. By the turn of the century it was a bustling country crossroads surrounded by vineyards, olive groves, and orchards and populated by small landowners, many of them recent immigrants from Ireland, Italy, the Balkans, or Japan. The name Cupertino was revived in a fit of historicism, and except for the destruction of the vineyards by blight, the place remained much the same for the next forty years, an unassuming country village adrift in a sea of apricot and prune trees. Every spring it attracted a swarm of sightseers who came to marvel at the endless expanse of blossoms, and every summer it attracted an army of pickers who cut the fruit and left it to dry in the sun. The inhabitants found all this so consonant with their dreams that they called it the Valley of Heart's Delight.

Even in these halcyon years, the electronics industry was beginning to take hold. Stanford University was the catalyst, and it set the pattern early on. The first start-up was the Poulsen Wireless Telephone and Telegraph Company of Palo Alto, established in 1909 by a Stanford engineering graduate, with venture capital from the school's president, to market something a local teenager had invented—the wireless telephone. The first spin-off occurred one year later, when two Poulsen engineers left the new company to start their own firm; before long they invented the loudspeaker, and their company became Magnavox. Poulsen was renamed Federal Telegraph in 1911, and the next year one of its engineers, Lee de Forest, discovered that the vacuum tube—an altered light bulb—could be used to amplify sound. It was the birth of electronics: the manipulation of electrons for some beneficial purpose, like radar or computers or TV.

Later, during the twenties and thirties, Stanford's radio lab—headed by Fred Terman, a former faculty brat with a doctorate in electrical engineering from MIT—became a mecca for bright young men with a technical bent. Terman thought electronics could change the world. When two of his students, Bill Hewlett and David Packard, set up a company in Packard's garage to exploit an oscillator Hewlett had invented, he gave them encouragement and funding. The new company's first oscillators went to Walt Disney Productions, where they were used in recording the soundtrack for *Fantasia,* Disney's high-tech, proto-psychedelic, animated fantasy film.

Terman was named dean of engineering after the war, and it was then that he hit upon the idea of setting up an industrial park on Stanford land. Leland Stanford had left his entire 8,200-acre farm to the university in his will, with the proviso that none of it be sold. By leasing it to nascent technology enterprises, Terman figured, the school could keep the land and still raise the money it needed to become a research institution of the first order. The first company to move in was Varian Associates, an instrument company founded by two Stanford research associates who'd invented the klystron tube, the device that made radar possible. Meanwhile, a few miles down the road, Lockheed was setting up its missile and space subsidiary next to Moffett Field, the naval air station where the National Advisory Committee for Aeronautics (the bureaucratic forerunner of NASA) had established its research center. IBM built a lab in San Jose to investigate new technologies for storing data on its computers. And in 1956, William Shockley, the physicist who'd led the team that invented the transistor at AT&T's Bell Laboratories back east, returned to his hometown of Palo Alto to start his own semiconductor company.

During the fifties, semiconductors—transistors and other devices which got their name because they're made out of materials like silicon, which conduct electricity less efficiently than metals but better than wood—created a revolution in electronics. Used in computers, radios, televisions, and telephone switching networks, they could do the same work as vacuum tubes, but they were a hundredth the size, infinitely more reliable, and drew far less power. Shockley, who'd grown up not far from the building where de Forest had done his work on the vacuum tube, returned with the dream of creating the best semiconductor company in the world. That dream was shattered a year later when his engineers, upset at the direction of his research and alienated by his condescending manner, walked out en masse to launch Fairchild Semiconductor with the backing of a Long Island company called Fairchild Camera & Instrument. Later, during the sixties, Fairchild itself disintegrated into a shower of new ventures—Signetics, Intel, National Semiconductor, Advanced Micro Devices—which soon gave rise to spin-offs of their own.

With the creation of Fairchild and the arrival of Lockheed and IBM, a sort of critical mass was reached, and thereafter the canneries and orchards that typified the valley gave way to an ever-multiplying number of electronics labs and semiconductor factories and tract houses for the people who worked in them. Encouraged by what they saw, San Jose's business leaders developed a vision of their town as a sprawling suburban metropolis—a Los Angeles of the north, based on electronics rather than show business. Land speculation replaced fruit growing as the main vocation of local property owners. By the mid-seventies most of the orchards had been uprooted and the land paved over with asphalt. From that point on, the Valley of Heart's Delight would be known as Silicon Valley instead.

Only a handful of agricultural landmarks remained, among them the grain elevators on Stevens Creek Boulevard at the Cupertino crossroads and, five miles in toward San Jose, a 160-room farmhouse that stuck out amid the suburban sprawl like some kind of pathologically overgrown "Addams Family" house plunked down in the midst of a Steven Spielberg movie. Built about the same time as the Romanesque revival quadrangles of Stanford University, this "Winchester Mystery House" had doors that opened onto blank walls, skylights that never saw the sky, and stairways that went down only to go up again. The story is that when Sarah Winchester came to California from Connecticut in 1884, having lost her husband and infant daughter to disease, she was convinced that she would share their fate unless she built continuously. She got her instructions by communing with the spirits of those who'd been killed by the source of her fortune, the Winchester repeating rifle—a bit of high-tech weaponry known as "the gun that won the West." As long as she kept building, the spirits assured her, no harm would come to her. So for thirty-eight years she kept workmen hammering away every hour of the day, every day of the year; and after she died anyway, an arthritic recluse of eighty-two, her home was turned into a tourist attraction and exhibited as a spook house.

Like Leland Stanford, whose transcontinental railroad knit California to the Union, Sarah Winchester was an avatar of progress. Her fortune was based on Yankee ingenuity, and she herself held the patent on an innovative laundry sink that went into her house. But if the Stanford University quads—ordered, intricate, rational—represented the architectural embodiment of progress, the Winchester house was the epitome of progress gone amok. And without anyone's realizing it, it was Sarah Winchester who set the pattern for the development that Stanford made possible. Ninety years after her arrival, the entire Valley seemed to feel that it had to keep building or die. Apple Computer was started during this stage of development, by two kids who'd grown up in the tract houses the land speculators had built and whose parents worked in the jobs the electronics industry brought. Its first offices were not more than a few hundred yards from the crossroads, right behind the Good Earth Restaurant, a health-food chain with Formica-topped tables and vinyl banquettes.

■ ■ ■

Apple's founders were true kids of the Valley—college dropouts who plugged state-of-the-art semiconductors into a board, wired them together, and created a rudimentary computer that almost anyone could afford. Their enterprise was an outgrowth of the computer-hobbyist culture that sprang up around the freewheeling semiconductor industry that Stanford had spawned in Silicon Valley. But there was more to the Valley than electronics. Things had been happening all around the Bay Area: The free-speech movement at Berkeley, the "summer of love" in Haight-Ashbury, Ken Kesey and his psychedelic Pranksters, flower power, the Grateful Dead, the birth of a counterculture. Apple was a technological manifestation of its environment, the product of a sensibility that encompassed Eastern mysticism, electronic wizardry, and "blue boxes" used to rip off the phone company.

The dominant institution in Jobs's and Wozniak's early life was Homestead High School, a low, prisonlike, concrete-block structure that sat on Cupertino's Homestead Road, surrounded by orchard land that had been taken over by homes. Wozniak lived a few blocks away in Sunnyvale, in a tract-house development that had been put up for Lockheed engineers like his dad, who had a degree from Caltech and designed satellites for a living. Jobs, the adopted son of a payroll clerk at Varian and a machinist at Spectra Physics—a company that made laser scanners that read bar codes in supermarkets—lived a mile down Homestead in a ranch-style house on the edge of Los Altos. They met through a mutual friend named Bill Fernandez, who lived across the street from Woz and was in the same grade as Jobs. They got to know each other at the beginning of 1970, when Jobs was a fifteen-year-old sophomore at Homestead and Wozniak, five years older and back home after flunking out of the University of Colorado, was trying to build his first computer.

All his life, what Wozniak had wanted more than anything else was a computer of his very own. But that fall, when he and Fernandez started trying to build one on a workbench in Fernandez's garage, the electronic components required to build even a tiny computer with no screen or keyboard cost twice as much as a car. Wozniak didn't have any money and Fernandez was still in high school, so Wozniak cadged surplus chips from local semiconductor companies—Fairchild, Intel, Signetics. They called it the cream soda computer because they guzzled Cragmont cream soda as they worked. When they were almost done, Fernandez brought Jobs over to look at it. He went away impressed: Wozniak knew even more about electronics than he did. But a short while later, when Wozniak's mom invited a newspaper reporter to see her son's new invention, it expired in a cloud of smoke.

Like Wozniak, Jobs was both a loner and an electronics nut; he entered science fairs, studied electronics at Homestead High, and hung out at the big electronics supply stores in Sunnyvale and Mountain View. He was brash and resourceful, too; he'd landed a summer job at Hewlett-Packard after calling William Hewlett at home to ask for some parts. But he wasn't as single-minded about electronics as Wozniak was. Intense, withdrawn, and self-absorbed, he was curious about things like Eastern mysticism and marijuana. He and Fernandez would spend hours walking the quiet suburban streets as they wrestled with life's Big Questions—why are we here? Is there a God? What is loneliness? When will I find a girlfriend? Aside from Fernandez, however, he had few friends of any sort. He wasn't interested in chugging beer or trying out for sports or hanging out with the right crowd. Most of the other kids thought he was weird.

Wozniak and Jobs had one other thing in common: They both

liked pranks. At Boulder, Wozniak had used an oscillator to jam TV sets in his freshman dorm, surreptitiously twiddling the controls to get his dorm mates to do acrobatics to get rid of the interference. Jobs's chief extracurricular activity was the Buck Fry Club, which specialized in stunts like parking a Volkswagen Beetle on the cafeteria roof. (With a little transposition, "Buck Fry" became a nasty remark about Homestead's principal, a Mr. Bryald.) The two collaborated on a spectacular stunt for the 1971 graduation ceremonies, painting a banner to show a hand with the middle finger extended and rigging it up so it would unfurl in front of the audience. The following fall— just as Jobs, who by now had shoulder-length hair, was starting his senior year—Wozniak left to study engineering at Berkeley. He hadn't been gone long when his mother sent him an *Esquire* article she thought might interest him.

The story described a mysterious "Captain Crunch" who built electronic boxes that mimicked the tones governing telephone-company switching equipment, giving him free access to the long-distance system. This Captain Crunch was the unofficial leader of an outlaw underground of creative misfits who styled themselves "phone phreaks" and performed amazing feats of technological wizardry while staying one jump ahead of the authorities. Wozniak was enthralled. He was on the phone to Jobs immediately, and for the next few months they pawed through technical libraries, looking for information they could use to build their own blue boxes. By the time they located Captain Crunch—it turned out his name was John Draper and he worked at a Cupertino radio station—Wozniak had already built a blue box that was smaller than his, more cleverly designed, and required $40 worth of parts instead of $1,500.

It was Jobs's idea to go into business. They set up a manufacturing operation and went door-to-door through the Berkeley dorms, selling the devices for $150 and up. To demonstrate their effectiveness, Wozniak would call London to book a suite of hotel rooms at the Ritz, or Rome to speak with the Pope. He grew so obsessed with phreaking that he all but forgot about school. Jobs, on the other hand, saw blue boxes more as a way to earn spending money to finance the torment of teen angst. He developed a taste for Beethoven and Dylan Thomas, went to freshman English classes at Stanford, hung out at coffee houses in Palo Alto and Berkeley, dropped acid in a wheatfield, and spent hours at the beach with his new girlfriend from Homestead. In the spring of 1972, when it was time to apply to college, the only one he was interested in was Reed, a small, hip, liberal-arts school in Portland, Oregon. He thought of it as a place where people went to find out about life, not to get ready for a career.

Reed was a fixture on the psychedelic circuit, a regular stopover for people like Timothy Leary and Richard Alpert and Ken Kesey; but Jobs didn't fit in there either. A brooding, solitary figure who had a disconcerting habit of staring directly into other people's eyeballs as he spoke to them, he made only two close friends: Robert Friedland, the student president, who wore Indian robes and was on parole for possession of 30,000 tabs of LSD; and Dan Kottke, a soft-spoken youth who shared his yearning for personal enlightenment and his delight in goofing on the world. Together Kottke and Jobs studied Alpert's *Be Here Now,* hitchhiked to the Hare Krishna temple for the free feast (curried vegetables), read about Zen Buddhism, and threw the I Ching. Jobs became a vegetarian and then a fruitarian, fasting for extended periods and watching his skin change color. He dropped out of school but stayed on in the dorm. When summer came, he rented a place in town.

Meanwhile, Friedland went to India and joined the followers of Alpert's guru, Neem Karolie Baba. Already the most mesmerizing figure on campus, he came back glowing with enlightenment, and Jobs and Kottke soon decided they wanted to go too. But Jobs didn't have any money, so early in 1974 he returned to the Valley to live with his parents and get a job. Wozniak was already back, having decided to stay on at the summer job he'd taken in Hewlett-Packard's calculator division after his junior year at Berkeley. Jobs answered a classified ad that said "Have fun and make money" and talked his way into a job as a technician for a new video-game company called Atari, the brainchild of a brash and unpredictable young entrepreneur named Nolan Bushnell. Jobs was a smelly, unattractive youth who liked to tell the engineers they were dumb shits, so he wasn't very popular at Atari; but that was okay, because he didn't want to be there anyway. Before long he got his boss to send him off to Germany to fix some video-game machines, and then he was on his way to India.

There he received a revelation, though not the kind he'd been expecting. India had more to offer in the way of poverty and disease than instant enlightenment: mud villages, appalling slums, starving beggars, funeral pyres in the Ganges. Seeking food, Jobs wandered into a religious festival and was seized upon by a holy man who led him to a mountaintop and shaved his head, laughing maniacally all the while. Later, Kottke flew into New Delhi and the two of them set off for Neem Karolie's ashram, only to discover that the guru had died and his followers had scattered. They went to see another guru who struck them as a phony, and on the way back they were nearly killed in a violent thunderstorm that broke as they were crossing a dry riverbed. They got scabies and dysentery, and Kottke lost his traveler's checks. Finally, disillusioned and exhausted, Jobs gave Kottke the few hundred dollars he had left, flew back to California, and went to work again at Atari, first as a technician and then as a consultant.

For the next year and a half, from the fall of 1974 until the spring of 1976, he Ping-Ponged between Silicon Valley and Oregon. He went to the Oregon Feeling Center for primal scream therapy, meditating in a womblike sensory deprivation box and screaming away at the pain of infancy. He hired a private detective to trace his real mother. He went back and forth to Friedland's new retreat in Oregon, the All-One Farm, where he worked in the apple orchard and sampled communal living. And he and Kottke started going to the Zen Center in Los Altos to meditate and listen to the master. Zen was intriguing because it was loaded with paradox and it defied rational analysis; unlike college, it called for intuition and spontaneity and direct action, not intellectual understanding. But most of his paths to enlightenment proved as disappointing as India. Primal scream seemed simplistic; the All-One Farm began to feel like all these people working for Friedland. As for the detective work, he kept the results to himself.

When he returned from India, Jobs had already begun to suspect that enlightenment might come through electronics rather than philosophy—that Thomas Edison, as he later put it, might have done more to improve the lot of mankind than Neem Karolie Baba. By the end of 1975, as he worked at Atari and watched his friend Wozniak build another miniature computer and listened to him carry on excitedly about a group of fanatics who met at Stanford and called themselves the Homebrew Computer Club, he was beginning to realize that he wasn't the only person who felt this way.

■ ■ ■

In the fifties, when Steve Wozniak was growing up, the idea that some college dropout in California might actually build his own computer was too outlandish for serious consideration. Computers were the domain of a technological priesthood that guarded their secrets on behalf of awesome institutional bureaucracies—the great corporations, the Pentagon, the major universities. The machines these institutions used were room-sized behemoths equipped with neither keyboards nor screens. Instead, data went in on punch cards ("Do Not Fold, Bend, Spindle, or Mutilate") and came out through a teletype machine. Even programmers had to submit their work in the form of a large batch of cards that had been laboriously punched by a keypunch operator. The priests would take the cards, and a few days or weeks later the programmer would get back a printout that showed what the computer had done with them. By poring over the printout, he'd discover that on card number 683, say, he'd foolishly forgotten to put in a comma, and the whole process would begin all over again. People called it "batch processing" because all the computer did was process batches of cards.

The sixties were the decade of the mini. First Digital Equipment and then other companies along Route 128 outside Boston began to challenge batch-processing, and the hegemony IBM enjoyed in it, with scaled-down machines that were called "minicomputers" (after the skirts). In place of punch cards and teletype machines, minicomputers used a typewriter-style keyboard for entering data and a cathode-ray tube, like a television screen, for displaying it. These innovations made it possible for the first time for the user—the person who actually needed the information—to interact with the machine directly. But though the mini was small and racy by comparison with the lumbering mainframe, it was still far beyond the reach of any ordinary individual. Computers remained big and expensive because the electronic devices that went into them—the silicon chips that stored the data and performed the calculations and did the work—were big and expensive as well.

But semiconductor researchers in Silicon Valley and elsewhere were already shrinking these electronic components, cramming more and more of them onto thumbnail slabs of silicon and bringing the price down dramatically. Working independently, Robert Noyce of Fairchild and Jack Philby at Texas Instruments invented the integrated circuit, a silicon chip that contained dozens of transistors, resistors, and other devices. In 1964, Gordon Moore, another of the "traitorous eight" who'd deserted William Shockley to found Fairchild, wrote a paper in which he predicted that advances in microelectronics would follow a curve that would make chips about 30 percent cheaper each year into the indefinite future. In 1968, Noyce and Moore left Fairchild to launch Intel, and three years later Intel introduced the microprocessor, a silicon chip that held all the electronic components of a computer's central processing unit. With a microprocessor and some memory chips to store data and a couple of other chips to handle input and output, you had the rudiments of a miniature computer. And Moore's Law, which mathematically predicted that in a few years the price of all these components would come down to a level even a Steve Wozniak could afford, turned out to be right.

The personal-computer revolution began in January 1975, when *Popular Electronics* ran a cover story on the first hobbyist computer, the Altair 8800, which had just been announced by a little electronics company in Albuquerque, New Mexico. The Altair (named after a star on "Star Trek") wasn't even a finished computer, it was just a kit, and once you assembled it there was almost nothing you could do with it; but orders flew in nonetheless, hundreds of them, then thousands. Many came from the San Francisco Bay Area, where for the past few years a handful of New Left techies had been promoting the idea of computer power to the people. Berkeley had Community Memory, an electronic bulletin board that relied on a rickety teletype in a record shop to access an obsolete mainframe lent by the Transamerica Corporation. Menlo Park, just north of Stanford, had the People's Computer Company, which published an underground paper about using computers to free the people. The idea was to seize control of technology, to transform the computer from an Orwellian instrument of oppression to a liberating force. But the Altair suggested they were relying on the wrong technology—that liberation would come not from massive mainframes but from computers so small they could sit on a table.

In March, the Altair inspired two guys who hung out at the People's Computer Company to announce the formation of a "Homebrew Computer Club." Steve Wozniak was among the thirty-two people who turned out for the first meeting. By June, ten times that number were showing up—renegade engineers at Hewlett-Packard and other local firms, researchers at the Stanford artificial-intelligence lab, political activists, veterans of counterculture institutions like the Midpeninsula Free University, and phone phreaks like John Draper, the legendary Captain Crunch. The meetings were held in the auditorium of the Stanford Linear Accelerator Center, a futuristic complex in the hills above the Stanford campus, and moderated by Lee Felsenstein, the guiding force behind the now-defunct Community Memory project and the founder of its parent organization, Loving Grace Cybernetics. A red-diaper baby from Philadelphia (his brother Joe was named after Stalin), Felsenstein ran the anarchic meetings with the same cool efficiency with which he'd once dissected street demonstrations as "military editor" of the *Berkeley Barb* in the late sixties. There were new-product demonstrations, sessions in which people announced their plans and breakthroughs, and a "random access" period in which they got together in small groups to trade components and share information, much of which actually belonged to local high-tech companies. No matter. Property was theft. If a Homebrew member knew about a secret chip design at Intel, he'd be happy to share the details.

Wozniak found the Homebrew meetings even more enthralling than blue boxes had been, and on several occasions he took Jobs along. They'd gotten out of the blue-box business by this point, but Woz, who was still working at HP, had started moonlighting at Atari for Jobs, who would let him in at night to play video games for free. On one occasion, Nolan Bushnell told Jobs his idea for a new game they'd call Breakout; Jobs got Woz to design it in four days, telling him they'd get $700 and split it fifty-fifty. But while Woz liked hanging out at Atari, Jobs found the obsessive attention to technical minutiae at the Homebrew meetings a little tedious. He was more interested in what Woz had just built.

About twenty of the guys at Homebrew had an Altair, and a number of others were building their own computers. But the Altair cost $395, and Wozniak didn't even have the $179 to buy the Intel microprocessor that did most of the work in it and design his own. A company called MOS Technology was selling a new microprocessor, the 6502, for $25, so he used that and some memory chips for storing data and a few other chips to tie everything together and built a computer that could do more than the Altair, even though it had a fraction of the Altair's hardware. The Intel 8080 was considered the chip of the future at Homebrew, so many of the more prominent members were unimpressed when he passed out the schematics for his machine. But Jobs was excited, and at his insistence Woz agreed to go into business, selling a computer that was nothing more than a printed circuit board stuffed with chips—no screen, no keyboard, not even a case. It was early 1976.

Jobs, who'd recently returned from the apple harvest at the All-One Farm, wanted to call their operation Apple. He thought of the apple as the perfect fruit—it has a high nutritional content, it comes in a nice package, it doesn't damage easily—and he wanted Apple to be the perfect company. Besides, they couldn't come up with any better name. They needed money to get started, so Jobs sold his Volkswagen van and Woz sold his programmable calculator and between them they netted $1,300. A Homebrew member named Paul Terrell had started a personal-computer store—one of the first—and he ordered fifty of Apple's machines. Jobs persuaded Dan Kottke to come from New York, where he'd been studying music at Columbia, and put him up on his parents' living-room sofa. At first they assembled the computers in his sister's bedroom; then his father—a laconic individual who liked to tinker with cars, restoring old Nash Metropolitans, installing a laser behind the grille of his station wagon—cleared out the garage for them. They sold their product for the odd sum of $666.66 and identified themselves with a curiously romantic logo that showed Isaac Newton under an apple tree and sported a legend lifted from Wordsworth: "Newton . . . 'A Mind Forever Voyaging Through Strange Seas of Thought . . . Alone.' "

It was no accident that the Apple and the other Homebrew machines were built by people who knew more about the components that went into computers than about computers themselves. The Homebrew people were passionate amateurs, not trained professionals, and they built their machines from the ground up. To serious computer scientists at IBM or Digital Equipment or even Hewlett-Packard, any computer with only four thousand bytes of internal memory—the equivalent of four double-spaced, typewritten pages—was too trivial to bother with. Internal memory means the amount of information a computer can hold in its own chips rather than on some external storage device like a cassette tape or a floppy disk—in other words, the amount of information it can get to without too long a wait. And what could you do with four kilobytes? Not much. At the Xerox Palo Alto Research Center—Xerox PARC, the sprawling lab on Stanford's rolling hills where scientists were supposed to be inventing the office of the future—personal computers with sixty-four kilobytes of memory had been in regular use for years. Most of the people there and at HP thought nobody would care about the tiny computers Woz and his friends at Homebrew were building. So when Woz offered his new computer to HP before Apple was formed, his bosses, not surprisingly, told him it wasn't a viable product.

By August 1976, however, Wozniak was already working on another computer, one that would come with its own keyboard and be able to display color on a TV screen. Like his previous model, it was cleverly designed to get maximum performance from the fewest number of chips. Meanwhile, Jobs was working maniacally to launch their company, and though Wozniak's parents considered Jobs an unsavory companion who was leading their son into a highly questionable venture, his efforts were beginning to pay off. Impressed by the sophistication of Intel's ads, he'd tracked down the man responsible for them, a Palo Alto consultant named Regis McKenna, and pestered him until he agreed to take them on. Banks weren't eager to lend money to a smelly kid with ripped jeans and bare feet, so McKenna sent him to see Don Valentine, a Fairchild alumnus who'd become a powerful venture capitalist. Valentine drove his Mercedes over to Jobs's garage, decided the two Steves were too small-time to bother with (they thought they might sell a couple of thousand computers a year), and called back and said, "Why did you send me this renegade from the human race?" But he did give them the name of a semiconductor man who might be able to help them, another Fairchild veteran named Mike Markkula. Unlike Valentine, Markkula was gadget-happy, and when he came over to look at their little machine in October he fell in love. Less than three months later, in exchange for $91,000 of his own money and his guarantee on a $250,000 line of credit from the Bank of America, Wozniak and Jobs gave him a one-third interest in the company. It was January 1977, and Apple Computer was about to move out of the garage.

Mike Markkula and Regis McKenna had lived a very different side of the sixties from the one Wozniak and Jobs experienced. They'd made good in the go-go business climate that had turned the once-peaceful Santa Clara Valley into the scene of a technological Gold Rush. Markkula had been marketing manager at Intel, the company that had come out with the microprocessor; he'd wanted to be a millionaire by the age of thirty, and when his stock options at Intel made it possible he'd decided to retire to a happy home life with his wife and kids. McKenna had earned a reputation as the top advertising and public-relations consultant in the Valley for the work he'd done for Intel. In taking on Wozniak and Jobs—a bumbling engineer and a wastrel of a youth with fire in his eyes—they weren't setting themselves an easy task. Wozniak, who didn't trust marketing types in the first place, was convinced that their enterprise would fizzle and Markkula would lose his shirt; when Jobs and Markkula tried to get him to give up his perfectly good job at HP to work for Apple full time, he almost didn't do it. As for Jobs, he was so brash as to be almost frightening. Unable to say where he'd come from, uncertain where he was going, he nonetheless made it clear that he was going there fast. Certainly his adoptive parents couldn't give him much direction, though they'd indulged his post-adolescent wanderings and helped agreeably when he decided to start a computer company in their garage. Practically speaking, they had little choice; when they brought this kid home, Paul and Clara Jobs must long since have come to realize, they'd landed themselves a live one.

Markkula forged ahead where they'd thrown up their hands, and under his tutelage Jobs learned the importance of wearing a suit and using the proper fork. Wozniak wasn't exactly polished either, but that didn't matter as much because he only wanted to build computers. Jobs wanted to build a company, and his role at Apple was to put the fever in everyone else—a task for which he'd be perfectly suited if only his energies could be properly channeled. Markkula supplied the marketing talent, and he brought in Mike Scott, a genial but short-tempered man with whom he'd once shared a cubicle at Fairchild, to run things. Scotty was the disciplinarian, the one who kept the company moving ahead and Jobs firmly in line. They got their sales vice-president from National, their financial VP from a smaller semiconductor company called American Microsystems, and their corporate spokesman from Fairchild. From the beginning, then, Apple was a partnership between two breeds of people: obsessed kids like Wozniak and Jobs, and older semiconductor professionals like Markkula and Scott. The hobbyists, long-haired dropouts whose main tether to society was a passion for electronics, provided the dream; the semiconductor guys, more mature and experienced, provided the skills, the drive, and the daring to make it real. So while in fact it was Markkula and Scott and their cronies who built the company while Jobs fired off ideas and Wozniak went on periodic engineering binges, in the myth it was Jobs and Wozniak who transformed their dream into an Horatio Alger story for our times—and it was the myth that was more compelling, and that was beginning to seem more real.

■ ■ ■

A half-mile or so down Stevens Creek Boulevard from the Good Earth Restaurant lies De Anza College, a modest two-year school whose palm-studded campus was once the country estate of a young millionaire from San Francisco's turn-of-the-century "fast set." After the college was put there, his house—a dazzling white pavilion modeled after the Grand Trianon at Versailles—was jacked up and moved away so that a large, concrete auditorium could be built in its place. Flint Center was as functional as it was ugly, a featureless gray mass looming over a vast parking lot. Because it doubled as Cupertino's civic auditorium, it was the logical place for Apple's 1983 annual meeting.

For most corporations, the annual meeting is a pretty cut-and-dried affair. First the company officers get up onstage and read financial results, and then the assembled stockholders—those who bother to show up—vote for a slate of directors and maybe a change or two in the bylaws. Things can get acrimonious if there's a takeover attempt or a stockholder revolt, but otherwise it's about as exciting as your average New England town meeting, which in theory it resembles. Apple, however, was not most corporations. Many of its stockholders were employees, thanks to its generous stock option and stock purchase plans; and since everyone was given the morning off to attend, its annual meetings were more like pep rallies. This year's meeting actually *was* a pep rally, because it was where Jobs would officially unveil Lisa.

There were hundreds of Apple people at Flint Center that morning, most of them in T-shirts and jeans, looking more like college students than like grown-ups. Plenty of other people came too. There were analysts from brokerage firms in New York and San Francisco—people whose recommendations would help determine whether Apple's outside stockholders, among them a number of giant institutions holding tens of thousands of shares, would maintain their faith in the company. There were also analysts from market-research firms with names like Dataquest and Infocorp; their job was to track high-technology enterprises for their clients—venture capitalists, retail chains, component suppliers, other high-technology enterprises. And there were dozens of reporters as well, from techie journals like *Byte* and *InfoWorld,* from the business magazines and the news weeklies, from *The New York Times* and *The Wall Street Journal.* They were there to witness the introduction of Lisa and to promulgate this latest chapter of the Apple myth, as invented by Regis McKenna and manufactured on a daily basis by the Regettes.

Aside from the gusher of cash provided by the Apple II, the myth was the main thing Apple had going for it—the myth of Jobs and Woz, two quirky, lovable kids who'd given computer power to the people. The story of how they'd sold Jobs's van to buy parts and built their first computers in his parents' garage had already become a hallowed chapter in the annals of entrepreneurship, taking its place alongside such legends as the mass defection of William Shockley's engineers to found Fairchild and the young Henry Ford's first encounter with a self-propelled wagon. By 1983 both founders had become millionaires many times over, transformed by the marvel of capitalism from techno-bohemian rebels to celebrities in the business world. Wozniak, who'd never really been interested in business at all, had left Apple to go back to Berkeley for his bachelor's degree in computer science. But Jobs had stayed on, sparking an enterprise that mirrored his own personality—brilliant, erratic, and messianic in its zeal.

As the leading man in America's sudden romance with entrepreneurship, Jobs was the embodiment of everything Apple represented—vision, opportunity, New Age idealism. To those who worked with him, however, he was known as a "reality-distortion field." To listen to him was to be ensnared by the warp of his beliefs, no matter how they might conflict with general opinion or objective reality or what he'd said the day before. He could convince you that up was down, that black was white, that apples were oranges—not because he wanted to trick you (this was the secret of it) but because he sincerely believed that it was so, believed it so fervently that he would not rest until you believed it too. And the next day, when he announced that up was up and black was black and apples were apples, it wasn't because he'd thought about it and changed his mind; he'd simply forgotten everything he'd said before, so caught up was he in the overpowering reality of the moment—of *his* moment.

When the reporters and stock analysts entered Flint Center, they stepped into a realm in which doubt did not exist. It wasn't just this event; Apple itself was the product of Jobs's reality-distortion field.

How else could he have gotten people like Regis McKenna and Mike Markkula to back him? And the remarkable thing was that the company they built out of this mind warp was as self-absorbed as Jobs was. People at Apple focused their attention inward—on their leaders, on their myth, on their technology, on everything except their customers. Though they talked a lot about being a "market-driven" company, what really drove them wasn't the marketplace but technology. The world outside couldn't compete with the ideas of their own engineers.

One of Apple's cardinal rules was "Never build a computer you wouldn't want to own." In the early days, when personal computers were new and the market for them restricted to hackers and hobbyists, that policy stood out as a badge of integrity. Now, as Apple consumers ceased to be an identifiable community and became an amorphous mass, it was beginning to sound arrogant. But the employee-stockholders who filled Flint Center didn't see it that way. The computers they wanted to own were ones that encouraged personal creativity and individual self-expression, and the idea of building anything else was anathema to them. They were children of the seventies, on a crusade to change the world. Their motto was "One person—one computer," and they fully expected the democratization of computer power to alter the balance between the individual and the institution. It wasn't just computers they were selling, it was a vision of society, a vision that was as liberating and utopian as it was wrapped up in the excitement of self—self-discovery, self-fulfillment. Jobs's company built computers for people like Jobs, people who wanted to enter society on their own terms. Its goal was to transform his dream into their dream, his computer into their computer, his "me" into their "me."

The archenemy IBM, on the other hand, remained what it always had been, a seemingly faceless monolith whose corporate identity could in fact be traced to the simple, small-town virtues of prewar America—Babbittry writ large. Thomas Watson, Sr., had imposed his personality on IBM as thoroughly as Jobs had his on Apple, and the qualities Watson valued were those that still infused the company: service to the customer, conformity to the norm, loyalty to the organization, and a rigorously Protestant belief in the spirituality of sales and the morality of profit. If Apple was an inward-looking corporation, IBM was an outer-directed one—everything about its white-shirt culture was designed with the customer in mind. Why did IBMers wear blue suits? Because Tom Watson, back in the twenties, thought they should wear what their customers wore. Not that Big Blue was incapable of change: Both the IBM PC and the in-house entrepreneurship that created it were in crucial ways modeled after Apple. But the final product was IBM all the way—dependable, uninspired, behind the times. Qualities for which Jobs had nothing but contempt.

There were no blue-suiters at Apple, not even on the executive staff. Everyone was young and enthusiastic and full of zeal. Apple had made so many of them millionaires—more than three hundred, thanks to generous stock options and a series of stock splits before the company went public that transformed one share in 1978 into thirty-two in 1980—that the parking lots looked like a Porsche-Mercedes dealership. But Apple was more than a get-rich-quick scheme. Apple was a twentieth-century David-and-Goliath story, a little team of people against the world, all of them so special and so bright. Most were motivated less by money than by the feeling that they could make a difference. It was all illusion, of course; the bulk of them couldn't make any difference at all, but because they felt they could, their productivity was so high that they were the object of scrutiny in business schools.

That productivity—sales per employee of nearly $200,000 per year—demonstrated that Apple was more than just a self-improvement society, too. There were many components to the Apple dynamic, and if one of them was the "Stanford mentality"—an upper-middle-class belief in personal growth as a consumer item—another was the Silicon Valley work ethic. The Stanford mentality wasn't just a product of the seventies; its roots went back to the school's beginnings, which combined democratic ideals and Western individualism in a cult of vigorous self-improvement. At Apple it found expression in Apple Values, a corporate code that was modeled on the HP Way, Hewlett-Packard's long-standing pledge of corporate humanism. Long before such ideas became fashionable, Bill Hewlett and Dave Packard had developed a philosophy based on the worth of each employee—a benignly paternalistic code that stressed job security, profit sharing, "management by wandering around," and a sense of the company as one big, happy family. But other HP attributes—the emphasis on organizational cohesiveness, on working together as a group, on following orderly procedures and doing things by the book—were considered hopelessly dull at Apple. All in all, HP was regarded as little more than an updated version of the womb-to-tomb environment at IBM, a corporation people joined in order to retire. The difference between it and Apple was the difference between a lumbering 747 and an F-14 fighter jet, and the F-14 characteristics all came from the semiconductor industry.

The Silicon Valley work ethic was diametrically opposed to the HP Way. The semiconductor industry prided itself on its "go-for-the-gold" mentality. This was the new Gold Rush. People had been flocking to California to hurl themselves at sudden wealth since 1849, and they'd been hurtling over the edge into oblivion ever since. The Valley had pioneers and outlaws and empire builders; Elisha Stephens would have packed up and moved to Oregon, but Leland Stanford would have felt right at home. Now as before, the prize went to those who moved fast and took risks. People were an expendable commodity. It really came down to a philosophy of crash-and-burn— move like hell, put your ass on the line, hang it over the ragged edge, and if you crash and burn that's the chance you take. The ultimate manifestation of crash-and-burn would be provided a few months hence by the forty-year-old president of a successful start-up called Eagle Computer, who went for a spin in his Ferrari the day his company went public (making him richer by $9 million), sailed off a freeway, and crashed and burned. But it happened on a less literal level every day, and could be measured in the number of aborted careers and ugly divorces.

What Apple tried to do—what it almost had to do, given that so many of its employees came from Hewlett-Packard and most of the rest came from the semiconductor industry—was marry the HP Way with the go-for-the gold philosophy. The result was a sort of New Age humanism that celebrated the self even as it set you up for eventual self-sacrifice. The benefits were manifold: profit sharing, bonuses, stock options for senior managers, a stock purchase plan for the rank-and-file, a "company store" where employees could buy Apple products at a discount, a "loan-to-own" program that gave every employee an Apple computer after a year on the job. "Apple University" offered training programs, inspirational speeches by business leaders, and an Outward Bound–type experience by the Pacific ("ropes on the beach," the cynics called it) in which managers were given a workout by a mountain-climbing instructor and encouraged to get in touch with their own personal summit. The point was to create a network of highly motivated individuals bound by a common vision.

They'd designed Lisa to appeal to the new breed of business people, the ones who were young and eager and willing to take risks—who were, in short, just like themselves. As they filled Flint Center this January morning, there was no doubt in their minds that these businessmen and -women populated offices all across America, just as there was no doubt that as soon as they saw Lisa they'd rise up and demand that their corporate data-processing managers purchase this marvelous new machine by the thousands. Compared with Lisa, the IBM PC was as clunky and soulless as one of those batch-processing mainframes from the fifties. And so it was with supreme confidence that Jobs proclaimed Apple's two new products, the Apple IIe and Lisa—"evolution/revolution," as the press handouts had it. The evolution got played down; there was little excitement in the fact that Apple was replacing the aging II+ with the re-engineered IIe—was rolling it over like last year's Chevy. The people here wanted to hear about *revolution*, and Jobs was ready to oblige. As he addressed the eager throng, he left no question where he stood. The future of computing was with Lisa technology, and Jobs was a man who lived always in the future.

3

The Dream

The future that Jobs envisioned had actually been set in motion some forty years before. The impetus was an article in the July 1945 *Atlantic Monthly* by Vannevar Bush, an MIT professor who'd become director of the wartime Office of Scientific Research and Development—America's chief scientist. The nation's leaders were beginning to turn their attention to the peacetime world ahead, and in his paper Bush addressed the question "What are the scientists to do next?" He thought they should turn to the problem of managing information.

The problem, as Bush saw it, was that scientific research had yielded too much knowledge for anybody to keep track of. He proposed a "memex," a microfilm device with a keyboard and with automatic indexing and photocopying capabilities. The memex itself held little appeal to others, but the idea behind it—the idea that the world is generating so much information so fast that we need some dramatically improved technology to keep track of it—inspired a number of people to seek more workable solutions.

One of them was Doug Engelbart, a Navy radar technician who went to work after the war as an engineer at NACA's Ames Research Laboratory at Moffett Field. Engelbart had read the *Atlantic* article in a Red Cross library in the Philippines shortly after Hiroshima, and in 1951, searching for a cause he could devote his life to, some way he could improve the lot of humankind, he remembered Bush's challenge. He had a sudden vision of people sitting in front of cathode-ray tubes (not unlike the radar screens he'd serviced during the war) working with text and graphics. From that point on he committed himself to the task of "augmenting the human intellect," not with microfilm but with the electronic digital computer, which had been developed during the war by a team of researchers at the University of Pennsylvania's Moore School of Engineering. He left Ames, got a Ph.D. in electrical engineering at Berkeley, and in 1957 went to work at the Stanford Research Institute, a think tank in Menlo Park, where he tried without much success to get funding for his ideas.

To think the way Engelbart did required a considerable leap of faith. The batch-processing computers of the fifties were hulking number-crunchers without keyboard or screen, programmed by stacks of laboriously punched cards ("Do Not Fold, Bend, Spindle, or Mutilate") and off-limits to all but the priests who knew their secrets. But in 1960, an experimental psychologist at the Cambridge research firm of Bolt, Beranek & Newman published a paper called "Man-Computer Symbiosis" in which he set forth an idea similar to Engelbart's. His name was J. C. R. Licklider, and he'd discovered that he spent a lot more time keeping records, plotting graphs, and looking up data than actually thinking. He thought computers ought to do all those things. He envisioned a symbiotic relationship between computers and humans, an intimate partnership between dissimilar organisms.

Licklider was one of the first to use the PDP-1, a brand-new computer from a start-up outside Boston called the Digital Equipment Corporation. It was far cheaper and smaller than mainframe computers, which cost millions of dollars and took up most of a room. It also introduced the idea of "interactive computing": It came with a keyboard and a screen, and it took programs and data from paper tape rather than punch cards—tape you could actually change while the machine was running. Licklider had what he called a "religious conversion" while working on it, and because he was well connected with the defense establishment in Washington—BBN was a military think tank, part of a sprawling Boston-area research complex that also included MIT and Lincoln Laboratories—he knew plenty of influential people he could tell about it.

In 1962, Licklider was asked to set up an information-processing office at the Pentagon's Advanced Research Projects Agency, which had been set up in the wake of the Sputnik scare to fund basic scientific research for the military. It was the height of Camelot: Idealistic young men, heeding President Kennedy's call to public service, were flocking to Washington, and Licklider abandoned his psychological research to become one of them. ARPA was a funding agency for bold ideas, and he had one of the boldest. At a time when most computer scientists were arguing about ways to improve batch processing, he was pushing something they considered straight out of science fiction: humans and computers working in tandem, thinking "as no human being has ever thought," processing data "in a way not approached by the information-handling machines we have today."

Licklider had vast sums of ARPA money to distribute to researchers who would advance his dream. One of them was Doug Engelbart, who set up an Augmentation Research Center at the Stanford Research Institute and led the development of a complex but exhilaratingly powerful computer system that included not just a screen and a keyboard but a drawing-and-pointing device that rolled across a desktop. Because its top was curved and its cord looked like a tail, they called it a mouse. At MIT, Licklider funded a "time sharing" project that would allow dozens of different people to use a single mainframe at the same time. (A computer runs millions of times faster than a human can type, so there was no need to make people stand in line for their turn at the machine.) At the University of Utah, ARPA-funded researchers began working on computerized graphics systems that could display three-dimensional models on a cathode-ray tube. By the time he left, Licklider had created a nationwide community of computer scientists who were committed to his dream—a vision they now referred to as "the ARPA dream."

The ARPA dream had radical implications. The high priests of data processing had created a technocracy so centralized, so rigidly authoritarian, it was almost a parody of the corporate and governmental bureaucracies they served. In their hierarchy, man was subservient to the machine. They considered time-sharing and interactive computing to be dangerous and irresponsible ideas. The ensuing debate had all the heat and fervor of a political contest; it was many years before it was clear that the forces of democracy had won. IBM clung to batch processing so long that Digital Equipment, the 1957 start-up that launched the minicomputer revolution, was able to outpace the "seven dwarfs" that competed with it in mainframes and become the second-largest computer company in America.

There was one problem, however. Most of these innovations were being paid for by the military, and by 1969 the military was not such a welcome sponsor in the academic community. In a few years the leadership of the country had passed from John Kennedy to Lyndon Johnson to Richard Nixon, and the idealism that brought people like Licklider to Washington did not survive the transition. Then Congress passed the Mansfield Amendment, which prevented ARPA from funding any projects that weren't "mission oriented"—in other words, connected to some specific military mission. By the early seventies, ARPA money was beginning to look decidedly tainted.

At precisely that time, however, Xerox, a company that had become a multibillion-dollar enterprise by exploiting technology IBM had spurned in the fifties, decided to move into the computer business. Xerox had a new president, Peter McColough, a Harvard Business School graduate who'd proclaimed his intention to make it "the architect of information." Researchers in physics, electrical engineering, and computer science were hired, and a lavish research center—the Xerox Palo Alto Research Center, or Xerox PARC—was set up near the Stanford campus. For the next ten years the ARPA dream took up residence at PARC.

The first thing the people at PARC's computer science lab did was build for themselves the kind of computer they thought other workers would want. It was called the Alto, and it was one of the first computers designed to be used by a single person. It had enough memory chips to store 64 kilobytes of information, or about 64 typewritten pages. And while that much memory cost $7,000 in 1974, they knew the miracle of Moore's Law would bring it down to about $34 in 1984. It also had a mouse (an adaptation of the one invented at Engelbart's Augmentation Research Center) and a high-resolution screen made up of some 500,000 individual dots of light. The screen, the keyboard, and the mouse sat on top of a desk; the computer itself was in a large metal box that rolled underneath it.

The Alto was the hardware prototype of the personal computer of the future. Most of the software to make it run came from a team headed by Alan Kay, a young researcher who'd been one of the ARPA crew at Utah. A few years before, on seeing the first flat-panel screen— a slab with an electronic display—Kay had thought about the implications of Moore's Law and realized that eventually all the components of a functioning computer would fit on the back. The resulting vision became his own interpretation of the ARPA dream: a computer no larger than a notebook, so powerful it could hold an encyclopedia full of information within its circuits, and yet simple enough for a child to use. He thought of it as dynamic paper—paper that would not only hold marks but look at the marks and do what they said. He called it the Dynabook, and at PARC it became for him a sort of Holy Grail.

Kay believed that for a computer to be truly personal it wasn't enough for ordinary people to be able to use it; they ought to be able to program it as well—to tailor it to their needs. To make that possible, he and his team at PARC developed a radically innovative programming language they called Smalltalk (because they thought programming languages were at about the level of cocktail-party conversation). Programming languages are what computer experts use to write the programs that tell a computer what to do. They're completely made-up languages, with made-up words and made-up grammar, and most of them are maddeningly complex. Kay wanted one that was simple enough for anybody to use; and to ensure that he got it, he brought kids from a local junior high up to the lab after school to try it. They came to be known as the "Smalltalk kids," and their presence was one reason most people at PARC thought of Kay's group as the lunatic fringe.

Kay was also concerned about *how* people used the computer— the quality of the experience. Most computer programs, no matter what language they were written in, required you to memorize an arcane set of commands before you could hope to do anything with them. Kay, building on some of the concepts developed at Engelbart's Augmentation Research Center, hoped to bypass all that.

He and his team created for the Alto (which they dubbed the "interim Dynabook") a screen that offered a simple visual metaphor for what was going on inside the computer. The screen was controlled by a technique known as "bit mapping," which allowed each of its 500,000 dots of light to be turned on or off independently. With bit mapping, it was possible for the first time to combine text and graphics onscreen. Many of the other features that were developed were simply onscreen representations of the way things looked on paper. There was a WYSIWYG (Kay-talk for "What You See Is What You Get") word-processing program that displayed documents onscreen exactly the way they'd come out of the printer instead of being littered with special codes to indicate things like underlining or italics. There were overlapping "windows" onscreen that looked like pieces of paper lying on top of one another; to open a new window or close an old one, you simply pointed to it with the mouse and clicked the button on top. There were visual "icons," little pictures onscreen that could be selected with the mouse—point, *click!*—and took the place of typed commands that had to be memorized.

One thing nobody at ARC or at PARC had counted on was the runaway market for tiny hobbyist computers that developed in the mid-seventies. They'd assumed that no one would want a personal computer until the state of the art in semiconductors made them cheap enough to afford, small enough to sit on a desk, and powerful enough to be useful. But by 1977, Apple, Commodore, and Radio Shack were selling computers that seemed like little more than toys, and people were buying them at an astonishing rate. Apple's sales alone went from $770,000 in 1977, the year the Apple II came out, to $7.9 million in 1978 to $49 million in 1979. And in the summer of that year, just as the financial community was working itself into a frenzy over the idea that Apple would soon go public, the company concluded a third and final round of private financing. One of the investors was Xerox.

In ten years, Xerox had spent more than $100 million on research at PARC—nearly twice as much money as Apple had generated in its entire corporate history. But Peter McColough was gone by 1979; and when the new management looked at what was coming out of PARC, they didn't know what to think. They didn't know computers, nor were they risk takers by nature. They were coupon clippers, which was why they wanted to invest in Apple—it seemed to be offering some good coupons. After years of hedging they'd finally okayed development of an office computer based on PARC research, but personal computers for office workers seemed pretty radical in 1979. The action was in low-cost home computers, and it looked to them like the best way to get into it was by buying into Apple. But they couldn't get in just for the asking; Apple stock was too much in demand for that. So in exchange for being allowed to buy 100,000 shares, Xerox agreed to open the doors of its Palo Alto Research Center to Apple's vice-president for research and development, Steve Jobs.

Jobs's tour of Xerox PARC turned out to be a signal event in the history of personal computing. Driven by financial and strategic considerations, it resulted in the union of two distinct elements of the personal-computer movement. The hobbyists, their roots in the Homebrew Computer Club, had been working their way up from microchips; the scientists, their roots in the ARPA research of the sixties, had been working their way down from mainframes. At this point their paths converged.

■ ■ ■

The research center Jobs went to visit looked like a Hanging Gardens of the Information Age: a terraced structure built into a golden hillside high above the bay, filled with the electronic marvels of tomorrow. He toured the place with John Couch and a handful of engineers, and when they were given a demonstration on the Alto, he flipped. Jobs always responded best to visual stimuli, and what was great about this machine was that it was *all* visual—you made it work just by pointing at pictures, and you could use it not just to write on but to create amazing graphic images. This was a computer he could actually understand. It made the Apple II look as archaic as an old Victrola. He and Couch decided to bring something out just like it.

So when Jobs went back to Apple, the ARPA dream went with him. But as an entrepreneur with the mentality of an engineer—a mentality focused on building gadgets rather than on seeking knowledge, which is what scientists do—he thought differently from people like Licklider and Engelbart and Kay. To them the point was to show how computers could be turned into partners in handling information; to him the point was to do it.

Apple had two computers under development then: the Apple III, which was supposed to be a simple upgrade of the Apple II, and Lisa, an experimental machine that was having something of an identity crisis. Both had been conceived of as nifty pieces of hardware rather than as products to appeal to a specific market: At Apple you designed a box and people bought it because it was neat, not because any thought had been given to what it would do for them. At this point, however, Lisa wasn't even a neat box.

Jobs had wanted a sixteen-bit machine, meaning one whose central processor would handle information in groups of sixteen "bits"—*bi*nary dig*its,* zeros and ones, the positive and negative charges the computer processes directly—instead of eight bits, as the Apple II did. The advantage of a sixteen-bit processor is that it runs faster. Woz had tried to adapt a technique used in minicomputers to build an entirely new sixteen-bit processor. When that didn't work, the project was turned over to Ken Rothmueller, who'd been hired from Hewlett-Packard. Rothmueller started building a computer most people at Apple regarded as absolutely typical of HP engineering, which is to say it was so dull it could have been made out of gray flannel.

The obvious solution was to transform Lisa into a PARC-style computer—to keep the new Motorola 68000 processor that was being used in place of Woz's failed attempt, throw everything else away, and build a machine with a bit-mapped display and a mouse and windows and icons and the whole thing. Jobs and Couch hired several people away from PARC, including the person who'd demonstrated the Alto for them, and for the next year they worked together to turn Lisa into an office computer that would capture the PARC vision. Then Apple proudly launched the Apple III, its first new product since the phenomenally successful Apple II, only to discover a few weeks later that its chips were prone to failure, its connectors tended to short out, its cables were too short, its circuit boards were unreliable, and its software was riddled with bugs.

One day in the fall of 1980, when Apple was reeling from the disastrous introduction of the III, Mike Scott walked into an executive staff meeting and, as Apple's president, announced that he'd decided to reorganize. Three years of rapid growth and six months of constant pressure to ship a product had produced chaos. Scott felt some accountability was in order, so he dispensed with the old functional organization—all of hardware in one division, all of software in another, all of marketing in a third—and carved the company into divisions based on product line. Under his new scheme, there'd be one division for the Apple II and III, one for Lisa, one for "peripherals" (floppy-disk drives and other data-storage devices), one for manufacturing, one for sales and service. Jobs begged to be put in charge of the Lisa division, but Scotty turned him down. He needed Jobs to serve as the company spokesman when Apple went public, and he didn't think Jobs was any good as a manager anyway. Instead, Scotty gave Lisa to John Couch, who, like Rothmueller, had come from Hewlett-Packard, where things were structured and professional and slow.

Couch had arrived two years earlier, when Apple was forty people in a dinky little building with Scotty firing off orders in a Black Sabbath T-shirt and Jobs running around like some sort of feral child. At first he'd gone into culture shock, but working with Jobs had taught him a lot. They'd made a great team, in fact—Couch helping to smooth Jobs's rough edges while Jobs taught him about risk-taking and innovation and vision. And now, with Apple employing hundreds of people all over the Valley and running factories in Texas and

Ireland and about to open another one in Singapore, Couch was ready to combine his HP experience with what he'd learned here. The problem was that Jobs was left feeling like somebody had stolen his baby.

There was a standoff. Scotty was a formidable figure, a squat, blunt, no-nonsense man with a stern manner and an explosive temper. He was the only person at Apple who could dominate Jobs. But not even Scotty could bottle him up in some kind of corporate-figurehead role, to be trotted out for the benefit of Wall Street analysts. Steve had to be involved; and if he couldn't be involved with Lisa, it would have to be something else. So early in 1981, after the stock offering had been successfully completed, he started hanging out around a tiny project headed by a former college professor and longtime computer hobbyist named Jef Raskin.

Raskin was a gnomelike individual full of nervous energy and ideas. In the early sixties he'd been on the fringes of the avant-garde art scene in New York; then he'd driven out west and taught music and art and computer science at the University of California at San Diego. In the early seventies he'd spent some time at PARC. Later he'd been a member of the Homebrew Computer Club, which was how he'd come to write the manual for the Apple I when Apple was still in the garage. Eventually he'd gone to work full-time writing manuals for Apple, and then he'd moved into the engineering side, and finally he'd gotten Scotty's reluctant go-ahead to build his own dream computer. He wanted it to be inexpensive, portable, and as easy to use as an appliance. He called it Macintosh, after his favorite kind of apple.

Raskin had no use for windows and icons and mice, but he did admire the graphics capability of the bit-mapped screen he'd worked with at PARC. So his Macintosh was going to have a high-resolution, bit-mapped screen, and it was also going to have a closed architecture—that is, it would lack an essential feature of the Apple II, the interior slots that would allow people to plug in special-purpose circuit boards in order to customize the machine. These slots, which allowed computer owners to adapt their equipment to an incredible variety of needs, had turned the Apple II into the Model T of personal computers—a workhorse that gave rise to a whole industry devoted to finding new ways of customizing it. But you had to open up the computer to plug these circuit boards in, and Raskin thought it was time to design a personal computer for people who would no more open up a computer than they would a toaster or a television set. His Macintosh was to be an all-in-one machine: no detachable keyboard or screen, no complicated instructions, everything built in—even the software, on preprogrammed chips.

Raskin's hardware designer, Burrell Smith, was a self-taught engineer and former Homebrew Computer Club member he'd discovered working in Apple's repair shop. Smith was a classic computer nerd—a Hobbitlike little man, short on social graces and all but innocent of personal hygiene, with the chopped-off blond curls of a fourteenth-century monk. By the time Jobs got interested, he'd already built two Macintoshes: one around the same microprocessor that was inside the Apple II, and then another around the Motorola 68000 that was in Lisa. He'd done it, moreover, in a way that was both quirky and brilliant. He didn't work like other engineers. His technique was to take home a bunch of parts, spread them all out on his bed, study the manuals that went with them, and sit there grooving on everything. Sooner or later, patterns would start to take shape in his mind (*this* to *that* to *that* to *this*—*click! click! click!*), and as quickly as he could he'd write it all down and move on to the next problem. It wasn't really anything he could explain; it was far too intuitive to bear any kind of rational analysis. But it worked.

Jobs, who admired brilliant engineering more than anything else, thought Burrell was the most inventive designer since Woz. He arranged raises for him and for Bud Tribble, a software wizard who'd been in some of the performance-art pieces Raskin had staged a decade earlier for his "Happenings and Events" course at UC San Diego. Then he started bringing in people of his own. He wanted Andy Hertzfeld, a friend of Smith's who wrote software in the Apple II division; when Hertzfeld said it would take him two weeks to finish the project he was working on, he started carrying Hertzfeld's belongings over himself. He went after the people he'd worked with in the early days, when Apple was still in the garage. He got Wozniak to sign up. He got Randy Wigginton, who'd been Woz's teenage follower at the Homebrew Computer Club. He got Rod Holt, the Marxist engineer who'd designed the Apple II power supply. He got Jerry Manock, the Hewlett-Packard veteran who'd designed the Apple II case. He got Dan Kottke, who'd been his best friend at Reed and trekked with him to India and then plugged microchips into the Apple I in his parents' living room. One day he told Raskin he was taking over hardware. Then he announced he was taking over software too, and Raskin could write the manuals. At that point, Raskin told him he could write his own manuals and went on a leave of absence.

Jobs was beginning to think of Macintosh as the next Apple II, the Apple II of the eighties, the Apple II carried a few orders of magnitude further. It was going to be a great computer—"insanely great," he liked to say with his wicked smile. Stung at being passed over to run Lisa, he wanted to show Scotty and Markkula and Couch how to do it right—how to build not just a great computer but a great organization. He had a small, hand-picked team, and he was going to create an environment that would encourage them to do really great things. Most people, he felt, don't do anything great because nobody ever demands it of them. Big organizations of the sort Couch had started creating for Lisa might guarantee a certain minimum level of competence, but nothing great would ever come out of them. His way was riskier. His way, they'd either fail completely or go down in history.

Woz's involvement was brief. On February 7, 1981, as he was taking off from a little airport near his home in the Santa Cruz Mountains, his single-engine Beechcraft shuddered and crashed. He woke up in the hospital several days later, unable to remember what had happened. For the next five weeks he could remember neither the crash nor anything that occurred after it, not even a conversation he'd had a few minutes before. Finally he woke up in the middle of the night and told his fiancée—who'd been with him in the plane, along with her brother and his girlfriend—that he'd just dreamed they'd had a plane crash. She told him it was no dream; and when he realized she was right, he decided it was time to take a break.

The others stayed, and it wasn't long before what they were doing began to take on—in their own minds, as well as Steve's—some of the aura, the mystique, of the garage in which Apple had been born. Apple was rapidly becoming a big company: Sales for 1980 hit nearly $120 million, and the reorganization that fall, when the company was split into product-line divisions, was accompanied by a hiring binge that doubled the number of employees in three months. Old-timers called it "the bozo explosion." The hackers and hobbyists were being edged out by degreed engineers from places like Hewlett-Packard, professionals who'd thought the Apple II was a dumb little toy in 1977 and who still thought that way today. It was obvious to these people that the Apple II would stop selling in a few months; they couldn't believe it had sold this long. And when it did stop, their job was to be ready with something real—if not the Apple III, then Lisa. Macintosh to them was just another toy, like the Apple II. They didn't understand that the Apple II was Apple's heart and soul—that Woz's dream of a computer you could know and understand and own and love was the essence of Apple, and that the Apple II was that dream made real.

But the people in the Macintosh group did know that. Take Hertzfeld, for instance. Andy had a face as round and as open as a pie plate, with hair all around it and an air of incredible impatience combined with total naiveté. He looked like a hippie, but he spoke techie jargon. Having first encountered computers through a time-sharing system in high school—he'd grown up on Philadelphia's Main Line—he'd majored in computer science at Brown and then come out to Berkeley for his Ph.D. But he was always frustrated by the computers in school, because he couldn't get close enough to them to understand what they were doing at a fundamental level. They were huge systems shared by hundreds of people, and you couldn't just go in and muck around because that would make them crash. But in 1976 he read that for $1,000 you could buy your own microcomputer, and in the spring of 1977 he went to the West Coast Computer Faire in San Francisco and saw the Apple II, which was being introduced there. It blew his mind. He didn't have the $1,800 to buy one, but nine months later a store had a $400-off sale and he took all his money out of the bank and did it. At that point he lost all interest in school. He became completely obsessed with his Apple II. He started writing programs for it and publishing them in hobbyist journals like *Dr. Dobb's Journal of Computer Calisthenics & Orthodontia,* and then he wrote a program that seemed good enough to sell. When he took it to Apple, they offered him a job. He took a master's instead of his Ph.D. and went to work right away.

So people like Andy became refugees from the bozo explosion. They worked in a place they called Texaco Towers, on the second floor of a little office building behind a Texaco station at the corner of Stevens Creek and De Anza, several blocks from the buildings on Bandley Drive. There was a pizza joint called Cicero's across the street, and every afternoon they'd go there to eat pizza and play Defender on the video-game machine. Jobs came over every evening from his office in Bandley 6 to see how they were doing. His patronage couldn't make the company care what they did, but it could buy them independence. They were mavericks like him. They thrived on excitement, on crisis, on the prospect of flaming out in fiery greatness. They weren't just trying to capture some market niche, they were out to change the way people thought about computers, which, after all, were the driving force of the twentieth century. They were out to change the world. They were building the new messiah.

Over on Bandley Drive, the traumas of rapid growth were taking their toll. Scotty was still frustrated by the kind of mismanagement that had led to the Apple III fiasco, and early in 1981, not long after Woz's plane crash, he summarily dismissed forty-one people—a purge that immediately entered Apple lore as "Black Wednesday." The uproar that followed was so great that Scotty himself was forced out as president and demoted to vice-chairman. Mike Markkula took over the job of running the company, and a few months later Scotty took his leave in a vitriolic outburst against "hypocrisy, yes-men . . . and empire-builders." The company was left reeling. Over at Texaco Towers, however, things perked along as before. To the little band of dreamers in the Macintosh crew, Apple seemed an increasingly distant place.

Not that there weren't points of contact. Bud Tribble was renting a room from the other veteran of Jef Raskin's early-seventies art happenings at UC San Diego, Bill Atkinson, who'd recently cashed in some of his Apple stock and bought a big house in Los Gatos, not far from where Jobs lived. Bill was designing LisaDraw—the graphic underpinnings of Lisa, the software that controlled its bit-mapped screen. It was Bud who'd seen what he was doing with Lisa and suggested to Burrell that they switch to the Motorola 68000 microprocessor so that Macintosh could take advantage of it. Lisa had sixty people working on software, and Bud was living in the same house with the guy at the center of it all—which meant they could rip it all off for Mac, just as Lisa was ripping it all off from Xerox. And in the process they could learn from Lisa's mistakes.

So Macintosh was beginning to look like a junior version of Lisa, with a mouse and a separate keyboard and windows and icons on-screen. All that remained of Raskin's ideas was his emphasis on low cost and his appliance concept—the closed architecture that meant it couldn't be customized. And yet, as the Lisa and Macintosh teams raced toward completion, they took increasingly divergent routes toward the end that had been defined at PARC. Lisa was a powerful office computer whose ever-increasing price tag could be justified by its large memory, its impressive data-storage capacity, and its sophisticated software. Macintosh was small and friendly like the Apple II, but much more powerful and easy to use. It wasn't meant for the kind of people who'd buy Lisa. It wasn't for people who read *The Wall Street Journal* and worked in giant corporations. Andy liked to say it was for his kid brother.

■ ■ ■

Now it was January 1983, two years after Jobs had taken over Macintosh. Lisa was out in the world. Scotty was gone, Markkula was president, Jobs had taken Markkula's position as chairman, and Couch had won the $5,000 bet. Macintosh was due to be introduced in August—the date had just slipped from May—and even though engineering realities had already precluded the hoped-for $1,000 price tag, the mood in the group was near-euphoric. The entire Valley was abuzz with rumors about Lisa's baby sister, the amazing little machine that could do everything Lisa could do for only $1,000 (or $1,200, or $1,500). The source of these rumors was Jobs, who was too enthusiastic about what he was doing to be very good at keeping a secret. "It's a strange ship that leaks from the top," as the saying went at Apple.

On the last Thursday in January, eight days after Lisa's introduction, the members of the Macintosh group piled into buses for a two-day trip to Carmel. There were a hundred people working on Macintosh now (the Lisa division had nearly that many in marketing alone), and this was probably the last time they'd all get together for an off-site retreat. They were going to the La Playa Hotel, a sedate establishment much favored by blue-haired ladies who wished to relax in a refined village by the sea. That's what Carmel had to offer: narrow lanes lined with art galleries and boutiques, flower-filled courtyards and twisted cypresses, a dazzlingly white beach, the bohemian charm of the artists' colony, all in an atmosphere of unbearable cuteness. It wasn't an obvious place for a business meeting, especially one that would be more like a college beer blast.

Ostensibly, this retreat was being held to bring everyone up to date on the status of the operation. In fact, they already knew the status: they were behind. Engineering wasn't finished. The disk drive was extremely iffy. None of the outside software developers had delivered anything. Marketing was out in the woods. The factory didn't even exist. But that wasn't really the point. The point was to build a little team spirit, to get everybody psyched up for the final push—and to have a good time.

Steve began with a little talk. That was part of the ritual—Steve standing up in front of them and turning on the reality-distortion field. He'd turn on the field and everybody would bask in it and pretty soon they'd all start to glow inside. So he stood at an easel at one end of a long, narrow conference room and unveiled the first of three epigrams:

REAL ARTISTS SHIP.

They were all artists. They knew that. But real artists don't hang on to their creations. Real artists ship. Matisse shipped. Picasso shipped. They were going to ship too. Next epigram:

MAC IN A BOOK BY 1986.

That was the vision. That was the ultimate dream. Alan Kay's Dynabook would be realized as a Macintosh. The next saying completed the picture:

IT'S BETTER TO BE A PIRATE THAN TO JOIN THE NAVY.

They weren't only artists, they were a band of renegades. And although he didn't mention names, it was clear that the contrast he was drawing wasn't just between Apple and IBM; it was between Macintosh and Lisa as well. It was between the future that had been taken away when Scotty split the company into divisions and the future he'd built for himself with Macintosh. The problem with Lisa technology was that Couch had screwed it up. With Macintosh, they were doing it right.

At the very least, they were doing it differently. These were kids, most of them still in their twenties, and they were all doing it for the first time. Burrell Smith had never designed a computer before. Mike Murray, the marketing director, had never introduced a computer before. Matt Carter, who was setting up the factory, had never manufactured one before. They were having an adventure. They were going to change the world. They'd missed the sixties—Murray and Jobs were both twelve years old when the hippies came to Haight-Ashbury for the summer of love—but they were young and idealistic all the same, and they certainly had a mission. Steve could make personal computers sound as important as Vietnam or civil rights. He could turn them into a crusade.

There were two veterans on the retreat. One was Jay Elliot, Apple's forty-two-year-old human-resources director, a tall man with a salt-and-pepper beard and the good-humored patience of a professional camp counselor. Elliot was calm. He knew how to chuckle. When he was eating dinner in the La Playa's primly starched dining room and saw a dozen Macintosh people swimming nude in the lighted pool outside, he chuckled softly and went on with his meal, oblivious to the polite strangling sounds of the blue-haired ladies all around. He was, after all, the official guardian of Apple's corporate culture, and if this was what he was supposed to guard, he was ready for the task. It was certainly more fun than IBM, where he'd worked for fourteen years before. At IBM the burning issue in personnel was whether the receptionists should be allowed to wear pants suits. Apple reminded him of his youth, when he'd dropped out of San Jose State to go surfing in Hawaii, then enrolled in the Don Martin School of Radio and Television Announcing in Hollywood and landed a job as a deejay at a Monterey radio station. He'd only gone into computers because IBM was hiring when he went back to San Jose State, and one of his professors said that's where the future was.

The other veteran was Bob Belleville, the Macintosh engineering director. Belleville came from a small farm town in the Midwest— Belleville, Illinois, to be precise—and with his straw-colored hair and baby face he looked as pale and unassuming as a glass of milk. Despite his appearance, however, he was Jobs's direct link to the ARPA dream. In the early seventies, after getting his Ph.D. from Purdue, he'd worked with Doug Engelbart at ARC. Then he'd helped build the Xerox Star, the $16,000 "office information system" that Xerox had introduced in 1981—the first computer based on PARC principles. Steve had hired him to manage software development for Macintosh because Andy didn't want the job. (Andy was an artist, and when artists become good they achieve recognition and acclaim, they don't start managing other artists.) He'd taken over all of engineering a few months later, when Rod Holt left to sail across the Pacific. And while he believed in what they were doing, he lacked the religious fervor of the newer converts. He didn't think they were going to change the world; they were simply designing a computer with a better "human interface."

After dinner that night, Bob stood up and gave a little talk—all very tongue-in-cheek, of course—about where they'd be a year from now, when Macintosh still hadn't shipped. Steve Jobs? Steve would be trying to get a job heading the Apple II division, which he claimed was the only decent part of the company anyway. Mike Murray? Mike would be running a clothing store in the Midwest and doing his own late-night advertisements on TV—phrases like "Hurry to Murray's!" wouldn't bother him. And Bob Belleville? He'd be driving alone across the West with a small box of semiconductors in his pocket. Whenever he ran into people, he'd open the box and show them what was inside; and if they knew what the little things were, he'd get back in his truck and drive deeper into the wilderness.

It was a great story, and after it was over, they all ran down to the beach and lit a bonfire, which was really fun until the police came and made them put it out. The next day they were invited gently but firmly never to return to the La Playa Hotel—whether because of the bonfire or the skinny-dipping they never knew for sure. But a curious thing happened in the bus on the way back. A woman had just been hired for marketing, and when she remarked to Bob that they were going to have to do some work to sell this computer, he told her he agreed completely. At that, a dozen people jumped up and said, "What? Are you crazy? There's no way!" They told her *everybody* was going to want a Macintosh. They told her Macintosh would sell itself.

Years later, when Steve had been fired and the Macintosh division had been subsumed in the corporate bureaucracy and Belleville was spending a large part of every day asleep, this exchange would reverberate through his dreams.

4

Twiggy

These off-site retreats were a way of life at Apple. There were off-sites for Lisa, off-sites for Macintosh, off-sites for the Apple II, off-sites for the executive staff. Some drew fifty to a hundred people; others involved no more than a division head and four or five staff members. Sometimes two or three off-sites would be going on at once—different parts of the company retreating to different parts of the region to consider this problem or that.

Of all the off-site locations, the one that was most frequently used was a beach colony on Monterey Bay called Pajaro Dunes—a sand spit at the mouth of the Pajaro River thirty-five miles south of Cupertino, on a stretch of coastline where the mountains and the headlands give way to a fertile plain that ends in a dune-protected beach. Pajaro Dunes was practically an extension of Bandley Drive. Its casual beach houses and rustic conference center offered solitude and comfort and the chance to measure your cares against the power and the vastness of the ocean—to keep things in perspective. Ten days after the Carmel retreat, however, Bob Belleville was sipping a drink at this Bandley-by-the-sea when he got some news that made the Pacific seem faraway and small.

The occasion was an off-site meeting of Apple's engineering council—the top engineers and engineering managers of the various divisions, a group whose only point of agreement was that the company ought to be run by engineers. Belleville was talking with Wayne Rosing, the engineering manager of the Lisa division, who was telling him about the problems they were having with their new disk drive—

the device that reads information from a floppy disk into the computer and from the computer onto the disk. For years, engineers in Apple's mass-storage division had been working on a high-performance drive that was code-named Twiggy. Twiggy was going into Lisa, and it was supposed to go into Macintosh as well. But now Rosing was telling him that Twiggy was in deep trouble. Rosing was telling him that the mass-storage division could barely turn out enough Twiggies to satisfy Lisa's demands, that most of those it did manufacture didn't work, and that the Twiggies Macintosh was depending on would never arrive on time. "Wayne," he cried, his voice cracking with panic, "there's no possible way!"

Twiggy was not, of course, the only disk drive Macintosh could use. Several of Belleville's engineers had already been pushing for a new, three-and-a-half-inch "microfloppy" recently introduced by Sony. Strictly speaking, the Sony disk wasn't really a floppy at all, since it was encased in a rigid plastic housing rather than a flexible plastic sleeve. That meant the Sony disks weren't as delicate as the ordinary five-and-a-quarter-inch disks, which were always in danger of being ruined by bends and fingerprints and spilled drinks. The Sony disks were also small enough to slip into a shirt pocket, and the drives they slipped into used less power than five-and-a-quarter-inch drives, which meant they generated less heat—always a plus in computer design.

So that Thursday, Belleville met with Steve and told him about Twiggy and suggested they explore the possibilities with Sony. Steve said to go ahead. Then he wrote a bitter memo to Mike Markkula in which he declared that he'd lost all confidence in the mass-storage division. If Twiggy went into Macintosh, he wrote, it would tank the project.

The next day, he and Belleville drove to the mass-storage division to check up on Twiggy in person. Mass storage was out on Orchard Parkway in San Jose, just off the Bayshore Freeway in an area of flat, featureless farmland that was rapidly going industrial. It was not an attractive place, and what they found when they got there was even less attractive.

They went onto the factory floor and started inspecting the Twiggies that were coming down the production line. When they talked to the people on the line, they discovered that most of them were temporaries who'd never built a disk drive before and didn't even know what one was. They discovered that engineering revisions were occurring so often that a single drive rarely got all the way through the production line without one. When they asked what the yield was—that is, how many drives coming off each step of the line actually worked—they were given figures like 30 percent. When they totaled up all the steps in the line and the yield for each step, they came up with a final yield that was virtually zero. In other words, a Twiggy that worked was a rare event. The more they learned, the redder Jobs's face became. Finally he began to sputter incoherently and talk about firing everyone in sight. Slowly, gingerly, lest he do something he'd later regret, Belleville maneuvered him into the parking lot. The two of them walked around the parking lot for a long time. Belleville kept repeating that it really wasn't these people's fault. He told him it was John Vennard, the head of the mass-storage division, they had to deal with, not these people. Finally they got in Steve's Mercedes and drove away.

■　■　■

Belleville was wrong about one thing: Twiggy wasn't just Vennard's fault. Twiggy was emblematic of all that had gone wrong at Apple. It showed what runaway success had done, how it had given them all the sense that they were so brilliant they could do anything, and it demonstrated how crippling such an attitude could be. Two years earlier, after the trauma of the Apple III introduction and the mass firings on Black Wednesday and the removal of Mike Scott as president, Markkula had decided it was time to formalize the values of the company. He'd appointed an eight-member task force to do it, and a few months later the task force had come back with nine "Apple Values": "One person/one computer," "We are all on an adventure together," "We build products we believe in," "We set the pace," and so forth. A tenth Apple Value might have been "We work here, so we must be brilliant." Twiggy was the most visible result of this hubris, but the attitude itself was pervasive. Everybody at Apple seemed to think he was Woz. And the result was Twiggy, an engineering project that had turned into a nightmare.

The basic idea of the floppy disk is simple: a thin sheet of Mylar plastic, encased in a square paper sleeve and coated with a magnetic material that stores information. It's like recording tape, except that it's round and flat instead of long and spooled. The circular Mylar disk spins around inside the disk drive like a record on a turntable, and information is taken off it and put back on through a hole in the sleeve by a head that's like the head in a tape recorder.

Minicomputers and mainframes had used eight-inch floppies for years, but they were too large and expensive for micros. So when hobbyist computers like the Apple II were introduced, people hooked them up to ordinary cassette tapes. That limited their computers' usefulness dramatically; cassette recorders were unreliable and slow, and computer owners who had to rely on them wouldn't get much done. A floppy disk, on the other hand, made finding information as simple as automatically cueing a record. Then a Silicon Valley company called Shugart introduced an inexpensive five-and-a-quarter-inch floppy-disk drive. But before it could be hooked up to any particular computer, someone would have to design a special circuit board to control it—to tell it what to do and when. So at the end of 1977, Wozniak began a binge effort to design a disk controller that would make the five-and-a-quarter-inch floppy-disk drive work on the Apple II.

This was a task that could occupy a team of engineers for months. Woz did it in a few weeks, staying up nights, working through Christmas Day, going without sleep, living off French fries from McDonald's. He came up with a brilliantly intuitive solution, one that did the job with eight chips instead of the usual fifty to seventy. "Poetry in electronics," Burrell Smith later called it. Apple bought the drives themselves from Shugart and then worked with the Alps Electric Company of Japan to design a less expensive clone. The resulting product, the Disk II, was almost obscenely profitable: For about $140 in parts ($80 after the shift to Alps), Apple could package a disk drive and a disk controller in a single box that sold at retail for upwards of $495. Better yet was the impact the Disk II had on computer sales, for it suddenly transformed the Apple II from a gadget only hard-core hobbyists would want to something all sorts of people could use. Few outsiders realized it, but in strategic terms, Woz's invention of the disk controller was as important to the company as his invention of the computer itself.

By 1983 there was no reason for Apple even to try to build its own high-performance drives; they could be bought off the shelf from other companies that already knew how. But the Twiggy project had been started in 1978, when the five-and-a-quarter-inch floppy disk was still a new invention. Apple had been so successful in adapting the floppy-disk drive to the Apple II that there was no reason to think it couldn't repeat that success again. Only this time, everything went wrong.

Certainly when Rod Holt—who as Apple's vice-president of engineering had redesigned the Shugart drive for manufacture by Alps—started thinking of ways to build a drive that would store more information on a disk and do it more reliably than the Disk II, it was only natural to think he could do it. Holt got together a few engineers and started working on concepts. But Mike Scott was an impatient man, and he decided that Holt's disk drive would be perfect for Lisa, the machine Wozniak was supposed to have ready in six months. This was in 1979. John Vennard, an Apple executive who'd worked with Scotty at National Semiconductor, took over the disk-drive project, promising to deliver a product in time for Lisa. Holt left the project in disgust.

As Holt suspected, Vennard gradually discovered that if the idea of a disk drive is simple, the engineering realities are tricky indeed. None of his engineers had actually designed one before, and the schedule they were committed to didn't give them time to learn how. The best they could do was take the ideas they already had and freeze them into a product definition. When those ideas didn't work, there was no time to go back and re-engineer anything; all they could do was apply Band-Aids, which invariably solved one problem while causing three others.

It didn't help that one of Steve Jobs's cardinal rules for Apple computers was that they should not contain a fan to dissipate the heat generated by their electronic circuitry. Fans, Jobs felt, were noisy and distracting, and any computer that had one was *ipso facto* a piece of shit. It also didn't help that someone in marketing decided, for no apparent reason, that Apple computers ought to run at an ambient temperature of 110 degrees. If you put a computer with no fan in a room that was 110 degrees, the temperature inside the computer would go to 140—hot enough to crumble the paper sleeve around the disk. And it most particularly didn't help that the engineers in mass storage lacked a firm mastery of the physics that governed how a disk drive worked. So Twiggy turned out to be a four-year exercise in missteps, coverups, and disasters, the fix for each one leading inexorably to the next. By 1983, this process had given Lisa a disk drive that was unreliable, expensive, and all but unmanufacturable.

■ ■ ■

One thing they did do well at Apple was throw parties, although they didn't always throw them on time. The Macintosh Christmas party was held in February, just as the Twiggy situation was nearing the crisis point. It was a formal dinner-dance at the St. Francis Hotel in downtown San Francisco, a black-tie affair with two orchestras playing waltzes. Jobs had to talk the group into it; most of them would rather have hired a rock band and worn denim. But Jobs had developed sophisticated adult tastes rather rapidly after Apple's public stock offering had turned him into an instant millionaire at age twenty-five: He wore bow ties and hand-tailored suits, and drove a shiny new Mercedes coupe, which he left in the handicapped zone whenever all the convenient parking spots were taken. His Christmas party had to be special and, like everything else he touched, it had to be perfect. There remained the problem of how to get the Macintosh people to go along. He told them to think of it as a costume party—a Halloween party, maybe—and that made it okay. He also gave them all waltzing lessons.

Jobs's date for the evening was Joan Baez, whom he'd met in the process of donating an Apple II to her relief organization, Humanitas. They made a singularly glamorous couple as they glided across the ballroom of the St. Francis, he in his black tuxedo, she in a long lace gown. They sat at a table with Burrell Smith and Andy Hertzfeld and some of the other key Macintosh people, several of whom were wearing sneakers with their rented tuxes. Baez, not relishing the prospect of small talk with a bunch of computer nerds half her age, remained serene and aloof. But while Jobs was charmingly deferential—he'd revered her as a teenager, after all—it was clear that he relished the juxtaposition. He could handle incongruity, he could move between different worlds, he could hold conflicting views in his head. It would take a lot more than a waltz with Joan Baez with the pirates in attendance to throw him off.

There was another party about that time, a company-wide party on Valentine's Day in a parking lot on Bandley Drive, right behind Eli McFly's. This was the party to celebrate Apple's achievement of a billion-dollar run rate. Sales for December had reached $100 million, and when you multiplied that by twelve months you got annual sales of over $1 billion—in other words, a billion-dollar run rate. It was the crowning achievement of Mike Markkula's stewardship. In six years—first as chairman, then as president—he'd taken the company from a garage operation to a billion-dollar enterprise. He was ready to retire. And this, in essence, was his going-away party.

There was no question that Markkula was largely responsible for Apple's success. He and his buddies from the semiconductor industry had turned the Apple II into a manufacturable product, had built a sales and distribution network from nothing, had constructed the platform that enabled Steve Jobs to become the avatar of personal computing. But there was also no concealing that he wanted out. He wasn't a man who liked to make tough decisions, and with Scotty gone the tough decisions had been deferred more and more. The popularity of the Apple II had been so phenomenal as to bury any problems in an avalanche of sales, but the problems were there. Twiggy was one. The Apple III was another. The rivalry between Macintosh and Lisa was a third. In his quiet, benign way, Markkula had been letting them all fester.

Basically, Markkula just wanted to play with his computers. He was the kind of guy who liked to go home after a hard day at the office and write programs until three in the morning. His idea of how to get the management team to work together was to pass out floppy disks in which every vice-president was asked to rate all the other vice-presidents on various points, then merge all the responses together and calculate the result. But it was all too easy to tell what most of the vice-presidents thought of each other simply from the way they talked in executive staff meetings. Unlike the vice-presidents of most American corporations, who are constrained by mortgages and college expenses and hope of advancement from being too forthright about their feelings, these people didn't give a damn what they said. Why should they? Apple had made them rich. Most of them were worth $10 million or more, and several were worth well over $100 million. They could walk away tomorrow and spend the rest of their lives happily managing their investments. So they tended to be frank with each other—often too frank. And the company was growing so fast that they were all in a perpetual frenzy. Markkula didn't need it. He'd proved himself twice, first at Intel and then at Apple, and now he wanted to go home.

Meanwhile, the company he was shepherding had devolved into a confederation of warring fiefdoms. Scotty's divisionalization had pinpointed responsibility for different projects, but it also created rivalries. After divisionalization, the drawbridges went up. Each division developed its own culture. Each division looked to its own leader for support. Each division was as strong as its leader and no stronger. Lisa was strong because John Couch was an ambitious and assertive man whose product, everyone agreed, represented Apple's future. Macintosh was strong because Steve Jobs was a founder of the company and its chairman and largest stockholder. Apple II was weak because its people were blamed for the failure of the Apple III, because its leader was unassertive, and because Markkula, unable to decide who should replace him, had decided its marketing and engineering managers should share authority. Mass storage was only as strong as John Vennard's credibility, and Jobs was determined to destroy that as soon as possible.

Still, Apple's success was undeniable, and it covered up a great many mistakes. So the celebration on Valentine's Day was lavish and festive, and employees and their families were bused in from all over the Valley to be part of it. An enormous white circus tent was erected in the parking lot, and tables beneath it were laden with cheeses and sandwiches and ice sculptures. Apples and balloons were everywhere, and crystal wine goblets etched with the Apple logo were given away to all present. The Stanford marching band and cheerleaders made a dramatic appearance. Markkula and Jobs gave speeches, and Rich Page and Bill Atkinson, the chief hardware and software wizards behind Lisa, were named "Apple Fellows" in appreciation of their work. For almost everyone there, it was a wonderful celebration. Only a couple of people noticed Jobs and Vennard in a remote corner of the parking lot, circling each other like dogs, fangs bared.

■ ■ ■

Meanwhile, in Japan, Alps wanted Apple's business. If it couldn't manufacture the Twiggy drive for Macintosh, maybe it could make the drive Sony had invented. It had already licensed the basic technology for the three-and-a-half-inch microfloppy-disk drive from Sony, and its engineers were scrambling to design their own version of it. Alps was in the second tier in the hierarchy of Japanese electronics firms—big, but not as big as Sony or Hitachi. Mostly it made little things, switches and connectors and the like. It was one of Sony's suppliers. Apple had gotten it into the disk-drive business with the Disk II, and now it was ready for more. So on the morning in early March when Jobs and Belleville and Rod Holt and Dave Vaughan, the man in charge of Macintosh manufacturing, got off the bullet train from Tokyo in the little town of Furukawa, two hundred miles to the north, they found what seemed like sixty people waiting for them. These people grabbed their luggage and whisked them into limousines and sped them directly to the Alps disk-drive factory a couple of blocks away. There they found Alps's chief disk-drive engineer beaming proudly over a chunk of aluminum that had some holes drilled into it. This was Alps's model of its three-and-a-half-inch drive. Steve thought it was wonderful.

So did Rod. Years before, Rod had worked with Alps's engineers to clone the Shugart drive for the Apple II, and he'd built up close relationships with people up and down the company. He liked the way Alps did things, and he liked the ideas Alps had for simplifying the Sony drive. Belleville, on the other hand, was appalled. The Alps drive was wonderful, all right, but it was also years away from production. He was supposed to deliver Macintosh on time, and Alps didn't even have a working prototype. They were still designing the thing. One look at this hogged-out model was enough to convince him it was in worse shape than Twiggy.

For the next three days they visited other companies and looked at other drives. They weren't impressed by anything. They'd be ushered into a room and rafts of engineers would come out to show them their drives and Steve would pick one up and examine it for a minute with a look of extreme distaste and cry, "What are you showing me *this* for? This is a piece of crap! *Anybody* could build a better drive than this." Then the engineers would murmur politely and disappear into another room, doubtless to commit hara-kiri. It was Steve's first trip to Japan, and he was indifferent to the niceties of doing business there. He'd show up wearing blue jeans at formal meetings with the heads of major corporations. The underlings were flabbergasted, but the corporate chieftains loved it. They'd all heard about this brash young California entrepreneur, this millionaire industrialist who'd started in a garage, and to meet him in person was—well, it was almost as good as going to Disneyland. And then, when he explained that the only reason he was holding their products up to ridicule was because he admired their company and he wanted their products to be the best in the world—when he did that, with that riveting intensity that turned his eyes into magnets, they nearly swooned.

Sony was last on the list. The Sony drives were made at a camera factory in Atsugi, a drab industrial suburb an hour's drive from Tokyo—a crowded little town full of dumpy-looking factories and gray concrete houses with bright blue tile roofs. When the team from

Apple got there and looked at the drive, Steve hated it. It looked like a pile of parts. It was complicated and messy and expensive to make. Sony was manufacturing it by hand, according to traditional Japanese techniques, and shipping a couple of hundred a month to Hewlett-Packard, its only major customer, which was using them in one of its own new computers. Until other companies adopted it, there was no reason to commit the resources it would take to make it cheap and easy to produce. In the meantime, Sony was essentially shipping prototypes. But Steve had a highly developed sense of engineering aesthetics, and the Sony prototype clearly fell short of his standards.

That evening they went back to the Okura, a sprawling and lavishly appointed businessman's hotel across the street from the American embassy and not far from the Imperial Palace. They had drinks in a lounge and debated their options. Bob Belleville and Dave Vaughan favored the Sony. Steve and Rod were convinced it was no good. As far as they were concerned, there was only one thing to do: work with Alps and design a better drive. Vaughan objected but was beaten down. Belleville decided there were forces at work here that were larger than he was, so he went along.

With Steve's encouragement, Rod set up a crash program to help Alps design the drive. He thought they could do it in three months. But Bob saw Twiggy repeating itself. Bob and Rod were good friends, but over the next few weeks Bob's distaste for the project—his "defeatist thinking," Rod called it—led to sharp words between them. Outwardly the two were quite similar: Both born tinkerers, they combined a fresh-faced Midwestern innocence with a childlike fascination with the way things work. In other ways, however, their personalities were radically divergent.

Rod, thin and angular, came from an old New England family in which a puritan sense of the elect coexisted with a fervent Marxist ideology. He had ancestors who'd prospered in the China trade and a grandfather who'd committed himself to socialism in the twenties, he saw no reason to let wealth from a capitalist business venture such as Apple interfere with his belief in the workers' revolution. His conflict was elsewhere. He wanted to stay at Apple, but he was tired of trying to manage people. He wanted to be an engineer, but he also wanted to race his sailboat across the Pacific. And while Bob was as soft-spoken and mild-mannered as they come, he was also ambitious and, as far as many people in the Macintosh group were concerned, way too uptight about his own status and authority.

A former vestryman of his Episcopal church, married to his high-school sweetheart, Bob couldn't help but regard the Macintosh environment as anarchic and crazed. He was supposed to be running engineering, and yet Steve was constantly changing things without telling him and turning everything upside-down and leaving him to deal with the mess. There were superstar engineers like Andy and Burrell who took direction only from Steve, and then there was Rod, who had enormous historical authority but didn't have much follow-through. Already Bob had had to go to Steve and Rod individually and patiently—calmly, he thought—explain how they were making his life impossible. It was insane, and he soon began to think of this business with Alps as the worst yet.

So one day in mid-March, he went to Mike Markkula and told him what was going on. Markkula listened quietly and told him to do whatever he had to do, but get Macintosh a drive that worked. From that point on, Bob had two positions regarding the disk drive. His public position was to go along with the plan to help Alps design one. His private position was to work with Sony to make its drive acceptable to Steve.

Several engineers backed him up on this, and together they developed a little conspiracy. Bob had dinner with an executive from Sony America. He told the man he couldn't promise anything, but if Sony would put some work into the drive they might be able to do some business together. A few days later, the drive's inventor came over for a week to work out the specs of a drive that would meet Steve's requirements. Hidetoshi Komoto was a pleasant young man who'd studied at Purdue and spoke fluent English, and he was aware of the constraints of the job—the need to work with the Macintosh engineers without Steve knowing he was there. Day after day they played a shell game with him. Every time Steve left his office in Bandley 6 and headed over to the engineering department, they'd shuffle him frantically from one cubicle to another. They had him running down the halls, hiding behind desks, stuffed into closets. Steve never saw him there, although they did run into each other once at the magazine counter in a drug store. Steve came back and remarked how peculiar it was, running into Komoto in Cupertino. As for Komoto, he couldn't help wondering, every time he had to crouch in some empty cubicle, why no one had ever told him that this was how Americans did business.

5

Package Goods

The change, when it came, was fast. For months the dozen or so vice-presidents on Apple's executive staff had known that Markkula would be stepping down and that a search for a replacement was under way. Only a couple of them knew that an outside candidate had been found and that Steve was courting him assiduously. Most still expected Floyd Kvamme to take over as soon as he'd been there long enough to learn the ropes. That was a reassuring thought: a nice, orderly transition to a new CEO from the ranks of the local semiconductor industry. Then, suddenly, John Sculley landed in their midst.

It began on a Friday morning in April, when Markkula called them together, all the executive staff, for a special meeting in the boardroom on the second floor of Bandley 6. There, in his calm, matter-of-fact fashion, he announced that Apple was getting a new president. His name was John Sculley, he was forty-four years old, and he was the president of the Pepsi-Cola Company and a senior vice-president of its corporate parent, PepsiCo, Inc. Sculley, he added, had an architecture degree from Brown and an M.B.A. from Wharton, was married to his third wife, "Leezy," and was an absolutely outstanding, though noncharismatic, individual—at which point Jobs jumped in to say that he disagreed, he thought Sculley was *very* charismatic. The reaction was muted. People were a little nervous, but the decision had been made. Steve was obviously in favor of it, and it certainly wouldn't do to appear unwelcoming.

Pepsi made a public announcement that afternoon, and on Monday morning *The Wall Street Journal* hit the stands with a major article. From the *Journal* they learned several intriguing facts: that Sculley had married and then divorced the stepdaughter of PepsiCo's chairman, Donald M. Kendall; that in coming to Apple he'd given up the chance to succeed Kendall, who was planning to retire in a few years; and that his decision had been eased by the promise of a $1-million salary, a $1-million bonus the first year, and a $1-million severance package, plus options on 350,000 shares of stock and a loan to buy a $2-million, Tudor-style house with a kidney-shaped pool in Woodside, a horsey little village set amid the peninsula's rolling hills. Two days later he was there among them, opening his first executive staff meeting. It was Wednesday, April 13.

The word for Sculley was understated. He wasn't dull, he wasn't nondescript, but he wasn't the kind of guy who could take over a room by walking into it. In that sense he resembled Markkula more than Jobs. But he didn't look like Markkula, or like any other executive they'd ever seen at Apple. He was wearing a business suit. He looked comfortable in it. He looked like he'd been wearing suits and ties all his life. There were people at Apple who generally wore a tie—Floyd Kvamme, for one, and Joe Graziano, the chief financial officer—but it was hardly the adornment of choice. It was constricting. It had to go with your clothes. You might spill something on it. Far better to go to work in an open collar and blue jeans, or polyester. Polyester was very big on the exec staff, especially among the semiconductor veterans. People often said that Apple was run by kids with money falling out of their jeans, but in fact it was run by guys with money falling out of their burgundy-colored Sansabelt slacks. Sculley had probably never even walked into a place where such a garment was sold. He was a product of the Ivy League: buttoned-down, corporate, and utterly alien. Here they were in sunny California, with its casual dress code and its go-for-the-gold business climate, and now it looked as if they were being taken over by some exponent of the Eastern establishment. It was the Porsche versus the limousine, and none of them were eager to make the trade.

What he said, however, was calming and reassuring. He said they had to avoid letting Apple lose its entrepreneurial values, suggesting that at least he didn't want to smother the freewheeling spontaneity of Apple under layers of corporate bureaucracy. He said his job was to build, not to change, because Apple was already in good shape. He talked about shifting from a one-product to a multiproduct company—an issue they'd been trying to deal with for some time—and he talked about the need to "leverage Apple's critical mass," a Steve Jobs phrase that meant using Apple's size to bomb out the competition. He went on and on for hours, and during all that time he said only one thing that was startling or new: that in entering the corporate marketplace, Apple was venturing into a "total systems environment," one that entailed a host computer and data communications and individual workstations.

That *was* startling, if you thought about it. It suggested a challenge, or at least an amendment, to the central tenet of the Apple belief system—Jobs's techie-populist notion of "One person—one computer." It suggested that in order to succeed in the business world, they were going to have to emulate IBM. But that was easy to overlook in the excitement Sculley generated when he talked about the need to "stay ahead of the power curve." So what if nobody was quite sure what a power curve was? It sounded like a good thing to stay ahead of.

Steve sat through all this like the proud owner of an ingenious new toy. He'd been wooing Sculley since Christmas—dinners, phone calls, personal visits, long walks, heart-to-heart talks. The search for a new president had begun more than a year before, when Ed Winguth, a local headhunter who'd brought in many Apple executives, was asked to find someone to help Markkula run the company. Winguth was looking for a technologist, someone who could function either in a strategic role as chief executive officer or a tactical role as chief operating officer. He'd approached several candidates, among them Don Estridge, the atypically easygoing IBM executive who'd led the development of the PC and who now headed IBM's personal-computer unit in Boca Raton, Florida.

Estridge had a reputation as something of a renegade within IBM's rigid hierarchy, and he had a track record that was hard to argue with. Under his leadership the PC had been a spectacular success—200,000 units sold in its first full year of production, according to outside estimates, and a market share that was beginning to encroach upon Apple's 26 percent lead. Of course, the product hadn't been his idea; the goal of building a personal computer to compete with Apple had issued from corporate headquarters in the leafy suburban hamlet of Armonk, New York.

Armonk had been caught sleeping on the minicomputer, and it didn't want to be caught sleeping again. Frank Cary, who was then the chairman of IBM, had decided to champion the cause of the personal computer as an IBM market opportunity. He'd pushed the general systems division, IBM's small-computer unit, to conduct a study. He'd overruled marketing's objections that they had no one to market such a product. He'd forced the creation of a small, independent team to develop it. General systems had identified Boca Raton, Florida, home of its Series 1 mid-sized computers and System 23 office workstations, as the optimum place to conduct product development, and Don Estridge, a bright young software manager for the Series 1, as the person to head the effort. Carey gave him a year to get the job done and told him to do it whatever way he could. Estridge took the assignment and ran.

Between 1980 and 1983, the PC development effort grew from a twelve-man task force to an independent business unit to a full-fledged division. Estridge mimicked Apple's entrepreneurial attitude throughout, breaking IBM rules and creating an atmosphere so tinged with excitement that people who worked with him thought of it as Camelot. Like Jobs, he was full of energy and intelligence and charisma; he also had a remarkable generosity of spirit. He could give you an idea and make you think it was your own, and he could put so much trust in you that you'd break down walls to get your job done. And although he wasn't well known outside the business world, within its confines he was nearly as famous as Wozniak and Jobs.

By the fall of 1982, headhunters for rival computer companies were stumbling all over each other in Boca Raton. If a senior executive there didn't get at least one call a week, he began to get worried. But Estridge, for all his charisma and his informality and his reputation for derring-do—all he had to do was cock a leg at a press conference and the press went nuts—was both a devoted Floridian and a devoted IBMer. On a trip out to California he spent a full day in meetings at Markkula's house; later, he and his wife met Jobs for dinner in Boca when Jobs flew out to make an offer. Apple was offering a package worth several million dollars—more than he or anyone else could ever hope to make at IBM. It was tough on all of them, staying with the corporation and watching all the entrepreneurial types rake it in. Yet in the end, after long talks with Armonk, he decided to stay.

There were many reasons. He and his team at Boca had set out to build an Apple-killer; he didn't like the thought of abandoning them now and going over to the enemy. And it bothered him that Jobs still talked about his blue-box escapades; he didn't like the thought of working for a guy who'd gotten his start through theft of services from the phone company. But when one of his vice-presidents asked him how he could turn the job down, all he said was that when he met somebody on a plane and that person asked him where he worked, he enjoyed being able to say "IBM."

In the latter part of 1982, in the wake of the Estridge episode, Jobs and Markkula had decided that Apple was actually a consumer-products company, not a technology enterprise, and that they didn't really want a technologist at all. So they met with Gerry Roche, president of the New York head-hunting firm of Heidrick & Struggles, and gave him a long list of attributes the new president should have: He should be someone with a strong background in consumer marketing and an interest in technology; someone who could fit into the Apple culture and serve as a mentor for Steve; someone who was both a natural leader and a visionary thinker. Roche came up with nearly 150 names, chairmen and presidents and senior vice-presidents of major corporations, among them such unlikely possibilities as Buck Rodgers, IBM's top marketing executive, and Charlie Brown, the chairman of AT&T. Most weren't interested.

The shorter the list grew, the more Sculley's name stood out. As president of Pepsi-Cola for five years—almost as long as Apple had been in business—he had obvious management experience. As the person credited with reviving the "Pepsi Generation" campaign, he was a recognized genius at consumer marketing. Jobs had decided he needed marketing expertise to sell Macintosh—in other words, to do the send-off for his crusade. And with Markkula stepping down and Woz gone, Jobs was the only one of the founders still active in the company. The choice of a new president was essentially his call. It would be subject only to board approval, and Apple's board—which consisted of Markkula, two venture capitalists, the head of Macy's California, the head of the high-technology conglomerate Teledyne, and Jobs—was unlikely to deny him any reasonable choice.

Jobs didn't seem to mind that Sculley's role in the "Pepsi Generation" campaign and the development of "lifestyle" advertising was more that of caretaker than of innovator. The campaign had been dreamed up in 1963, well before his arrival at Pepsi, by John Bergin, the creative director at Pepsi's Madison Avenue ad agency, working with Pepsi's advertising chief and its new president, a former fountain syrup salesman named Donald Kendall. Kendall's predecessor, Alfred Steele, had, with the help of relentless publicity appearances by his wife, Joan Crawford, transformed Pepsi from a perennial loser into a soft drink that could challenge Coke. Inexplicably, however, their ads touted Pepsi as a high-society beverage. Then Bergin, working from research that showed that most cola drinkers over the age of twenty-three wanted to be younger than they actually were, developed a campaign built around the slogan "Now it's Pepsi, for those who think young." Kendall pushed him to do something with even more pizzazz, and the result was a series of terrifically exciting spots, full of athletes, sports cars, and motorbikes, all building to the theme of "Come alive—you're in the Pepsi Generation!"

In 1965, Kendall merged Pepsi-Cola with Frito-Lay and assumed the presidency of the new PepsiCo, Inc., putting Pepsi in the hands of a former bottler, who thought, like most bottlers, that advertising ought to feature the product. He was wrong, and at the end of the sixties the "Pepsi Generation" returned, bolder and more exciting than ever. Sculley played a part in its revival. As a thirty-year-old marketing whiz viewing the riots and protests of the sixties, he thought a campaign that captured youthful exuberance could use the turbulence of the times for Pepsi's advantage. He also realized that if you put soft drinks in bigger bottles, people would buy more. Pepsi's market share began a six-year spurt of almost uninterrupted growth. In 1975, having made the youthquake safe for consumerism, Sculley was put in charge of PepsiCo Foods International, the overseas snack-food division. By the time he was brought back to head Pepsi-Cola three years later, the drink was outselling Coke in food stores for the first time since its invention by a North Carolina pharmacist some eighty years before.

The driving figure in the transformation of Pepsi-Cola from purveyor of a backwoods elixir to multinational junk food empire was Donald Kendall. Sculley was Kendall's protégé. The son of a Wall Street lawyer, he'd had a very proper childhood in the moneyed precincts of Manhattan's Upper East Side. He'd gone to grade school at Buckley, where everyone except the Greek shipowners' sons lived carefully circumscribed lives. Most of his summers were spent at Head of the Harbor, a small, discreet beach community in the picturesque village of St. James on Long Island's north shore. At age eleven he was sent off to St. Mark's, a boarding school in the woods outside Southborough, Massachusetts. St. Mark's was a training ground for the Episcopal elite, cliquish, conservative, and so select as to make Exeter and Andover and Choate seem wildly democratic by comparison. Along with St. Paul's, St. George's, Groton, and Middlesex, it made up the legendary "St. Grottlesex"—a New England archipelago of tiny, isolated, all-male communities where adolescent boys assembled for chapel every morning and learned well the meaning of competition and caste. There were no Kennedys among them, nor any Jews.

The point of such an education was to turn out well-buffed young men, thoroughly inculcated with Protestant Anglo-Saxon values and ready to move on to the Ivy League on their way to a career in law or finance, preferably on Wall Street. Young Sculley showed more interest in electronics than he might have, but he adjusted well enough to be selected captain of the soccer team and head monitor. When it came time to go to college, however, he could muster no interest in law, the field his father had picked out for him. He wanted to go to art school and study to be an architect, or maybe an industrial designer. So after St. Mark's he went to Brown, the least fashionable of the Ivy League schools, because Brown was in Providence and he could also study at the Rhode Island School of Design. It was there, in 1960, that he met and married Kendall's stepdaughter.

He went on to the University of Pennsylvania, where he was planning to get a master's degree in architecture until events conspired to lure him into marketing. At a summer job with Donald Deskey's design firm in New York, he saw that most of the creative decisions were being made by marketing people. Working on a shopping center for the Philadelphia Redevelopment Authority, he realized that market research could tell him where people really like to sit. Kendall thought some marketing training would be helpful, so he decided to go to Wharton to be a better architect.

There he got hooked on marketing for its own sake. He was fascinated by products because they offered a chance to create and to build. He got so interested in advertising that after he graduated in 1963 he went to work for McCann-Erickson, the agency that handled the Coke account. Madison Avenue was no more an acceptable substitute for the buttoned-down world of Wall Street than architecture, but Sculley by this time had a powerful mentor in Kendall. A rough-hewn, hard-driving man, large in stature and crowned by a thatch of white hair, Kendall cut quite a different figure from Sculley's father, who'd grown increasingly weighed down by his obligations. Young

Sculley divorced his wife the same year Kendall divorced her mother, a unique form of male bonding. Then, in 1967, he joined Pepsi as a trainee—the first M.B.A. in a company where most of the executives were bottlers who hadn't been to college at all. In three years he was vice-president of marketing.

Like Estridge, Sculley had spent almost his entire career inside the corporate cocoon—a 120-acre park that was just a short drive, psychically as well as physically, from Armonk. He'd never seen any place like Apple before, nor had he met anyone like Steve—with the possible exception of Kendall. The two men were totally different, of course—Kendall a great bear of a man, a captain of industry, Jobs lithe and young, a social revolutionary and corporate gadfly—but in some ways they were oddly similar. Both had intense personal charisma. Both had interests outside business, like art and architecture. Both saw the world in black and white. And both had total and unfailing confidence that they were right. Sculley maintained the cool, remote exterior of the successful corporate executive, but he struck those close to him as a shy and insecure little boy still acting out the role he was expected to fill. Jobs could show him how to break away from St. Grottlesex completely. Jobs was doing what he might have done if he'd grown up in Silicon Valley instead of the Upper East Side. Apple offered the chance to reinvent himself, which was the California dream; and Sculley, like generations of uptight Easterners before him, responded to it as a drowning man.

At first, however, he was just curious. Jobs and Markkula flew to New York to meet him in December, but he was cool during the meeting and afterwards told Roche he wasn't interested. That didn't deter Roche; the good people always put up a fight. It left Jobs absolutely intrigued. So they kept up the pressure. Roche told Sculley that Silicon Valley was like Florence in the Renaissance—it was where the best minds of an era had congregated. In January they showed him Lisa and went out to dinner at the Four Seasons. In early March, when Pepsi had a bottler meeting in Hawaii, Jobs persuaded him to stop in Cupertino on his way back. He told the Macintosh software team that this good friend of his who was the president of Pepsi-Cola was thinking of buying Macs for his company, and they prepared a nifty little demonstration program for him that had Pepsi bottle caps bouncing across the screen.

Sculley liked the bottle caps; like Jobs on his tour of Xerox PARC, he thought this was a computer he could do something with. But he realized the job they were talking about wasn't really the CEO's. The chief executive officer of a corporation like Apple is the person who sets the agenda, who makes the directional decisions, who leads the company. That was what Jobs thought he did, although he didn't have the title or authority of CEO. So the position he was being offered, apparently, was that of Jobs's partner in running the company. He began to wonder if Jobs was someone he could work with, the way he worked with Kendall.

There were a number of reasons why Jobs wanted Sculley so much. First, of course, was his reputation as a marketing whiz. He wasn't full of hot air like most corporate types. He was bright and articulate and he had outside interests—literature, art. He was also a gadget person: As a teenager he'd built his own ham radio and designed a cathode-ray tube, and in college he'd built projection television sets. He was shy and introverted, and he clearly responded to Jobs's charisma. He didn't seem a threat. And as time went on, Jobs simply got caught up in the challenge of luring him to Apple and converting him to Apple's cause. Jobs was one of the richest men in America; he could buy anything he wanted; he had so much money it was embarrassing. Nothing made him salivate like the thing he couldn't get. Yet two weeks after the Macintosh demo, when Jobs made an offer, Sculley turned him down, bouncing Pepsi bottle caps and all.

Jobs flew to New York the next day. He and Sculley spent that entire Sunday afternoon walking around Manhattan. They walked through Central Park. They walked through the Metropolitan Museum of Art. He told Sculley he had a choice: He could sell sugar water to kids, or he could lead Apple in its crusade to change the world. By the end of their walk it was clear that Sculley wanted the job. There were three issues that would have to be settled before he'd take it, however. One was money: He'd made less than $320,000 the year before at Pepsi, but he was taking a big career gamble in coming to Apple, and he wanted to be compensated for it. The second was his family: If his wife and daughter didn't like the idea, he wouldn't do it. And the third was Don Kendall. Kendall had been his mentor throughout his entire career in business. If Kendall didn't approve, Sculley would stay at Pepsi.

Over the next two weeks, everything fell into place. Kendall admitted it was too good a chance to pass up. Leezy found the house in Woodside, which was cozy despite its eleven rooms and reminded them of the houses they were used to seeing in Connecticut. The board approved Jobs's financial offer—the salary, loan, stock option, parachute (in case things didn't work out), and bonus. It also agreed to pay $1.3 million for the house Sculley had helped design for himself in the estate section of Greenwich, thus sparing him the risk and trouble of having to resell it. Sculley said yes. And now he was in the driver's seat.

■ ■ ■

By the time Sculley got to Cupertino, Silicon Valley was waiting anxiously for the "shakeout," the seemingly inevitable downturn in growth that would signal the end of the gravy train in personal computers. The shakeout had been predicted for so long it was beginning to seem like the next earthquake; some people were even predicting it would never come. But it *would* come, and it would produce the same sick, queasy feeling you get when the earth starts to roll beneath your feet. The nervousness could be gauged by the sudden vogue for Eastern management, for CEOs with proven marketing savvy in the package-goods industry. Apple had Sculley. Osborne Computer, another meteoric success story with its roots in the mid-seventies hobbyist underground, had Robert Jaunich of Consolidated Foods. Atari, the video-game company which predated them all, was about to get James Morgan of Philip Morris. The industry was hedging its bets.

Unlike Apple, Osborne and Atari were in real trouble. Osborne, founded in 1980 by a onetime Homebrew Computer Club member and born huckster named Adam Osborne, had enjoyed phenomenal success with the world's first portable computer, an inexpensive but bizarrely designed contraption with a screen so small it could display only one side of a page at a time. (The designer was Lee Felsenstein, the Homebrew leader who'd scoffed at Wozniak's schematics for the Apple.) Osborne's management was far worse than its product design: When Jaunich got there he discovered $10 million unaccounted for and a looming loss of as much as $4 million, leaving him no choice but to cancel the company's imminent plans to go public. As for Atari, a sudden stall in the Christmas video-game market led Warner Communications, the entertainment conglomerate that had bought the company from Nolan Bushnell in 1976, to predict an unexpected slump in quarterly earnings, and that announcement sent Warner stock into an astonishing dive—from $54 to $35 in a single week, cutting the market's valuation of the company by $1.3 billion.

Atari president Raymond Kassar, the underwear manufacturer and onetime Egyptian rug merchant whom Warner had brought over from Burlington Mills, found himself under investigation by the Securities and Exchange Commission over the stock trading he'd done to supplement his $3 million in salary and bonuses. Meanwhile, Atari laid off twenty-two hundred workers.

Apple, on the other hand, was a healthy-looking enterprise. It had more than $200 million in cash, and its profits for the Christmas quarter were nearly double those of the year before. But the marketplace was in flux, and after the Christmas video-game debacle no one could be certain that the personal-computer business, which in six years had shot to $6 billion, would in the end amount to anything more than just another hula hoop. Low-cost home computers like those sold by Atari, Radio Shack, and Commodore International looked particularly iffy; the higher-priced Apple II, still the best-selling product in the business, was clearly vulnerable to competition from IBM. Price wars were looming on the hardware side, giving a clear advantage to companies that could manufacture cheaply and sell enough units to achieve economies of scale. The software front was shaping up as a battle between operating systems—the code that acts as the machine's central nervous system, handling all the signals to and from the keyboard, the printer, and the screen. Because computers that run on different operating systems are incapable of using the same programs, the marketplace was being forced to settle on a standard, just as the marketplace in videocassette recorders was being forced to choose between VHS and Beta—a brutal process that was sure to leave the losers gushing red ink. And there'd be no shortage of losers, for in the past few years more than 150 companies had jumped into the business—start-ups like Osborne, established technology firms like Hewlett-Packard and Texas Instruments and Digital Equipment, Japanese electronics giants like Sony and Nippon Electric. Obviously, only a handful would survive.

In the high-flying environment of Silicon Valley, land of the hot tub and the Porsche, the buttoned-down corporate culture of the Eastern business establishment was anathema. But with the increasing dominance of IBM and the spectre of a personal-computer shakeout ahead, Wall Street was demanding caution, maturity—companies that acted a little more like IBM. Firms such as Apple, which little more than two years before had depended on venture capital for their financing, were now being funded by giant institutional investors—

insurance companies, pension funds, banks. Big institutions tended to like Apple; a lot of them had enjoyed nice gains on its stock. But they didn't like the idea of its being led by a volatile twenty-seven-year-old multimillionaire with, as the saying went on Wall Street, "no adult supervision."

A maverick firm with a pronounced sense of adventure, Apple had long excited the admiration of analysts at the brokerage firms which did the trading on the institutions' behalf. Many had had their work lives transformed by VisiCalc, a dynamic spreadsheet program that turned the Apple II into a powerful tool for forecasting economic results. Invented by a pair of Apple fanatics at MIT and marketed by a Harvard Business School graduate who'd been selling video-game cassettes out of his apartment, VisiCalc was the program that ushered the personal computer into the American office. Its release in 1979 led the analysts to Apple, and what they saw—looking at Cupertino from the perspective of fifteen or twenty office towers packed together in Manhattan, three thousand miles away—was a bunch of long-haired kids who were having a lot of fun developing products and selling them to a vast extended family. When you bought an Apple II, you felt like a friend of Jobs and Woz and Markkula; and somehow when you bought an IBM PC, you did not feel that way about IBM chairman John Akers.

But something funny started to happen after the PC came onto the market in 1981, and the analysts were keenly aware of it because it was happening on their turf. In '79 and '80, when the Apple II got into the business market, it did so by effectively making an end run around the data-processing manager—the corporate functionary who sits at the top of the data-processing hierarchy and approves all the purchase requisitions for data-processing equipment. Any reasonably senior individual in a medium-to-large corporation could get an okay to buy a $3,000 item without too many questions being asked, and many thousands of those individuals bought Apples so they could run VisiCalc. But the arrival of IBM "legitimized" the personal computer in the eyes of corporate management at just about the time that the proliferation of these little machines around the office was starting to attract attention. By the end of '82 it was beginning to seem like a good idea to have a single corporate strategy for personal computers, and the obvious person to coordinate that strategy was the data-processing manager—a person who more likely than not had spent his entire career buying IBM mainframes. He felt comfortable with IBM: They serviced their computers, they supported their computers, they held his hand whenever anything threatened to go wrong, and he took it as an article of faith that from the moment the old Computing-Tabulating-Recording Corporation had been transformed into the International Business Machines Corporation in 1924, not one person in American business had been fired for buying IBM. Apple? Who were they? And what assurance did he have that they'd still be around next week?

The analysts in their aeries were aware of all this, and it colored their assessment of Apple's stock—especially since they expected the home market for personal computers to be hit much harder in the coming slump than the office market. Friendship was nice, but it wasn't enough. Like the data-processing managers, they were looking for security. Every day in the stock market, millions of dollars of other people's money were gambled on their recommendation, and these people wanted reassurance that it was all safe. That's why, when you walked into a brokerage house on the fifty-seventh floor of some glass-walled high-rise and gazed out the floor-to-ceiling window in the reception area and saw the street rise up to meet you, you were always surrounded by paneled walls and mahogany furniture and gilt-framed oil portraits of sober-looking men in nineteenth-century garb—the founders, presumably. There you were, suspended in space, dizzy and helpless as these people hurled your money out the window in a vertiginous spree; and to reassure you that this money was coming back, they'd tricked the place up to look like a men's club. Disembodied traditional—it made for a soothing decor. In this context, Sculley's consumer marketing skills didn't matter to Apple so much as his Wharton M.B.A. and his solid, corporate background. He was like one of those heavy oil paintings on the walls. He could make the Street feel safe.

■ ■ ■

The company Sculley came to head was dramatically different from what he'd known back East. Don Kendall's PepsiCo enjoyed a reputation as a place where entrepreneurial values thrived—"the biggest small company in the world," the people who ran it liked to say—but it was not a place anybody went to have fun. Its headquarters, in the aptly named Westchester County hamlet of Purchase, was a modern, corporate interpretation of the English stately home. A grand approach led through sweeping lawns to a formal Edward Durrell

Stone "house," an inverted ziggurat in alternating horizontal bands of concrete and glass. The grounds held not just parking lots but ponds and fountains, ducks and seagulls, willows and dogwood, sculptures by Henry Moore, David Smith, Alexander Calder, Isamu Noguchi. But life inside was as starched and grueling as in any other stately home, for behind this serene facade lay a jungle in which only the adept could survive.

The other thing people liked to say about Pepsi was that it was like a Marine boot camp. If so, it was a boot camp straight out of *Mommie Dearest*, with Joan Crawford playing the drill instructor. There was a predatory air, as you might expect of a business in which millions were spent to gain half a share point. Impeccably groomed young men in blue suits and white shirts applied their finely honed minds to the marketing of Chee-tos and Funyuns and Teem, their success a constant reaffirmation of the appeal of sugar and grease. These were the buttoned-down and the carnivorous, people who concealed their feelings, guarded their territory, and waited impatiently for their neighbors to stumble and fall. When one of them cracked one day under the strain, locking himself in his office and howling maniacally as he flung the furniture about— "AAAAOOOWW, fuck *meeeee!!*"—none of his co-workers thought to call an ambulance or even a security guard. Instead they gathered in the hallway to laugh and cheer him on.

Apple was like a hot tub at Esalen by comparison, all touchy-feely and warm. Steve viewed it as a model for the "vanilla companies" of corporate America—an example of how great an American corporation could be. The Macintosh group was a prototype, a management lab for the rest of the company. To his mind, the greatest challenge he and Sculley would face in the next few years, as Apple grew into a huge corporation, would be taking it there without losing its soul. Would it still be the kind of place where new ideas could flourish, where there weren't multiple layers of management, where anyone could get in to see the CEO?

To ensure that it would, he worked closely with Apple's human-resources director—Jay Elliot, the onetime surfer who took such a benign view of antics like the nude swimming at Carmel. Elliot was a fourth-generation Californian, the descendant of the American military attaché who'd served the Mexican governor at Monterey before the Bear Flag Revolt; he'd grown up on a farm on Ano Nuevo Point, on the Pacific coast some forty miles south of San Francisco, and he felt an entrepreneurial enterprise like Apple was not unlike farming in the amount of individual responsibility it required. Together they spent endless hours talking about ways to unleash the true entrepreneurial style within the self. One way was to keep things small—to get small groups of people working toward a shared goal in an environment where they can communicate openly, free from political considerations. Another way was to get people so excited about their work, so involved with the Apple cause, that they began to lose sight of everything else. If you wanted to change the world, of course you'd have to work all night. That's why half the Macintosh team was wearing T-shirts that read 90 HOURS A WEEK AND LOVING IT—T-shirts Jobs himself had had made.

Sculley had no beef with the culture. True, he'd been born in pinstripes, but if he had to dress down to fit in, that was okay. Within a week he'd put the suits in mothballs and switched to Top-Siders and chinos and L. L. Bean shirts, which was what he always wore on weekends in Connecticut or at the summer house in Maine anyway. And he certainly had no problem with the pace. The pace was constant—morning to night, meeting to meeting, back to back, weekdays and weekends. That was fine. He liked to get up and go running about four, get into the office by six, and grab lunch in his office—a couple of peanut-butter-and-jelly sandwiches and three or four cans of Diet Pepsi, following up on the two or three cans he'd swigged down in the morning and leading into the five or six he'd chug in the afternoon. ("Don't you worry about this stuff?" one of the exec staff members asked him. "If I worried about it, I wouldn't drink it," he replied.) He even tried to move the weekly exec staff meetings from 7:30 A.M. to 6:30, but too many of the vice-presidents protested—the period from five to seven was the only time they could get anything done.

It was other things that confounded him—the incredible amount of time it took to develop new products, for example. At Frito-Lay, a new chip could be on the store shelves in a test market six weeks after it had been dreamed up. At Apple, to get a new computer out the door seemed to take eighteen months or longer. All the other computer companies took the same amount of time. How were you supposed to do any rational planning when you had a product-development cycle that was nearly two years long? You'd start down a path only to find somebody blocking your way when you were halfway there. It was crazy.

And then there was the whole issue of compatibility. The Apple II wouldn't run software for the IBM PC; the PC wouldn't run software for Lisa; Lisa wouldn't run software for the Apple II; and none of them would run software for Macintosh. That was really crazy. You had eight-bit machines, sixteen-bit machines, thirty-two-bit machines. You had DOS machines, MS DOS machines, CP/M machines. You had 6502-based machines, 68000-based machines, 8086-based machines. Who knew what any of it meant? Certainly not Sculley; this stuff had about as much to do with the prehistoric electronics he'd dabbled in as a kid as it did with soft drinks and potato chips. But he was running a computer company, so he'd better know. He spent hour after hour with Steve going over the basics. By the end of April his speech was peppered with jargon. Convincing people he knew what he was saying took longer.

On organizational issues, he was able to look more decisive, in part because Markkula had left him so much to do. He didn't say much—he wasn't warm or friendly or outgoing—but he did listen, silently, and when he made a move it was invariably a quick one. His first move was to fire John Vennard—no great shock, since Steve had been demanding his head since February. Vennard was in Japan, working with Alps to fix a problem on a new disk drive for the Apple III, when Sculley summoned him back to get the ax. Then he got rid of Wil Houde, who'd been running the Apple II division until the previous fall, when Markkula had decided to replace him and, unable to decide between the division's marketing director and its engineering director, had put them both in charge. Houde had been named to head a special task force to look into ways of streamlining the company. His task force was already streamlined: He was the only one on it. Everyone knew that heading a task force at Apple was like being named vice-president in charge of looking for a new job. Sculley was merely completing the process.

Shortly after his arrival, Sculley asked the executive staff what the big issues were that had to be dealt with. They all agreed that the one that needed immediate attention was product-line strategy—how to position Lisa and Macintosh and the IIe and III so they made sense together. Thanks largely to Steve, Apple had an entire family of computers none of which talked to one another. There were valid technological reasons for this: It's the hardware that determines what operating system will be used and what software will run on it, and Steve was never a fan of old hardware. He valued technological innovation above all else, and to build a computer that was compatible with other computers meant conforming to a standard that was by definition obsolete. Compatibility, he liked to say, was the noose around creativity.

Because Lisa and Macintosh ran on the powerful new Motorola 68000 microprocessor, it was all but impossible to make them compatible with the Apple II and III, which were built around the old 6502 microprocessor Woz had used in the Homebrew days, or with the IBM PC, which was built around the Intel 8086. But Lisa and Macintosh weren't even compatible with each other. The people in sales, who got regular feedback from the dealers, at least wanted to make Lisa and Macintosh compatible, but the two engineering organizations could never agree on how to do it.

In developing a family of products that didn't talk to one another, Apple was in effect mimicking its own organization. But to customers who'd invested several thousand dollars in an Apple computer and software only to discover that to move ahead technologically they'd have to throw it out and start over, Apple's organizational squabbles were of no more interest than the intricacies of hardware design. If they couldn't be compatible, Lisa and Macintosh were at least intended to be complementary, but the indefinite delay that the disk-drive crisis had caused in Macintosh's introduction had thrown even that out of whack. Partly to sort it all out, partly just to get it straight in his own mind, Sculley scheduled a three-day retreat for the division managers at Pajaro Dunes. It was set for the first week of May.

■ ■ ■

The week began with a presentation from Chiat/Day, Apple's ad agency. After almost a year without TV, Apple would be spending $50 million to support its existing products and launch Macintosh. The man in charge of developing the ads was Chiat/Day's creative director, Lee Clow. Chiat/Day was as unconventional an ad agency as Apple was a computer company—small and distinctive, with headquarters in Los Angeles and a reputation for work that had a zingy California flair for which Clow was largely responsible. Like Jobs, he was adopted, the son of an aerospace worker. Tall and lanky, with a long gray beard and a droopy moustache and soulful, hound-dog eyes, he looked more like a sixties beach bum than an ad man. He'd come to Chiat/Day in 1972 after a brief and not-too-successful stint at the Los Angeles office of N. W. Ayer, a big Madison Avenue agency. To get himself hired he'd launched a one-man ad campaign with himself as product. Its theme was "Hire the Hairy," and after promoting himself on T-shirts, coffee mugs, bumper stickers, and TV ads and finally offering a three-months-free sale on his services, he'd gotten the job.

Chiat/Day, primarily a West Coast agency at the time, had gotten the Apple account nine years later, when Regis McKenna sold his ad business to Jay Chiat so he could concentrate on public relations. The first thing Steve said when he met his new creative director was "Am I getting anything I should give a shit about?" That was the kind of treatment Clow liked. He found it challenging. Steve wasn't just aggressive, he was smart—always ahead of everybody else, always making them struggle to keep up. He was Svengali-like in his ability to mesmerize you with his vision. And he not only forced you to pull out all the stops, to give him nothing less than great; he was even willing to sign the check for it. From a creative point of view, he represented the opportunity of a lifetime. So what if he was bratty in the bargain?

A couple of months before Sculley's arrival, about January or so, Steve had started talking excitedly about something he called "the Apple Generation"—a whole generation of people whose lives had been changed by personal computers. Where was he coming from, Lee had wondered, with this Apple Generation? When he heard about Sculley, it all clicked. Sculley had a long-standing relationship with Batten Barton Durstine & Osborn, Pepsi's agency, and the prospect of Chiat/Day's keeping the account seemed iffy. But Clow had been wanting to do corporate-image advertising for Apple for some time, and that's what he took this lifestyle idea to be—an opportunity to capture the spirit of the people who use Apples.

To make it work, his team first did an A&U study—attitude and usage—to understand customers' feelings about Apple and IBM. They discovered, not surprisingly, that people thought of Apple as an entrepreneurial, innovative, trend-setting, young company whose products were used by enterprising and creative people. IBM was considered bureaucratic and conservative. They plugged this data into a psychographic profile of the American public that had been developed at SRI International—a profile that combines psychology and demographics to help advertisers understand what motivates different segments of the population. This way they hoped to figure out what was really going on in the marketplace.

Researchers at SRI's VALS program—VALS is short for Values and Life Styles, a "holistic" and essentially Maslovian approach to viewing people's needs and wants—had worked up a detailed typology in which the American public was neatly divided into nine different lifestyle categories. At the bottom were "survivors"—people so poor and disadvantaged they have no hope of betterment. In the middle were "belongers," the largest group (38 percent of the adult population) and the most conservative—the proverbial Middle Americans, strong believers in church and family. Near the top were "achievers"—business and professional leaders, hard-working, success-oriented, and materialistic. Each group has its own patterns of consumption. Achievers buy high-performance German road machines; belongers drive Chevies and Fords; survivors take the bus.

Fred Goldberg, who as Chiat/Day's management supervisor on the Apple account was responsible for the strategic direction of the campaign, had worked with VALS at Young & Rubicam, the agency whose campaign for Merrill Lynch was the classic VALS success story. By switching the image in the Merrill Lynch ads from a thundering herd of bulls to a single, proud specimen, Y&R's "A Breed Apart" campaign replaced an obvious belonger symbol—a herd—with one perfectly attuned to the individualistic self-image of the achievers who play the market. Clearly what Apple should do was appeal to that sense of individualism in the achievers who buy computers. What it shouldn't do was try to emulate IBM.

Goldberg began the presentation that day by outlining the strategic issues. There was a high skew on owning personal computers among achievers—competitive, risk-taking individuals who respond to computers that offer high quality and advanced technology. And it wasn't the Fortune 1000 companies that were producing new jobs; it was small, entrepreneurial enterprises. What were the implications for Apple? Advertising that appealed to the self-perception as well as to the practical needs of the target prospect. IBM's personal-computer ads, which featured Charlie Chaplin's lovable "Little Tramp" character and a single red rose to symbolize individual creativity, were clearly an attempt to soften the company's image; but among computer owners that image remained large, institutional, and conservative. Apple's communications opportunity, then, was: *IBM is what people think they ought to be, but Apple is what people feel they'd like to be.* And the copy strategy—the unspoken message of all the new ads—was: *You know where you're going, and Apple can get you there faster.*

Next, Clow began to present the ads—mock-ups of the print ads, story boards for the TV spots. There were fifty in all—lifestyle ads, benefit ads, ads for the IIe, for the III, for Macintosh, for Lisa. The lifestyle spots—"Apple People," they were called—featured creative young people hard at work in unconventional situations. The psychographics showed that Apple users were much like Apple employees in terms of being free-spirited and entrepreneurial, so these ads were like mirrors held up to the company. One showed a team of young architects playing basketball on their lunch break and then going back to work in a loft. Another showed a young guy in jeans bringing his dog (a pit bull) into the office on a lonely weekend morning and then answering the phone. "Hi, honey," he said. "Yeah, I'll be home for breakfast." All ended with the same line: "Soon there'll be just two kinds of people—those who use computers, and those who use Apples." Steve thought the ads were great. So did John. He nixed a couple of print ads for the Apple III, but otherwise everything sailed through.

Finally there was the Macintosh presentation. Steve had shown them all Macintosh months before and filled them with the vision of a computer so revolutionary it would change the world. Its announcement was viewed as an event of roughly the same magnitude as the Second Coming. The strategic problem was that what made it different was that it was so incredibly easy to use, and yet every other computer was already being touted as easy to use and nobody believed it. Chiat/Day had a "clutter reel" on which dozens of different TV spots for personal computers had been spliced together, copy point by copy point, and they all made precisely the same claims: "Faster" "Faster" "Faster," "More Software" "More Software" "More Software," "Easier" "Easier" "Easier," "Cheaper" "Cheaper" "Cheaper." No wonder people chose IBM. But Apple had a computer that was radically easier to use than anything else, and the solution was to use that word—"radical." Radical ease-of-use. The computer for the rest of us—for all the people who'd been intimidated by computers to date. That was Macintosh.

The ads were all very specific, explaining exactly why this new machine was so easy. But to launch it you needed something spectacular, something to rise above the clutter, something that would make your socks roll up and down when you saw it. They had two possibilities. One was "King Kong Gates"—a spot that would feature a gargantuan set of iron gates, two hundred feet tall, that would open just a crack so a handful of tiny people could squeeze through. The Apple II opened the door for a few people, the ad would say, and now Apple is introducing the computer for the rest of us—as the gates burst open and nine thousand people rush out. There was a problem with that idea, however: Nine thousand people aren't cheap.

The other idea was "1984." A year earlier, Steve Hayden, the chief copywriter on the Apple account, had written a little essay on "Why 1984 Won't Be Like *1984*" as one of a series of institutional ads Apple was running in *The Wall Street Journal*—ads that took the form of thoughts from Chairman Jobs. The idea had been nixed by Apple's advertising staff; but then Brent Thomas, the art director on the Apple account and the third key member of the creative team, had resurrected it as a way of introducing Macintosh—assuming the introduction would be made at the beginning of the year. The Orwellian theme seemed so great, why not do a spot in which Apple destroys Big Brother? Lee got excited about it, and in ten minutes they'd knocked it out—girl smashes Big Brother with baseball bat. Great. Next idea. Now Lee was presenting the story boards, and Steve and John were intrigued. John said yes. Lee flew back to L.A. and got started.

■ ■ ■

That evening Steve and John joined Mike Markkula and the division managers at Pajaro Dunes, where for the next two days they would hole up in a beach house with only one telephone and thrash out a product-line strategy for the company. This was Markkula's only official act of transition; he hadn't even met with Sculley when he'd arrived, just sent him a stack of boxes full of papers. A long list of issues was on the agenda. Should Apple's office strategy be built around Lisa or Macintosh or both? Should they try to make Lisa and Macintosh compatible? How could Apple coexist in an office market dominated by IBM? Should it build an IBM-compatible Apple II? Should it phase out the Apple III? Should it go into the software business? What business posture should it assume anyway?

A few days after his arrival, John had sent out a memo outlining the requirements of a "go-for-it" strategy: "Get in front of the power curve . . . continued success of our Apple II products . . . nothing major can go wrong . . . must preserve our incredible entrepreneurial environment. . . ." He'd told the exec staff that Apple had an opportunity to break away from the pack and make this a "two-horse race" with IBM. But to do so, he'd warned, meant adopting a high-risk, high-reward strategy that would put heavy stresses on the organization—and, he might have added, on the people in it.

Well, they were going for the gold. Why not? Excitement over Lisa, coupled with a general infatuation on Wall Street for high-tech companies, had just pushed the stock up to $55 a share, up from $39 when Sculley arrived and $29 at the beginning of the year. In the past four months the net worth of everyone present—in most cases already measured in the millions of dollars—had nearly doubled. Almost 12,000 Lisas were on order, with shipments to begin in two weeks; over the next twelve months they were expecting to sell 57,000 units. Fiscal 1983 was going to be a billion-dollar year, and when they added up the projections for fiscal '84 it looked like they could hit $2.5 or even $3 billion. John declared that he hadn't come here to take Apple from a $1-billion company to a $2-billion company; he'd come here to take it from $1 billion to *$10* billion. There was excitement in the air, and a touch of euphoria.

They spent both days hashing out the issues. They had breakfast sessions, lunch sessions, dinner sessions, and in between they sat around on sofas in the living room. John kept asking questions, some of them tough. How was all this going to play together? What was it going to mean in the office? Was Apple a bunch of disparate parts or a coordinated whole? Gene Carter, the vice-president of sales, wanted to make Lisa and Macintosh fully compatible; Steve didn't. He wanted to sell Macintosh at $1,000, and he knew he couldn't do that if he had to equip it to run Lisa's sophisticated but cumbersome software. Macintosh had been cleverly engineered to capture the 20 percent of Lisa that gave 80 percent of the benefit. So they compromised on the idea of a Macintosh "window" on Lisa—a technique that would enable Lisa to use a fraction of its power to run the software that was being developed for Macintosh.

Making the Apple II or Macintosh compatible with IBM was more of a problem. John wanted to do it because he was concerned about staying in the mainstream of the personal-computer business, and he didn't understand why you couldn't just use the microprocessors the II and the Macintosh already had. But the Intel 8086 microprocessor at the heart of the IBM PC was radically different from either the 6502 in the Apple II and III or the Motorola 68000 in Lisa and Macintosh. The MS DOS operating system was crafted to work on the Intel chip, and all the software for the IBM PC was designed to run on that operating system. It was all but impossible to build a computer that ran IBM software without using either the 8086 or one of the newer chips in the same series.

On the other hand, you could always build a circuit board with an Intel chip and plug that into a slot on the Apple II or III or on Lisa (Macintosh, of course, didn't have slots), giving you essentially two computers in one box. But was that a good idea? Nearly everyone there thought it wasn't. If Apple became a second source of IBM-type computers, it would have to compete on price, which was not what it was good at—it had never tried to build the cheapest computer, only the best. It would be vulnerable if IBM ever decided to introduce a new model with a proprietary operating system. And it might as well forget about Macintosh; why would anyone go to the trouble and expense of developing entirely new software for it when Apple was tacitly admitting IBM's superiority in the marketplace? For that reason as much as for any other, Steve argued vehemently against IBM compatibility. Apple had decided years before to go its own way, to set its own standards, and he saw no reason to change now.

The second evening, as they sat around after dinner, the talk turned to things that could get in their way. One problem they could see was divisiveness—in other words, Steve's attitude toward the other divisions. John Couch of the Lisa division made the point, and Paul Dali and Dave Paterson, whom Markkula had made co-managers of the Apple II division ("the dull and boring division," as Jobs had taken to calling it) backed him up. Wayne Rosing, the Lisa engineering manager, had come to bring some technical expertise to the meeting, and he weighed in against Steve as well. Later Steve and Couch took a long walk on the beach, trying to make things right.

Floyd Kvamme closed the meeting the next afternoon by drawing a target on a blackboard and asking everybody to name the most important thing Apple had to accomplish in the coming fiscal year. He called it a TAP session—short for "target analysis process," a focusing gimmick that had been developed by the human-resources people at National Semiconductor. He got about forty answers and wrote them in the outermost ring, and over the next hour they whittled them away until there were twenty and then seven and then five. Finally only one goal was left. That one he wrote in the bull's-eye: "Successfully introduce Macintosh." It was unanimous. Steve's project, long considered marginal, was now regarded as vital to the company's future.

But when would he be able to deliver it? They all knew that the demise of Twiggy had left it without a disk drive, and none of them were convinced that the drive Rod Holt was trying to engineer with Alps would be ready in time. The August intro date was obviously dead; would they be able to make January 1984? Steve couldn't promise. That made them angry. You're out of your mind, they told him—you can't ship, you don't have a disk drive, you don't know what you're doing. Why don't you quit screwing around with our sales forecasts, they said, and tell us if the product is going to be ready in January?

In sixty to ninety days, Steve said, we'll know for sure. Every head turned to Belleville. John said, "Well, Bob?"

Bob knew something the others didn't. Komoto was due back from Japan the next week with a working model of the Sony drive, re-engineered to the specifications Bob had given him. "In thirty days," he said quietly, "we'll know for sure." Steve looked puzzled for a second; then, as it dawned on him what Bob must have done, his face broke into an enormous grin. "You son of a bitch!" he cried.

6

Bermuda Triangle

One of the few calls that went out from Pajaro Dunes that week was made by Del Yocam, Apple's head of manufacturing. Yocam—Delbert W. Yocam, age thirty-nine—was an uncharacteristic vice-president for Apple. Short and pear-shaped, with curly hair and a neatly trimmed beard, he rarely impressed anyone with his brilliance; but his effectiveness was something else again. Yocam was a plodder, the kind of man who often wins in the end—fastidious, methodical, and utterly thorough. Though he'd come to Apple from Fairchild, he'd gotten his start at Ford, first in southern California and then in Detroit, and his calm, unexciting demeanor seemed more reminiscent of the auto industry than of Silicon Valley. Unlike Detroit, however, Yocam could manufacture product. His secret was the black notebook he kept: Whenever he wanted something done, he made a note of it, and nothing he wrote down ever failed to happen. So when it was agreed at the retreat that they should terminate the Apple III because it was old and embarrassing and its positioning in the office market conflicted with Lisa's, Yocam made a note in his black book to have his office send out an electronic-mail memo to tell his purchasing agents not to buy any more parts for the Apple III. He called Cupertino that evening.

While the general managers were trying to make sense of their product lines in Pajaro Dunes, the key people in the division responsible for the Apple II and III were holding a retreat of their own at Rickey's Hyatt House in Palo Alto. Rickey's was a low-slung, rustic-looking motel on El Camino Real, the neon-lit "Royal Highway" the padres had supposedly built to link the early California missions, and its dark and clubby lounges were almost always full of semiconductor executives, computer entrepreneurs, venture capitalists, business journalists, and industry analysts. The Apple people were there to discuss the projects they had going in the division, one of which was the impending introduction of the Apple III+, an updated version of the now-classic Edsel. Dave Fradin, the young man who two weeks before had been made product manager for the Apple III, was in the middle of this meeting when he got a phone call from one of his staff members in Cupertino. A call had just come in from a vendor who supplied Apple III parts to the factory and wanted to know what was going on. Was Apple abandoning the III?

Fradin figured he was out of a job. To his mind, the III was a good product which had never overcome the disastrous launch it had received nearly three years earlier. Conceived at the end of 1978 as a stopgap improvement on the Apple II until Lisa could be developed— by then it had already become apparent that Lisa was not going to be out in six months—it had become such an embarrassment that most of the exec staff, Jobs in particular, only wanted it to go away.

As with Twiggy, the problem could be laid to the fatal combination of hubris and inexperience. None of them had really known what they were doing, but they had known they were doing it right. The first thing they'd done, before the engineering was completed, was settle on a case and commit to millions of dollars' worth of tooling. It was no slouch of a case, either: The Federal Communications Commission was about to issue new guidelines on radio emissions to keep personal computers from interfering with broadcast reception, and since nobody knew how stringent the regulations would be, they decided to shield the III inside a heavy piece of cast aluminum. Then they started adding features they hadn't planned on.

Everybody had a wish list: Jobs, who was then vice-president of research and development; Tom Whitney, the executive vice-president of engineering; marketing people of all stripes. The III would have more memory than the II, a better display, an upper-and-lower-case keyboard, and a better operating system. The only thing they couldn't expand was the space inside the case. Everything had to be shoehorned in there, and the chief hardware engineer— Wendell Sander, an ex-Fairchild man who'd signed on at Apple after bringing Jobs a souped-up version of the Apple I—was so good that he actually managed to do it. But to pull it off he had to put all the memory chips on a separate printed circuit board that was piggy-backed on top of the main board, and even then it was so crowded he had to use a fine-line board—one on which the printed circuits connecting the chips were only seven microns across.

It might have worked if they'd had time to figure out how to manufacture it properly. But in 1979 and '80 Apple was still operating on a hobbyist mentality, and the thought of spending more than a year developing a new computer seemed crazy. The marketing people wanted to bring it out immediately because they were convinced that the Apple II, already three years old, was going to be overwhelmed by the competition in six months. Legally the company had to ship it, because it had been included in the prospectus for the public stock offering that was about to take place. And while the engineers who were working on it kept telling people there were problems, their warnings got filtered out before they reached the people who were running the company.

After assuring Mike Scott that everything was fine, Whitney took off on a business trip to Europe. While he was gone, the first models came off the production line, which screeched to a halt because they didn't work. When a technician unbolted the cases the machines worked fine, but when he bolted the cases back they stopped again. Then they discovered they couldn't get more bolts. It was a nightmare, and that was only the beginning. The real trouble started after the computer hit the market, when they discovered corrosion in the connectors between the main board and the memory board. Suddenly, for no apparent reason, the computer would simply forget what it was doing. That was in addition to the clock display that went flooey, the fine lines that shorted out, the manuals that were full of errors, and the software that wasn't there. Whitney was fired as soon as the stock offering was completed in December 1980, and Black Wednesday followed soon after.

What gnawed at everyone most was the gradual realization that the failure of the Apple III was what gave IBM the chance to establish its PC as the leading computer in the business market. The PC was introduced in August 1981, one year after the III, and it wasn't until more than a year after that that it began to look like a success—two years during which Apple did nothing except bring out a re-engineered version of the III, which it didn't publicize because Lisa and Macintosh were supposed to come out momentarily. Worse yet, the PC in many ways resembled the III, particularly in its operating system. The III's operating system—which was known as SOS, for Sophisticated Operating System—imposed a level of standardization that ensured that any Apple III would run like any other Apple III, regardless of whether it had add-ons like extra memory. But while MS DOS—the Microsoft Disk Operating System, developed for the IBM PC by programmers at Microsoft, a company that, like Apple, had emerged in the mid-seventies from the hobbyist underground—had by late 1982 become the standard in business, all SOS had done was create dissension between the Apple III people, many of them computer professionals from Hewlett-Packard, and those who took the hard-core hobbyist position that all operating systems were more or less bullshit.

The problem with an operating system, from the hobbyist point of view, was that it made it more difficult to reach down inside the computer and show off your skills; it formed a barrier between the user and the machine. Personal computers meant power to the people, and operating systems took some of that power away. Of course, to most of the people who were actually using personal computers by this time, an operating system meant more freedom rather than less—the freedom to hook up any printer you wanted, for example, without having to worry about whether your software would get it to work. But the hackers didn't see it that way. Operating systems were something you found on IBM mainframes. If God had wanted the personal computer to have an operating system, Woz would have given it one. It wasn't a design issue; it was a threat to the inalienable rights of a free people. Or so the hard-core hobbyists said, and they had Jobs's ear.

There was a certain irony in the fact that the man who spurned compatibility because it meant being a slave to the past was himself so tied to the legacy of the hobbyist underground. Idealism and naiveté mingled with a childlike fascination with what the machine could do—that was the hobbyist mentality. When personal computers were toys for macho demonstrations of technological wizardry, the hacker ethic had made sense. Now that they were being used by people who had no feeling for or interest in their inner operations, the rules had changed. Jobs knew that—that's why he envisioned Macintosh as an "appliance" computer, one you could take out of the box and plug in and start using without bothering to look at a manual. But his was to be an appliance computer that incorporated the hacker ethic—one built by the heirs of Woz, not by degree-packing engineers from Digital Equipment or Hewlett-Packard. He'd gone back to the garage. He was building the kind of machine Woz might build if Woz were still around. But it was hard not to notice that in his drive to create his own computer, he seemed equally driven to bury Woz's.

When Scotty divisionalised the company after the Apple III introduction, the II and the III got lumped together in a single unit under Whitney, who was soon to be fired. Then Jobs took over the Macintosh project, and one by one he lured the hobbyists away. Whitney was replaced by Wil Houde, a former Hewlett-Packard man who'd been in charge of service and distribution—"the distribution orifice," Jobs liked to call it, in a phrase that fully captured his feelings about its necessary but lowly function. Houde looked the part of a division manager, with his square jaw and his trim gray beard, but there was no way he could stand up to Jobs's ferocious attacks. Jobs—Steven P. Jobs, chairman of the board and chief stockholder, multimillionaire entrepreneur, hero of the personal-computer revolution—would walk into their cramped quarters on Bandley Drive and peer over the shoulder of some hapless engineer and say, "What are you doing here? That's a dumb idea. That's *shitty!*" Houde would make a presentation to the exec staff and Jobs would cry, "That's the shittiest thing I ever heard!" He called them all "Clydesdales" because they seemed so slow and deliberate. He said they were HP plodders. He called them "the dull and boring division." Macintosh was going to be out in January 1982 for $995, he reminded them; and once that happened, there'd be no need for them at all.

Macintosh didn't come out in 1982, but it seemed like there was no need for the Apple II people anyway. That fall they found themselves exiled from Bandley Drive: Macintosh was outgrowing its quarters and Jobs wanted their building. There was no more room on Bandley, so the whole division packed up and moved to a new building a mile down Stevens Creek Boulevard—a six-story, three-sided office building, its black glass skin scarred across one side by an ugly white portico, the whole thing awkwardly situated on an oversized traffic island between a major expressway and the freeway to San Francisco. They called it the Triangle Building. In their grimmer moments they called it the Bermuda Triangle, because obviously Apple had sent them there to get lost.

The division's new managers, Paul Dali and Dave Paterson, took offices on the fifth floor, where all the rooms were named after Monopoly positions; theirs were called Free Parking and Chance. They were not much more effective than Houde. Paterson was a mild-mannered engineer who'd gotten sucked to the top in a leadership vacuum, and Dali was so much on the defensive he defined his job as keeping the bombs out. But two years of neglect and abuse had turned the whole division into an embattled underground. These weren't hotshot professionals like the men John Couch put in charge of Lisa or messianic hackers like the wizards Jobs had recruited for Macintosh, who were known behind their backs as "Moonies." They were practical people who worked on a practical computer. They'd been called "C players" for so long they hardly heard it anymore, but their stoicism was tempered by the knowledge that they were the heirs to Woz's dream.

With its immense library of available software, the Apple II had become the Volkswagen beetle of personal computers, an unassuming yet useful little machine with a personality as distinctive as its inventor's. Since what the dealers paid Apple was three times the manufacturing cost, it was also a cash cow of incredible proportions. And by that May of 1983 the Apple IIe—the evolutionary advance on the II+ that had been introduced with Lisa—was turning out to be the most successful II of all. It was selling sixty to seventy thousand units a month, more than double the average sales of the II+. But what was most remarkable about the IIe was the way it had been developed—by a handful of engineers, working almost in secrecy from the rest of the company.

The main force behind it was Walt Brodener, an engineer who'd worked with Woz on an earlier, abortive attempt to update the II and who pursued this one in the face of Jobs's ridicule. Jobs wanted him to work on Macintosh; he told Brodener any idiot could do the IIe. Brodener told him this was one idiot who was going to finish. He did it because he loved the II. It was going to die of obsolescence if somebody didn't do something, and it was all that was carrying the company. That was the division in microcosm: loyal to the memory of Woz, stubborn in their resistance to Jobs, committed to the Apple dream, and resentful that the dream seemed to have passed them by.

■ ■ ■

One day in early June, Steve Wozniak walked into the Triangle Building and asked for a job. Nobody—not Jobs, not Markkula, not

Sculley, whom he'd never met—knew he was coming. He didn't have an appointment; he didn't even know whom to see. He just walked in the front door and asked whom he should talk to and ended up with Dave Paterson, the co-manager of the division. They sat in Paterson's office for twenty minutes or so, and Wozniak told him he wanted to go to work on the Apple II. He was eager to do some engineering again; he felt really motivated and inspired. Paterson said they'd have a desk for him within a week.

It had been more than two years since Woz's plane crash, and although he'd been drawing a minimal salary in exchange for promotional appearances—he didn't want the computer system to lose track of him—he hadn't done any engineering work at all. After recovering from amnesia he'd decided to take a year off and go back to Berkeley. He registered under an assumed name—"Rocky Clark," which he got by crossing his dog's name with his wife's—and started taking classes in economics, psychology, and computer science. Then one day, while listening to the car radio on the way to his home in Scott's Valley, it came to him: Why not put on a huge Woodstock-style music festival with progressive country-and-western bands and have maybe a million people come? He had no idea how to put such an event together, but then he ran into a nightclub owner in Santa Cruz, the beach town at the foot of the mountains below Scott's Valley, who told him about a local New Age businessman named Peter Ellis.

Ellis turned out to be a former sixties radical and est graduate who was now offering his services as a management consultant. He was exactly the kind of person you'd expect to find in Santa Cruz, a surf center and retirement community that had become a haven for hippies in the early seventies. Santa Cruz was where the tribes of the Rainbow Nation had retreated after Altamont and Kent State and Jerry Rubin's defection to Wall Street. Sixty miles south of Haight-Ashbury, blessed with cheap rents and mild winters, shielded from development by high mountains and redwood forests, it was a refuge to those who clung to the dream of a counterculture. But though they came with visions of milk and honey, they found themselves scraping by on food stamps and mantras—while just across the mountains, Silicon Valley was growing into a humming electronic web of freeways, shopping centers, ranch houses, and office parks. A spillover occurred, and soon the denizens of Santa Cruz were talking about "the tech" that was emerging from "the Pit" as if it offered some sort of nirvana. By the time Woz had his car-radio epiphany, this once-sleepy little resort town had become the southern terminus of an eighty-mile chain of scientific brainpower, high finance, and weird ideas that snaked northward through the Valley to San Francisco and Berkeley and ended in Marin County, home of Lucasfilm and *Star Wars.* The adjective everybody applied to Santa Cruz was "flaky." Of course a club owner there would network Woz with Pete Ellis. No problem.

So Woz wrote a check for $2 million and Ellis put together an organization. They called it UNUSON—short for "Unite Us in Song." While Woz went to school, Ellis met with concert promoters and hired est people and generated concepts. If the seventies were the "me" decade, the people at UNUSON reasoned, the eighties were going to be the "us" decade. Instead of asking "What's in it for me?" people should ask "What's in it for *us?*" They dubbed it the US Festival and promoted it as a combination rockfest and technology fair whose aim was to generate a spirit of world cooperation. To ease tension during the stressful planning process, they'd interrupt business meetings to hold "centering sessions" in which they'd close their eyes and hold hands and think relaxing thoughts. Bill Graham, the feisty San Francisco rock impresario Woz had hired to book the performers, called them "séances" and refused to believe what he was seeing. Woz, viewing the chaos as he continued to write checks, concluded that Ellis and his people must be building tension into their lives so they'd have something to defeat.

The festival took place on Labor Day weekend, 1982, and had all the harmonic resonance of a New Age blowout. An estimated 200,000 people showed up at the desert site, on the edge of the barren San Bernardino Mountains some forty-five miles east of Los Angeles. Bruce Springsteen wouldn't come, but Fleetwood Mac was there, along with Jackson Browne, Tom Petty, Talking Heads, and the Police. The outdoor amphitheatre looked like a makeshift shopping center, lined as it was with concession stands, beer tents, and air-conditioned marquees exhibiting the latest electronic gizmos. An enormous Mitsubishi video screen suspended high above the stage gave everyone a view; great banks of amplifiers sent the music booming across the desert floor. There was a "Sensonics Theater," an inflatable dome wired for wrap-around video and eight-channel sound. There were laser shows, parachutists, a Goodyear blimp, a hot-air balloon emblazoned with the Apple logo. At one point a Soviet rock concert was beamed in by satellite and projected onto the screen—although Graham didn't believe he was seeing *that,* either, so Woz had to go out and announce it himself.

When it was all over, Woz decided to do it again. His friends, who'd watched helplessly as he poured money into the first festival, were aghast. But Woz was having a good time: "I think the fans got their money's worth," he told interviewers. "I know I got mine." Expenses had come to $12.5 million, but while he was writing checks a bull market had caused the value of his Apple stock to rise by $18 million—and next time, he figured, with better ticket-collection procedures, he could even make money. So UNUSON staged a second US Festival on Memorial Day weekend, 1983, and this one was a disaster. By the time it was over, 145 people had been arrested, 120 injured, and two killed—one of a drug overdose, the other from being beaten with a tire iron. Meanwhile, Ellis, who was not unaware of the stress-reduction potential of large sums of money, was passing out five-figure bonuses to himself and his favored employees. And Woz, having lost $25 million in two weekends, was ready to go back to work.

■ ■ ■

On Friday, June 24, a little more than seven weeks after he'd gotten the phone call from the vendor at Rickey's, Dave Fradin was walking out of Apple's gleaming new building on Mariani Avenue, around the corner from Bandley, when he heard someone calling his name. It was Ida Cole, the acting marketing manager for the II division. She was in a meeting with Sculley, Del Yocam, and the chief financial officer, Joe Graziano, and they had something they wanted to talk to him about. Sculley had just been presented with a spreadsheet that held an unexpected surprise: an $18-million inventory of parts for the Apple III in warehouses and factories around the world. If they followed through on their plan to scrap the III, they'd have to write all this off. He wanted to ask Fradin what he thought they ought to do about it.

As product manager for the Apple III, Fradin was responsible for coordinating everything that was done for it in sales, marketing, manufacturing, and its own division, the Apple II. A native of Detroit with a B.S. in engineering from the University of Michigan, he'd gotten his product-management training at Hewlett-Packard—an excellent credential—and had managed the Disk II and then Twiggy before being tapped for the III. His willingness to accept the last two assignments made it clear he didn't mind living dangerously. But he didn't feel suicidal, and as he sat there in front of Sculley, he found it hard to get a reading on the man: He seemed cold, calculating, yet willing to listen. So he told Sculley that for weeks he'd been trying to put together a sales promotion for the III to respond to the PC XT, a souped-up version of the PC which IBM had introduced in February at half the price of Lisa, but that getting anything through all the sales and marketing groups that had to approve it was like trying to push a wet noodle. He'd had meeting after meeting after meeting, and nobody could agree on anything.

Sculley asked what they should do. Fradin said he thought they ought to give one person or group of people full authority over the product and full responsibility for it—in other words, set it up as an independent profit-and-loss center. Sculley was about to tour Europe with Ken Zerbe, Apple's executive vice-president for finance and administration, who'd been sent over to clean up the European operation by Markkula. He told Fradin to have a proposal ready when they came back.

For the next two weeks Fradin and a small team of people pored over every aspect of the III—inventory, manufacturing, financials, marketing, engineering. Sales, which had peaked at 4,400 for the month of December, had dropped to 2,000 a month after the Lisa introduction. At that rate the company had enough III's to last until November, on top of which it had nearly 12,000 III + 's ready to build. They discovered that Apple's computerized inventory management system was responsible for all the extra parts: It had automatically ordered a six-month supply at the December sales rate, which turned out to be a twelve-month supply once sales started to tumble. Then, in a single thirty-six-hour burnout session, they pulled together an eighty-page business plan in which they proposed setting up an independent P&L center, selling off the existing IIIs, introducing the III + , and promoting it in niche markets—legal, medical, real estate—where it could be coupled with available software to offer the customer a well-tailored solution.

One afternoon in mid-July, standing at the head of a three-sided table in a five-sided conference room in the Triangle Building, Fradin presented his findings to Sculley and the executive staff. While not a charismatic man, Fradin was certainly a committed one—that's why he was at Apple instead of at Hewlett-Packard, where if you talked about your commitment to a product they looked at you like you were some new species of chump. Still, it took a lot to show commitment to the Apple III, even with Jobs absent from the meeting. At the Pajaro Dunes retreat they'd decided they were a high-volume/low-cost/high-technology company, and anybody could look at the Apple III and see that it was a low-volume/high-cost/low-technology product. It didn't fit. They might be making money off it, but were they making enough money to justify the attention it consumed?

Fradin examined the options from two vantage points: their impact on the bottom line, and their consistency with Apple Values. They could drop the product now, taking a loss on the inventory and abandoning the nearly 100,000 people who'd already bought one. They could shut it down after selling off the inventory, or they could shut it down after introducing the III +, or they could keep it going and make a long-term commitment. He wanted to pursue the last option, but he asked for at least the chance to introduce the III + and re-evaluate the situation in six months. Sculley hung back, listening carefully, gathering input, asking for their help but giving away nothing. At the end he thanked them all and said he'd have to think about it.

Ten days later, Fradin got a call from Ken Zerbe, a Pennsylvania Dutchman with a Humpty Dumpty silhouette and a penchant for polyester. Zerbe had just made a triumphant return from Europe, where he'd set Apple's operations in order, and now Sculley had given him the task of quenching flames in Cupertino. "I hear you know something about the Apple III," he cracked. Sculley had decided to give it another chance.

■ ■ ■

Wozniak's first encounter with Apple's new president came when he wandered into a meeting of engineers in the Triangle Building. Sculley was explaining the staff cutbacks he was making on the III. The company would support it, he said, but only in relation to what it earned. Wozniak didn't try to introduce himself, since he didn't like to make a big deal about who he was, but he went away impressed by Sculley's hard-headed business sense. In 1981, when he'd had his plane crash, the company was doing flips to make the III look profitable. Most of the work in the newly created Apple II division was being done on the III, but it seemed like all the expenses—for engineering, advertising, office space—ended up being charged against the II. Yet to make sure the II and the III didn't compete with one another, the II's capabilities were deliberately kept limited. It was perverse.

Now things seemed different. When Woz showed up at the Triangle Building, he discovered that a new-generation Apple II was in the works, a project they called the IIx. While the IIe was an incremental improvement over the old II +, the IIx would be a dramatic update. It was being built around the 65816 microprocessor, a successor to the 6502 that was currently under development at the Western Design Center, a semiconductor laboratory in Phoenix. What was amazing about the 65816 was that it promised to be as fast and as powerful as the Motorola 68000 at the center of Macintosh—which meant that this new-generation II could be the equal of Macintosh, and yet it could run all the Apple II software as well. Woz got really excited. He signed up immediately. And the people who were working on it were thrilled to have him, because obviously any project he was involved in wasn't likely to get canceled.

Having him back was great for morale: With Woz around, the people in the dull and boring division didn't feel so dull and boring anymore. But it didn't do much for their status in the company, because he wasn't interested in helping to run Apple. It was too high-pressure, having to hire and fire people and make decisions all day. Besides, he didn't like to take advantage of the fact that he was famous. He just wanted to be an engineer.

It was easy to stay out of management—you just didn't try to throw your weight around. It was a lot harder to duck celebrity. The phone kept ringing and the mail kept coming in, and even with a full-time secretary he couldn't keep up with it. But he'd read in a book that you ought to be accessible to people, so he was very conscientious about answering every letter and returning every call and doing as many interviews as he could fit in. And in fact he liked being a hero. He liked the myth they'd built up around him, this myth of the nerdy engineering whiz who'd made good. It didn't feel like reality, but it was a good myth to have and he tried hard to live up to it. And he liked the people who believed in it. He wanted them to have a hero, and he resolved to be the best hero he could. But it did keep him from doing much engineering work, because being a hero was a round-the-clock job. In a sense it was like being caught in his own personal Bermuda Triangle. But he never complained; that wasn't his style. He just answered the phone and was famous.

7

The Honeymoon

It was a golden moment, there on the lawn before the mansion, its red tile roof glinting in the midsummer sun, its marble porticoes draped with wisteria and framed by cedars: a Maxfield Parrish moment, with Macintosh inserted. Steve and John were lying on the grass at Villa Montalvo, the onetime summer home of San Francisco's turn-of-the-century mayor, James Duval Phelan. The villa's namesake was García Ordónez de Montalvo, the sixteenth-century Spaniard whose depiction of a golden isle, ruled by Queen Califia and peopled by Amazons riding winged griffins, inspired the conquistadors who discovered California in 1535 and gave it its name. It was not quite four centuries later that Phelan, a millionaire banker and real-estate developer with extensive interests in the Santa Clara Valley, built his estate on the edge of Saratoga, a quiet town nestled in the foothills of the Santa Cruz Mountains a few miles south of Cupertino. He called it Villa Montalvo in testament to his faith in the California dream—a romantic vision of a Mediterranean land, bountiful, idyllic, enchanted. And though the nature of the dream had changed since Phelan's day, the dream itself endured.

In Steve Jobs's version of the California dream, technology replaced nature as the bountiful provider, but poetry and romance still held their place. He thought of himself as an artist—a trapeze artist, without a net. He thought of his people, particularly the software team, as artists. He'd persuaded Jean-Michel Folon, the graphic artist whose dreamily surrealistic work he found so appealing, to create a character that would capture the spirit of the machine they were building.

When that didn't work, he'd hired first one and then a second graphic artist to do a simple line drawing of Macintosh. He wanted something that would express the freedom it promised—the freedom to imagine, to soar, to create. The drawing had been presented that very morning, and Jobs in his enthusiasm had dubbed it "the Picasso artwork." In fact the artist had had Matisse in mind when he'd done it. No matter. What mattered was that all that was special about the machine had been communicated with just a few simple strokes and a palette of primary colors.

There was a lot of nervousness that day. They were coming down to the wire. They'd missed one launch date, then another, and then another; they'd been missing launch dates for a year and a half. They still didn't have any fully functional software, either from their own programmers or from the outside developers they'd been courting. And they didn't even have a factory yet; the building they'd been planning to use outside Dallas, where the rest of Apple's computers were manufactured, was needed now to satisfy the runaway demand for the IIe, and their new factory across the bay in Fremont was still just an empty shell. Steve hadn't dwelled on any of these problems when he'd spoken earlier that afternoon. Instead he'd painted a glorious picture of the future—the 750,000 units they were going to sell in 1984, the Big Mac with its fifteen-inch screen they were going to introduce in 1985, the network Bob Belleville had devised to link them all together. But he ran into trouble when he mentioned the price they were thinking of selling it at.

Burrell and Andy and the rest of the hobbyists who formed the Macintosh group's core cult had long since resigned themselves to losing their original goal of a $995 price tag. They'd accepted reality in the form of $1,495 and then even $1,995. But now Steve was telling them that this guy Sculley wanted to charge $2,495. It was hot in the little outdoor amphitheater at Villa Montalvo and they were getting irritable. The whole point of doing Macintosh was to develop an insanely great little machine their friends could use. What could their friends pay? That was the marketing question they cared about. Then Steve tried to explain why John wanted to charge $2,495—to pay for a multimillion-dollar ad campaign and to establish a clear-cut price differential between Macintosh and the IIe. This kind of reasoning didn't wash. They'd met their goal. They'd engineered it to be manufacturable for less than $500 apiece, and now the company was breaking its end of the bargain. They were pissed.

To no avail, apparently. After his talk, John and Steve strolled off and lay on the grass together. They could almost have been lovers. For weeks they'd been gazing worshipfully at each other, finishing each other's sentences, parroting each other's thoughts. It was as if they were on a perpetual honeymoon which they had to share with a great many unruly children.

They ate dinner on the lawn as the shadows lengthened, Steve and John and the Macintosh team. Liz Story, the Windham Hill pianist, was there too; she was going to play for them after the evening meal. And then the inevitable happened: The dessert cart arrived, and Randy Wigginton, Woz's onetime teen disciple who was now writing the word-processing program for Macintosh, took a bowl of whipped cream and, acting on a hundred-dollar bet, poured it down Steve's back. That did it. Instead of making sundaes, they were spattering the grass with ice cream, and by the end of the evening they couldn't go back to Villa Montalvo either.

■ ■ ■

The summer honeymoon between Steve and John was the talk of the company. The two were inseparable. John was listening and learning, and the person he was learning from was Steve. He seemed so in awe of Steve—of his brashness, his charm, his charisma—that he saw everything through Steve's eyes. He'd make a decision in the afternoon, but then he and Steve would spend four hours on the phone that night and he'd come back in the morning and reverse himself. Steve seemed to be his Svengali. It was the reality-distortion field. John was helpless.

But the infatuation wasn't one-sided. It was almost like a father-son relationship in which the two had adopted each other. Sculley's expertise was marketing, and in that area he tutored Steve. This created an awkward situation for Fred Hoar, Apple's vice-president for communications—a Fairchild veteran who ran everything from public relations to advertising to community affairs. Hoar was a flush-faced, easygoing, laugh-a-minute kind of guy who liked to open his speeches with a dramatic flourish. "Hi, my name is Fred Hoar," he'd say, putting the emphasis on "Hoar"—"and that's spelled F-r-e-d." He was a wonderful speaker, but on the exec staff it was generally agreed that marketing strategy was not his strong point. As for advertising, Steve and John were going to handle that directly.

Hoar made a well-timed exit to another computer company.

Meanwhile, John and Floyd Kvamme had been searching for a consumer-marketing person to back up Kvamme, who as executive vice-president was responsible for sales and marketing both. The man they wanted was Bill Campbell, a former account executive at J. Walter Thompson, the New York ad agency. Campbell had been vice-president of marketing at Eastman Kodak for the past year. Kvamme had dealt with Kodak at National Semiconductor—Kodak buys microchips to sit in front of the lens of its automatic-focus cameras—and he liked the idea of an expert in consumer marketing who understood the long development times that high-tech products require. Also, Campbell had been head football coach at Columbia before going to Thompson, and the prospect of a team builder amid Apple's jealous fiefdoms had definite appeal. Campbell was about to move to London to run Kodak's European marketing, but Apple wooed him relentlessly. In one sixteen-hour visit he was greeted at the airport by Sculley, introduced to Jobs, and then turned over to Kvamme, who took him wine-tasting in the remote Uvas Valley and finally told him at the bar at Rickey's Hyatt House at one in the morning that this was the opportunity of a lifetime. Eventually he succumbed.

Jobs was indifferent to Campbell's beefy charms. He liked artists, musicians, writers, but not football coaches. Team play wasn't his strong point either. But marketing was Sculley's call. Technology was Jobs's area, and there he took over.

In the original triumvirate—Scotty as president, Markkula as chairman, Jobs as visionary—Jobs's brash enthusiasms had been leavened by Scotty's stern hand and Markkula's persuasive manner. With Scotty gone, there'd been less of a brake against his fits of recklessness, but other executives still felt free to challenge him. Markkula was a skillful arbiter, listening to everyone, siding with Jobs when he was right, getting him to see things differently when he wasn't. Jobs may have been chairman and largest stockholder, but there was no penalty for disagreeing with him. Sculley's arrival changed all that. John made Steve his partner, not realizing that Steve had never been a partner in running Apple before. Suddenly there were no restraints. Sculley unleashed him—and Steve unleashed was an astonishing spectacle. People began to liken it to Godzilla being let out of his cage.

John Couch, who as head of the Lisa division was Jobs's chief rival technologically, got his first taste of life under the new regime when Sculley referred to Jobs in a meeting as "my boy genius." From that point on, Couch knew that as far as technology was concerned, Steve was going to get whatever he wanted. Couch wanted to develop a family of large office systems—bigger and more powerful, with two to four times the memory of Lisa and screens that could display a full page of text at once. He wanted to position Macintosh as a compatible home computer, so you could take your Lisa disk home at night and slip it into your Mac. But Steve was interested in developing consumer products, not office systems, and compatibility was something he valued not at all. So Couch found himself on the sidelines. With Lisa out the door, he was ready for a sabbatical. Sculley wanted him to spend it working up a business plan for a new division that would develop software. Couch moved out of the picture.

Because Macintosh was quasi-portable, Jobs wanted control of all small computers. So while leading Macintosh to completion, he was simultaneously overseeing the development of a smaller Apple II, a "book-sized" II that was known within the company as the IIb. The idea of a portable II had been around since the summer of 1981, but it hadn't gone anywhere for a year and a half, apparently because Jobs was afraid it would compete with Macintosh. Then, one day late in '82, Paul Dali showed him a photograph of a Toshiba portable and they started fooling around with the idea of an Apple II that would look like the Toshiba but come with a built-in disk drive. They took out a IIe circuit board and a disk drive and a keyboard and played with them until they arrived at a promising configuration—keyboard in front, disk drive in back, circuit board in between. What got Jobs excited about this idea was the engineering difficulty of squeezing it all into a package not much bigger than a notebook. And a machine so small wouldn't have the expandability that characterized all the other II's. Like Macintosh, it could be taken out of the box, plugged in, and put to work—no extra parts to buy, no cables to figure out. It was the II reinvented as an appliance.

As it happened, the IIb idea coincided with another of Jobs's pet projects—"Snow White," an effort to develop a new look for Apple's computers. After engineering, design was Jobs's hot button. His early insistence on a modular plastic case for the Apple II—a significant advance over the aesthetics of the Homebrew members, who liked their gizmos with wires sticking out—had been crucial to the company's initial success. But Apple's early products were still pretty homely, and the aesthetic sophistication he'd acquired after sudden wealth was thrust upon him when Apple went public in 1980—with 15 percent of the company, his worth in one day shot up to more than $256 million—rendered previous standards of taste unacceptable. Nerdy-looking boxes of beige plastic (that ubiquitous Silicon Valley brown) might have been fine when Apple was a small company selling mainly to enthusiasts. But a world-class enterprise could afford world-class design, just as Jobs himself could now afford hand-tailored suits from Wilkes-Bashford, the San Francisco clothiers.

Early in 1982, ten months before Dali sold Jobs on the IIb, Rob Gemmell, a twenty-four-year-old designer in the II group, had suggested that they look for a design firm that could bring Apple's products up to the standards of Olivetti or Sony. This was just the sort of idea to set Jobs on fire. He sent Gemmell and two other Apple designers to Europe to interview candidates. They went to London, Stuttgart, Paris, Milan. They met with Mario Bellini, Italy's leading industrial designer, and Ettore Sottsass, whose Memphis group was beginning to turn design on its head. But the Memphis look was too avant-garde for Apple, and by the end of the trip it was apparent that the most appealing prospect was Hartmut Esslinger, a German designer who worked in the rural village of Altensteig in the Black Forest, twenty-five miles southwest of Stuttgart. Esslinger, who called his firm frogdesign after the green frog that symbolized the town, was best known for the motorcycles he'd done for Yamaha. His specialty was translating technology into human terms, which made him perfect for a company like Apple.

Esslinger responded to Apple's proposal with a look that was fresh, clean, and sophisticated, and in the spring of 1983, shortly before Sculley's arrival, he opened a Silicon Valley office and was given authority over Apple's new product design. Everyone agreed that the IIb should be the first product with the "Snow White" look. That shouldn't have been a problem, because Gemmell and Esslinger had been trading sketches all winter. But the project was on a crash schedule, and Esslinger wanted to make refinements just as the IIb team was hurtling into tooling. In separate meetings, Jobs would tell Esslinger and Gemmell they each had final say. The ensuing "frog-wars" turned an already frantic situation into chaos. Soon they were screaming at each other about whether the case should be two millimeters longer and whether the radius of the corners of the keyboard should be six millimeters or eight. Such minute changes might cost hundreds of thousands of dollars in retooling and delay the product for months; but imperfection was something Jobs could not abide, whether it was a subtle flaw in the monitor or the deliberate scratch someone had just made on his new Mercedes—a point he made very loudly one morning before storming out of Sculley's office in a rage.

Jobs wanted to control the engineering as well as the design, so he bypassed Paterson and Dali to work directly with Peter Quinn and David Larson, the engineering manager and the marketing manager who were running the project. Quinn and Larson didn't mind having their bosses cut out—they could never get them to talk with each other anyway—but they didn't like interference from Jobs. They'd managed the IIe before this, and by now they'd been moving so fast for so long with so little supervision that everything was going past in a blur. How could they be expected to slow down long enough to listen to anyone else? So when Jobs said he wanted the IIb mouse to work like the Macintosh mouse, Quinn, a fearless young man with bright red hair, declared it couldn't be done. Jobs made him do it anyway.

Then Jobs insisted it have a connector in back so it could be hooked up to the network Belleville was developing for Macintosh. Quinn kept saying this was a mistake—it would take too long and the chip you needed to make it work was too expensive and nobody would want to link them up anyway. Paterson would go forth to argue Quinn's case in meetings, and every time he'd come back whipped. When the final decision was reached and Jobs won, Quinn—who'd been working eighteen hours a day for two years and was losing his wife and kids in a divorce and was getting that fried-hair look of the terminal crash-and-burn victim—called Jobs on the phone and started screaming at him. "What the hell's going on here?" he cried. "I thought the idea was we build computers we *believe* in!"

This caught Jobs's attention, and while he had no plans to give way on the network issue, it did suggest that the troops were unhappy. He didn't mind being yelled at; he respected people who stood up to him. Quinn to him was like the sergeant in the World War II movie who leads his men up the hill against incredible odds and throws the grenade that wipes out the Nazi machine-gun nest. Quinn was a good guy. It was the colonels who needed fixing. So one day near the end of August he arranged for Quinn and Larson to air their grievances on the network issue before Sculley, and as they were doing so, he suggested in a not-so-subtle way that Sculley wasn't getting all the facts from his division managers. There were sides of the story they weren't telling him. They were filtering information. Shortly after that, Paterson and Dali were gone. Paterson, who'd already complained to Sculley that he had no authority, took a demotion and went to work managing an engineering project in the Lisa division. Dali was named to a task force.

There was no one else in the division who was qualified to take over, so Sculley decided to manage it himself for a while. It would give him a little "hands-on experience," as they said in the computer magazines, and since the division was generating virtually the entire revenue stream, it would be a good idea to find out what was going on over there. Apple was in a critical period, with the shakeout looming ever larger on the horizon and the whole industry agog over IBM's new "Peanut," whose introduction was thought to be imminent. Analysts were expecting the Peanut—a small, inexpensive version of the IBM PC—to take over the home market in personal computers the way the PC had taken over the business market. Their use of the term "Peanut"—an early code name that had been used in Boca because a peanut is smaller than an acorn, which was the original code name for the PC itself—only reinforced the idea. The Peanut, people said, was going to eclipse the Apple II before Macintosh even got out the door. The Peanut was going to put Apple out of business.

So Sculley took a desk in the Triangle Building and started spending nearly half his time there, trying to make sense of the place. He rarely ventured out of his office; management-by-walking-around was not his style. But he did meet frequently with Quinn and Larson and Ida Cole, the marketing manager who'd taken over the IIx project, and he began to get some very disorienting information as a result. He was dumbfounded, for example, to learn that it was Wozniak who'd designed the original Apple II; he thought Jobs had done half the work. Worse, the division seemed rudderless, and Sculley's experience in the soft-drink industry gave him no clues about how to proceed. All you do in soft drinks, he admitted one day, is mix sugar with water and mark it up a lot—it's a no-brainer. Here you've got all these technical decisions to make—MS DOS, IBM-compatible, and even after you'd mastered the terms, how could you foresee all the implications? He confided too that he didn't believe in Lisa, though he'd always admired the Apple II. But when they tried to get him to be their champion, he told them no good would come of his being at odds with Steve.

■ ■ ■

What was bugging the Lisa people was that damn pirate flag. Susan Kare, the artist who was designing the Macintosh icons, had painted the skull-and-crossbones on a piece of black cloth, and at the beginning of the summer, when the renovation of Bandley 3 had finally been completed and the Macintosh division was moving in, she'd stolen onto the roof with one of the software guys and hung it from a pole on top of the building. It had been flying there for weeks, right across the street, waving in their faces, as if the Mac group were going to seize their building with grappling hooks and swarm aboard with cutlasses between their teeth and send them all to the bottom of the sea.

Band of pirates indeed. The way it looked to the rest of the company, the Macintosh crew lived more like kings than like pirates. Bandley 3, which as headquarters for the Apple II division had been packed knees-to-elbows with some two hundred people, had been renovated for Macintosh to hold half that many. For a while there'd even been talk of calling in an exorcist to rid the place of the lingering vibes of the Apple III, but Jay Elliot had put a stop to that. Steve wanted his team to be inspired by great products, so he parked his BMW motorcycle in one corner of the spacious atrium and a Bösendorfer piano in another corner. They got great fruit juices too—free juices, which they stocked in their refrigerator at company expense. They got business cards with funky titles—"hardware wizard" for Burrell Smith, "software wizard" for Andy Hertzfeld, "Macintosh artist" for Susan Kare. And because Steve considered them all artists, the conference rooms on either side of the atrium were named "Picasso" and "Matisse." They were mirror images of each other, and the funny thing was that nobody could ever keep them straight.

But it was the pirate flag that really galled the Lisa group. They ran up their own flag, one that bore the Lisa logo—a brave gesture, but an empty one. The whole thing was unnerving, especially with Couch gone and all the bad press they'd been getting. The pride and euphoria of January were gone. In their place were nervousness and fear.

The euphoria had been based mainly on the response Lisa had gotten in sneak previews, when reporters and representatives from Fortune 1000 corporations were led in more or less blindfolded and given a few well-orchestrated moments to play with the machine. The reaction then was uniformly favorable. But in June, when Lisa started shipping and potential customers finally got a chance to spend some time with it, the response wasn't so good. People complained about its $9,995 price tag. They complained because to buy it you had to buy the six integrated software packages that came with it. They complained that it was slow—that to do anything on it required an agonizing wait, because the software was so complex and the computer code that made it run was so voluminous. They complained that it couldn't share information with any of IBM's computers. And worst of all, they weren't ordering it. In May there'd been a backlog of 12,000 orders; by midsummer that backlog was gone. Something was wrong.

Certainly that was how it looked to Wayne Rosing, the engineering director who'd taken over the division from Couch. Rosing had been running mid-range systems development at Digital Equipment when Couch hired him; Digital had just turned down his proposal to build a minicomputer using the same Xerox PARC technology that Apple wanted to build into Lisa. Couch's offer came at just the right time. But two years later, in September 1982, when they were about to introduce Lisa to the world, it had suddenly occurred to Rosing that maybe they shouldn't go through with it. At that point everything was ready to go: Marketing was giving sneak previews to potential customers, and his own engineers were already working on data-communications networks so Lisa could be integrated into the corporate office environment, sharing information with other computers. But when he looked at what Jobs was doing with Macintosh, how he was creating a computer that was personable and winsome and *charming,* as only the Apple II had been charming before it, Rosing realized that the corporate office environment was not for Apple.

Apple built computers for individuals. Lisa was taking it into the systems business—complex and expensive products that had to be sold directly to corporate customers by an Apple sales force and serviced by a trained support staff. IBM played the systems game flawlessly. For Apple to do so would require exponential increases in commitment. Did Apple really have the follow-through needed to win? Maybe, Rosing thought, they ought just to cancel Lisa and put the Lisa people to work writing software for Macintosh. The idea was preposterous, of course. He'd suggested it to Couch one day as a joke and they'd tossed it around for a few minutes, but marketing had these sales projections that said they had all these computers sold—what were they, crazy?

Now it was summer 1983, nearly a year later. Couch was gone and Lisa was out and things were going sour. On a Tuesday morning in early August, Rosing got a phone call from Roy Weaver, Apple's vice-president for distribution. Because Weaver was running the warehouses the dealers ordered from, he had a better idea of what was happening than anybody else in the company. He had his fingers on the numbers. "Wayne," he said, "the backlog has broken on Lisa."

The backlog had broken: That meant they'd filled all their orders and new ones weren't coming in. The dealers weren't reordering, Weaver explained, and the direct sales force Apple had built to woo corporate accounts was dribbling in orders of five and ten machines. The demand just wasn't there. Rosing called Gene Carter, the vice-president of sales—the semiconductor veteran who'd built up Apple's dealer base from scratch when personal-computer dealers barely existed. "What gives?" he asked. Gene didn't know, but he told Wayne not to worry—they'd sell more this month. Wayne was worried anyway. So far they were only manufacturing these things on a Volvo-style assembly line—that is, virtually by hand, each worker assembling an entire machine—right there on Bandley Drive; the major production lines in Dallas were still being ramped up. The sales forecast called for them to sell 59,000 units the first year, 5,000 a month, and 5,000 a month was what they were building. At a wholesale price of $5,000 per machine, Wayne could be building up inventory at the rate of $25 million a month. He'd better do something right away.

The next day, after conferring with his staff, Rosing grabbed Sculley between meetings. He explained what was happening. Sculley asked what he wanted to do. He said he wanted to stop purchasing. He wanted to shut down production in Cupertino and move those people to the Macintosh factory in Fremont. He wanted to make a presentation at the exec staff meeting that afternoon. Then he'd figure out what to do next.

The backlog of orders on the IIe had already broken. With IBM's Peanut looming, the home-computer market had gone into paralysis. They'd been counting on Lisa to see them through. Crisply, for there wasn't much to say, Sculley told him to put his plan together.

■ ■ ■

While Rosing scrambled to shut down Lisa, Jobs and his lieutenants were scrambling to launch Macintosh. The hardware was fixed at this point, but software was still barely visible on the horizon. For more than a year Macintosh had had a "software evangelist" whose job was to spread the gospel of Macintosh in the programming community. His name was Mike Boich, and he had both an M.B.A. from Harvard and a hobbyist's interest in personal computers, having started with an Apple I while a math major at Stanford. Apple wasn't paying anybody to develop software for Macintosh, so Boich had to convert people to the Macintosh cause. He'd walk into a little office somewhere and unzip his bag and pull out a prototype Macintosh and demo MacPaint, the graphics program Bill Atkinson had done. It looked so whizzy the programmers would all go, "Whoa! This is hot! How do you do this? Can I keep one?" Before they knew what hit them, they were hooked.

Certainly that's what had happened with Mitch Kapor, the founder of Lotus Development, the Cambridge software start-up that was enjoying phenomenal success with its first product, a business program for the IBM PC called 1-2-3. Kapor was an early Apple II enthusiast who'd worked briefly for the company that sold VisiCalc. Like many in the industry, he'd been profoundly influenced by Jobs: He liked the style, the excitement, the sense of possibilities at Apple, and even the name Lotus—short, nontechnical, suggesting a flower, a race car, inner peace—was reminiscent of the name Jobs had chosen for his enterprise. What he didn't like was Jobs's charisma, which seemed to him little more than a license to persuade other people to do things that weren't in their own self-interest. But when he saw Macintosh, he was blinded by the light. Steve was doing it right, and IBM wasn't. Lotus went to work on a Macintosh product right away.

Boich had persuaded several other top software companies to develop programs as well, but they were all behind schedule, because Macintosh was so different from other computers that programmers had trouble adapting to it. While most computer screens were equipped to handle only the standard assortment of letters, numerals, and punctuation marks arranged in the standard twenty-four lines by eighty columns, the sophisticated graphics capabilities of Macintosh meant that programmers had 160,000 individual dots to turn on and off. The machine had so little memory that programmers kept running out of space, a disaster that was signified by sudden and mysterious crashes: The computer would cease to function and all their work would be lost. And because Jobs insisted on a uniform look and feel for every program, many of the features that programmers generally design themselves had been burnt into the circuitry. Buried within the system were some five hundred special routines they could call upon for help, but mastering them was no small task. The system was like a genie in a bottle that would do five hundred favors for you, but only if you knew what to ask for. The upshot of all this was that even MacWrite and MacPaint, the word-processing and graphics packages that were considered the bare minimum of what had to be ready when the computer was shipped, were late and full of bugs.

Right now, however, the critical issue was manufacturing. Apple's other computers were all built by Del Yocam's manufacturing division, which ran factories in Dallas and Ireland and Singapore. Jobs thought Yocam was a joke. Yocam got the job done, but he had no finesse whatsoever. He wasn't into low labor content or good materials management or any of the ideas that were generating excitement at other companies; his people just punched out computers like doughnuts. That might be okay for the Apple II, but it wasn't good enough for Macintosh. The Macintosh factory was part of the vision. It was the machine to build the machine.

To build the Apple II, Yocam used a cumbersome system that relied on cheap offshore labor: Parts were stockpiled at a Silicon Valley warehouse, shipped to Singapore for assembly by hand, then shipped back to Dallas for final production. The whole process, from pile of parts to finished computer, took ten weeks. Macintosh would be manufactured in the United States in a single, fully automated plant. Parts would come in one end and machines would go out the other. Inventory would be kept to an absolute minimum through the use of a marvelous new concept known as just-in-time delivery. Just-in-time—or *kanban,* as it was known in Japan—meant that instead of warehousing parts, the company would keep just enough on hand to fill a single day's orders. Instead of tying production to sales projections that were months old, it could respond to actual demand. Toyota was credited with the idea, but in fact it was nothing more than a return to Henry Ford's assembly line, a revolutionary concept that had been corrupted over the years by managers who built up inventory buffers to protect themselves from all the disasters that could halt production—strikes, breakdowns, defective parts, delayed deliveries. Jobs, recalling the vision of the ultimate factory that Ford had realized in his phenomenal River Rouge plant, even fantasized about a factory in which the raw materials that came in would be not semiconductors but sand—the natural source of the silicon from which semiconductors are made. Even without such extremes, just-in-time was not for the faint of heart: It demanded a perfectly tuned system in which managers, workers, and suppliers all worked as one. But the benefits for the daring were many, and Jobs was never much for risk avoidance.

In 1982, Jobs had gotten board approval to build his own factory for Macintosh and bring it up to speed before handing it off to Yocam. He had a site picked out in Fremont, but Mike Markkula had insisted they put it in Dallas, partly because they had empty factory space there and partly out of fear that the Apple II would stop selling, and if they had to start laying off factory workers it would signal that Apple was in trouble. Jobs had hired Dave Vaughan, who ran a Hewlett-Packard manufacturing plant in Oregon, to set up the operation. Vaughan knew all about zero defects and just-in-time delivery and getting in touch with your suppliers, but he didn't know how to cope with his new boss. Steve would worry about things like what color the robots should be painted—maybe he should hire an interior designer? This was worth thinking about, given that just-in-time demanded such commitment from the workers, but it wasn't top priority under the circumstances. Bob Belleville told Vaughan he should simply ignore a lot of what Steve said. Steve spun off hundreds of ideas every day and never bothered to write any of them down; there was no way he could remember them all, so the thing to do was seize the ones that made sense and forget about the rest. But Vaughan wasn't used to working that way.

A more serious problem was the factory's cost overruns. The board, against its natural instincts, had authorized a capital expenditure of $3.6 million to equip it, and this figure had since crept up to nearly $8 million. But that spring, when the finance people rolled the numbers, they discovered they'd need $12 million to get it finished. Steve went before the board with his controller, Debi Coleman, and asked for $16 million, just to be on the safe side. This got the board members so angry they ordered Coleman out of the room and demanded to know why they shouldn't turn the factory over to Del. But they contented themselves with a brutal admonition, and shortly afterwards, with the IIe selling beyond anyone's expectations and all the excess capacity in Dallas taken up to produce it, Markkula gave his permission to move the factory back to Fremont. Then Vaughan walked into Steve's office and announced that he'd accepted a job with another computer company.

A few weeks later, at the end of August, with a still-empty factory and nobody to run it, the Macintosh division staged a two-day vendors' conference at the Red Lion Inn, a concrete slab that had just been put up near the airport in San Jose. It was really a pep rally for the companies whose components would make Macintosh happen— for Sony and Motorola and Samsung and dozens of smaller firms with names like AB Plastics Corporation and Deluxe Die Mold and United Chemi-Con. Together they were Team #1, high-technology partners at the cutting edge of American industrial innovation. Steve and Bob Belleville laid out the essential message—the critical importance of quality and of on-time delivery, the threat that they'd shut the factory down if their standards weren't met. Then everyone was given a look at the machine itself, followed by a quick trip to Fremont for a tour of the factory and then a banquet back at the Fir Room with Liz Story playing piano. They all left in a flush of warm feelings and high expectations, fully convinced that Macintosh was real.

There was another factory tour the next day, this one for the Macintosh people themselves. For most it would be their first, sobering look at the multimillion-dollar facility where the dream they'd been nurturing for so long would soon take substance. The buses pulled up outside Bandley 3, and the band of pirates got on in a blaze of anticipation and excitement, and then the buses drove away. Bob watched it all from his office window. I'm supposed to be on this bus, he thought to himself, but I'm not on it.

What Bob liked to do at moments like this was go for a long walk. He left the empty building, climbed into his oversized beige camper in the parking lot, and drove off. He got on the freeway and headed north to Page Mill Road. Instead of swooping down into Palo Alto, he went west, where the road turns narrow and winding as it wends its way up the ridge that separates the bay from the ocean. The Valley fell back behind him as he climbed: the Stanford campus, its Hoover Tower standing red-tipped and engorged above the trees; the vast dirigible hanger at Moffett Field, where the Navy P-3 Orions sleep between forays over the Pacific in the never-ending hunt for Soviet submarines; the Lockheed missile plant, with its array of radio dishes locked into orbiting satellites; the red flats of the salt evaporators at the southern end of the bay. He pulled over near the top, not far from the deceptively subtle cleft of the San Andreas Fault, and parked beneath some oak trees.

Off to the left, behind a gate, was a dirt road that cut across an open field. Two miles up that road was the summit of Black Mountain, at 2,800 feet the highest peak along the ridge. Bob had been walking to the top of Black Mountain for nearly a decade now, ever since he'd left Purdue for California. The hippie squatters who'd been living on the ridge top when he first came were long gone. The air was damp and foggy, though the grass was still brown from the long summer dry season. Bob climbed out of the camper and headed up the road, an awkwardly boyish figure in baggy khaki shorts and thick, gold-rimmed glasses, a blond cowlick sticking up behind his head.

The summit was more a gentle knoll than a mountain peak, but because it was so high it had been transformed into a node in the invisible information web that had been spun above the Valley. In a small clearing surrounded by ghostly live oaks and red-barked madrones stood a cluster of concrete bunkers enclosed by chain-link fences laced with barbed wire. Atop these information forts stood radio transmitters, while all around them were microwave reflectors and repeaters—flat screens like billboards and shiny round disks mounted on metal towers to refocus microwave transmissions and bounce them from one location in the Valley to another. This vista, strangely pastoral to the naked eye, was in fact buzzing with raw information in its densest form, in imperceptible waves moving through the air at a billion cycles per second. In the midst of it all was a gunmetal gray slab from which issued a loud, static hum. It was a transformer. Bob sat cross-legged on the transformer and closed his eyes and communed with the energy around him—the trees, the winds, the buzz of electricity rising up his spine, the pulse of information passing noiselessly above his head. Mists swirled through the trees, while the headwaters of Stevens Creek gathered strength in the canyon far below.

Months earlier, Bob had written a paper that outlined the strategy he thought Macintosh should pursue to develop a simple office automation system. It was the direct antithesis of the strategy the Lisa division had formulated. It called for a small, unassuming network linking inexpensive computers with each other and with "file servers" that would store data for everyone on the circuit. His hardware engineers were done with Macintosh by this time. All summer they'd been working on the network and a file server and a laser-controlled printer that would produce documents of almost typeshop quality. As Bob rose from the transformer, he realized that Apple should cancel the Lisa network and concentrate on his own. Lisa was all but dead. Apple's office of the future would have to be built around Macintosh.

□□ **8** □□

Flashdance

That fall the shakeout hit. The first warnings came in late July, when jitters on Wall Street sent technology stocks into a sudden free fall. IBM, Hewlett-Packard, Apple, Commodore, Texas Instruments, Motorola, National Semiconductor: The dive was universal, and analysts and portfolio managers were at a loss to explain it. From then on the news only got worse. Osborne, which had zoomed from $0 to $100 million in two short years, laid off three-quarters of its employees in September and then filed for bankruptcy to seek protection from its creditors. Atari's losses for the year were edging up toward $400 million, enough to make the foundations tremble at Warner headquarters in New York. Texas Instruments lost $230 million in six months in a mad attempt to seize the market for low-cost home computers—a market whose bottom dropped out over the summer, just as it had for video games the previous Christmas.

The public's fascination with the idea of computers had led to a proliferation of tiny machines like Texas Instruments' 99/4A and the Timex 1000 and the Commodore VIC 20, which sold for as little as fifty dollars and were supposed to be hooked up to a television set. They were useless except as toys, and even as toys they were unsatisfactory; the people who bought them got little of the taste of computing except how frustrating it could be. But more functional machines, like the $1,400 Apple IIe, weren't all that useful in most homes either. What were you going to do with them—balance your checkbook? Organize your recipes? Play video games every night? Unless you were running a small business out of your living room, there was only one thing you could do: give them to the kids so they wouldn't grow up to be computer-illiterate. Yet with IBM about to introduce its Peanut, no responsible parent was likely to buy a computer now.

The demand for office computers was stronger, but that didn't help Apple. In early September *Electronic News,* the leading trade journal in the industry, reported that Lisa sales weren't up to expectations; a few days later, Hambrecht & Quist, the San Francisco securities firm that had financed the better part of Silicon Valley, revised its estimate of Apple's earnings downwards. That sent the price of Apple stock skidding below $35 a share, nearly half the level it had been trading at in June. A couple of weeks later, shortly before the end of the fiscal year, Sculley announced that sales were flat and that, as a result, earnings for the final quarter would be sharply lower than they'd been for the same quarter the year before. Wall Street took this as a sign to stop hurling money out the window and start dumping Apple stock instead. Because so many giant institutions held huge blocks of Apple stock, a handfull of Wall Street professionals could send the stock price plummeting if they all decided to sell. And so in one day Apple stock fell more than $8—not as bad as what had happened to Texas Instruments, which a few months before had dropped $51 in two days, but clearly not good for a company's health.

If investors were skittish, it was because buyers were too. At least 150 companies were selling personal computers, and the experts were saying that no more than thirty would survive. What if you bought the wrong computer? What if you bought the wrong stock? Smaller companies, like Victor Technologies in Scotts Valley and Vector Graphic in Los Angeles, found themselves bereft of credibility as analysts and business reporters fingered them for extinction. Such forecasts became self-fulfilling, for lost credibility meant fewer sales and fewer sales meant bigger losses and bigger losses meant lowered credibility and on and on in what could only result in the whole business going spiraling down the drain. And it wasn't just start-ups that were having trouble; in the wake of the Texas Instruments debacle, major corporations like Digital Equipment and Xerox found their commitment to personal computers in question as well. The beneficiary of all this was IBM, the only company no one thought was going to either go out of business or pull out of the market. As for the rest, "I'd do better picking winners in horse racing than survivors in personal computers," a market researcher at the Cambridge consulting firm of Arthur D. Little told *The Wall Street Journal.*

■ ■ ■

"A two-horse race": That's how Sculley had seen it when he'd arrived at Apple a few months before. Now, suddenly, the race seemed over. In a cover story that hit the stands at the end of September, *Business Week* proclaimed IBM the winner. Apple was coming off its biggest year ever—$982 million in sales, up from $583 million in 1982— and yet its future seemed completely up in the air. It was no secret in the industry that Lisa sales were far below expectations, or that the IIe—the cash cow of the company—was languishing on dealers' shelves, or that IBM was about to deliver the final blow with the imminent announcement of its Peanut. And in the midst of all this, Apple was betting the future of the company on an entirely new computer that was incompatible with anything else on the market.

If Macintosh was to have any hope of succeeding, they'd have to establish it immediately as a sexy and easy-to-use alternative to the safety and security of IBM. To accomplish this, they'd set a budget for the launch—advertising, publicity, promotion—of $15 million. The task of marketing it—that is, of figuring out how to spend all this money—had been given to Mike Murray, a Stanford graduate with both an engineering degree and an M.B.A. Murray liked to think of himself as a "marketing hacker." It would be the first time he'd introduced a computer.

Mike Murray was the perfect sidekick for Jobs: a kinetic little guy, no older than his boss, with a million ideas and enthusiasm to match. He generated concepts so fast it left him breathless, and what he was best at was taking a complex situation and capturing its essence in a single, memorable phrase. With his Beatle haircut and well-trimmed moustache and his coat-and-tie style, he had the faintly hip look of a junior record-company executive. His only previous experience had been running marketing for a new product being built by Hewlett-Packard in Corvallis, Oregon, a bucolic little town on the Willamette River. Several other Macintosh people had come from Corvallis too, among them Mike Boich, the software evangelist, and Dave Vaughan, the recently departed manufacturing manager. The product HP was supposed to be building there was a dead ringer for Macintosh, but the work wasn't like Macintosh at all—it was strictly eight-to-five, no weekends, no passion, no commitment. And while Murray was remarkably straitlaced in certain ways—a family man, a nondrinker, a Mormon—he liked to think of himself as a sixties idealist who'd been born too late. So when Jobs called and offered him not just a job but a chance to change the world, he took it. Now he was working at Jobs's side, helping to orchestrate the Second Coming.

From the first, Macintosh had been conceived of as the ultimate personal computer. It had been defined in terms not of what it was but of what it wasn't. It wasn't for people who read *The Wall Street Journal.* It wasn't for people who worked in big corporations. It wasn't even a computer in the usual sense of the term. It was an information appliance—and when Murray looked up "appliance" in the dictionary, he found it meant a tool that was a means to an end. So he tried to position Macintosh as a productivity tool for "knowledge workers," a buzzword he'd picked up from an old Booz Allen & Hamilton management study. (They'd gotten it from Peter Drucker, the management guru, who'd come up with the term in the late sixties to describe the office workers who'd create the wealth in an economy based not on production of goods but on knowledge.) From there he'd ricocheted off into a never-never land in which Macintosh, the information appliance, was seen as a Cuisinart for the desk—a concept he liked to illustrate with a slide presentation that showed mushrooms dancing out of the refrigerator, their creativity unleashed.

There was a natural conflict between the early, hobbyist definition of Macintosh—the list of "wasn'ts"—and Murray's evolving concept of it as an information appliance for knowledge workers. Obviously, many knowledge workers read *The Wall Street Journal* and worked in big corporations. Unfortunately, Macintosh hadn't been designed for them. When Bob Belleville arrived from Xerox—in March 1982, the same month Murray came down from Hewlett-Packard—he'd viewed the prime markets for it as business and college, just as Murray did. But Jobs and his chief designers, Burrell Smith and Andy Hertzfeld, had always regarded it as a consumer item with a $1,000 price tag, so they were more concerned with keeping the cost down than with pleasing the kind of people who had corporate bucks to spend. When Belleville pointed out that Macintosh stored files in a way that made it all but impossible to use a hard disk—a type of disk that would store twelve to twenty-five times as much information as an ordinary floppy disk—they looked at him as if to ask what planet he'd just jumped in from. Obviously Macintosh wasn't going to need a hard disk. Macintosh was going to be a *people's* computer.

At the conceptual level at least, Murray was remarkably adept at conflict resolution. He and his staff managed to bury the conflict between Macintosh the people's computer and Macintosh the information appliance in a welter of enthusiasm and creative phrase mongering: "The crankless computer." "The desk appliance." "A Cuisinart for the office." What would it offer? Not just ease of use but enhanced productivity . . . enhanced creativity . . . enhanced *life*. They took a caustic view of this sort of thinking over in the Triangle Building, where cartoons circulated with captions like "MAC . . . Think of it as a typewriter for your kitchen" and "MAC . . . Think of it as an enchilada for your desk" and "MAC . . . Think of it as a trash compactor for your mind." But in Bandley 3 the reality-distortion field held sway. In Bandley 3 it was easy to believe that Macintosh was so easy to use, so revolutionary, so life-enhancing that everybody would want one, software or no software.

This was the problem Floyd Kvamme ran up against in his monthly forecasting meetings, when he and his staff met with Del Yocam and the marketing directors from the different product divisions to decide how many computers they were going to sell and how many they had to build. It had been the same way with Lisa. By any rational standard, Kvamme thought, Lisa should be considered a resounding success. Clearly Apple was going to sell twenty thousand of them the first year, which at a wholesale price of $5,000 apiece made it a $100-million business—not bad for a computer that was expensive and slow and incompatible with every other computer on the market, from a company with no experience selling into corporate accounts. But the business plan called for a $300-million business, and by those standards it was a disaster.

Murray estimated that there were 25 million office workers in the United States alone, and he saw no reason why they couldn't start out selling eighty thousand Macs a month, or nearly a million the first year. Kvamme, in his calm and understated way, pointed out that at $2,500 apiece, that called for a total world outlay of $2.5 billion—not a likely prospect. There was only one product in the history of mankind that had ever experienced that kind of sales, he told them, and that was the Boeing 727. So the numbers in Apple's business plan for the coming fiscal year had been constrained to a mere 425,000 Macs sold, for a total of just a little more than $1 billion. The fact that Lisa had tried and failed to become a $300-million business its first year didn't matter. Macintosh was going to be a billion-dollar business, just like that.

■ ■ ■

In the meantime, Apple's only weapon against IBM was advertising. The first of the new lifestyle ads was a Lisa spot called "Alone Again," which was meant to suggest that with Lisa technology, Apple was alone again at the forefront of the computer revolution. Chiat/Day liked to use British directors, because they thought of ads not in conventional terms but as sixty-second films, and this one—directed by Ridley Scott, the director of *Alien* and *Blade Runner*—perfectly encapsulated the Stanford mentality that the Apple generation was thought to have. Set to the New Age jazz of Windham Hill, it closed with a shot of a young man alone with his Lisa in a room that seemed suspended in air. Cynics remarked that, yes, alone again was exactly where Lisa put you.

The "Apple People" ads aired shortly afterwards—the lunchtime basketball game, the home-for-breakfast guy with his pit bull. But the crucial spot—the one that would introduce Macintosh—was still under wraps. Neither Jobs nor Sculley had been terribly excited about "1984" when they'd seen the storyboards, but Ridley Scott would agree to direct "Alone Again," which they *did* want, only if he could do this one as well. Scott, with his fine eye for period detail, was clearly the right person to direct a sixty-second mini-film with an Orwellian theme. The idea was to portray a totalitarian state that didn't work, like East Germany in 1953, and to give it the air of the dank and leaky spacecraft in *Alien*. The sets were modeled after those used to create Everytown, the art-moderne "city of the future" in the 1936 science fiction classic *Things to Come*. They were planning to use a fashion model as the woman who smashes Big Brother with a sledgehammer, but at the casting call in Hyde Park one model let fly the hammer a second too early and nearly took out an old lady who was walking down a nearby path, so they decided to go for a more athletic type instead. They shot it at Shepperton Studios in September, and after it was done they added Maoist gibberish to the soundtrack. When they finally showed a rough cut to Jobs and Murray, the two were dumbstruck.

The first airing of "1984" was to be at sales conference. Every October, as a new fiscal year began, Apple flew all its sales reps—the independent representatives who sold its wares to dealers on commission—to Hawaii or Acapulco or some other lush and exotic locale for a week-long pep rally to psych them up for the coming year. Every meeting had an inspirational theme, and the inspirational theme of this year's was "Leading the Way": With Macintosh, Apple would be leading the way to a brighter tomorrow. So 750 sales reps, Apple execs, and Apple support people arrived in Honolulu on a Saturday afternoon to be decked with leis and ushered to the Sheraton Waikiki for mai-tais and pupus. Regis McKenna and the Regettes were there, as were Jay Chiat and Lee Clow and the rest of the creative team from Chiat/Day. It looked like your typical loose-as-a-goose Apple sales meeting—equal parts tent revival, show-biz extravaganza, and drunken blowout. But there was a disturbing undercurrent to this one, for as the reps checked into this glittering tropical paradise of plate glass and palm fronds, some of them were wondering out loud how much longer their employer would be in business.

Their anxieties were lent credence by the absence of several customary faces. All the top legal and financial people—Ken Zerbe, the executive VP for finance and administration; Joe Graziano, the chief financial officer; Al Eisenstat, the chief counsel—were back in Cupertino, trying to divine the impact of the Lisa debacle. They had no time for any sales conference. The operations of the entire company had been based on sales projections that now turned out to be chimerical. Inventory, capital investments, hiring—suddenly there was excess everywhere. And because their earnings were going to take such a hit, it made sense to write off everything that looked the least bit doubtful. With every week that went by their position seemed worse. It had been bad enough at the board meeting at the beginning of September; and as new information came in, they had to revise their earnings estimates downward and then downward still. Before it was over, they were looking at profits for the quarter of only eight cents for every share of stock, down from forty cents a share for each of the three quarters before.

That was the harsh reality, but sales meetings are never about reality. At 7:45 on Sunday morning the reps boarded buses for the ride to Honolulu's civic auditorium, where the hoopla was to begin.

Then, still jangled from jet lag, they were blasted into their seats by a laser-powered song-and-dance routine with special lyrics set to the music from the summer's hit movie, *Flashdance:*

> We are Apple
> Leading the way
> We are Apple
> And we're making a better new day!

Then there was the usual morning full of speeches and presentations, all leading up to the main event: the unveiling of Macintosh.

While the sales reps were getting the warm-up, Jobs and Murray were sprawled on the floor of a hallway outside, writing Jobs's speech. Jobs never bothered to prepare his talks in advance. Why should he, when he was blessed with perfect timing and a flair for drama and total faith in his own ideas? Macintosh was an artificial arrangement of silicon and metal designed to manipulate electrons according to the strict rules of logic; but its appeal transcended logic, and so would his pitch for it. This was no mere "productivity tool" but a machine to free the human spirit. It was wizardry at work, the electronic embodiment of the hobbyist ideal. It was a mystical experience. All you needed to use it—all you needed to *respond* to it—was your own intuition. And to sell it, Jobs had only to play to the emotions.

Ten minutes later he took the spotlight on a darkened stage. Blue jeans, white shirt, bow tie, reality-distortion field. Oration was his gift, and in its throes his voice, normally high-pitched and slightly nasal, assumed stentorian tones, a great, rolling, majestic quality that swept you up in its passion. "It is 1958!" he declared. "IBM passes up the chance to buy a young company that has just invented a new technology called xerography." And he retold the wondrous and horrifying tale of how IBM, offered the technology for dry photo-copying, deemed it insignificant and *turned it down.* "It is ten years later," he went on, "the late sixties. Digital Equipment Corporation and others invent the minicomputer." Yet another horror story: the sorry saga of IBM trying to squelch the minicomputer revolution. "It is now ten years later," he intoned, "the late seventies. Apple, a young company on the West Coast, invents the Apple II, the first personal computer as we know it today. IBM dismisses the personal computer as too small to do serious computing and therefore insignificant to its business.

"It is now the early eighties—1981." Everyone in the hall knew that date: the year IBM entered the market for personal computers. Cheers erupted as Steve told the story; the hysteria was building. Steve quieted the throng with an upturned hand, then slowly, dramatically, began his takeoff roll. "It is now 1984. It appears that IBM wants it all." Gathering speed, he told how Apple was perceived as the only hope against IBM, how dealers were turning to Apple as the only force that could ensure their freedom, how IBM had turned its guns at the last remaining obstacle to industry control, how IBM wanted it *all*. "Will Big Blue dominate the entire information age?" he cried at last. "Was George Orwell *right?*"

"No!" they screamed. "No! No! NO!" And as they did so, an immense screen descended from the ceiling. In a sixty-second microburst the drama unfolded: a world of gray, the slack-jawed drones, the pulsing sound, the drones assembling in a vast hall, Big Brother on the screen before them, his crazed harangue, the young woman with the hammer, the security police behind her, the woman running, faster, faster, the hammer flying, the drones' astonished faces, the screen exploding in a million tiny fragments. "On January 24, Apple Computer will introduce Macintosh," a voice intoned, "and you'll see why 1984 won't be like *1984*." And then, with the stage wreathed in dry-ice fumes, a laser barrage revealed a descending Macintosh, its screen lighting up in mid-air. At that point the auditorium erupted. People stomped, people whistled, people stood on their chairs and cheered. It went on for five minutes, ten minutes, forever. Jobs looked at Murray, waiting in the wings, and in that moment they both knew they had it. They knew how everything would play for months to come. They knew the public would go wild.

The sales conference was transformed in that moment—all defeatism banished, euphoria in its place. With Macintosh they could challenge IBM and win. To show that they'd have all the software they needed, Jobs emceed an elaborate "software dating game" in which the three leading figures in the business—Bill Gates of Microsoft, Mitch Kapor of Lotus Development, and Fred Gibbons of Software Publishing—came onstage and each vowed to go steady with Macintosh. At any other meeting that would have been the high point, but not this one. For the rest of the week, wherever they were— at coffee breaks, at receptions, at "breakout" sessions in the hotel conference rooms—the reps insisted on watching Ridley Scott's little movie again and again. And at their *M*A*S*H* theme party out past the sugar-cane fields on the north side of the island, the party Jobs and Gene Carter and Floyd Kvamme flew out to by helicopter wearing surgeons' garb, they gathered in the dark with their K rations and booze and broke into hideously off-key choruses of their theme song:

> Leading the way, leading the way!
> Aaaooww wwooowww, Aaaap-ple!

They were ready to charge into 1984. They were ready to change the world.

■ ■ ■

When they got back from Hawaii, Jobs screened the ad once again, this time for the board of directors. He had little doubt that they'd approve it. Apple's board members, while hard-nosed and business-like, generally kept a hands-off attitude toward the running of the company. The most influential among them was Mike Markkula, the man who'd led it out of the garage. After that came Arthur Rock, at fifty-seven the most powerful venture capitalist in the Bay Area, a weathered, laconic man who'd helped finance first Fairchild and then Intel and then Apple. Like Markkula, he and his wife had taken Steve under their wing; they shared nights on the town in San Francisco, weekends at their condo in Aspen. Henry Singleton, the founder and chairman of the Los Angeles–based technology conglomerate Teledyne, was the grand old man of the group, the oldest and most distinguished. Philip Schlein, the president of Macy's California, was there to lend retail expertise. The only East Coast representative was fifty-one-year-old Peter Crisp of Venrock, the venture fund the Rocke-feller family maintained for its high-technology investments. He had a reputation for being tough on the numbers.

While some of the board members—Markkula and Rock in par-ticular—took a paternal interest in Steve, his relationship to them, complicated as it was by fame and money, was something other than filial. He was at least twenty years younger than all of them except Markkula and Sculley, and yet it was he who ran the meetings. He listened to their advice; but in strategic matters, matters of global direction—hiring Sculley, for instance—he also did what he wanted to do. And he certainly never went out of his way to cultivate them or curry favor or ingratiate himself with them; brown-nosing wasn't his style. He simply managed to be more restrained around them than he was with most people.

He wasn't restrained in his enthusiasm for "1984," however. As the board meeting began, he was almost quivering with excitement. The seven directors were assembled in the boardroom on the top floor of Apple's dramatic new headquarters on De Anza Boulevard, a long, low building that was known around the company as the Pink Palace. The room was modest by the standards of most corporations, but in the California-casual atmosphere of the Pink Palace, where the corridors were painted mauve and pink and trees seemed to sprout every ten feet, it looked formal, even imposing. It faced south, toward Saratoga, its wall of windows affording a dramatic view of Cupertino's antiseptic streetscape, which was ringed by the distant Santa Cruz Mountains and punctuated by the incongruously antiquated grain elevators of the R. Cali & Bro. feed store on Stevens Creek Boulevard. The view disappeared as the shades were drawn and a television screen lit up at the far end of the table.

There was a long silence when the sixty seconds were over. Phil Schlein was sitting with his head on the table. Finally a deep voice spoke up. It was another of the board members, wanting to know if they could vote to find a new agency. The others quickly joined in. They could think of only one explanation for what they'd just seen, and that was that Chiat/Day had gone completely amok. Not only did the ad not show the product; it barely mentioned the word "computer." And they were going to show this on the Super Bowl, where air time cost $1 million a minute? That wasn't how you launched a computer.

What they failed to realize—what they couldn't realize, being businessmen and capitalists rather than dreamers—was that Macintosh wasn't a computer; it was a crusade.

□□ 9 □□

Compatibility

On November 1, at a press reception in New York, IBM finally unveiled the Peanut—the PCjr, as it was more formally known. There were two Peanuts, actually: a $669 model, which could only store data on a cassette tape recorder the buyer had to supply, and a $1,269 model, which came with a single built-in disk drive. The screen had to be bought separately. In place of ordinary typewriter keys, the keyboard had little domes under a rubbery membrane. The $1,269 version came with 128 kilobytes of internal memory, which wasn't enough to run the sophisticated programs that had been developed for the IBM PC—programs like Lotus 1-2-3, an "integrated" software package that allowed users to do complex financial analyses, display the results in chart form, and sort through piles of data in a flash. In March, 1-2-3 had replaced VisiCalc as the best-selling personal-computer program in America; it was so hot that people were buying the PC just so they could run it. But it was also a business program, and the fact that Junior couldn't run it—along with other drawbacks, like the creepy rubber keyboard and the single disk drive (or none)—suggested that Don Estridge and the folks in Boca Raton thought there was a market out there for a $669 recipe file.

The real news, however, was that it wouldn't be available until after Christmas. Originally it had been scheduled for announcement in June and then by Labor Day, but problems with the manufacturer had delayed it for months. Unlike all of IBM's other products, the Junior was being built by an outside supplier—a division of Teledyne, the conglomerate headed by Henry Singleton, who sat on Apple's board. Teledyne had put up a $6-million factory in the middle of Tennessee to manufacture it, but it was having trouble trying to ramp up to the capacity that IBM and its dealers thought necessary. The success of the PC and the mushrooming expectations of analysts and reporters for the Junior had sent everyone into delirium. Dealers told IBM it had better have thirty or forty thousand machines on the shelves before it was announced; one early IBM forecast predicted that 1.7 million would be sold the first year. Finally, in a desperate attempt to forestall further speculation in the press and tie up the Christmas market, IBM had decided to announce it even though it wouldn't be available until sometime the following year.

At Apple, all this was regarded as great news. The pundits had gotten so used to predicting that the IBM logo would work the same magic in the home that it had in corporate America—that it would bring order to a chaotic market, introducing a standard for the citizenry to follow—that they kept right on predicting it, even after IBM's unveiling of this obvious clunker. In Cupertino, however, the announcement was greeted with incredible relief.

Apple's fear was that the Peanut would hit Christmas, undermine the IIe, and already be well established by the time the IIb hit the market. Lacking even a rudimentary industrial surveillance program, the company had had to rely on press speculation to find out when the Peanut was coming and what it would be. Woz's brother Mark owned a computer store, and he got the first one to come into the Valley. He brought it to the Triangle Building the day it came in. The engineers there tore it apart immediately, and by the time they'd torn it down to a pile of parts in the middle of the lab they'd proclaimed it a kludge. Not only was it unable to run most of the programs for the PC and cursed with a keyboard that felt like it was made out of Chiclets; it required all sorts of cables and add-ons before you could make it work. To hook it up to a cassette recorder, you'd have to go back to the computer store and buy a thirty-dollar cable. To hook it up to a TV you needed a twenty-dollar cable. To hook it up to a computer monitor, you needed yet a third cable. As an appliance computer, the IIb was intended to be the simple solution—everything you needed in one box. The PCjr looked like the endless problem.

■   ■   ■

A new leader had just taken over in the Triangle Building: John Cavalier, the man who'd been heading the computer division at Atari. Like Bill Campbell, the Eastman Kodak executive Sculley had hired to run marketing, Cavalier came from consumer goods—in his case, paper cups and toilet tissue. With his jowly face, overhanging brows, and chunky physique, he looked more like a member of the Politburo than like an East Coast corporate executive. But for thirteen years he'd been at American Can, first in finance, then on the "metal side," and finally on the "paper side," running businesses like Dixie Cups and Northern paper products. Ray Kassar, the former Egyptian rug merchant, had lured him to Silicon Valley to run Atari's foundering computer operations. When Kassar was replaced a few months later by James Morgan of Philip Morris—a man who didn't seem to understand that he had weeks rather than months to deal with Atari's losses before they caused Warner Communications to collapse—Cavalier allowed himself to be wooed by Sculley. Obviously Sculley couldn't run the Apple II division and the whole company at the same time, and Cavalier seemed to have the right credentials. He was a package-goods man with experience in computers. What could be better?

Cavalier didn't just come from package goods; he came from the packages themselves. At American Can he'd managed soap boxes, shampoo bottles, toothpaste tubes. He'd dealt with some of the biggest consumer-goods outfits in the world—Proctor & Gamble, Anheuser-Busch, General Foods. Packaging was a stodgy, old-line sort of business, and he'd been one of the Young Turks who'd shaken things up by pushing through innovations like the seven-layer laminated toothpaste tube. He knew marketing too. He'd licensed the *Star Wars* characters from Lucasfilm and put them on Dixie Cups and discovered that no matter what you charged, kids would create such a racket in the supermarket that their parents would break down and buy them. Just about the only thing he didn't know—having been at Atari for less than a year—was computers.

Like PepsiCo, American Can was a pretty starchy place. In 1970 it had joined the corporate exodus from New York City, forsaking the grime and crime of Park Avenue for the bucolic splendor of Greenwich. The wooded hills of Westchester County, New York, and Fairfield County, Connecticut, where sturdy Yankee farmers once tilled the flinty soil, seemed hospitable to the dimly remembered Protestant virtues of American business. There, in Greenwich and

New Canaan and Bedford and Pound Ridge, the Mr. Blandingses of mid-century had built their dream houses—rambling, colonial-style farmhouses of white clapboard, with clay tennis courts out back. And in nearby Stamford and Danbury and Harrison they were building their corporate headquarters as well—imposing edifices of stone and concrete and glass, the stately homes of industry, superimposed on a Norman Rockwell landscape of stone walls, scarlet maples, and white picket fences.

The executives who worked in these places—people like Sculley and Cavalier—were Organization Men who carried with them a certain set of expectations. They expected a steady, upward progression in their careers; they expected a relatively fixed universe; they expected the respect of their subordinates. And in return, they dressed in the proper way and acted in the prescribed manner and did their best to promote the spread of soft drinks or junk food or toilet paper or whatever.

Atari was altogether different. At Atari there was no fixed universe, only a world racked by seismic convulsions. At Atari there were young people in blue jeans who brought sleeping bags into their cubicles and seemed to work twenty-four hours a day. Before long, Cavalier was so caught up in the excitement of the place he was running 180 miles an hour. But that was nothing compared with Apple. Apple was *crazy*. At Apple they treated you like some kind of bozo if you didn't understand every little technological subtlety. The engineers at American Can were genuinely appreciative if you took an interest in what they were doing, and even at Atari they were helpful and polite; but at Apple they were moving so fast it was all you could do to get the hell out of the way before they mowed you down. And Jobs—Steve Jobs could be worse than rude. He could tear you apart for no reason whatsoever. Cavalier had never seen anything like it.

And in the midst of all this was John Sculley. Cavalier couldn't figure it. He knew Sculley's reputation back East. The guy wore eight-hundred-dollar suits, and here he was at Apple running around in khaki pants and flannel shirts. Cavalier was the kind of person who didn't feel comfortable without a tie around his neck. Every day he came in wearing monogrammed white shirts with French cuffs and gold cuff links. That was how you dressed in a sophisticated business environment. On weekends, if you wanted to relax, you might put on a blue blazer. Of course he had kids, he knew they had to express themselves, but he didn't know why Sculley would want to ape them. Even worse, he couldn't understand why Sculley would put up with the other stuff that went on—like the letter one of the engineers in the II division sent out attacking him for coming in as president and getting a million-dollar bonus. What kind of place was it where somebody could do a thing like that and get away with it?

It quickly became clear that Cavalier wasn't going to adjust to the quantum universe of the Triangle Building. He just wouldn't buy into the program. His staff stood outside with their mouths agape as he paraded a string of aliens through his office—people with imposing desk chairs for him to try out, people with IBM clones for him to sell under Apple's logo, people with cheap manufacturing facilities in the Far East. At Atari he'd closed the factories in San Jose and shifted all production to Hong Kong. He tried to do the same thing at Apple, even though manufacturing was Del Yocam's job, not his, and offshore manufacturing was the antithesis of what Apple represented. (Assembly work in Singapore didn't count.) He got quotes from factories in Hong Kong that showed they could build the IIe for a third less than what they were spending to produce it in Dallas, and Yocam went berserk. Another company came to him with an IBM clone that was manufactured in the Far East; all Apple had to do was slap its label on it and get an easy $500-million business, but Steve wouldn't get in bed with anybody like that. No, Steve cornered him at an exec staff meeting and told him it was a crazy idea—told him Apple was the technology leader and there was no technology in clones. And it wasn't just Steve; the whole division regarded IBM clones as inferior technology.

Technology was Cavalier's bugaboo. His own staff could see he didn't know it, and soon they were treating him with all the deference they'd give a bump in the road. Finally he informed them that more technology went into putting that thin layer of air between the sheets of Charmin toilet tissue than into the entire Apple II. After that they didn't even give him the deference due a bump.

Sculley, on the other hand, was buying into the program. He was dressing like a kid—a kid who bought his clothes at J. Press and L. L. Bean rather than Esprit, but subtleties like that went unnoticed at Apple. He was acting like a kid, too—fired up with enthusiasm, working incredible hours, spewing forth ideas. Only Cavalier was disturbed by these things. What disturbed everybody else was the way he acted like Steve's sidekick. Ken Zerbe, the executive vice-president who'd come back from Europe to fix the Apple III and the mass-storage division, told him it wouldn't work. Zerbe tried to explain that Steve consumes everything around him, that he only respects authority, that he turns any equal into a subordinate. Sculley, ever close-mouthed, said he appreciated his comments. Zerbe assumed he was simply trying to live up to the image everyone had of them—the dynamic young entrepreneur and the seasoned corporate manager, working in tandem. Others found it difficult to imagine him remaining in such a role indefinitely. They began to take bets on how long the honeymoon would last.

■ ■ ■

Now that he'd handed the Apple II over to Cavalier, Sculley was free to turn to the organization of the company itself. He liked to tinker with structure. Maybe it was his architectural training, maybe just his natural cast of mind, but he was always thinking about how things fit together. Jobs's thinking tended to be intuitive, emotional, and visionary; Sculley was more a systems man, rational and analytical. Form and process were what interested him. So within days of his return from the maelstrom of the Triangle Building, he began drawing charts on the board in his office.

Sculley's office was as unassuming and informal as his new wardrobe. A small, square room in the rear corner of the Pink Palace, it overlooked the car wash on one side and a parking lot on the other. The furnishings were standard issue for Apple executives: no grand desk, no imposing office chair, just a work surface running along two walls and a round table in the middle of the room for meetings. The wall that overlooked the area where his secretary sat was all glass, creating an illusion of openness. But the board where the new org charts were taking shape was behind the door, hidden from view to all who passed by.

Sculley's immediate problem was that Steve wouldn't give up manufacturing. The original plan had been to swing the Fremont factory over to Del Yocam's organization as soon as Steve had gotten it set up; but as the time approached, it became obvious that this wasn't going to happen. Then Steve came up with an alternative solution. Why not give Yocam the Apple II division and let him take the Dallas factory with him? Cavalier was a bozo, the Apple II was basically a manufacturing issue anyway, and there wasn't much else for manufacturing to do. And if Del took the Apple II and the Dallas plant, then Steve could have Macintosh and the Fremont plant.

That was an appealing idea. With Macintosh and the II responsible for their own manufacturing as well as for marketing and engineering, they could be managed as independent profit-and-loss centers, the way Pepsi and Taco Bell and Pizza Hut were at PepsiCo. That left Lisa and the corporate staff groups—human resources, finance, sales and distribution, and the central marketing organization, which was mainly concerned with implementing the product divisions' plans.

Lisa was a problem. Sculley's big question all fall had been how to use Lisa to support Macintosh. The solution he'd come up with was to turn Lisa into Mac's big sister. Lisa engineers had taken out the Twiggy drives and put in Sony drives so people could use the same disks in either machine, and they'd developed a program that would allow Lisa to run Macintosh software. (Macintosh had about one-eighth Lisa's memory, so there was no way it could run Lisa software.) That meant Lisa and Macintosh could finally be united in what Sculley liked to call, with his marketeer's flourish, "the Apple thirty-two-bit supermicro family." But while the two machines might be moving toward compatibility, the teams responsible for them were not. The only way to make Sculley's strategy work was to combine them under one person.

The choice was between Wayne Rosing, the former Digital Equipment engineer who'd taken over Lisa, and Steve. Clearly it would have to be Steve. The only problem was that Steve didn't want Lisa anymore. All he cared about now was what was good for Macintosh. Lisa was somebody else's problem.

The day before Thanksgiving, at the regular Wednesday exec staff meeting, Wayne and Steve had a run-in. Nothing unusual about that. John suggested they take it up after the meeting. So one evening the following week, he and Steve and Wayne and Bob Belleville got together for dinner in the boardroom. Things got heated, especially after John brought up the idea of merging Lisa and Macintosh. Wayne didn't like the idea any better than Steve did; but as he put in some resistance, Steve came at him with his left hook, too many bozos, *bam!*, don't know what you're doing, *chop!*, whole thing's a failure, *pow!* That got Wayne upset, and pretty soon he was landing a couple of his own—you don't have any software, you're not going to have fifty programs in eight weeks, you're going to have *nothing!* "Boys,

boys!" John cried. "Calm down." But they wouldn't calm down; they kept at it for half an hour, until finally, after they'd thoroughly demonstrated their inability to work together, John simply stood up and announced what was going to happen: Steve was going to run a consolidated division; they were going to find something else for Wayne to do. That was it; end of discussion. The naughty miscreants promised to keep silent about what had just happened until Macintosh was introduced, and then they were sent home.

The next day, Steve started making calls. Whom should he get rid of? Was there anybody in the Lisa division who was worth a damn? Then Wayne told his staff what was going to happen, and by the end of the week word was out. To quell the rumors, Jay Elliot and his human-resources people persuaded Steve to make an announcement to the Lisa division, which consisted of about four hundred people, and explain what was going to happen. It was a move they'd soon regret.

By this time the Lisa division was ready to cave in with fear. The product wasn't working, Steve was out to get them, John had a reputation for ruthlessness, nobody else was able to defend them, they were about to be overrun by pirates. Steve wasn't in great shape either. He'd promised John a January introduction, and everything at Macintosh had gone into time-to-completion mode: three months to completion, two months to completion, seven weeks to completion, six weeks to completion. . . . Four years of work and dreams had been reduced to a final, desperate push. Everyone was frantic, trying to finish in time, to get rid of the bugs, to ship a machine that worked. The factory tour at the end of August—the one they'd taken while Bob hiked to the top of Black Mountain—had impressed on them all the hard dollars-and-cents reality of what they were doing. Macintosh wasn't just a fun thing they did every day in a nice building on Bandley Drive, it was a gamble with tens of millions of dollars of the company's money. The stockholders' money. Other people's money, out the window, on their dream. Now they had to deliver. The pressure was on, and it was on Steve more than anybody else. Macintosh was his baby. Macintosh was his vision. Everything he'd worked for was about to become real. He could barely sleep at night. He was blitzed. He was headed for overload. And now he had to absorb this crew of bozos?

It started out calmly enough, a mass meeting in the defunct manufacturing area of the Lisa quarters on the west side of Bandley Drive, across from the Macintosh building. Wayne Rosing got up and announced that the two divisions were going to be merged and explained the strategy behind it. Then he turned the meeting over to Steve. Steve was obviously trying to be conciliatory. He said they were going to move people from Lisa to Macintosh because they were desperately needed there. He told them what a great product Macintosh was going to be. But he couldn't resist pointing out that Lisa 2—the Macintosh-compatible Lisa with the Sony disk drives— was not going to be a successful product. The meeting went downhill from there, and it completely fell apart as the question-and-answer period began, when people started needling him and he began to let fly.

In attacking the Lisa people, calling them bozos and C players, Steve was fighting the ghosts of people long gone—of Mike Scott, who'd denied him the chance to head the project, and of John Couch, who'd been given that chance instead. But when the hard core on the Macintosh team found out what was happening, they went nuts as well. They were only a tiny band of pirates, after all, not much more than a hundred people, and though they'd won they were sure to be overwhelmed by the losers. Even if Steve fired half the Lisa division, they'd be outnumbered two-to-one. They might get to run things, but the incredible camaraderie they'd built up would be destroyed. They couldn't believe it. They were ready to sacrifice themselves for the dream, and this was their reward?

Steve couldn't call off the merger, but he could go back across the street to explain how things were going to be. He called a spur-of-the-moment meeting in the plant-filled atrium at the core of the Lisa building, and this time he didn't try to hold back. He told it like it was. He said there were too many bozos in the Lisa organization. He said the Mac group was in fear of them and he wasn't going to let them in. They were C players, bozos, and there wasn't room for any more bozo engineering at Apple. As he spoke, the whole atrium went numb. Wayne went comatose. When it was over, people retreated white-faced back to their cubicles. For the rest of the day they streamed into the human-resources office, begging to know if they'd have a job after Christmas. Was Steve going to cut them out of the company? Was he going to make them walk the plank?

Yes, actually, he was. Across the street in Bandley 3, Steve was planning layoffs. He saw no reason to wait. He wanted to terminate them the day before Christmas vacation. That way they could have the holidays to get ready to look for a new job.

There was only one person left at Apple who could talk him out of something like this: his personal HR man, Jay Elliot. Calm and authoritative, with a deep, soothing voice, Elliot could get through to him in a crisis in a way no one else could. But Elliot was in Ireland, visiting the European manufacturing operation in County Cork. So Mary Fortney, the HR woman for the Lisa division, called him at two in the morning and got him to call Steve.

Jay talked him out of the Christmas firings, but the meetings to decide who would go and who would stay went on, and the carnage mounted daily. "Bloody awful," Bob Belleville wrote in his journal as he sat in his office on Christmas day. He was there because life at home was even more unbearable than life at Apple. His home, his kids, his marriage to his high-school sweetheart from Belleville, Illinois—all those things were sliding away under the strain. Like Steve, like Lisa, like all of them, he was a victim of the vision.

At the systems level, however, a certain rationalization had taken place. At the systems level, Apple was about to be streamlined into two quasi-autonomous operating entities, the Apple II division and the Macintosh division, each with its own independent engineering, manufacturing, and marketing functions. The corporate staff would serve as a common appendage, providing support in the form of sales, distribution, finance, and HR. The product divisions would be headed by two individuals whose talents seemed well suited to the task: for Macintosh, a visionary leader; for the mature Apple II, a master manufacturer. And one of those divisions, if Steve's predictions held true, would ultimately fade away. When that happened, the whole company would be Macintosh.

II.
1984

January–December 1984

The Children's Crusade

"You guys ready to go?"

Steve waited impatiently for an answer. It was already a week into 1984; the formal introduction of Macintosh at the shareholders meeting in Flint Center was just sixteen days away. Now he was in a suite at the Grand Hyatt Hotel on Forty-second Street with Mike Murray and Bob Belleville, both of whom were as anxious as he was. At the other end of the line was the software crew in Bandley 3. It was snowing outside.

New York was the first leg of a three-city rollout. Jobs was doing New York, Chicago, and Toronto; Sculley was leading a separate tour of San Francisco, Dallas, and Atlanta. They were unveiling Macintosh for the dealers, several hundred of whom would be checking in downstairs that evening for a first look at the machine they'd been hearing rumors about for more than a year. The demonstrations they'd be giving would be carefully circumscribed to avoid the bugs they knew were there, the glitches in the software that could cause the machine to crash. But in eight days the final version of the software had to go out to be duplicated, and all the bugs had to be eliminated before then. A lot was riding on the answer to Steve's question.

The software crew had a nerve-wracking job, tracking errors that reveal themselves momentarily only to dart back inside. Bugs tend to show up only after a long and often improbable series of events. Tracing all the steps in the sequence can take hours, days, sometimes weeks. Fixing the bug once it's been found can introduce new bugs.

Since few things repel potential computer buyers as much as strange and catastrophic errors, new software is normally tested for months by outside guinea pigs before being put on the market. But the Macintosh group had run out of time. A week from Monday at six in the morning, a courier from the factory would be at the door to take their disks away.

They had problems all over, but the worst was in the finder, the piece of code that was supposed to find programs and data files on the disk. The finder was crucial. It was the first thing you saw when the machine came on, a beaming Macintosh happy face that quickly turned into an arrow you could use to point to all the little icons onscreen—the hand-and-pen icon that represented MacWrite, the hand-and-paintbrush icon that represented MacPaint, the file-folder icon that represented a data file, and so forth. Unfortunately, it tended to get lost if you asked it to do too many things. You could point to a file and drag it across the screen to the trashcan to throw it away, and then change your mind and drag it back; but then if you pointed to a program and tried to run it, the finder would go nuts and the deep shit manager (officially known as the "system error manager") would take over. When that happened, a cute little bomb icon would appear onscreen and the computer would go dead. That's if you were lucky; sometimes the deep shit manager itself would go haywire and start flashing weird, pulsing patterns across the screen while the computer beeped and belched.

The finder was being written by Bruce Horne, a twenty-three-year-old programmer who'd gotten his start in junior high school as one of Alan Kay's "Smalltalk kids" at Xerox PARC. Horne was a perfectionist with a particularly tough job. The finder had to sit on top of the rest of the systems software—Andy Hertzfeld's "firmware," the code that would be burned into programmable memory chips within the machine to govern what happened onscreen and elsewhere in the system. The systems software was the closest Macintosh came to having an operating system, and it was still being changed, months after it was supposed to have been frozen. Horne had started to panic that summer, so Steve Capps, who'd been helping Andy on the firmware, had pitched in, and the two of them had been holed up in a tiny room in another building since November. They didn't have time to venture outside or sleep more than a few hours at a stretch. Somebody would come by a couple of times a day to bring them food, and otherwise they barely saw another human face. Even without any distractions, however, they were too frazzled to make much progress. By January, with the weight of the entire project resting on their shoulders, they were nearly incoherent.

They were also having problems with MacWrite and MacPaint, the word-processing and graphics programs, which were supposed to be shipped with the machine. Both were prone to weird glitches that caused the computer to crash; and every time one glitch was fixed, two new ones would crop up. And because there were still bugs in the systems software, it was all but impossible to figure out if the problem was caused by a bug in the system or a bug in the program. So when Steve called from New York that morning and asked if they were ready to go, the answer was pretty clear: They weren't. Andy and the others crowded anxiously around the speakerphone, and Jerome Coonan, the software engineering manager, told him they needed another two weeks to finish.

Two weeks wasn't much, they thought. It wouldn't delay the introduction. It would simply mean that instead of having computers in the stores on the day Macintosh was announced, as they'd all planned from the beginning, they'd have demonstration units in the stores. People could look at it right away, and a couple of weeks later they'd be able to buy it. Certainly the last thing they all wanted was to ship a computer that crashed all the time; that was what had killed the Apple III. If the same thing happened to Macintosh . . .

Steve looked across the hotel room at Bob, but he knew how Bob felt without asking. Two weeks wasn't enough for these people to do anything. If you gave them two months off, then maybe they could come back and finish up in two weeks; but if you just gave them two weeks, they'd spend the whole time in Brownian motion, bouncing randomly off the walls like molecules of superheated gas, and at the end they wouldn't be any more finished than they were now. Steve's inclination was always to give the software crew whatever they wanted. They had free fruit juice, they had the best stereo equipment on the market, they had their own food fund. They were artists, after all. But real artists ship.

He spoke softly into the phone. "Gentlemen, ladies," he said, "I'm going to ship the code a week from Monday, with your names on it."

■ ■ ■

That was the week the photographer came from *Newsweek*. While Steve and Bob and Mike were leading the Macintosh road show across the Snow Belt, the software hackers back in Bandley 3 had to juggle the conflicting demands of vanity and panic. *Newsweek* was supposed to put them on its cover, but if they didn't get the bugs out soon they wouldn't want to be on anybody's cover. Four years' work was riding on one week's effort, and that was the week they were supposed to be immortalized.

The publicity campaign for the Macintosh launch had been in planning for two years. It had started with special peeks for key "influencers"—people like Ben Rosen, the New York venture capitalist who'd helped orchestrate Apple's initial public stock offering in 1980. A former semiconductor analyst at Morgan Stanley & Co., Rosen had started publishing his reports as a newsletter—the *Rosen Electronics Letter,* which was regarded as an oracle by every technology watcher on the Street. As an analyst he'd been entranced by each new electronic toy to come out of the Valley—pocket calculators, digital watches, and finally personal computors. In 1981 he'd formed a venture partnership with Dallas semiconductor entrepreneur L. J. Sevin; one of their first investments was Lotus Development. A year and a half ago, Rosen had been invited to speak at a Macintosh retreat and initiated into the cult with the gift of a Macintosh T-shirt that they'd all signed. As a key influencer, he'd been romanced with as much care and calculation as the software developers.

There was no logical reason any of them should go wild about a new computer that was totally incompatible with the Apple II and the IBM PC and everything else on the market, so they had to be won over emotionally. The point was to get the buzz going. The buzz had been building over time; and now, suddenly, it was about to explode into a firestorm of publicity. Banner headlines! Magazine covers! The evening news! Macintosh wouldn't just be a computer, Mike Murray thought, it would be an event. It would begin with "1984" on Super Bowl Sunday; and by the time the annual meeting was over on Tuesday, the whole country would be talking about it. People would stop whatever they were doing and huddle by the radio for details. *What happened?* they'd cry. Mike started waving his arms every time he talked about it.

Months earlier it had been decided that one focus of the publicity campaign would be the Macintosh design team—the people who'd built the machine. Of course they'd set up interviews with Sculley and with Jobs, whose quotability and charisma Regis was promoting as Kennedy-esque. But they could also promote a handful of key engineers as the core team, the Apollo astronauts of personal computing: Burrell Smith, the onetime Homebrew member and former repairman whose intuitive brilliance had yielded a hardware design worthy of Woz himself; Andy Hertzfeld, the systems software hacker who'd given Burrell's hardware its lovable personality; Bill Atkinson, the graphics wizard who'd left a promising future in neurochemistry to write software that would enable anyone to paint a computer-generated masterpiece; plus Bruce Horne, Susan Kare, and a handful of others who were personable and colorful and empathetic. They were turned over to Regis and the Regettes, who reduced their life stories to capsule form and coached them on what to say and then made them available to the press, which took its cues as readily as an orchestra does.

All the stories were timed to come out the week of the introduction. They'd started giving "sneak previews" in October—eight-hour sessions in which a team of journalists from a particular magazine would come into Bandley 3 for a secret unveiling. They'd be ushered into the Picasso room at eight for an orientation session with Steve Jobs—*dis*orientation would be more like it—before being turned over to Mike Murray, who'd hit them with his dancing mushrooms slide show. Then they'd get to play with the machine itself for an hour. Sculley would come in to answer questions during the lavishly catered lunch, which he invariably ignored in favor of his two peanut-butter-and-jelly sandwiches and his row of Pepsis. Then they'd get to meet the engineers or hear about the factory or explore whatever preapproved angle was of interest to them. The entire day was scripted, and yet it was all carefully designed to seem impromptu. America loves spontaneity, Mike liked to say, as long as it's neatly packaged.

The sneak program had begun with *Byte* magazine, the oldest and most technical of the glossy microcomputer monthlies. *Byte* had conducted an extensive question-and-answer session with Steve, Burrell, Andy, Bill, and eight other team members in which they'd talked about the wonders of the 68000 microprocessor and the things they'd done to make it sing. All the other computer magazines had followed—*Popular Computing, Personal Computing, Microcomputing, Computer Update, Computers & Electronics*. So had the business magazines—*Forbes, Fortune, Business Week, Venture, Inc.* David Bunnell, publisher of the phenomenally successful *PC World*, which came out every month and was as thick as a phone book and was one of two slick magazines devoted entirely to the IBM PC, had been persuaded to launch another magazine that would be all about Macintosh. *Rolling Stone* had flown a reporter out from New York and hired Norman Seeff, the rock photographer (he'd shot the Rolling Stones, he'd shot James Taylor, he'd shot Ike and Tina Turner) to do everybody's portraits.

Seeff was a cool guy, an artist just like they were. But the *Newsweek* photographer was something else. He'd been given instructions to shoot them all in their work place, and to him that meant Bandley 3. He didn't realize that Bandley 3 was a total zoo and that if a photographer came in now, everybody would get so bent out of shape they wouldn't be able to get anything else done all day. So Andy told him he did most of his work at home, and if he wanted to see his work place he ought to come to Palo Alto, where he and Burrell had bought neighboring houses on a quiet, tree-shaded street a few blocks from downtown. The photographer got there and found them living like college students with no dorm counselor—overgrown yards, beat-up furniture buried beneath heaps of records and magazines, computers and stereo components and musical instruments lying around all over the place. He shot Burrell sitting cross-legged on the floor, strumming a guitar and looking doe-eyed, like a folksinger practicing for talent night at the local fern bar. He was lucky to get that much, for by this time Burrell and Andy were virtually the only ones who were still coherent.

They worked frantically all through the weekend—Andy Hertzfeld, Bill Atkinson, Randy Wigginton, Bruce Horne, Steve Capps, and about ten others. They'd sleep for an hour or two at their desks and then go back to work. What started as a mad, desperate party quickly turned into a nightmare. By Sunday they were hallucinating. They did a new release every two hours through the night; each one was terrible. Randy's MacWrite program was crashing all the time. MacPaint had a weird bug that would cause it to run out of memory after a complicated sequence of events and crash horribly. Andy discovered a bug in his firmware that caused the screen to highlight improperly. It was a rare occurrence, and his first impulse was to pretend he hadn't seen it; but the others encouraged him to dive in and fix it, so he did. And then the incredible happened. They did a release at a quarter to six and passed it out for everybody to test and they couldn't get it to crash. They couldn't believe it. All the bugs were gone.

Except one. This one they hadn't noticed before. It was in the disk-formatting package—the piece of firmware that was supposed to format a new disk so it would be ready to accept data—but it showed up only when you were using MacWrite. If you were in MacWrite and you tried to format a disk, the computer went dead: Nothing happened. Nobody could explain it. They all sat there in front of a machine, trying to figure out what was going on. Then Andy reached over and pressed a key on the keyboard, and the computer came alive again.

The courier arrived at six. They could finesse the disk-formatting bug by writing in instructions to press any key; but Jerome Coonan decided that wasn't the thing to do, so he rode to the factory with the courier to tell them not to start mass-duplicating the disks yet—to treat these as demo units rather than as final takes. Most of the others staggered home, but Andy couldn't leave. He had to find out what had happened. When he went home, he wanted to sleep for two days; he didn't want to come back and do a final release.

For the next three hours he sat bleary-eyed in the lobby of Bandley 3, dimly aware of all the people arriving for work. The sun was rising and the light was streaming in and Bandley Drive was filling up. This was something he'd never seen before, since he never got in before ten.

Finally Steve came in and wanted to know what was going on. Andy showed him the problem. "Are you kidding?" Steve cried. "This is nothing!" He called up the factory and told them it was a go. At that point Andy climbed into his pale blue Volkswagen Rabbit with its MACWIZ license plates and drove home, praying he wouldn't get any phone calls.

■　■　■

Around the corner in the Pink Palace, Floyd Kvamme was trying to figure out what to do with "1984." The board hadn't actually ordered them not to run it, but the reaction against it was so strong that both Steve and John had to think again. Had Chiat/Day indeed taken leave of its senses? So far the indications weren't good. The "Alone Again" spot for Lisa had turned out to be a disaster, a sixty-second TV special that managed to expose exactly what was wrong with the product. The "Apple People" spots had been summarily pulled after dealers started howling that they were too mellow, too laid-back, too California. One dealer described them as "nice foreign movies." So much for the Apple generation. Now the question was: After these two missteps, did Apple really want to come out with an Orwellian rock video that cast IBM as Big Brother? Steve still thought the ad was great, but if the board was right it could kill the introduction. He and John decided to try to get rid of the airtime they'd bought on the Super Bowl. The details, including whether to run it if nobody bought the time, they left to Floyd and Bill Campbell.

The Super Bowl was six days away. On Tuesday the spot was due to start airing in a five-day teaser campaign in eleven major markets across the country—actually, ten major markets and Boca Raton, Florida. (Boca had been Steve's idea.) Then, after a week on late-night local news shows and the like, it was supposed to explode across the nation's consciousness on Super Bowl Sunday. Some 43 million Americans were expected to watch Super Bowl XVIII that afternoon, and as they sat in their living rooms, transfixed by the highly kinetic electronic image of the Washington Redskins taking on the Los Angeles Raiders in Tampa Stadium, their synapses would be blindsided by this micro-spectacle—not once but twice, for Apple had bought two chunks of airtime.

ABC had a buyer for thirty seconds, but no one was willing to pick up the remaining ninety. Floyd's advertising people were on the phone all week to Chiat/Day's media office in San Francisco, and Chiat/Day was on the phone all week to ABC in New York, trying to find out if there were any takers. On Thursday they sold another thirty seconds. They had sixty left.

While their media people were trying to get ABC to sell the airtime, Lee Clow and Jay Chiat were lobbying Steve and John to keep it. Circumstances were in their favor. With its bungled introduction of the PCjr, IBM had made Apple's Christmas. The fabled Peanut wasn't even in the stores for people to look at; dealers were supposed to have demo units on the floor, but few wanted to tie up space at the height of the Christmas season with something they couldn't sell for months. And it was getting such lousy reviews that a lot of consumers didn't see any point in waiting for it. They turned to the IIe instead. Apple sold every IIe it could build that Christmas, more IIe's than it had ever sold before, and it hit the new year on a roll. Now they were betting the future of the company on Macintosh. It was a bold move, and with this commercial, Lee and Jay declared, they could trumpet their confidence. They could prove they weren't intimidated by Big Blue. They could beat their chests in the jungle.

Bill and Floyd were sitting that Friday afternoon in Floyd's office on the top floor of the Pink Palace, overlooking the car wash. A few minutes before three, someone from advertising came running up with the news they were waiting to hear. ABC had a buyer, she said as she stuck her head inside the door—but the buyer was willing to pay only $725,000 for the minute. Apple had paid $900,000 for it, and $400,000 to produce the ad. Floyd and Bill looked at each other, two coaches plotting an offensive play: Should they punt now, or go for a touchdown?

"Floyd," said Bill, "if you don't mind, I think we ought to run it."

"Bill," said Floyd, "I believe you."

■ ■ ■

This is what happened on Super Bowl Sunday: IBM aired an ad for the PCjr which showed the Charlie Chaplin character pushing a baby carriage while a female voice-over effused about "the bright little addition to the family." Then, early in the third quarter, the Raiders began a seventy-yard march that ended in a touchdown. At that point, instead of the usual instant replay, the screen went black—totally, ominously black, for two seconds—and then the "1984" ad unrolled. When the camera returned to the sportscasters, they had that stunned, "What was that?" look on their faces. The phones lit up at ABC, at Chiat/Day, at Apple. Steven Spielberg had his secretary call to find out who made it. NBC, CBS, and ABC featured it in their evening newscasts that night. So did the BBC. By Monday morning it was the talk of Madison Avenue. The creative director of Ogilvy & Mather told *Advertising Age* it was sophomoric. His counterpart at Leo Burnett thought it was sensational. Puzzling, said the creative director at Young & Rubicam. But none of them could deny that it was more memorable than the game.

Those who were smart showed up at Flint Center early on Tuesday morning. The Super Bowl spectacular had started a buzz, a glow, a spreading force-field of excitement that emanated from the nation's TV screens like an irradiating shower. By Tuesday morning it was generating a mob scene. People hurried across the vast parking lots to the concrete auditorium, which rose fortresslike from the bionic green of the De Anza campus. They snatched away the free copies of *MacWorld* that Apple employees were handing out at the door. A stack fell to the pavement; they dove for them, scrambling, tearing, clawing to get one as they rushed inside. By 9:45, fifteen minutes before the meeting was to begin, every seat in the 2,600-seat auditorium was filled, and more than a hundred impatient stockholders were still outside, pushing to get in.

In the front row, center stage, sat Apple's board of directors and executive staff. Directly behind them, filling the next four rows and providing a focal point for all the hysteria in the hall, were the wizards of Macintosh, each one clad in an identical Macintosh T-shirt. Beyond them were all the customary spectators—analysts, investors, business reporters, Apple's other employees. A hush fell as Steve strode across the stage to offer the invocation, which he'd culled from Bob Dylan's third album and which he recited now with the solemnity of a priest:

> Come writers and critics who prophesize with your pens
> And keep your eyes wide the chance won't come again
> And don't speak too soon for the wheel's still in spin
> And there's no tellin' who that it's namin'
> For the loser now will be later to win
> For the times they are a-changin'

In a staff meeting the week before, Steve had gotten so overwrought that he'd broken down in tears as they discussed the introduction. No one was sure he'd be able to make it through this morning. But as he spoke now, stylishly dressed in a double-breasted gray blazer and crisp white shirt and bright red bow tie, he was focused, intent, in control. The lines he was quoting struck the perfect note of defiance and portent. They'd hit the airwaves exactly twenty years earlier, in January 1964, to electrifying effect. Their anger and self-righteousness had signaled the beginning of the protest movement, the children's crusade of the sixties. They sounded strangely different here, in an auditorium filled with investors, recited by a highly polished young entrepreneur whose personal net worth was on a par with that of Jay Rockefeller or Henry du Pont or H. J. Heinz II. It was as if the sixties had undergone a bizarre inversion in which demonstrators became stockholders and protest rallies turned into business meetings. These stockholders were protesting against IBM.

They were demonstrating for the personal-computer revolution. It was a new revolution, a new cause, a new children's crusade.

But first there was business to discuss. Steve turned the meeting over to Al Eisenstat, the chief legal officer, who took care of the formal agenda—the re-election of board members, the vote to issue more stock. Then Sculley came out and gave a reassuringly conventional business speech. He portrayed the bottom line in flattering terms. He explained the new product-line strategy, which grouped all of Apple's products into two families, the Apple II family and the new family of Apple thirty-two-bit supermicros—Lisa and Macintosh. He laid out a comprehensive business strategy, which called for a lot of money to be spent on marketing. He sounded earnest, committed, sincere. "We are returning to our roots," he declared, "of offering high technology at low cost." People clapped. Finally he told the story of the reporter who'd asked him what was the most important thing that had happened to him in the nine months since he'd come to Apple. "The most important thing that's happened to me in the past nine months," he said, "was the chance to develop a friendship with Steve Jobs. . . ."

Steve gave the same performance he'd given three months before in Honolulu—the same recitation of milestone dates in information-processing technology, the same anti-IBM harangue, the same equation of Apple Computer with truth and freedom. He was mesmerizing, spellbinding, magnificent. Behind him his image glowed larger-than-life on a video screen as he spoke. When he asked his final, rhetorical question—"Was George Orwell right?"—the audience went into a paroxysm of excitement. "No! *No!* NO!" they cried, as "1984" exploded before their eyes.

There was a stillness after the ad, a brief, stunned quiet. Then Jobs talked about their accomplishments: how they'd pulled Lisa technology down to a mainstream price point, how the 68000 microprocessor eats 8088s for breakfast, how the three-and-a-half-inch floppy disk would be the innovation of the eighties, how Macintosh was only one-third the size and weight of an IBM PC. Finally he opened a bag, pulled out a Macintosh, and remarked that he was giving the machine a chance to speak for itself.

"Hello, I am Macintosh. It sure is great to get out of that bag." The voice was a little shaky, which made it seem vulnerable and endearing. The crowd reacted as if ET had stumbled out.

"Unaccustomed as I am to public speaking," it went on, "I'd like to share with you a maxim I thought of the first time I met an IBM mainframe—never trust a computer you can't lift!" It paused for the laughter to subside. "Obviously I can talk, but right now I'd like to listen. So it is with considerable pride that I introduce a man who's been like a father to me—Steve Jobs."

Steve beamed, his thin lips tightly sealed, as if that way his excitement could be contained. There was no question of paternity here, for Macintosh was his and his alone. The crowd, led by the Macintosh contingent before the stage, cheered wildly, tumultuously, standing on the seats, in the aisles, waving their arms, almost berserk. It went on for twenty seconds . . . thirty seconds . . . forty . . . fifty . . . nearly a minute. Steve basked and grew radiant. No executive, not even an entrepreneurial wunderkind, had ever received such an ovation. It was the sort of adoration Dylan used to receive: ecstatic, frenzied, almost worshipful.

The reporters and analysts in the hall were used to the idea of entrepreneurs as economic trailblazers, as the modern-day incarnation of the frontier spirit that once possessed men like Elisha Stevens. Thanks to Jobs, they were even getting used to the idea of personal computers as a crusade, a democratic force that would assault the bastion of information control held by IBM. What they weren't prepared for—what few in fact even grasped—was the force that drove it: a mystical faith in technology. There was nothing rational going on here, nothing that could be expressed in the binary logic of the machines themselves; it was more like a new religion, or a new drug. The personal-computer revolution wasn't about word processing and electronic spreadsheets, it was about altering human consciousness. Human/computer symbiosis was just another form of mind expansion. This was the LSD of the eighties. Twenty years before, in 1964, Ken Kesey and his band of Merry Pranksters had been dropping acid in a log cabin nestled among the redwoods of La Honda, high on the ridge above Palo Alto. Jobs was Kesey's heir too, as much as he was Elisha Stevens's or Leland Stanford's. A pioneer on the electronic frontier, he was pushing toward a place where Kesey and Stevens might meet, toward a nonexistent node in space and time, a blank spot on the map of human experience which he alone could fill in.

Near the end of the meeting, as the exuberance was ebbing into a warm glow, Steve turned the stage over to a videotape that, as he said, captured the spirit of the artists who'd built Macintosh. There was Andy, and Burrell, and Bill Atkinson. The soundtrack was a

Windham Hill guitar, soft, moody, and introspective. "We started in a very tight-knit, small group," said Andy, "and we had this dream that was sort of us against the rest of the world." "No compromise," Bill declared. "Do it right. Do it really good, the way you would want it. And then figure out how to make it cheap so people can afford it." Mike Murray: "You know, when people ask me who the Macintosh is for, we like to say that the market for Mac is the desk. Over the last few years we've sold between three-quarters of a million and a million Apple IIs, and that seems like a real large number—but an even bigger number is 25 million, and that's the number of knowledge workers in the United States alone who are sitting behind desks every day doing their work. And the way they do their work really hasn't changed since probably the start of the Industrial Revolution. So our marketing goal is really very simple. . . ." The camera showed the steel-and-glass office towers of San Francisco's Embarcadero Center; students in the Stanford quads; an office overlooking Central Park. "You know," Mike said in a faraway voice, "for us in the Macintosh group, the product is like—it's like this torch being carried into a pitch-black room." He smiled. "We like to say that it's incredibly, insanely great."

The room was still. Nobody made a sound. But anyone who'd been able to see through the darkness into the ranks of the Macintosh group would have gotten a surprise. For one by one, as their turns came up onscreen, the members of the little band of pirates were mouthing the words on the tape as they boomed out over the loudspeakers. Like *The Rocky Horror Picture Show*, this little movie had a fanatical cult following. In this case, however, it wasn't the fans who recited each line as they watched enraptured; it was the stars themselves. An uncharitable observer might have thought these people in their Macintosh T-shirts had more in common with the shuffling drones of "1984" than they were prepared to admit. Anyone else would simply have understood why the rest of the company called them Moonies.

□□ 11 □□

The Forever Day

That was Day One. Jobs, following Franklin Roosevelt's example with the Depression, had given himself a Hundred Days to establish Macintosh as the alternative to IBM. There was to be no letup, for to do it that quickly meant following up the prelaunch advertising-publicity-promotion blitz with an even more intensive postlaunch advertising-publicity-promotion blitz. Ten million copies of a twenty-page advertising insert went into *Time, Newsweek, Business Week, Fortune, Forbes,* and *Inc.* TV spots were aired to follow the tremendous uproar caused by "1984" with a look at the benefits of the product. The Macintosh crew, their pictures adorning half the magazines in the country, set off on an elaborate road show to demonstrate Macintosh to computer clubs. Burrell went along, and Andy, and Dan Kottke, Jobs's friend from Reed, and Steve Wozniak. Andy was reading a book about Atari that had just come out, and when they were on their way to Florida he passed it on to Woz. As he read it, Woz learned something he didn't like: Years earlier, before they'd started Apple, when he was working at Hewlett-Packard and Jobs had gotten him to design "Breakout" for Atari for a fifty-fifty split, the fee wasn't $700, as Jobs had said, but $5,000. He was so upset he started to cry on the plane.

Jobs was frantic. This was the test, he thought. This was it. He'd put himself on the line. Why was he doing it? Not for the money, he knew that—he already had more money than he could ever spend in his entire lifetime. He didn't even particularly think it was for his ego. He was doing it because he loved it—because this was what he wanted to do with his life. The way he saw things, it was like computers and society were out on a first date, and for some crazy reason he just happened to be in the right place at the right time to make the romance blossom. He was Cupid, and this was his best shot. By the end of the decade it would all be over: Computers would be everywhere, and society would have chosen his way or IBM's. If he failed, then his entire world view must be wrong. If he failed, he might as well go climb a mountain somewhere, go back to Tibet, retire from this material life. And in a hundred days they'd know if he'd failed or not.

It wasn't as if the Hundred Days were some secret hidden away in internal memos. On the contrary, the Hundred Days itself became part of the publicity campaign. "100 Days Will Make or Break Macintosh" cried *MIS Week,* a trade paper for corporate information managers. "We need to make Mac the next milestone product of our industry," Jobs declared inside. "And we have 100 days to do it." As analysts murmured that, well, maybe Apple ought to give the new machine a chance to build up a little momentum, Jobs set even more extravagant goals. Sculley told *Fortune* he wanted to sell 250,000 computers the first year; Jobs said he wanted to sell 500,000. "The Macintosh is just the best we can do," he announced. "If it fails, we deserve to fail."

Some sales were already in the bag. Peat, Marwick, Mitchell & Co., the first of the "big eight" accounting firms to commit to using personal computers for on-site audits, had an order in for 2,500. Two years earlier, dissatisfied with what was on the market, Peat, Marwick had asked Apple, IBM, and Hewlett-Packard to reveal their development plans; it decided to go with Macintosh after IBM refused to play. Then there was the Apple University Consortium—twenty-four colleges, including Stanford, Chicago, and the entire Ivy League, which had agreed to buy 50,000 Macintoshes by the end of the year. The universities would buy directly from Apple for less than half the $2,495 retail price, then resell them to students and faculty. Not only would Apple sell a lot of computers, it would get them in the hands of people who were likely to develop important new software. After all, VisiCalc had been invented by college students, and look what it had done for the Apple II.

And of course there was "Stars Can't Wait." In 1982, Jobs had launched an emotional but unsuccessful campaign in Congress for his "Kids Can't Wait" program, which would have allowed a corporate tax write-off in exchange for donations of Apple IIs to elementary schools. He had more luck with the California state legislature in Sacramento; Apple responded by giving away ten thousand computers. "Stars Can't Wait" was what Bob Belleville called his current efforts to ensure that every star in America, from Michael Jackson down, had his or her own Macintosh. Shortly after the introduction, Jobs and Mike Murray and Andy Hertzfeld and Bill Atkinson all flew to New York to present one to Mick Jagger, whom Jobs had met at a party. They went to his brownstone on a weekend afternoon and were directed by the bodyguards to a third-floor room where Jagger sat in a T-shirt and Levi's. There were keyboards in various corners of the room; Jagger looked like any other middle-aged musician practicing his craft. He didn't seem too interested in the Macintosh. His daughter Jade was, however, so Bill and Andy gave her a demonstration while Jobs and Murray chatted with Jagger. After a while they left.

That took care of 52,501 Macs: only 447,499 to go. This was where event marketing kicked in. A week after the Cupertino event, when Jobs staged a repeat performance for the Boston Computer Society, the oldest and most influential of the personal-computer users' groups, nearly 1,200 people packed a Back Bay auditorium and 300 more stood outside in the snow. Dealers found themselves mobbed with customers eager to try out the new machine. Macintosh became the hottest-selling computer in the country. Stores were sold out. The University Consortium was put on allocation. Even Lisa sales began to take off, as customers who came in to look at Macintosh decided they really needed a more powerful model. "Sales are phenomenal," declared a store owner in New Jersey. "We'll sell the machine even better when there's software available," added a salesperson in Texas.

Software *was* a problem. Mike Boich, the software evangelist, had managed to get commitments from more than a hundred independent developers, including the top companies in the field, but so far that's all they were—commitments. The only programs that were actually available at introduction were MacWrite and MacPaint, both of which were being shipped with the machine, and a spreadsheet from Microsoft. MacWrite was great for writing letters—you could even write them in Old English script if you wanted to—but not for much else, since it couldn't handle anything longer than ten pages. For more ambitious documents you'd have to wait until Microsoft Word was finished, sometime in the spring. If you wanted to create business graphs, you'd have to wait for Microsoft Chart. And if you wanted business graphing and a spreadsheet combined, you'd have to wait for Lotus to deliver its promised Macintosh version of 1-2-3, the program that sold the Fortune 1000 on the IBM PC. Small wonder, then, that most of the ads in the first few issues of *MacWorld* were for Macintosh carrying cases.

There were other problems as well, most of them the result of attempts to keep the cost down. The machine came with only one disk drive, which was one too few for any serious user; you could buy another drive to sit next to it, but that cost $495. It only had 128 kilobytes of internal memory, which wasn't enough for most serious software to run on; Apple was promising a 512-kilobyte version as soon as chips were available, but nobody could say when that would be or how much it would cost. The appliance concept made it impossible for owners to increase the memory or otherwise customize it; a notice on the back declared that once the case was opened, the warranty would no longer be valid. The only printer that could be used with it was a dot-matrix type, which formed letters and numerals out of patterns of dots—great for graphics, but not good enough for business correspondence. And its compatibility with Lisa was largely imaginary, for while Lisa could run Macintosh software—what little there was of it—Macintosh could not run Lisa's.

All the same, the biggest problem with Macintosh in the first hundred days was that Apple couldn't build enough of them. The highly touted, highly automated factory in Fremont had ended up costing more than $20 million, and still the manufacturing manager Steve had hired to replace Dave Vaughan had been unable to whip it into shape. It was supposed to churn out a finished computer every twenty-seven seconds, but that was assuming just-in-time delivery of zero-defect parts. Instead they had to shut the place down for ten days because video display screens from Samsung were marred by barely detectable colored spots. Another time they shut it down because of a problem with the Samsung power supply, and another because of a problem with Sony on the disk drive. Analysts and pundits were blaming Lisa's failure partly on Apple's inability to deliver it until six months after its introduction. If Macintosh wasn't available when people were excited about it, it seemed unlikely they'd come back when it was.

So on February 11, the day after the Macintosh Christmas party (another formal dinner-dance at the St. Francis), Steve flew to Japan with Bob Belleville and Al Eisenstat to find out what was wrong with the suppliers. Jay Elliot, the vice-president for human resources, went along because Steve liked having him to talk to. Burrell Smith went along because Steve wanted him to patch up his relationship with Bob, which had deteriorated so badly that it was threatening Burrell's progress on the laser printer he was working on. Bob's proposal for a little office automation system had by this time become the technological blueprint for the campaign to convert America's knowledge workers to the Macintosh cause, and the laser printer—an adaptation of a Canon product that, combined with Mac's superior graphics capabilities, could produce documents of near-printshop quality—was a key component. Keeping Bob and Burrell on speaking terms was high on Steve's list of priorities.

With Macintosh finally out the door, the group that had built it was on the verge of splitting apart. For the hackers and hobbyists who made up the core of the cult—Burrell and Andy and most of the software crew—the introduction was followed by an enormous psychic letdown. Emotionally and physically drained to the point of collapse, they had continued to work on it until the last possible moment; and now, suddenly, it was over. To cover their sense of loss, they'd set out on their road show, speaking to computer clubs and demonstrating the machine at expos. This only added to their exhaustion. And their reward for all they'd done was to see their little maverick operation turned into a gargantuan bureaucracy by the influx of Lisa engineers.

This didn't improve their feelings for Bob, who was idiosyncratic and aloof and less than a model of tact. He'd never been able to manage them anyway; his real role was as Steve's court technologist. He was the power behind the throne. With his Ph.D. in engineering and his experience at SRI and at Xerox, he was a tap to the source of what Apple called "Lisa technology"—just as Burrell and Andy and the software team were the link to the magical electronic wizardry of "Woz-level" engineering, to the suburban roots-myth of the furry genius in the garage. Steve took what he needed from each and played them off one against the other, granting or withholding his approval as his moods and needs dictated. It was a complex psychic interplay in which both parties vied for his attention but neither side could win; for once that happened, the game would be over.

Andy, being the most assertive of the core cultists, was the least shy about expressing their feelings. To him, Bob was this total organization man who was on some kind of power trip that made him want to squelch all individual initiative. The HR people drew diagrams of their personality traits to help them understand their differences, but it didn't help. The truth was that Bob didn't really care if Andy hated him; his marriage was falling apart, his life was a shambles, and he was tired—much too tired to be dealing with this kind of thing. Always a quiet soul, he was now growing so detached that it left the others unnerved. They responded by voting him most likely to walk in and blow everybody away with a shotgun. Finally, the week before they left for Japan, Steve walked him around the parking lot and told him everybody hated him because he was on a power trip. Bob's immediate response was to resign—which meant that the next day, at a Macintosh staff retreat at Pajaro Dunes, Steve had to walk him around the beach and talk him into staying.

Steve had his own problems. His love life was making him miserable. As one of America's more eligible bachelors, he dated a number of women; and though he was self-conscious about his looks—his smile in particular—he was always getting letters from women he'd never met who were madly in love with him. Recently he'd been seeing Maya Lin, the architecture student who'd designed the Vietnam Veterans' Memorial in Washington, but she'd turned noticeably cool. He couldn't seem to form a lasting relationship with anyone—not surprising, since his primary relationship was with Macintosh. If only he could change the world and be in love at the same time! He envied people who had love and companionship in their lives, and he couldn't help feeling sorry for himself for being so alone. There was a great deal of the child in Steve—the wondering child, the impatient child, the self-indulgent child, the feral child—and to reap the benefits of one, it was necessary to put up with all the others. Right now it was the self-indulgent child that was showing itself, which meant that life would be difficult for everyone around him.

It was snowing in Japan. Things went well at their meetings with Sony and Canon; the next day they were scheduled to visit Epson to look at printers, disk drives, and flat-panel display screens. They left Tokyo by car at five in the morning for the trip to Epson headquarters, high in the Japan Alps west of Tokyo. But when they got halfway there, they discovered that the highway was blocked by an avalanche and they'd have to turn back. They went back to the edge of Tokyo and boarded a train, only to be stuck in the snow for hours by the same avalanche. By the time they reached Epson it was almost noon, and nobody had prepared lunch for them. Steve was furious. He was rude to everyone. He hated every product they showed him. They didn't get back to Tokyo until after midnight.

The next day they visited an Hitachi factory outside Tokyo, a just-in-time manufacturing plant that Floyd Kvamme had pulled some strings to get them into. A raft of engineers came out one after the other to explain how it worked; each one would bow politely and say his name and begin his spiel, only to hear Steve say he already knew everything there was to know about *that;* he wanted to know about *this.* Then that engineer would disappear and another one would come out and the whole process would start all over again. Finally Steve announced that he wanted some cookies, so everybody had to scurry around looking for cookies for him. Bob was disgusted. The next day, he gave Steve an ultimatum: He could start to behave like a human being, in which case Bob would continue to keep him in Japan, or he could keep on behaving as he had been, in which case Bob would telephone the American embassy and urge that he be requested to leave.

■ ■ ■

The org chart on Sculley's office wall was continuing to evolve. No longer did it show more than a dozen vice-presidents reporting to him, as had been the case when he arrived. Now there was a distinct hierarchy, with two powerful product divisions responsible for their own manufacturing, marketing, and finance and a small central organization for sales, distribution, corporate finance, and human resources—in essence, two companies, each reporting to Sculley and his staff, each competing with the other.

There were further refinements to be made. Gene Carter, the vice-president of sales, stepped down in January; and with marketing being split up between the Macintosh and Apple II divisions, it made sense to give his job to Bill Campbell, the marketing vice-president they'd hired from Kodak. Carter was leaving largely because he disagreed with another structural change—Sculley's plan to "restructure the dealer channel," as they put it, by adding more dealers. Having rationalized the product-line strategy and restructured the organization, Sculley was now ready to turn his architect's eye to the network of stores that sold Apple's products to the public. Apple computers could currently be bought at some 1,500 stores across the country, and by adding a handful of big chains—ComputerLand, Businessland, Sears—he could nearly double that figure overnight. It all came down to "shelf space," as they called it in package goods—getting your soft drinks or potato chips or whatever onto the shelves. To sell more goods, you had to have them in more stores. It was simply common sense.

But would it work that way with computers? Carter thought not. He'd built the dealer network from nothing, having started at a time when computer stores were as rare as head shops in the fifties. He thought personal computers were like cars, not like soft drinks. You had new cars, used cars, service centers, and warranties. You had Chevy dealers, Ford dealers, Chrysler dealers, and imports. You didn't try to sell Fords through four dealers at the same intersection, because if you did, the dealers would undercut each other until they all went broke. You sold selectively, through the best dealers you could find.

There were other points on which Carter and Sculley disagreed. Rather than maintaining a salaried sales force to sell computers to the dealers, Carter had always relied on a network of independent manufacturer's reps—twenty-three different organizations, employing about four hundred people and operating entirely on commission. That meant that Apple's cost of sales was tied directly to the amount of sales, because Apple wasn't responsible for their salaries or expenses or overhead. Sculley wanted to replace the manufacturer's reps with his own sales team of Apple employees. He wasn't happy with the way some of the rep organizations were performing, and he thought it was time Apple had the prestige of its own sales organization—the prestige and the control.

And then there was the question of management style. Under Markkula, each division had been its own little fiefdom with its own distinct identity. Carter's turf had been his own; nobody tried to tell him how to do his job. But Sculley had more definite ideas about how things should be done, and he expected his managers to try them out. The organization he was creating was one in which decisions came down from above. That was a corollary to the hierarchy he was constructing; it flowed from the org chart that was growing on his wall. Years before, when Apple was tiny and Carter was flying around the country constantly to set up a dealer base, he'd promised his wife that when sales hit $1 billion, he'd quit. Fat chance of that ever happening, he'd thought. Now it *had* happened, and it was time to live up to his word. So he stepped down as vice-president of sales and went on sabbatical to do a study on whether Apple should have its own product centers like IBM—company-owned stores that would serve as repair centers and as a base for Apple's other sales force, the national account team that had been set up to sell Lisas directly to Fortune 1000 corporations.

Kvamme was having his own problems fitting into the new organization. Markkula had hired him to head an "Apple sales company" on the IBM model, a central sales-and-marketing organization that would supervise the reps and be responsible for products from half a dozen different divisions—Apple II, Lisa, Macintosh, peripherals, and so forth. But Sculley's arrival had made Kvamme the number-three marketing expert in a company that only had room for two—Sculley and Jobs. They were on the phone to each other night and day while Kvamme sat in an office down the hall. With marketing going to the two product divisions, he wouldn't even have it on paper. All you had to do was look at the org chart to see there wasn't much need for an Apple sales company anymore.

Kleiner Perkins, Caufield & Byers, a powerful San Francisco venture capital firm, had been trying to recruit Kvamme for a year and a half. He started talking with them shortly after the Macintosh introduction, and in March he accepted their offer. With Carter gone, that left only three vice-presidents who'd come out of the semiconductor industry—Ken Zerbe, Del Yocam, and Roy Weaver, who was in charge of distribution. The new Apple taking shape on Sculley's wall would be run not by semiconductor veterans but by Sculley and Jobs. And even though lifestyle advertising had been tried and discarded, it would still rely on consumer-marketing techniques to sell computers.

■ ■ ■

The next test of Apple's consumer-marketing abilities would come in April, when they introduced the sleek new book-sized version of the II—the II reinvented as an appliance. Though smaller and less versatile than the IIe, the new IIb was both more powerful and far simpler to set up. It had twice the memory. It lacked the expandability that made the IIe so versatile, but it came with all the most popular options built in. If you wanted your IIe to display the standard eighty columns of text instead of forty, you had to open it up and plug in a special eighty-column card—a little circuit board that went into a slot on the main board. To connect it to a printer, you had to plug in a printer interface card. And if you wanted to equip it with a second disk drive, you had to plug in a disk-drive interface card. All you had to do with the new model was take it out of the box, flip the switch to select the forty-column or the eighty-column display, and plug a printer or a disk drive into the back. And it was slim and attractive, with a clean, white look that underscored its hoped-for appeal to the novice computer user.

The II was Del Yocam's division now. He took over from Cavalier at the beginning of February, and life in the Triangle Building started to change almost immediately. Del was not without vanity, but he was never visibly concerned about things like what kind of desk chair he sat in. He *was* concerned about keeping all the papers on top of his desk in their proper piles. He'd come to the Valley from Ford, and though many of the free-and-easy accoutrements of Valley life—the sporty European cars, the casual clothes—had somehow insinuated themselves into his existence, the values they reflected had not. When it came to business, Del was still in Detroit. Risk and passion were his watchwords, but what mattered was keeping things neat and tidy—his desktop, his division. What he lacked in charisma he made up in fastidiousness.

Del had come to Apple in 1979 as director of materials—purchasing, in other words—and quickly demonstrated a way with the balance sheet. Stable, reliable, and almost frighteningly efficient, he held his footing in Apple's earthquake-prone terrain. Steadfastness comes in handy in any company, but at Camp Runamok it made him invaluable. He always did his homework, which was what it took to keep Steve from savaging you in meetings, and he was politically astute as well. Unlike Cavalier, he could see that with a new II about to come out and Steve and John both excited about it, he should be enthusiastic too. By that time, of course, it was far too late for him to have any say in the product itself; and because his experience was in manufacturing and finance, he didn't have much to say about the marketing or advertising or promotional strategies for it either. So the posture he maintained was one of watchful waiting. The person he was watching most closely was Dave Larson, the marketing man who'd been working on the project from the beginning.

Like Mike Murray, his counterpart in the Macintosh division, Larson was young and enthusiastic and inexperienced, a family man who hurled himself into his job and continually worked at the edge of his abilities. He and his wife had come to California from Minnesota, and being free spirits, they'd settled not in the Valley but in a charming little ranch-style house a block from the Pacific in Santa Cruz, surrounded by a postage-stamp yard in which the previous residents had grazed goats. In the summer of 1981 he'd joined Apple, an astonishing place that had just been showered with riches. There were something like fifteen millionaires within a few feet of his desk; and the amazing thing was, they were ordinary guys, not geniuses or anything, though in fact they were beginning to think of themselves as such. Every morning when he got to work a new Porsche or Mercedes would be sitting in the parking lot, and every afternoon when he went to the coffee pot somebody would be talking about a new tax shelter he'd just heard about or a new airplane he wanted to buy. And it wasn't just individuals who were rolling in dough; the whole company was. When Dave asked what the budget was for his first job he was told, "Hey, you're smart! Spend what you need." Now, three years later, things had calmed down a little. Now there were constraints. To launch the new II—advertising, publicity, merchandizing, promotion—he'd been given a budget. He had $13.7 million to spend.

Larson was a cool guy. He kept his hair in a shag cut and wore a thin black goatee and drove a little yellow Porsche. He wanted to be a leader, not a manager, and as a leader he wanted to create a peak work experience for his people. For many it became a peak life experience. Making a lot of money was the least of it, and in any event they'd joined too late to become millionaires. They were there because Apple was a company where business was a creative endeavor. They weren't just pimping products, they were doing something they could believe in. Like the Macintosh group, they had a ready-made external threat in IBM. Apple was the great American experiment; IBM was the big blue steamroller. One of them liked to claim that IBM was a Marxist-Leninist organization sponsored by the Soviet Union for the sole purpose of destroying the American entrepreneurial spirit. It was an absurdist joke that revealed the essential truth: At Apple they'd transformed capitalism into a crusade, and in IBM they had their Evil Empire.

The other thing Larson's team had was momentum. Most of them had come off the IIe introduction the January before, and the

IIe was a powerhouse. Over Christmas they'd sold 110,000 of them, and the new II promised to be just as big or bigger. But they were on a crash-and-burn schedule, and as the launch date approached, the symptoms grew unmistakable. Larson was routinely working eighty-hour weeks, rising at five, driving the steep and winding expressway over the Hill (as the Santa Cruz Mountains were euphemistically called) to Cupertino, getting home at nine or ten. Peter Quinn, the engineering manager who'd run the project, had been sent to Fiji for two weeks in March because his hands were shaking and his attention span was no longer than a minute, but there was no way they could send Dave away. They were counting on him to bring the product out.

First, though, they had to decide what to call it. The IIb, for "book"? The IIc, for "compact"? Pippin, after the apple? Sculley told them to call it some kind of II, he didn't care what; so they settled on IIc. That was easy. The hard part was deciding how to price it. The original goal had been to sell the complete package—everything except the monitor, which was optional—for $995. That way it could be positioned as an entry-level machine, and the more expensive and versatile IIe could provide a path for those who wanted to move up. But by the time the design was finished, it was clear there was no way they could hit that magic $995 price point. To arrive at a price point that would work, they had to predict the ratio of peripheral products that would sell against the main unit—what percentage of buyers would purchase an extra disk drive, what percentage would buy a monitor or opt for a flat-panel display or just hook it up to their TV sets. Then they had to come up with a price point that would allow them to hit the right gross margin for the entire product portfolio—the computer itself and all the peripherals. And once they had it all figured out in retail, they had to work it out in other sales channels where the pricing was different, such as education. And finally, after all this analysis had been done, after all these calculations had been made, it came down to a handful of guys in an office playing power poker. Sales wanted one price; the division wanted another; and at the end it was Del who got to call.

They ended up with a retail price of $1,295, with the monitor an additional $199. At the same time, they dropped the price of the basic IIe—just the computer and a single disk drive—to $995. And they decided to price a fully configured IIe—two disk drives, a monitor, and an eighty-column card—at $1,795. So the IIc was bracketed in price between the stripped-down IIe and the fully loaded version, which completely disrupted its positioning.

The IIe was a product that sold to all sorts of customers—high schools, elementary schools, small-business people, home-computer enthusiasts. The IIc had been designed as a complementary consumer item with a special appeal to women, on the theory that the wife is likely to be involved in any family decision to buy such an expensive item. The previous spring they'd done focus groups—intensive interviews with small groups of potential buyers—to determine what hot buttons they could press to motivate women to buy a personal computer for the home. This was the first time Apple had done consumer research on a product that was still in engineering, and they found that except for women with kids, who wanted a computer that would run the same software their kids used in school, most women had the same hot buttons as men. Most people bought a home computer because they had some kind of home business going—a real-estate investment, some stocks and bonds, that kind of thing—so it had to run business software. Being able to pull it out of the box and plug it right in without buying a lot of extra cards and cables was important, and so was its not taking up too much room. But would people actually pay more for a smaller computer?

The small size of the IIc was, in fact, a significant technological achievement that would never have been possible without advances in the semiconductor industry, in disk drive technology, and in Apple's own engineering. Yet Larson's research showed that while people appreciated a computer that was compact and easily transported, they didn't value smallness for its own sake. If anything, they tended to be suspicious of a computer that looked too small. The hundred-dollar home computers from Timex and Texas Instruments were small, and when you got them home they turned out to be just toys. One thing that was impressive about the IBM PC was that it was so big and hulking; it looked like a computer was supposed to look. So did the IIe. The IIc actually gave you more than the stripped-down IIe, but how do you explain that to a first-time computer buyer? It was like trying to explain why a BMW costs more than a Buick to somebody who's never driven a car before.

Chiat/Day's solution was a series of print and television ads that began with the line "Announcing a technological breakthrough of incredible proportions." The underlying assumption was that the growth in personal-computer sales was expected to be in serious "productivity tools" rather than game-playing machines and novelty items. To figure out how to appeal to the market, Chiat/Day had superimposed the VALS typology on another psychographic profile, the bell curve that shows what percentage of the population will adopt a product innovation over time. The classic adoption curve begins with a tiny group of "innovators," moves steeply upward with a larger group of "early adopters," goes over the top and down the other side with the "late adopters," and ends with those who can only be described as "laggards." The comparison revealed that the VALS "achievers"—quite apart from being the 28 percent of the population that accounted for 45 percent of all retail sales—matched the early adopters of the adoption curve. The IIc's market was made up of early-adopting achievers, and the job they faced was to convince these people that the IIc was the superior productivity tool—superior to the IBM PCjr, superior to the Commodore 64, and (by implication, at least) superior to the IIe.

Apple was planning to spend $15 million advertising the IIc through the summer months, and nothing was being left to chance. Ads, packaging, promotional materials—all were designed to portray the IIc as the ultimate digital consumable, the perfect companion for an "achiever" lifestyle. The computer was packaged in a bright red box with a picture of a lighthearted young woman holding the computer in her hand. That picture became the visual symbol for the IIc, just as the "Picasso artwork" had come to represent Macintosh. The look was casual, natural, spontaneous. The woman was not a model but a member of the product marketing team; and because the original photo had been taken merely to get a feel for the product, it lacked the professional quality it might have had. The woman's teeth weren't quite straight. Her hair was a little messy. She was holding a prototype rather than the actual computer. But when they tried to reshoot it later, none of the other pictures had quite the same sexy, vivacious charm. So they digitized it. Dot by dot they straightened her teeth, combed her hair, moved the prototype out, inserted the finished computer in its place. The result, to anyone looking closely, was strangely denatured; yet the image it conveyed was that this box contained the computational equivalent of sportswear from Esprit.

■ ■ ■

April 24, the day Apple was planning to unveil the IIc, was also the day after Ansel Adams died. Bob Belleville, seeing the news on the front page of the morning *Chronicle,* sat on a San Francisco sidewalk and started to cry. Belleville had met Adams seven times, had studied at his Yosemite Workshop, and had himself made thousands of Adams-like photographs in Death Valley, in the Sierra Nevada, and in the Santa Cruz Mountains above Cupertino. Nine of them were on display in the atrium of Bandley 3, along with three vintage prints by Adams (including his "Moonrise over Hernandez" of 1941) and, of course, the Yamaha motorcycle and the Bösendorfer piano. Photography of this sort was a natural mode of expression for Bob, who shared Adams's precise and austere vision and was adept at using technology to express mood and feeling. He and Steve had been planning to visit Adams at his house in the Carmel highlands to give him a Macintosh, but his health was bad and the date had been pushed back several times. Now he was gone.

So Bob sat on the sidewalk and sobbed. It was a brisk, clear day in San Francisco, and people were hurrying past him into the steel maw of Moscone Center. The Stars and Stripes snapped in the breeze alongside the Bear Flag of the California Republic. Apple had invited four thousand people to this gleaming semiunderground bunker in the seedy strip south of Market Street—dealers, software developers, analysts, and reporters, all there to witness the launch. This was event marketing in action, marketing so focused and intense it was an event in itself, the way the Macintosh launch had been in January. There was a mammoth software exposition; an Apple II museum with a replica of the garage where it all began; a vast auditorium equipped with a three-screen video projection system and "presidential" TelePrompTers, the kind the White House uses. (The prompters were Sculley's innovation; Jobs had little use for them.) It was a $2.5-million party, and the theme was "Apple II Forever." The engineers were so proud of themselves they walked in wearing tuxedoes.

But if the message that day was that the II would last forever, the subtext was that its development path would be constrained. Only three weeks before, the IIx—the project Wozniak had started working on when he returned to Apple—had been canceled. The Western Design Center in Phoenix was developing a new microprocessor for it, a powerful successor to the 6502 that had gone into the original II. But when the first samples had come in—in February instead of November—they hadn't worked. The second samples came three weeks later and didn't work either. Clearly the IIx couldn't make its scheduled ship date of September. Then a variety of forces conspired to kill it.

The IIx had an extreme case of "creeping elegance," which is what happens when engineers pile new features on top of one another with such abandon that the original idea is lost completely. The IIx had grown a co-processor slot which would allow its owner to open up the case, plug in another processor, and turn it into an entirely different computer. You could use an Intel 8088 and turn it into an IBM PC-compatible, or you could use a Motorola 68000 and enable it to emulate Lisa or Macintosh or to run UNIX, an extremely powerful and sophisticated operating system that was used mainly in the academic research community. Woz, who had a great deal of mail to answer in any event, had long since lost interest in it. Jobs could hardly be expected to champion it, since it promised to do everything Macintosh could do and more. And Ida Cole, the woman who was managing it, projected they'd sell only 25,000 a month, while everybody was expecting the IIc to sell 100,000 a month. So why should they invest any more effort in it?

The Apple III was quietly phased out as well. After the Macintosh introduction its sales dropped by three-quarters, and then the sales reps and the dealers started hearing rumors that Apple wasn't behind it. They were right. To Sculley and Jobs and most of the exec staff, the III made no sense: They weren't making enough money off it. It had taken them four years to sell 85,000 units, while in seven years they'd sold nearly two million Apple II's. The rumors hurt sales even more; by April they were down to 1,000 a month. So when Larson told Dave Fradin, who was managing the III, that he could display only one Apple III among the seventy Apple II's at Moscone Center, Fradin decided it was pointless to go on. He'd been fighting for a peculiar sort of shelf space—shelf space in the minds of the sales force and the dealers—and with two new computers coming out in four months, he obviously wasn't going to get it. So on April 24, while the dealers and the sales reps and the reporters and the software developers were witnessing the launch of the IIc in San Francisco, he quietly sent out a memo announcing the demise of the III.

What Fradin didn't understand was how hard Larson and his boss had to work to keep the focus of this event on the II. Del Yocam wanted to give the IIc as big a launch as Macintosh had had, and it bugged him that Steve kept trying to work Macintosh into the picture.

Del couldn't keep Mac out altogether, but he was determined to minimize it. He wanted to focus their excitement on the II.

■ ■ ■

"Let's get fired up!" Campbell cried, a real coach-to-team rah-rah job, and that was how the day began. Steve came out in his suspenders and bow tie to give a report on Macintosh on Day 92 of the Hundred Days. Good news: more than 60,000 shipped to date. Then Woz took the mike and announced he was going to tell some jokes—political jokes, since the Democratic Convention was going to be held in this hall a few months hence. Jobs stood behind him, looking like a teenager who was embarrassed to be seen with his parents.

And with good reason. He'd been talking about the personal-computer market with Jesse Jackson, Woz said, and Jackson had quipped, "Well, now Apple knows what it's like to be a minority."

Mondale told him that 80 percent of the components of Apple computers should be American-made. When Woz protested that an Apple II would have to cost $8,000, Mondale said, "Well, that would be good for Apple—and good for Jobs."

Jobs hid his face in his hands and cringed, but Woz was just getting started. He'd just bumped into Ronald Reagan downstairs, Woz announced. And when he asked Reagan what he thought about the PCjr, Reagan said he was against abortions!

That got a good response, but when Sculley took the mike it became clear that this day was really his. The II might be Woz's machine and Del's division, and this II might be Jobs's concept, but its success would depend on Sculley's marketing abilities. "We are changing forever the ground rules for competition in the personal-computer industry," he told his audience. "Apple is going to become not just a great product company but also a great *marketing* company. McDonald's and Burger King are great marketing companies in their industry, just as Pepsi and Coke are in theirs. The Apple challenge is built on firm foundations—that product innovation and marketing innovation can play the major role in shaping this dynamic growth industry. If we are right—and we believe we are—Silicon Valley will never again be the same."

Later, as if in ironic counterpoint, an earthquake rippled through the city. It was a small one really, just a rumble. But it was enough to make people queasy, and it sent a wave of nervousness through the hall. Jobs, deep in conversation when it came, failed to notice.

□□ **12** □□

Metamorphosis

Isn't it funny, Jay Elliot thought as he fed the outstretched hands, how millionaires will scramble for a free T-shirt just like anybody else? He'd had a couple of dozen made up for the occasion; they said SCULLEY'S BILLION-DOLLAR BATTALION, referring to the $M*A*S*H$ party at last fall's sales conference. Now the vice-presidents and directors of the company were grabbing them out of his hands. It was Sculley's first anniversary at Apple.

They were at the Mouton Noir, a French restaurant on Big Basin Way in Saratoga. Despite its Laura Ashley look—the pink floral wallpaper, the cream-colored woodwork—and its traditional menu, the Mouton Noir was Steve's favorite restaurant. He lived nearby, in a rambling house in the hills between Villa Montalvo and Los Gatos, the last town in the Valley before the expressway climbs the Hill to Santa Cruz. Los Gatos had been a pretty hip town in the sixties, when the mountains above it had been home to Wavy Gravy and his psychedelic troupe, the Hog Farm. The proliferation of techie millionaires had changed its character in the years since, but many of the millionaires it attracted were renegades, like Steve. Saratoga, nestled in the foothills of the Santa Cruz Mountains just south of Cupertino, was different—a magnet for capitalists since the 1860s, when its name had been changed from McCarthysville. To drive its wooded lanes was to understand what made California a golden land: the Mediterranean air of the cedared hills, the earthy shadows of the redwood groves, the sybaritic intensity of sun and sky. The money came from electronics now rather than gold and silver, but the appeal of the place remained the same.

Mike Markkula was there that evening, and Arthur Rock, and Peter Crisp, and all the vice-presidents and their wives. The waiters brought out cold cucumber soup in hollowed-out apples. The vice-presidents and the board members gave testimonials, and then Steve presented John with an elaborate collage he'd had made, a massive, memento-studded plaque with a Pepsi logo on one side which evolved into an Apple logo on the other. John thanked them all and told them how excited he was to be at Apple—how he'd come to Apple because of Steve, how he wouldn't want to be there if Steve were gone. It was a remark they'd all heard before and one the exec staff members found more than a little irritating, since it cut them out of the picture. But John was oblivious, and in the excitement of the moment he even went a little further. "As far as I'm concerned," he declared, "Apple has only one leader—Steve and me."

The man from Pepsi was becoming the man from Apple. He was merging with Steve. A transformation was taking place. Not everyone thought it boded well.

■ ■ ■

The anniversary dinner came on Day 101 of the Hundred Days. That morning, Apple had issued a press release announcing that the campaign to establish Macintosh had been a stupendous success. They'd shipped 70,000 units, considerably more than the publicly announced projection of 50,000 and only slightly less than the internal figure of 73,500. Even with $15 million in marketing costs, the Macintosh division was showing a profit for its first quarter. Mike Murray was predicting sales of 80,000 Macs per month by September, and in April the board had approved Steve's proposal to double the capacity of the factory in Fremont. With the new production line they ought to be able to meet Murray's forecast—exceed it even, if they really pushed.

But the original production line still wasn't up to speed, and red lights were going on in Steve's mind about the way Fremont was being managed. He took it up with John one day near the end of May, at a general managers' retreat at Pajaro Dunes. They decided to offer the job to Debi Coleman, the Macintosh division controller, who'd wanted it all along.

Debi looked the part of a factory boss. She was forceful and blunt, with incredible drive and a no-nonsense approach that was sadly lacking in most of the men associated with the place. She watched "Dynasty" and "Dallas" religiously, knew every detail of every character's life, but in every other respect she was a hard-nosed businesswoman. Steve hadn't given her the job before because no one was convinced she could do it—and besides, he needed her running finance. Now he was ready to give her a shot. He called her down to Pajaro Dunes from the Sonoma Mission Inn, a gourmet spa in the wine country, where she'd taken a couple of weeks off to lose weight. It was a 150-mile drive across the Golden Gate and down the coast. When she got there, he took her for a walk on the beach.

Debi was thrilled. Manufacturing was her mission, her goal in life, her way to change the world. She'd grown up hanging around her father's machine-tool shop in Rhode Island, she'd worked summers in college as a production supervisor at Texas Instruments, she'd served on the manufacturing manager's staff at Hewlett-Packard's technical-computer group in Cupertino. At HP she'd joined a task force looking into ways of reducing factory inventory, and by the time they were done she'd been converted to the gospel of zero defects and just-in-time delivery. Then, when she was twenty-eight and having lunch one day at the Good Earth Restaurant on Stevens Creek Boulevard, she'd run into a Stanford Business School classmate who'd become the marketing director for Lisa at Apple Computer. With him was another Stanford M.B.A., the Lisa controller, who was about to move to Boston. Would Debi like to apply for the job? She would. Then she discovered there were two jobs available—controller for the Lisa division, which was grandiose and bureaucratic and committed to this ridiculous one man–one machine production system, and controller for the secret task force that was building Macintosh— Steve Jobs and thirteen other people. There was no question which she'd take. She joined Steve's staff in October 1981, the same day as Matt Carter, who'd been hired to run production engineering—to build the factory and get the machine ready for production.

Now, with Debi getting to run the factory at last, the job of Macintosh controller fell to the woman she'd been grooming for it ever since the first manufacturing director made his exit. Susan Barnes was as passionate about accounting as Debi was about manufacturing. She saw it as a creative endeavor: You had to respect the parameters, of course, but within those bounds it was all a free zone— and you got to play in everybody else's territory. She was a slim and eager young woman with blond hair and a dress-for-success wardrobe, and that suited her fine.

Barnes was the daughter of a Mobil geologist and a physician. She'd grown up in Texas and Mexico, earned a degree in archaeology at Bryn Mawr, and gotten her M.B.A. from Wharton. He brother was an analog engineer, her sister a technical writer, and during the seventies the two of them moved to Silicon Valley. They kept telling her she had to come out because this was the center of the world. She made it as far as the tax department of the San Francisco office of Arthur Andersen, the Big Eight accounting firm, and then a friend who'd left Andersen for Apple persuaded her to interview there. She ended up taking a finance job in the Lisa division, working for a Stanford M.B.A. who was about to leave for Boston—the same one Debi met a short while later. It was 1981, and she was twenty-eight.

After Debi joined Apple the two had become friends, and eventually Debi offered her a job on the Macintosh special task force, which by this point had grown to nearly thirty people secreted away in the little building they called Texaco Towers. Before she could take it, however, she had to be approved by Steve Jobs. She'd heard he could be ferocious, and she was scared. When she showed up at Bandley 6 for the interview she was told he was running late, which was customary, and in a terrible temper, which wasn't unusual either. Finally he stalked in and said, "Hi! I'm Steve Jobs, and I'm pissed." "Hi," she replied, "I'm Susan Barnes, and thanks for the warning." They hit it off right away.

With finance in Susan's hands, Debi moved over to Fremont and proceeded to whip the factory into shape. She shut it down for a month. She threw out $7 million worth of equipment that didn't work. She fired some people and "outplaced" others. She cleaned up the dirt and repainted the walls—with semi-gloss this time, so they could be washed. In July she got out 43,000 machines—more than double what had been produced in May. But while Susan was taking over a smoothly running finance operation and Debi was pulling manufacturing together, engineering and marketing were falling apart. The boys in Steve's organization weren't doing as well as the girls.

■   ■   ■

Bob Belleville and Mike Murray were under constant pressure—Belleville to develop new products that would make Macintosh work in the office market, Murray to come up with new schemes to make them sell. The merger with the Lisa division and the subsequent "infrastructure phasedown" had given them both more people than they could manage and, paradoxically, fewer than they needed for the job. The Macintosh Office development project had transformed them into just what Belleville had feared—a systems division that was getting mired in complexity. And while earlier Steve's staff had always stood together whenever one of them caught Steve's ire, under stress they began to point fingers.

Mike was simply unable to convince himself that the Macintosh Office was a good idea. With Macintosh itself he'd felt a deep personal attachment, almost a symbiotic relationship, as if it were he and he were it. But the Macintosh Office seemed wrong to him—forced, unnatural. Macintosh was never designed to be a work station in a large office system; it was designed to be used by individuals in their homes or offices. But the failure of Lisa, the success of the IBM PC, the shakeout in home computers, the promise of the office market—all these were forcing them to try to turn Macintosh into the whole list of things it wasn't.

In March, Mike's marketing people had begun planning the introduction of the various components of the Macintosh Office—the file server, the laser printer, and the network. As the process wore on, he increasingly divorced himself from it. Instead he concentrated on things he enjoyed, like advertising. The woman he put in charge of the introduction *was* enthusiastic—too enthusiastic, Bob thought. She was beginning to sound like a Xerox marketing person. "Workstations," "electronic mail," "interconnections with the IBM environment," "completely integrated office of the future": Macintosh marketing was soon inventing an office system so powerful it could take Macintosh engineering years to develop. And they wanted it right away.

Bob persisted in thinking of the Macintosh Office as nothing more than a simple, inexpensive little network linking three or four people together so they could exchange computer files and share a high-quality graphics printer. Anything else was simply beyond the capacities of his people, who were still reeling from the effort they'd put into Mac itself. They were all crash-and-burn victims, Bob as much as any of them. His wife and children were gone, he was in the midst of a divorce, and all he felt was tired. But even if he and his engineers had been fully functional, they couldn't have built anything more than a rudimentary system in the few months remaining before January.

When the Lisa veterans came in, the engineering lab had suddenly bloated to 150 seriously disoriented people—too many to forge quickly into productive teams, yet not enough to deal with the intricate difficulties of systems development, which involves building not a single product but a suite of interacting ones. Without these products, however, Macintosh was never going to make it in the office, so all they could do was hurl themselves at the task. The critical problem was software. Because Macintosh had been designed with a file system that couldn't cope with a large-capacity disk drive— only a creep from Planet Xerox would want *that*—an entirely new file system had to be developed before it could be equipped with a hard disk or connected to a file server. Because some 70,000 people had already bought a Macintosh with the old file system, the new one had to be fully compatible with it. And the only engineering manager who seemed capable of designing such a file system was already bogged down developing the software to make the network function.

That spring saw the return of Bud Tribble, the original Macintosh software architect. The software team remembered him from happier days, and he brought with him a ray of hope. He'd been the fourth and last person Jef Raskin had brought onto the Macintosh team, when it consisted only of Jef, Burrell, and Burrell's assistant. He'd left Apple and software both after a few years to go to medical school in Seattle; Bob Belleville had been hired as his replacement. And as Bob, with his alien point of view and his competing rapport with Steve, became a villain in the eyes of Burrell and Andy and the rest of the people who made up the core cult, Bud had been elevated to near-sainthood. So when Steve persuaded him to give up neurosurgery and come back as software manager—his old job, but with twice as many people reporting to him—the software team cheered. Bob wasn't thrilled, since he hadn't been informed about it, but over dinner one night the two of them agreed that Bud would work for Bob and they could both work together. It wasn't as if Bob were getting a warm and fuzzy feeling when he walked past software anyway.

There was less rejoicing in Mac's core contingent about Steve's other snare, Alan Kay, the forty-three-year-old computer scientist whose Smalltalk project at Xerox PARC had inspired so much of their work. Steve had been after him for a year and a half, but Kay, who was living in a verdant Los Angeles canyon and commuting six hundred miles a day by limousine and jet to his job as chief scientist at Atari, kept telling him no. Apple was strictly an engineering company, and like most research scientists, he regarded engineering with disdain. He considered the Apple II a Tinkertoy—clever, but a Tinkertoy nonetheless—and Macintosh little more than an implementation of $100 million worth of Xerox research. When he'd left Xerox in 1980, it was partly out of frustration with his own researchers, who wanted to spend their time developing Smalltalk as a commercial product instead of getting on with the real task, which was inventing the Dynabook. He and Jobs had been having lunch together every couple of months at Atari's executive dining room (a habit that drove Atari executives wild), but even after Atari started racking up incredible losses and Atari's president announced that he was going to cut spending for research, Kay was reluctant to go with Apple. Finally Steve got him to name what he wanted in a job and then made him a better offer. He arrived with the position of Apple Fellow, reporting directly to Steve and flying to Silicon Valley no more than once a week.

Steve envisioned Kay as a sort of natural resource for the Macintosh division: a walking, talking library of who's doing what in the universe; a technological bumblebee, flying around pollinating things. In a different world it might have worked out that way. Tousle-haired and still rather boyish-looking, Kay brought with him a breadth of knowledge that was rare in any field, much less the hermetic world of computers. He had degrees in computer science, math, and biology; he was up on quantum and classical physics and on Western and Oriental philosophy; he was well versed in child cognition and passionately devoted to music, with a personal repertoire that included jazz and rock guitar, Bach organ fugues, and eighteenth-century chamber music. Curiously, he often professed to finding his music more significant than computers. Some of his peers thought that might be a pose: If he took his research too seriously, he might be constrained from thinking up crazy ideas—and no one could accuse him of that.

At Atari he'd been secretly working to develop "fantasy amplifiers"—electronic information toys equipped with artificial intelligence, stereophonic sound, and full color, and capable of simulating Robespierre's Paris or the view from van Gogh's asylum window.

Just as he'd once argued that Xerox was really in the business of amplifying communications, he told Atari executives they were in the fantasy-amplification business—fantasy being nothing more than the process of building a convenient microworld, a world inside our heads that's smaller and more manageable than the world that really exists.

Kay's work at Atari was still far from fruition, but his accomplishments at PARC had already transformed him into a legendary figure, a sort of Buckminster Fuller of personal computing. Unfortunately, Macintosh already had its visionary; Kay was arriving a little late. In any event, he was far too outspoken to participate successfully in someone else's reality-distortion field. While visiting the engineering lab he exhibited a deflating tendency to say things like, "Oh, yeah, we did that at Xerox back in '76." Worse yet, his first official memo to his new boss was a critique of Macintosh entitled, "Have I Got a Deal for You: A Honda with a One-Quart Gas Tank"—a reference to Mac's solitary disk drive, which didn't allow you to store enough information to make it fast or convenient. Looks good in your driveway, the message was, but don't try to drive it across town. Steve was livid, Kay nonplussed. After all, he could have written *much* worse. Hondas were good cars. He drove one himself.

■ ■ ■

A couple of buildings away, in their third-floor offices in the Pink Palace, Sculley and Bill Campbell were piling on shelf space. Gene Carter was gone, his recommendation for a chain of Apple product centers rejected. Instead, Apple would go with the established chains, outfits like Businessland and ComputerLand and Sears. Businessland, with twenty-five stores stretching from Washington State to Texas, was the first to sign on. Analysts, well aware that most of Businessland's sales were in IBM machines and the rest in IBM-compatibles, hailed the move as a big boost for Apple's new "32-bit supermicro family." Then came Sears—not the department stores, though there'd been talks with them as well, but Sears Business Systems, a Sears-owned chain with sixty stores across the country and plans to open forty more. And finally, in July, they landed the biggest deal of all—with ComputerLand, the world's largest retail computer chain, a franchise operation with nearly seven hundred outlets in the United States and abroad.

There was a funny aspect to the ComputerLand deal, however.

Apple had been in ComputerLand for years, but in 1982 Carter had pulled out because too many of the stores weren't producing sales. As far as he was concerned, they just wanted to use the Apple line to sell against. The salesmen weren't good enough to figure out what the customer needed, so they'd take the path of least resistance, which was usually IBM. Carter considered ComputerLand part of the clutter. He'd continued to sell through hundreds of individual ComputerLand franchises, but he wouldn't have anything to do with the main office, across the Bay in Hayward. Months earlier John had asked him to add ComputerLand to the dealer base and he'd explained why he couldn't and John had seemed to agree with his point. But then John kept coming back every few weeks after that to find out when they could put them on. With Carter out of the way, the answer was now.

The addition of ComputerLand, Businessland, and Sears put Apple in some fifteen hundred stores. It seemed like a good move, but from Sculley's point of view it wasn't enough. The ferocity of the previous fall's shakeout seemed to suggest that the industry itself was in for a basic restructuring. The market for information-processing equipment, which just a few years before had been neatly segmented into mainframes for big business and big government, minicomputers for the scientific-research community, microcomputers for hobbyists and small-business people, and telecommunications equipment for everybody who had a phone, was blurring rapidly. Digital Equipment, the dominant manufacturer of minicomputers, was making personal computers as well. IBM, long dominant in mainframes, had pushed into minis and micros. AT&T, after decades as the telephone monopoly, had just been dismembered and was now trying to compete in computers and telecommunications simultaneously. Even the long-respected boundaries between products were disappearing with the advent of new machines like Digital's VAX line of "superminis," which offered the power of a mainframe at the price of a minicomputer. A whole new world was taking shape out there, and if Apple was to survive, it might well need to move beyond the "one person— one computer" philosophy that had been its guiding vision. The Macintosh Office was a step in that direction, but in John's view, what Apple needed was outside help.

Everybody was doing it. Strategic alliances were very much in vogue in the information industry, and suddenly they were going beyond simple joint ventures and licensing deals to include stock swaps and management involvement. Big companies were looking for a technology edge, small companies for management and marketing muscle and a little financial stability. IBM had acquired 20 percent of Intel, the Santa Clara chip manufacturer, which supplied the microprocessors for the IBM PC line. A few months later it bought 23 percent of Rolm, a fast-growing Santa Clara company that built electronic switchboards to handle voice and computer communications over the phone lines. AT&T bought a quarter-interest in Olivetti, the Italian office-equipment maker, with the idea that Olivetti would sell AT&T's products in Europe while AT&T sold Olivetti's in the States. Two years earlier, on January 8, 1982, the Justice Department had won its seven-year effort to break up AT&T and abandoned its thirteen-year suit against IBM. Now, with a post-antitrust era taking shape in Washington, AT&T and IBM seemed free to slug it out without fear of undue interference. Ultimately, industry observers agreed, the business would come down to little more than the two of them, along with a couple of Japanese giants, offering an across-the-board line of computer and communications equipment, with a much larger network of manufacturers supplying them. There was a limited pool of candidates, so the pressure was on to partner up soon.

John and Steve were talking deals with AT&T and with Wang. If Apple could join forces with either one of them, it could gain real credibility in the marketplace. Wang had a sales force that was skilled in dealing with corporate accounts and a line of office workstations that was built around the same Motorola 68000 microprocessor in Macintosh, raising the possibility of a joint effort to challenge the IBM standard in software. AT&T, newly shorn of its local operating companies and eager to compete in the brave new world of telecommunications, brought immense resources, vast technical expertise, and its own kind of prestige. This was a company that operated on a scale no one on Bandley Drive could even comprehend—thirty thousand engineers to the few hundred Apple employed. Obviously it was still staggering from the sudden, heady rush of deregulation; Steve considered it a stagnant giant, hopelessly mired in the mentality of monopoly. On the other hand, the deal it had struck with the Justice Department made it the only American behemoth in a position to take on IBM.

So they toured Bell Labs and met with executives in the "Death Star" building, an obsidian-glass office tower in the middle of a New

Jersey traffic interchange, where limousines bearing vice-presidents seemed to arrive in waves. High-ranking visitors came to Cupertino under various guises. Dinner was catered, sometimes in the board-room, sometimes in Matisse or Picasso. Murray showed off existing products; Jobs and Belleville showed off future products. In the early stages, neither party really knew what it was looking for. At the end of one such show-and-tell, Bob and Mike eyed their guest—a Texan by birth, kind of a backslapper, not cold and calculating like the well-tailored Eastern types—and realized as much. "Well," the AT&T executive asked, "what do you want to do?" Bob, sitting on the conference table in the middle of the room, patted the little Mac beside him and grinned. "That's what we got," he said. "Would you like some?"

■ ■ ■

John soon had other things to think about than trying to forge a strategic alliance. In the Triangle Building and on the third floor of the Pink Palace, panic was building over the IIc's performance in the stores. After a $14-million launch, it was dead in the water. They were hurling money at television, trying to use air time on the Olympics to burn it into the consciousness of America, but it had no effect. What people wanted, oddly enough, was the IIe—but they couldn't get it, because Apple couldn't meet the demand. All the marketing forecasts showed IIe sales dropping off, so Dallas had cut production. Now the market wasn't behaving according to their forecasts.

Dealers attributed the IIc's difficulties to a shortage of peripherals—monitors and external disk drives in particular. The IIc had been designed so you could hook it up to a television set, but most people who were willing to shell out $1,300 for a computer seemed to prefer the crispness of a monitor. TV sets were what you used with the cheap little home computers that Timex and Texas Instruments had lost millions on the year before. Unfortunately, the accessory-products division, which built monitors and disk drives and other peripherals at its factory outside Los Angeles, wasn't making good on its commitments. They were still scrambling to build keyboards and mice for Macintosh; there was no way they could meet their build schedules for the IIc as well. Besides, they'd never counted on the IIc actually making its scheduled announcement date. Why should they? No other Apple product had ever been announced on time.

Sculley and Jobs thought the problem was in the packaging. The bright red box with the picture of the woman holding the computer in her hand—that was what was keeping buyers away. The red box was frivolous. It created a lowered value perception. In soft drinks, perceived value is what you sell. In personal computers, perceived value meant differentiating yourself from the cheap home computers. The IIc needed a more businesslike package, they decided, one that would communicate more value. In the Triangle Building they called it "the Murine solution": Get the red out. Larson's marketing people ran intercept tests that showed the red box was quite effective in drawing consumers, but it still didn't square with the message Sculley was feeding the press—that the IIc wasn't a "home computer" at all but a computer "for the serious user in the home."

Del was embarrassed by the IIc's performance—not a feeling he found familiar or enjoyable. He'd been concerned for years about the way the II division had been drifting, and now he moved quickly to assert his control. He brought in people from Dallas, people from purchasing, people from materials. Within weeks the atmosphere was different. Everybody began to stake out his own little piece of territory. Before, if someone needed help you might jump in and do it. It was a communal effort, and the goal was to get the job done. Now you did your job, and other people did theirs. If you were successful, you won; and if they weren't, it was their problem. It was the antithesis of the freewheeling craziness that had always propelled the place, but Del liked to run a buttoned-down division.

Despite the screw-up on peripherals and the red-box controversy, Del named Dave Larson, the marketing guy behind the IIc, his marketing director for the entire division. But Peter Quinn, who'd been Larson's partner on the engineering side of the IIc, failed egregiously to fit the new mold. Quinn had a mouth. He'd been operating in a power vacuum for years, first on the IIe, then on the IIc. Now the vacuum had been filled. Del didn't want any more underground product development. Del wanted everything done by the book, and he wanted an engineering director who'd do it that way. He interviewed one candidate after another, without success. Finally Wayne Rosing, who'd been given a job developing computers for the education market after the Lisa takeover, went in for his monthly meeting with Sculley one day and was informed that he'd be taking over engineering in the II division. He started to protest; he was doing nicely with his education research group. But when Sculley remarked that they wouldn't be able to afford his research group if the II division wasn't making a profit, Rosing realized right away that he wasn't going to get to vote on the matter. So he moved into the Triangle Building, and Quinn fled the company a few weeks later.

The Apple II division had only one thing going for it that summer, and that was the PCjr. The Junior was in even worse shape than the IIc, and the press was so transfixed by its difficulties that Apple's troubles went virtually unnoticed. After so many extravagant predictions of runaway success, IBM's embarrassing sputter in the home market had the grisly appeal of an airplane crash. A Texas market-research outfit which in January had predicted sales of half a million Juniors the first year had trimmed that figure to 100,000 by May. At IBM's annual meeting at the Los Angeles Convention Center, chairman John Opel admitted that sales were disappointing and hinted that changes would be made soon. They'd have to be: In Silicon Valley, some stores were actually giving away a PCjr to anyone who bought an IBM PC.

PC sales weren't so great, either. In early June, the Dow Jones news wire reported that Ulric Weil, an influential computer analyst at Morgan Stanley, was saying the sales channels were "choking" on IBM personal computers. A few days later, amid a flurry of rumors, IBM announced price cuts. This gave Wall Street the jitters, since price cutting was what had started the debacle the year before in low-cost home computers. The prospect of a price war sent Apple stock on a slide at the end of the month. Michele Preston, the personal-computer analyst at L. F. Rothschild, Unterberg, Towbin, a Wall Street firm that specialized in high-tech stocks, took it off her "buy" list, observing that while the company was in fine shape, investors' fears were likely to drive the stock down still further. Other analysts followed. Fear and greed ruled the Street, and that summer it was mostly fear.

In any case, price cuts alone were not going to do the trick for Junior. Many observers felt that IBM had deliberately limited its usefulness to avoid undercutting sales of the PC itself. The team in Boca had indeed made some unwise trade-offs, chief among them the "elastomary" keyboard, which felt as crawly as it sounds, and the paltry 128K of memory, which wasn't enough to run Lotus 1-2-3 and the other programs that defined the IBM standard. These were the machine's basic problems, and not until the end of July were they corrected. By that time the momentum was clearly and inexorably against the little fellow. Redefine the home market, indeed: It was beginning to look as if IBM might be booted out of it.

The consensus in the industry was that IBM's moves were going to squeeze the clone makers much harder than they were Apple. That feeling intensified a couple of weeks later when IBM brought out the PC AT, a version of the PC that was more powerful than any yet available. Ironically, many of the features it was being touted for, such as on-screen windows and the ability to do several tasks at once, were ones Lisa had been offering for a year and a half. Yet by this time Lisa had ceased to be a factor in the office market. The industry was focused on IBM—on its success in the office, on its failure in the home. By August, despite two splashy new product introductions and millions of dollars worth of advertising, Apple might almost have ceased to exist.

■ ■ ■

By August, Apple's product and sales divisions were deep in planning for the October sales meeting. Hawaii in '83 had been successful beyond belief, and '84 had to surpass it. All summer Bill Campbell had been building his own sales force, replacing Gene Carter's network of manufacturers'-rep organizations with three hundred new employees. Human resources was running a "boot camp" in the Santa Cruz Mountains to train them in the Apple philosophy. Hawaii would be their final send-off, and an absolute blowout was on the boards. What they needed was a theme to pull it all together. A committee had come up with nine or ten concepts, and Campbell had cobbled two together to get one that emphasized the importance of the individual. But "Pride in Performance/You Make the Difference" was an all-too-conventional industrial sales slogan. It lacked the pizzazz of, say, "Leading the Way," which had had them dancing on the tabletops the year before. Steve wanted something with a little excitement. So one day he came roaring into a meeting with a new idea—"Bluebusters," after the summer's hit movie. If Dan Aykroyd and Bill Murray could strut around Manhattan exterminating poltergeists, why couldn't Apple do the same to IBM? They could write parody lyrics and dress up in *Ghostbusters*-type outfits and totally annihilate Big Blue.

It was such an outrageous concept that at first the sales-conference organizers just sat there with their mouths gaping, trying to take it in. As soon as they realized he was serious, they decided just to go for it, to let it all hang out, without even a thought about such mundane concerns as decorum or convention or good taste. Obviously they'd need a "Bluebusters" video. The first step was to license the song rights and rewrite the lyrics. Then they designed "Bluebusters" outfits—white jumpsuits with computer screens strapped to their backs and keyboards to their chests. They rented a soundstage in Culver City and built a Gozer Temple to destroy. And in the end they got the ultimate industrial comedy—a six-minute rock video that portrayed IBM as evil incarnate and showed Apple operatives hosing down store shelves to transform its boxes into theirs.

Mike Murray, not to be outdone, flew down to Hollywood as well and made a nine-minute, sepiatone movie of his own. His idea was to show why 1984 was like . . . 1944. Macintosh had taken the beachhead, and now it was time for the final assault. Intercut with World War II combat footage were camp scenes of a crack commando unit called "the Fighting 32nd." Murray starred as "the general," a diminutive figure with five stars on his shoulder and long curls sticking out from under his hat. Was it the curls that gave him such a tinhorn look, or was it the sunglasses and moustache? In any event, the high point was Jobs's cameo as FDR, placing a call to the field from his desk in the Oval Office as he flicked a cigarette holder in the air. "I am sure your victory will be great," he intoned. "*Insanely* great."

But what was the Apple II division to do? Sculley was worried that they'd look dull and, well, boring. They didn't have any new products to introduce, and Del certainly didn't seem to give off a lot of creative spark. It wouldn't be good if the new sales people went away so bowled over by Macintosh they forgot about the cash cow of the company. So Sculley wanted to throw in ideas, help them look creative, get them to do some wild stuff. He spent forty minutes brainstorming in his office with Dave Larson, but nothing came. Then, just as Larson was leaving, it occurred to him. He ran out to call Larson back. Macintosh was always taking potshots at the II group—why not fight back for a change? Why not dress people up as Mac Munchkins? They were all so short! You could hire midgets and dress one up as Steve and one up as Mike and get a real thing going. *That* would get everybody's attention.

13

Bluebusters

Ah, August in New York! Whose idea was it to hold a staff meeting there, anyway? When the heat transformed the city's rational, republican grid into a skittering concrete griddle, with garbage bags piled up in reeking heaps and everybody who could manage it lying prostrate at the beach? Yet there they'd been for days, Steve and the six of them—Jay Elliot, Debi Coleman, Mike Murray and his wife, and Bob Belleville and Steve's assistant, who were now living together. They'd seen *Cats, La Cage aux Folles, Sunday in the Park with George.* They'd toured the $2.5-million apartment Steve had bought in the San Remo—three stories of prime New York real estate at the top of an Italian Renaissance tower on Central Park West, with the park on one side and views of the Hudson on the other. Diane Keaton and Mary Tyler Moore lived downstairs; atop the matching tower at the other end of the building was Robert Stigwood, the Australian-born entertainment mogul behind Eric Clapton, the Bee Gees, and *Saturday Night Fever.* In 1930, when the San Remo was built, these glamorous tower apartments had made quite a contrast with the shanty-filled "Hooverville" springing up in the park below; now the park was looking spiffy, while Steve's apartment was just a rubble-filled shell undergoing an I. M. Pei renovation.

There'd been business to conduct as well. They'd met with a *Newsweek* team that was doing an article about fabulous young management. They'd met with Mitch Kapor, the founder of Lotus Development, and gotten a preview of Jazz, the Macintosh version of 1-2-3, now grown to include word processing and telecommunications in addition to its spreadsheet, business graphing, and data base functions. They'd had dinner with Jay Chiat at Café Luxembourg the night before. And now they'd taken a limo to Odéon, its sister restaurant downtown, a sleek art-deco café that drew its crowd from the neighboring worlds of art and finance.

Odéon was one of those late-night places, so common in New York, where the moneyed commingle with the hip and even the waiters have drop-dead hair. A beacon of light on a lonely street, it looked inside like a stage set for the young and the damned—Genet in a Hopper setting. Steve, feeling mischievous and perhaps a bit full of himself as he basked in its creamy neon glow, asked if anyone at the table wanted to stand up and ask the other patrons if they'd ever seen a Macintosh. That got a laugh. But it was a challenge, too, and how could they not take it up? In a few minutes Steve was pulling out money and urging them all to ante up. Soon they had a pile of cash on the table. They chose a spokesman, who stood up rather suddenly, cleared her throat, and started to speak.

She'd not gotten more than a dozen words out before the manager was at their table. "Please leave," he intoned. He was very polite, but the phalanx of waiters that materialized around them lent urgency to his words. Odéon had its reputation to think of. Who were these people? Why were they calling attention to themselves? What would the Eurotrash think? Did they care about this Macintosh? Certainly not. Within moments, Steve and his entire party were excised from the premises in an operation that had the precision elegance of an Israeli commando strike. They weren't even entirely aware of what was happening until they landed on West Broadway and the hot flush of August hit them full in the face. It was all horribly, grotesquely embarrassing. But the really awful thing was, no one had even answered their question. *Had* the diners in Odéon heard of Macintosh? Had anyone?

■ ■ ■

It wasn't long after their return to California that Debi Coleman began to sense something wrong. Macintosh wasn't moving. She could feel it. She'd had to shut down the factory for three weeks in August because the screens were coming in with spots on them, and everybody was saying the computer wasn't selling because it wasn't available, but she knew that wasn't the case. She talked to Roy Weaver, the vice-president in charge of distribution, who told her he sensed the same thing. It was selling to universities, but everywhere else it was dead.

They were about to introduce "Fat Mac," a Macintosh with four times as much internal memory as the original—512 kilobytes, enough to allow it to run sophisticated business software. That would take care of one criticism Macintosh was getting in the marketplace. Another complaint was the lack of a hard disk, which would allow users to store far more information than they could on the little Sony diskettes. Steve and Bob had decided to take care of that issue in June with TurboMac—a Macintosh with a built-in hard disk. TurboMac would address the limitation Alan Kay had so rudely pointed out—the problem of the one-quart gas tank. Burrell himself was designing it, having already gotten the laser printer ready for production.

Burrell was working in a corner of Bandley 2, across the street from Macintosh headquarters and right next door to the old Lisa building, which was now Macintosh territory as well. Since the merger, the Macintosh division had more or less taken over Bandley Drive. But Burrell and the handful of people who worked around him weren't trying to colonize, they were trying to escape. They'd staked out a little piece of the building and dubbed it TurboTown. They saw TurboTown as a place where genius-level, Woz-style engineering could flourish without bureaucratic interference. Just as Macintosh had been set up years earlier to recapture the back-to-the-garage mystique that had disappeared from Apple, TurboTown was an attempt to recapture the hobbyist spirit that now seemed endangered at Macintosh. Above all else it was a refuge from Belleville, who to Burrell and the core cultists represented the very personification of the big-organization approach to life. Burrell wasn't an engineer, he was an artist, and he was too temperamental to be managed. He needed to follow his own vision. He needed TurboTown.

But TurboMac had run into a problem. Burrell was trying to design for it a pair of custom chips that would do the work of several dozen off-the-shelf semiconductors, and in the process he'd gotten in over his head. One of the chips was under control, but the other was a mess. Burrell had always worked beyond the level of his capacity; that was the very essence of Woz-style engineering. But his strength was in laying out circuit boards, not designing the semiconductors that plugged into them, and with the custom chip for TurboMac he'd finally reached a level of complexity in which it was no longer possible to sit stoned and cross-legged in bed and intuit where the connections should go.

Because Bob and Burrell didn't really communicate, Bob had only the vaguest idea of the intensity of Burrell's dislike for him. He thought the work Burrell had done over the past five years was spectacular, but he was aware that Burrell was in trouble on the chip he was designing for TurboMac. And he knew that even if it did work, it wasn't going to address some of the other shortcomings that people were beginning to complain about. TurboMac wouldn't have a bigger screen. It wouldn't have internal slots that would allow you to plug in extra memory. And Mike Murray had convinced him that they should go to a modular approach, with the computer and the monitor in two separate boxes, like the Apple II and the IBM PC and most other personal computers. So he thought about TurboMac one morning and said to himself, Bob, this isn't going to work. He calculated that in the time it would take them to develop TurboMac, they could build a Macintosh that would have memory slots and a fifteen-inch screen that could display an entire page of text. So why shouldn't they do that instead?

When he brought it up, at an exec staff retreat at Pajaro Dunes, he used the analogy of the boa constrictor and the elephant. Apple was as incapable of developing two different Macintoshes as a boa constrictor was of digesting two elephants simultaneously, he said, so they might as well swallow the elephant that was going to do them the most good. Steve was against the idea; he thought the Macintosh with the hard disk was just what the public wanted. But later, in a hallway during a break, John came up to Bob and told him his idea wasn't so bad. They could develop the full-page machine just as easily and offer a hard disk as an option and give much more flexibility to the customer. Flexibility, after all, was what the market was saying it wanted. Together they argued the case, and that evening Steve finally saw their point. "That's what we'll do!" he cried. "It'll be great!"

Steve returned to Bandley Drive full of what Bob liked to think of as "Bellevillean zeal"—so full of it that he immediately set up a committee to define what the new product should be. A committee! The very word was enough to make the denizens of TurboTown cringe. The committee approach to doing things was exactly what they objected to most. A committee will always tear apart whatever is personal or idiosyncratic and replace it with an endless series of compromises. Each committee member needs to feel he's making a contribution, so each one will pick away at some little detail until everything that could make a product great has been eliminated. The wizards of TurboTown were the custodians of the Homebrew tradition; they couldn't be subjected to the whims of a committee. And to learn that TurboMac was being canceled in favor of some product a committee would define—it was unthinkable, and yet it had happened. Bob had just nuked TurboTown.

Burrell, never much of a communicator, fell inchoate in his rage and defeat. He was almost physically incapable of speaking to Steve; so Andy, who was just coming back from his leave of absence, spoke for him. Andy saw Burrell as the one person who needed above all to be shielded from the committee, the person the committee would most like to attack and destroy—and yet Steve was just throwing him to the wolves. So he told Steve how incredibly screwed up things were, how he ought to get rid of this Belleville guy and start a little group again, just him and Burrell and a handful of others, so they could get away from these awful managers who were trying to ruin everything. It was time they built the *next* insanely great computer. They shouldn't be making incremental changes on Macintosh, they should be designing a computer that was as much an improvement over Macintosh as Macintosh was over the Apple II.

But Steve was no longer so interested in going back to the garage. Why should he be, now that he could go to parties like the one Yoko Ono had just given for her son Sean in New York? It was Sean's ninth birthday: Andy Warhol was there with his Instamatic, snapping photos of everybody; Keith Haring, the hot young graffiti artist, brought a painting of the number 9. Steve's present was a Macintosh. Oblivious to the crowd, he and Sean retreated to a corner of the vast and starkly beautiful apartment in the Dakota, just down Central Park West from the San Remo, and set up the computer on the floor in Sean's room. Sean was fascinated, and Steve was thrilled with his response. After a while Andy wandered in, and as Steve showed him how to use MacPaint he shed his blank demeanor long enough to utter a brief exclamation of delight—a singular event indeed.

No, Steve had moved well beyond the garage. He and John had a Fortune 500 corporation to run, and the pressures of this bicoastal business and social life were such that the balancing act he'd managed for so long between Bob and Andy—between the ARPA dream and the hacker ethic—was too much to sustain. So he simply told Andy that things were better than they'd ever been. Andy was stunned. Better than they'd ever been, when engineering wasn't doing a thing because all these people were running off on their own little power trips? He couldn't believe what he was hearing.

So Andy took the only course he had left: He went to Sculley. In desperation he poured out his story. As final proof of the dire state that affairs had reached, he announced that Burrell Smith, the genius who'd created Macintosh, was about to quit the company. Sculley listened and gave no response.

■ ■ ■

Even as engineering was flying apart, marketing was shifting into hyperdrive. For the third straight year, Apple would have a dramatic new product announcement to make at its January meeting—not a computer this time but an entire suite of office accessories for Macintosh. The laser printer. The file server. The network. Jazz, forthcoming from Lotus Development. Mike Murray had opted out, but the people he'd put in charge thought these products would transform Macintosh into a complete office system. They'd introduce American business to the idea of "work-group computing"—small groups of people working together and exchanging information electronically. In two years they'd make Apple the equal of IBM in the business market for personal computers.

"Work-group computing," like "Lisa technology," had actually been invented in the seventies at PARC. There, in the research labs that Xerox had built into Stanford's golden hills, the heirs of the ARPA dream had created the Ethernet—the first local-area network, developed in tandem with Alan Kay's Smalltalk—and the Alto, the prototype of the personal computer of the future. When Xerox had brought the Ethernet to market, at a time when personal computers had barely begun to appear in corporate offices, the concept was too rarefied and the cost too great to have much appeal. But it grew more and more compelling as personal computers proliferated, and by the fall of 1984 such networks were being offered by a variety of technology companies, including Digital Equipment, Wang, and 3Com, a Silicon Valley start-up whose founder had headed the Ethernet team at PARC.

In May, IBM had announced the most grandiose network of all, one that would link its mainframes, minicomputers, and personal computers in a single powerful system. On closer inspection, however, IBM's announcement came to nothing more than a statement of what it intended to build. Delivery was promised in two to three years. The only thing you could buy now was the IBM Cabling System—the physical link the network would someday use. "I didn't realize IBM was in the copper business," quipped a Wang product manager in *The Wall Street Journal*.

Shortly afterwards, IBM did ship a much less powerful network—smaller, slower—designed to link only its personal computers. Machines in IBM's "PC Clusters" could transmit memos back and forth to each other via "electronic mail" and share files stored on a hard disk in one of the computers in the cluster—a file server, in effect. The cost of a PC Cluster "five-pack," which would connect four PCs and one PC XT with a hard disk, was more than $2,500. The marketplace was not overjoyed, because corporate users expected high-speed performance, while smaller users—lawyers, doctors, other professionals—could already buy comparable networks from companies like 3Com.

The product introduction plan for the Macintosh Office—an inch-thick blueprint for "implementing the vision," as Steve and his aides liked to say in staff meetings—began by contrasting Apple's people-centered world view with IBM's. In high-flying language it outlined the difference between a world run by people and a world run by corporations. The vision itself was to improve the productivity of small work groups, whether in two-person firms or in Fortune 500 corporations, by improving the efficiency of their communications—a remarkable goal, given the state of affairs on Bandley Drive. Marketing interpreted this to mean products that would offer electronic mail, shared data storage, and the ability to communicate with IBM mainframes. But that kind of talk made Bob crazy. It was like promising the equivalent of twenty years of IBM engineering, deliverable on January 20. He told them they'd get wiped out, because people would see they were offering things they didn't have. He wanted a staged approach—one step at a time.

The little computer network he was hoping to have ready by January was considerably less impressive than the IBM Cluster, although at a connection charge of only $50 per machine it would also cost one-tenth as much. It was a low-speed network that would do nothing more initially than enable several Macintoshes to share a single laser printer. Software that would allow people to share files or send memos via electronic mail would come later. So would the file server, the hard-disk device that would act as the central file-storage facility. The question was, how much later? As far as Mike could tell, the file server was lost in space. Prototypes weren't available. Completion dates kept slipping away. No one seemed accountable. And yet whenever the subject came up in engineering meetings, the response was that they'd build one as soon as marketing told them what they wanted.

The problem was that no two people could agree on what a file server was supposed to be. What Bob had in mind was simply a hard disk that could store files for three or four people on different computers. Anything more complicated than that would bring up a whole raft of issues that nobody at Apple outside engineering understood. With twenty or thirty people linked together on a network, who decides if they're allowed to read each other's files? What happens if one of them tries to alter someone else's file? What happens if two or three people try to work on the same file at the same time? What happens when the disk runs out of space? Who makes backup copies in case something goes wrong? In engineering these were known as the "sociological issues," because in order to deal with them the engineers would need a clear picture of the sociology of the group using the network. Then they could establish what amounted to a whole system of government for the network, which could be anything from a rigid hierarchy to a near-total democracy.

Normally engineering would take its cues from marketing on something like this, but the Macintosh marketing people couldn't give any direction here because they weren't aware of the implications. Engineering—Bob Belleville and the new software manager, Bud Tribble—hoped to sidestep the sociological issues by targeting the office system at groups of three or four people who could decide among themselves who would have access to what. That way they could avoid situations like having to network General Motors, where you'd have to keep low-level employees out of their bosses' files and build special safeguards around the finance department's files and design elaborate password systems so the people who needed the information could get it. And yet, with Mike Murray having removed himself from the picture, they didn't seem able to communicate any of this to the marketing people who were handling the Mac Office introduction.

Even if he'd been willing to get involved, Mike had more immediate problems. By early September it was apparent to everyone that sales were a fraction of what they'd predicted. He needed a quick fix, not something he could announce in January. The only possibility on hand was a special marketing blitz called "Test Drive a Macintosh" that they could have ready to kick in at the beginning of November, seven weeks before Christmas. "Test Drive" was a $12-million campaign with a gimmick: Drop by a computer store and take Macintosh home for a spin. As long as you had a major credit card, you could sign one out overnight for free and discover for yourself how easy it was to use. The week after it broke, a special election-week edition of *Newsweek* would hit the stands with forty pages of Macintosh advertising inside, culminating in a pitch for "Test Drive." Everybody in Bandley 3 was excited. They all loved the machine, and they knew that if people could just take one home and *touch* it, they'd never be able to return it to the store. Mike himself wasn't sure, but he went along.

With or without "Test Drive," Mike had a heavy forecasting problem on his hands. Even as sales for the month of August were slipping below 15,000, marketing and finance were putting the final touches on a business plan based on projected sales of 80,000 a month in the fiscal year that would begin in October. When these figures got to the Pink Palace and the corporate sales and finance organizations added them to the Apple II division's projections, Apple came out with projected sales in 1985 of $3 billion—double its totals for the year just ending. This hardly seemed credible, even on Bandley Drive, so representatives from the two product divisions held endless meetings with the heads of sales and finance to reach a consensus. It wasn't easy, because Steve considered it important that the Macintosh division contribute just as much revenue—and have just as much power—as the Apple II division. Finally, after weeks of negotiations, they all agreed to constrain the two divisions' projections to $1 billion each. But they also agreed that Christmas—always Apple's best season—might be tremendous this year, and that they should be ready to take advantage of demand should it surge out of control.

And so a go-for-it strategy was devised. Even though the company would base its operations on sales of 50,000 Macs a month, it would go through with plans to expand the factory's capacity to 80,000. And it would run manufacturing full-tilt all fall on the chance that Christmas might be a $1-billion quarter. Apple had more than $150 million in cash on hand, at least two-thirds of which would have to be spent building up inventory. All the factories—Dallas, Singapore, Fremont, Ireland—would have to run flat out, double and triple shifts, building every product they had. It would be an expensive gamble, and Joe Graziano, the chief financial officer, wondered out loud why they had to take it. Wouldn't a $600-million quarter be enough? Did the company have to hang its ass out over the ragged edge all the time? But they presented it to the board at its September meeting, and though Phil Schlein—the board member from Macy's—expressed the same reservations Graziano had, the plan was approved with Markkula's support. They were going to take the risk. There was a Gold Rush on, and the ethic of the Valley prevailed.

■ ■ ■

The announcement of Fat Mac a few days after the board meeting meant that finally you could buy a Macintosh with enough memory to run programs as powerful as Lotus 1-2-3. But the programs themselves weren't available, because neither Lotus nor Microsoft had delivered the software they'd been promising. All the same, the new machine was positioned squarely against the IBM PC. Apple was going to "duke it out" with IBM, Mike Murray told *The Wall Street Journal*. Yet a study by a market-research firm showed that of all the Macs sold in April, only 12 percent had been purchased by corporations in the Fortune 2000. Most had gone to small business people, professionals, and those hard-to-define "home users."

Clearly it would take more than raw memory to overcome corporate resistance to Macintosh. Software was an obvious lack, but beyond that lay a cornucopia of complaints. A professional industry watcher at Arthur D. Little in Cambridge thought one of the biggest problems was the comfort people felt buying from IBM. Across the river in Boston, a pundit at the Yankee Group lamented the lack of any kind of networking capabilities. At Future Computing outside Dallas, they were complaining about the lack of a hard disk. What the market needed was some kind of signal, some indication that management had a plan.

Two days after the Fat Mac announcement, Jobs was scheduled to speak at an investors conference sponsored by Montgomery Securities in San Francisco. Analysts from about six hundred major institutional investors would be there, each one worth a few hundred million dollars in the portfolio of this pension fund or that bank. Business reporters would be on hand, as would senior representatives from each of the other 111 companies present, a list that included Coca-Cola, Lockheed, IBM, Lotus Development, and Toys "Я" Us. Sculley when making such a presentation would have been rehearsing it for days, trying out lines on his vice-presidents, working his assistant overtime typing up drafts. He would have stayed home the night before and turned in early. All Jobs had to do was turn on the field.

The limousine showed up at his house in Los Gatos an hour before he was due at the Mark Hopkins Hotel, which was at least an hour's drive away, more if there was traffic. But Steve wasn't home. Joe Graziano, who as chief financial officer would be making a presentation as well, sat in back and fidgeted with his watch. Finally Steve roared up the driveway, dashed into the house and then out again, and scrambled into the waiting car with his coat and tie in one hand and his socks and shoes in the other. The car whooshed down the hill and was already on the freeway before he'd finished dressing. All the way to the city he complained about how lousy he felt—just flew in from Texas, not enough sleep, really tired. Fifty nerve-wracking minutes later, with the limo stuck in traffic halfway up Nob Hill, he turned to Graziano and said, "Now, what am I supposed to talk about at this thing?"

Jobs gave a brilliant speech that day, totally off-the-cuff but with perfect timing, in which he described the network Apple would soon introduce as cheaper than IBM's and easier to install than a stereo. But he could afford to be casual about public speaking; he didn't feel so confident about other areas. His job now was to deliver profits. It wasn't something he'd ever had to do before, and as sales dropped he was beginning to panic. He was feeling the heat. He had to perform. He had to measure up to John's expectations of him.

This was causing the air to crackle around him. Murray and Belleville, Coleman and Barnes—all caught the heat. But it wasn't Steve's style to dwell on his own organization's shortcomings when outsiders might be responsible. His inclination was to lash out, to spread the blame around. And now he had a plausible rationale for doing so, because as a division manager he was being held accountable for a bottom line that included expenses he couldn't control. How could he be judged on his own performance when so much depended on factors beyond his authority—sales and distribution, for example? A couple of weeks earlier, when Roy Weaver had presented the distribution organization's business plan to the exec staff, Steve had gone on the attack. Why, he demanded to know, did the cost of distribution come to 3 percent of sales? Why wasn't it 2 percent, or one and a half?

Fate, in the form of Memphis millionaire Fred Smith, was about to offer him an answer.

In the annals of entrepreneurship, the name Fred Smith looms large. Though not as famous as Wozniak and Jobs, among the cognoscenti—venture capitalists, Wall Street analysts, other entrepreneurs—he was celebrated beyond words. He was the John Wayne of modern business, the ur-hero of the unwritten Ayn Rand story, the model for all who'd followed. As founder and chairman of Federal Express, he'd not only created a $4-billion industry from scratch; he'd also led his company to phenomenal success through obstacles that would have destroyed an ordinary man. So when he came to Cupertino to speak at an Apple "leadership forum," a seminar sponsored by human resources to offer inspiration to Apple executives, it was only natural that he and Steve would have dinner together the night before.

Like many entrepreneurs, Smith was a product of the sixties—a Yale economics major whose dad had founded a Memphis bus company. After school he landed a commission in the Marines. He was much decorated in Vietnam, where he served first as a platoon leader and then as a company commander and finally flying ground-support missions. Afterwards, working for his stepfather's aircraft-repair business in Little Rock, he resurrected an idea he'd had in college. He'd written a term paper one night in which he'd laid out the concept of an express delivery service that would fly letters and packages from any city in the United States to any other city overnight. Unlike other delivery services, the company he envisioned would maintain its own fleet of planes. They'd fly in the dead of night, when airports are all but deserted, and to save time and money they'd all fly in to a central location and then fly back out to their destinations. The paper got only a C, and Smith, an indifferent student, counted himself lucky to do that well. But a few years later, frustrated at his inability to get quick delivery of aircraft parts in Little Rock, he decided his term paper idea hadn't been so bad after all.

Smith was not innocent of the transportation business. His grandfather was a Mississippi riverboat captain; his father was known as "the Bus King of the South." But aside from the lack of any proven market, his idea had one major problem: You had to have everything ready to go—planes, trucks, people—before you delivered your first package. Smith put down $4 million of his inheritance and raised $72 million more from such institutions as Citibank, Chase Manhattan, and New Court Securities, the investment arm of the Rothschild banking family. He opened for business in the spring of 1973, delivering eighteen packages the first night. Then the Yom Kippur War broke out in the Middle East; within weeks the Arab oil embargo was on, and by the end of the year the price of oil had shot from $3 a barrel to $12. Federal Express was as energy-intensive as it was capital-intensive. Soon it was losing $1 million a month.

Smith had to raise money fast. Things were so desperate that his pilots were helping to sort packages and paying for fuel with their own credit cards; meanwhile, his sisters were suing him for misinvesting the family fortune. Finally, unable to meet his payroll, he found himself stuck at O'Hare Airport after getting the turn-down from some Chicago investors. There was nothing better to do, so he decided to hop a plane to Vegas and try his hand at blackjack. By the end of the night he'd parlayed the few hundred bucks in his wallet into $27,000. He went on to raise another $11 million from investors, and though the company lost $29 million before it turned the corner, by 1984 it had grown into a billion-dollar business. His personal stake was worth some $200 million, and he was still running the show at age forty.

Under different circumstances, Jobs and Smith might have seemed unlikely dinner companions—the visionary dropout and the flying leatherneck. Smith bore himself like a general, and it was hard not to notice that everywhere he went, a squadron of lieutenants followed. But vast personal wealth and the entrepreneurial mystique can form a powerful bond; to Steve, long schooled in the Fred Smith myth, the man across from him was almost a father figure. Besides, Smith hadn't become the air-express king of the nation for nothing. He treated dinner that night as an opportunity to make a sales call on a potentially very important customer. He told Steve he ought to see what his competitors were doing, and as he did so he pulled out photographs of IBM PCs pouring out of a factory in Boca. Federal Express, he said, moves out every one of those units. Yeah, Steve said, but you're expensive. No, we're not, Smith replied; we're probably cheaper than your own distribution channel.

Since Steve was already upset about the cost of Apple's distribution system, he was a more receptive than he might have been to Smith's sales pitch. In fact, he was more than just receptive; he was seized with the brilliance of the idea. The way Smith put it, Federal Express offered distribution for the electronic age—fast air delivery, backed by computerized tracking of every item. Suddenly Steve envisioned a landing strip right alongside the factory in Fremont; he saw 747s full of Macs taking off every day. No need for warehouses all over the country or for any of the people who worked in them. No need to worry about inventory buildup in the distribution channels, either; all you had to do was look in a corner of the factory and see how many Macs were stacked up there. It was just-in-time distribution. He could hardly wait for dinner to be over so he could get home and phone people with the news.

■ ■ ■

The Hilton Hawaiian Village was a pretty crazy place. Imagine all the magic of the islands crowded into twenty acres of palm-shaded paradise and sprayed with see-through plastic coating. Imagine thousands of fun-seeking vacationers and slaphappy conventioneers roaming the halls of three high-rise slabs, wearing colorful Hawaiian shirts and fresh-flower leis. Imagine all the fun and exciting things to do: sipping piña coladas by the peaceful tropical lagoon . . . pupus at poolside . . . sun-filled afternoons on the largest beach in Waikiki . . . luxurious catamaran cruises to historic Pearl Harbor . . . the enchantment of hula dancing . . . lei-making classes . . . palm-frond-hat-weaving classes . . . shopping centers . . . island entertainer Don Ho and his Polynesian extravaganza. . . . The list was endless, and yet somehow it all ended up seeming just like Miami Beach.

As always, however, Apple created its own reality. In later years, Hawaii '84 would be remembered as the video battleground, the slickest and most lavish Apple sales conference ever, the one in which the company girded for battle with IBM, not with carefully thought-out sales and marketing and product strategies but with lasers and dancers and smoke and mirrors. They were Bluebusters every one, and just to show what great and amazing Bluebusters they were, they began the opening session, which was being held in one of the hotel's two enormous ballrooms, with a demonstration of what would happen if an IBMer were to wander onstage by mistake.

So at 8:30 Monday morning, with the ballroom full of Apple convention-goers in T-shirts and shorts and leis, a prissy little man in a three-piece suit came out and introduced himself as Frank

Splotto, sales administrator for the Northwest Quadrant. He had a fringe of hair around his head and large square glasses on his face and a look that said he might give you an F for penmanship. "We at the corporation have put a lot of work into this morning's agenda," he announced. "We trust you'll find it useful, instructional, informative, educational, helpful, and beneficial. But first, let me say a few words about your responsibilities to the corporation."

Boos and catcalls were already rolling in from the audience. Before Mr. Splotto could go on, Bill Campbell broke in on the mike from backstage. "Excuse me," his disembodied voice cried at the figure onstage. "Excuse me! What the hell do you think you're doing?"

Mr. Splotto looked confused. "Aren't you guys from IBM?" he asked. Loudly, rudely, he was told they weren't. "What company are you from?" Oh, Apple. "How do *you* start?"

"Like *this*," Campbell cried, sounding like the voice of God addressing the wimpiest guy in gym class. "I'm Bill Campbell! Good morning! *Let's get fired up!*"

"Let's get fired up!": that was Bill's signature cry, the one he let loose whenever the occasion demanded a little extra excitement. He didn't have to say it again. In a flash they were screening "Bluebusters," which after that intro was like throwing a hand grenade. Suddenly there were blue-clad androids onscreen filling store shelves with big boxes marked "IBM," only to be chased away by guys with computers on their backs as the loudspeakers pumped out the "Bluebusters" theme song:

> When the big machine
> Wants to take control
> Who ya gonna call?
> Bluebusters!

Then the Bluebusters dancers came marching down the aisles, each one wearing an identical blue suit, rep tie, blue fedora, and glossy ceramic mask. They swung their leather briefcases high and did a syncopated strut, prancing forward with a swagger in an elaborate parody of corporate self-importance. They were doing a cakewalk, the same kind of dance that slaves had done in the Deep South when they wanted to make fun of their plantation masters' fancy ballroom manners, only this high-stepping Bluebuster strut was a jab at the whole stiff-necked, buttoned-down, tight-assed IBM approach to life. As Campbell put it, *Let's get fired up!*

They stayed fired up for hours, through introductions and speeches and skits and lunch and more videos and product presentations, through everything Apple could throw at them. And then, finally, midway into the afternoon, they got Chiat/Day's sixty-second show-stopper for the Super Bowl. Lee Clow and the creative team had been under a lot of pressure to outdo themselves this year, and it showed. This was a spot with all of the cinematic sweep of "1984" and none of the heart. As a pitch for a suite of office products, however, it was truly remarkable. It showed a line of dressed-for-success business people wearing blindfolds and singing a dirge as they trudged lemming-like off a cliff. "Heigh-ho, heigh-ho," they chanted as, one after another, they plunged into space—all except the last, who pulled off his blindfold just as he was about to step over the edge.

The basic idea hadn't originated with Apple at all. It was something Chiat/Day had come up with for General Electric several years earlier, when GE was moving into factory automation—in other words, robotics. Maybe scare tactics were in order, they'd thought. How about suggesting that if computers weren't brought into the production line, American business (represented by men in Brooks Brothers suits) might as well dive off a cliff? It was certainly a good time to make the case. Chrysler was in the toilet; the industrial heartland had turned into the Rust Belt; steel mills were reopening as discotheques, if they reopened at all. But GE had opted instead for a spot that showed Uncle Sam being slapped in the face, and the "Lemmings" concept had lain forgotten in the hopper until after the Macintosh introduction.

Then Steve Hayden, the copywriter on the Apple account, had revived it for the suite of office products Apple was developing for Macintosh. Lee had flipped. As much as anyone on Bandley Drive, he felt a personal and emotional commitment to Macintosh. He'd had something approaching a religious experience when the first Mac had arrived at Chiat/Day and he'd realized it was a computer he could actually use—just the kind of reaction the ARPA folks had dreamed of in the sixties, as they probed the frontier of human/computer symbiosis and experienced their own religious conversions. So when Lee said "the computer for the rest of us," he meant for himself. The Macintosh Office he saw as simply "the computer for the rest of us" in business—the vision extended. It was the business solution for the Apple generation. It wouldn't sell to traditional corporate computer purchasers—the data-processing bureaucracy—but to creative people who saw Macintosh as a tool that could help make them more creative. "Lemmings" declared Macintosh as the alternative to IBM in the business world. It said to the viewer, "You can go on buying IBM like a lemming, or you can be creative and break away."

The enthusiasm on Bandley Drive was more muted. Mike Murray thought it was a downer. Susan Barnes hated it—what would her friends at Arthur Andersen think? Only Belleville was a real fan, because, like Lee, he believed what it said: If IBM won the personal-computer wars, he was predicting a dark age. Apple was willing to take technological risks; IBM wanted to take cash out of the environment. They did cut out the vultures at the bottom of the cliff, and then they'd decided to try it out at the sales conference. But when they played it that afternoon at the Tapa Ballroom of the Hilton Hawaiian Village, the deflation was palpable. They'd been getting these people fired up since 8:30 in the morning, pumping them full of hot air, and in sixty seconds "Lemmings" let a lot of it fizz away. There were those who liked it, but others came up afterwards and said, "Are you really going to show that on TV?"

But even with "Lemmings," it was a knockout meeting. The signs were good. Sales for the year were up dramatically, despite the summer slump. All that new shelf space promised big things for the future. The new sales force was wowed by all the razzle-dazzle. Even the two reporters who were allowed inside to cover it, one from *Business Week* and one from *The Wall Street Journal*, came away favorably impressed—but, of course, their view was carefully limited. Most sessions were off-limits, and everywhere they went there was a Regette at their side. They were accompanied on interviews. They were followed to the pool. They were followed to the beach. At a cocktail reception, when Bill Gates of Microsoft asked the woman from *Business Week* to dance, she turned to her Regette and said, "Would you like to dance with us?"

In any event, the elaborate product demonstrations they were barred from were little more than a sham. The network, the file server—what seemed to be functioning onstage was in fact running on jury-rigged software that had been set up for the show. There was nothing behind it, only hope and wishful thinking. The real action at the Hilton Hawaiian Village that October was neither at cocktail receptions nor at fake product sessions but in small conference rooms and private suites. No more than a dozen people witnessed it, but the tensions from the summer sales scare were making themselves felt. Susan Barnes and Debi Coleman got into a scrap in Sculley's suite. Jobs lit into Campbell, furious because sales weren't what they should be, furious because he was being stalled on the distribution issue, furious because so many of the new salesmen he was meeting were bozos.

The reason Macintosh wasn't more profitable, Jobs was convinced, was that the company—sales and distribution in particular—wasn't supporting it. Take distribution. He'd gone to Sculley with his vision of 747s loading up computers at the factory gates, but other people were trying to block him on it—particularly Bill Campbell, whose bailiwick had recently been expanded to include the distribution network that was already in place. Jobs wanted to fire all those people and close down their warehouses and go with Federal Express right away. Campbell was angry about it, and Sculley was hedging. He wanted to appoint somebody to study it. Jobs saw no need for study. At Apple, a study was something you gave a vice-president to do to get him out the door. And while *they* were studying it, *he* was being held accountable for his product's profitability—even though there was a major chunk of the pipeline he didn't control.

And so he was beginning to question Sculley's performance. He was beginning to wonder why the CEO he'd picked wasn't providing the leadership he needed. The public image the two men projected would be perfectly captured by *Business Week*, which hailed them on its cover a few weeks later as "Apple's Dynamic Duo." Yet even as they rode together in the limousine at dawn, chatting amiably with the reporter as they headed toward Diamond Head for the photo shoot, the undercurrent was sweeping them apart.

14

The Steve and John Show

While Steve and John were posing for candids in front of Diamond Head, Wall Street was buzzing with rumors that Sculley would soon be leaving—returning to PepsiCo, perhaps as chairman. He and Steve had dodged the issue all week in Hawaii. But back in Cupertino, on the Monday after the sales conference, he mounted a podium in a parking lot filled with several thousand Apple employees and denied it outright. He'd come out there that day to announce a profit-sharing plan—a bonus of three-and-a-half percent of each employee's fourth-quarter earnings. The bonanza days were clearly over: Previous bonuses had gone as high as 30 percent, and this was the first profit-sharing of any kind since the Lisa debacle. But the most significant thing he had to say wasn't about money, it was about those rumors.

The Valley seemed particularly golden that day, a flat, suburban, technological paradise neatly paved and ringed with mountains; the faint autumn chill in the air made for a tingling contrast with the heat of the afternoon sun. With his jogger's physique and his open collar and his boyishly tousled hair, John looked very much at home. Standing in the back of a truck, he faced an homogeneous sea of humanity—casual, easygoing, free-spirited, and young—that seemed but a reflection of the image he himself now projected. "I love Apple," he declared. "I'll never leave. I'm having a ball working with Steve Jobs. Why in the world would I want to leave Apple?"

And the funny thing was, it was true. He *was* having a ball. Despite Steve's growing frustration with the way the rest of the company was run, and John's own mounting irritation at the way Steve yelled at him in meetings, and the tension that was beginning to build between them, they were having the time of their lives together. And why not? They had a major corporation to run. They were a dynamic duo. They could get together on weekends and make changes on a whim and spring them on the exec staff as *faits accomplis*. They could tinker with the price structure. They could rework all the marketing programs. The honeymoon was actually intensifying, and the rest of the exec staff couldn't believe it. They called it "the Steve and John show" and clucked and shook their heads.

But the most alarming aspect of the Steve and John show wasn't the sudden policy shifts or Steve's increasingly common outbursts, it was the secret talks the two were conducting with far bigger corporations about buying into the company. Apple had come out of fiscal 1984 a $1.5-billion corporation, half again as large as the year before. It was the third-largest enterprise in the Valley, after Hewlett-Packard and National Semiconductor. But it was growing only because the market was growing; its share of the market was continuing to shrink, despite an ad budget so swollen that profits went down while sales went up. Analysts were calling 1984 a "survival year," and with two-thirds of the personal computers sold now going into a business world totally dominated by IBM, some wondered if 1985 would offer even that much. Everyone—analysts, pundits, Steve and John—agreed that for Apple to flourish, it would have to challenge IBM successfully in business. And no one believed it could do that alone.

Some still argued that Apple ought to go the IBM-compatible route. As it happened, Ben Rosen, the former Morgan Stanley analyst turned industry prophet turned venture capitalist, had recently called to see if Apple had any interest in Compaq. Buttoned-down but very spunky, this little Houston outfit was making a name for itself among corporate customers with its IBM-compatible portable computer, which was both cheaper and more versatile than anything IBM could offer. Rod Canion, its president, was a former Texas Instruments engineer who'd sketched out a business plan with his partners on the back of a diner placemat. In 1983, its first year of sales, Compaq had grossed a remarkable $111 million. But profits were low and margins were slim, and with IBM cutting prices, even analysts were having second thoughts about the advisability of riding its coattails. Compaq seemed in for a tough time.

Rosen, who was the chairman of Compaq's board and whose

venture partnership, Sevin-Rosen Management, was a principle investor, was calling at Floyd Kvamme's suggestion. Kvamme, now ensconced in the Palo Alto office of Kleiner Perkins—the San Francisco venture firm, also a major investor in Compaq—recalled that Apple had never entirely rejected the idea of an IBM-compatible computer. With Compaq's stock trading at around $3.50 a share, the company could have been bought for not much more than $100 million, which was about the amount of cash Apple was furiously transforming into inventory in anticipation of a runaway Christmas. Sculley was due in Europe soon for an investor-relations tour, a whirlwind series of breakfast, lunch, and dinner meetings with important European analysts. Rosen was going to London. While he was there, it would be a simple matter for Sculley to fly in and talk it over with him.

But nothing came of the Compaq discussions; Steve was still adamant against the idea of going into the IBM-compatible business, and at this point the market seemed to be proving him right. In any case, he and John had far bigger deals in the works. Discussions were still going on with AT&T and with Wang. General Motors and General Electric had come into the picture as well. And their thinking had progressed far beyond a simple partnership that would give them credibility in the business market. Now they were talking about selling a quarter of the company to some giant corporation and using the money to finance a truly major acquisition—Xerox, for instance.

Their motivations were not hard to fathom. Sculley was leading them in a game of "brute-force marketing"—a high-stakes contest in which failure would be tantamount to oblivion, for in a two-horse race, as he liked to say, no one remembers number three. They needed critical mass to win. They were in a desperate race to reach the size and the stature necessary to go up against IBM. There were two ways to get it: They could grow it, which could take years, maybe decades; or they could do a deal. With a billion-dollar Christmas quarter in the offing, this looked like the time for a deal.

An agreement with General Electric was already in the works, a simple, straightforward deal that would add Macintosh to the line of computer products carried by GEISCo, a GE subsidiary that sold equipment from Wang and IBM and other manufacturers to major corporations. That would be a nice little boost for the Macintosh Office. But discussions were also being held at a much higher level about the possibility of marrying Macintosh with the engineering workstations built by Calma, the young Silicon Valley company which GE had recently bought.

If Apple wanted a partner, GE was a natural place to look. A $27-billion conglomerate that built everything from toasters to turbines, from jet engines to light bulbs, it was a high-technology powerhouse on the Westchester-Fairfield corporate axis, alongside PepsiCo, IBM, and Xerox. The company was headed by John F. "Neutron Jack" Welch, a chemical engineer who'd gotten his nickname because taking him on a plant tour was like getting hit by a neutron bomb—the building would still be there at the end, but everybody in it would be dead. Welch had done more than two hundred deals in his three years as chairman, selling off subsidiaries that weren't pulling their weight, buying up other businesses that could, but the divestitures so outweighed the acquisitions that now he had something like $5 billion in cash. With that kind of money he could have bought Apple three times over. Over the next few months, Steve and John met repeatedly with him and with the team of execs he sent out to look them over. They toured factories, touted the company, expounded the vision, talked deals. Bob and Debi were brought in to talk up Apple's technology and manufacturing. Del and Bill heard about it mainly through the rumor mill.

General Motors was another possibility, a $75-billion auto giant, a company so big its sales dwarfed even IBM's. Its chairman, Roger Smith, was a colorless accountant who'd turned suddenly and unaccountably visionary upon taking control three years earlier. Faced with imminent extinction, he'd decided to go the high-tech route, simultaneously automating factories, campaigning against bureaucratic inertia, trying to get better cars, and transforming the company from a car maker to a diversified technology enterprise. Already he'd started a joint venture with a Japanese robot maker, bought a stake in a Palo Alto artificial-intelligence firm, and paid $2.5 billion for Electronic Data Systems, the Dallas data-processing concern. EDS was supposed to straighten out GM's hopeless tangle of data-processing operations—a mammoth task that entailed designing software to run everything from computer networks to automatic parts-ordering systems. In the past, EDS had automated entire industries—banking, insurance, the U.S. Army. Now it was going to take on its new owner. And maybe, the thinking went, it could use Macintosh as the standard terminal for accessing GM's vast data banks. In other words, maybe it could turn Macintosh into an "intelligent front end" for IBM mainframes.

Roger Smith had even more cash in his pocket than Neutron Jack—about $9 billion or so—and he was more eager to spend it, too. He sent out a team headed by EDS's founder, H. Ross Perot, a free-marketeer who'd built his fortune on a contract to process Medicare claims for the state of Texas and now found himself on the board of the biggest, fattest, most overstuffed dinosaur in Detroit. The son of an East Texas horse trader, Perot had quit his job as an IBM salesman in 1962 and started his company with $1,000 in savings after encountering a quote from Thoreau in *Reader's Digest:* "The mass of men lead lives of quiet desperation." Now he was one of a handful of American billionaires, on a list that included David Rockefeller, David Packard, oil-and-movie magnate Marvin Davis, and the Hunt sisters of Dallas, who'd wisely stayed out of their brothers' ill-fated silver scheme. His new job was to help Roger Smith make GM competitive. The first thing he'd done was put up a Norman Rockwell painting of a weary leatherneck telling war stories to kids as he held a Japanese flag in his hands—a reminder that America had whipped them once and could do it again.

The negotiations were time-consuming and stressful. Smith toured the Macintosh factory when he came to Fremont to inspect GM's new factory there, an experiment in joint management with Toyota. Perot flew out to Cupertino, got a presentation from Steve and John in the boardroom, and took his own tour of the factory. He was charming and friendly, and he seemed to take an almost paternal interest in what the Mac team was doing, but meeting him in the context of beige, suburban Bandley Drive was like encountering Dirty Harry in a Steven Spielberg movie. A pint-sized Texan with a paramilitary management style, he had a presence that could make the hair on the back of your neck stand up on end. He was no Mac Munchkin. On the other hand, his crew-cut operatives seemed all too much like a band of pirates—not surprising for a man still basking in the afterglow of the successful rescue of his own personal Iranian hostages, a feat that had just been breathtakingly retold in a Ken Follett best-seller. And strangely enough, he got along famously with Steve. They had chemistry. They hated middle management. They liked each other's charisma. And later, when he told them GM would be interested in a deal only if Steve agreed not to leave, John had to confront the awkward realization that General Motors seemed a lot more interested in Apple's founder than in its president.

AT&T remained tempting as well, not only because of its aggressive stance against IBM but also because of its potential product synergy with Apple. It was beginning to look as if the telephone and the computer would soon become one, enabling people to communicate over the same lines by voice and by data transmission—by word and image, transmitted instantaneously.

At the moment, computer phones were still a tiny business ($350 million annually) controlled by a handful of privately owned companies. But market researchers were expecting the number of computer phones in use to jump from 35,000 in 1984 to 1.9 million in 1988, and already the big boys were leaping in. At the beginning of November, IBM and Rolm announced a $4,600 desk-top model that could send and receive data and speed-dial calls from numbers stored in memory. AT&T was working a deal with Convergent Technologies, a Silicon Valley company which would supply it with a pair of products—a small executive model with a touch-sensitive screen (point at a name and the computer dials the number), and a much bigger model that would be as powerful as IBM's new PC AT and come with a telephone built in. The same AT&T executive who set up the Convergent deal was also working with frogdesign and the Macintosh engineering lab in a hush-hush project to develop a "MacPhone"—a Macintosh with a built-in telephone for simultaneous voice and data transmission. Belleville's little AppleTalk network, while slower than other computer networks, had been designed to conform to standards that were being developed for worldwide data communications. At some point in the future, then, AppleTalk users would be able to throw away their cables, plug in to the phone lines, and—using their existing software—send data around the world in a fraction of the time it took to fax documents or send them by modem. When that happened, MacPhone would be ready.

There was a certain nervousness associated with all these meetings and presentations and negotiations, an edge that came not just from the thrill of big-money wheeling and dealing but also from the ever-present danger of going too far, of making the wrong move, of being swallowed up. In a sense, they could always tell themselves, it didn't matter who owned what; they were all publicly owned companies, so the important question was who *controlled* what—or, more precisely, who controlled whom. But missteps were certainly possible. These were strange times on the corporate takeover front, times when anything could happen. Texaco had taken over Getty. Mobil had taken over Superior. Standard Oil of California had taken over Gulf. Vast pools of liquid cash were sloshing around the banking system, all but unencumbered by antitrust considerations and kept in constant motion by a cabal of investment bankers, Wall Street lawyers, arbitrageurs, greenmailers, con men, and takeover artists. Only IBM and Exxon were valued highly enough by the stock market to be considered safe. Apple was a small fish indeed, and only nimble maneuvering would keep it whole. The idea was to sell a significant fraction of the company—25 percent was the figure usually discussed—with an agreement not to go any higher. But agreements like that have a way of not lasting. In September, for example, IBM had suddenly and unexpectedly announced that, having bought a chunk of Rolm under an agreement that restricted its ownership to 30 percent, it was now negotiating to buy the whole company.

It wasn't hard to figure out why. The emerging networks for voice and data transmission were made up of three essential elements—cables to carry the information, software to encode it and decode it, and switches to direct it to the proper place. Rolm was a leader in switching systems, and with AT&T moving into the computer side of the business, IBM had decided to buy some of Rolm's expertise. But the arm's-length relationship wasn't working, and with the threat of antitrust action out of the way, what reason was there not to move? It didn't matter that Rolm was one of Silicon Valley's entrepreneurial legends, not as famous as Apple but equally celebrated in the lore of the Valley. Founded in 1969 by four guys from Rice who wanted to build minicomputers for soldiers in the field, it had gotten its start not in the proverbial garage but in an empty prune-drying shed. Its subsequent move into electronic switchboards brought on a period of spectacular growth. Annual sales hit $20 million, $200 million, $660 million. With the skyrocketing numbers came a campus that defined the state of the art in corporate coddling—vine-shaded patios graced with artificial waterfalls, wood-beamed offices hung with macrame and ferns, a gym that would excite envy in an Olympic hopeful's heart. Now it was about to be devoured by the Colossus of Armonk.

Yet the Steve and John show didn't dwell too heavily on such real-world possibilities as that. No, the Steve and John show was much more a chance for John to create his own reality-distortion field, to share the giddy high of unbridled executive fantasy with Steve, to serve as a mentor in the most seductive sense of the word. During the day they might quarrel and snap at each other, but alone together in the boardroom, late at night, they sensed no limit to the things they could do together. They could get a billion-dollar loan from GM or GE or AT&T and float enough junk bonds to take over Xerox and dominate the office-automation market. They could run for president together and take turns being vice-president and run the country between them for sixteen years. They could . . .

■ ■ ■

Meanwhile, the world around them was crumbling. Macintosh sales in September were less than two-thirds of the 30,000 projected; October sales were projected at 50,000 and came in below September's. In November, after the October sales figures came in, Steve walked into his regular Wednesday-afternoon staff meeting and cast a chill across the room. The usual cocky dynamism was gone; he looked like a man who'd been blind-sided by—fate, numbers, whatever.

I've failed, he announced. What's the price I have to pay? What's the cost?

This was so radically out of character that no one knew what to say. Steve usually dealt with blame by assigning it to somebody else. After a day or so he'd announce his forgiveness and then he no longer had to worry about it—it wasn't *his* fault, it was theirs, and he'd forgiven them so they could all put it behind them now and move ahead. It was fairly effective if you had the emotional stamina to go along. This was different. This was Steve owning up to failure and trying to tally the bill.

It was obvious what the cost would be, but none of them dared speak it out loud. We're all going to lose our jobs, Bob thought to himself. We're not going to get to do it again. Months earlier his children had asked him what he was going to get for all this work he was doing days, nights, and weekends, and that's what he'd told them—he'd get to do it all over again. They didn't think it was funny. They thought he was going to get rich. They didn't understand about a career—that the journey is the reward, and the important thing is to be allowed on the next one.

In fact, of course, they hadn't failed at all. They'd sold a quarter-million computers since January, and even at 20,000 a month they were still doing a $300-million-a-year business. But success is relative, and the success they were having was so out of line with the success they'd predicted that it could only be interpreted as failure. They were missing their revenue targets by huge margins. They were failing.

Steve's fit of self-excoriation quickly passed, and when it did, the fault became Mike's, or Bob's, or Debi's, or Susan's, or Bill Campbell's, or John's. His weekly staff meetings turned into a shifting kaleidoscope of blame. The four of them were on his staff because they each believed in his vision; their ties were to him, not to each other. They were like jealous siblings competing for a parent's praise. That gave him a manipulative edge which he used instinctively.

In a staff meeting he'd acknowledge Mike's progress with satisfaction and then turn to Bob and ask what *he* was going to do to make it work. He'd pull Debi aside and tell her she should think about running the division someday; later he'd tell Bob the same thing. One day he'd be telling Mike he might become the next president of Apple in a few years; another day he and Bob would rip the guy apart. They'd want to know who these people were who'd been buying Macs. Did they have any friends? Could somebody call them? And when that happened, Mike just threw up his hands. He told them tracking sales wasn't his job; sales belonged to Bill Campbell. And he couldn't be held personally responsible for how Macintosh was selling, because he didn't control the sales force. His job was *marketing*.

One of them always had to carry the weight, and always with the knowledge that the others would offer little in the way of public support. If it wasn't Mike it was Susan, who'd come into a staff meeting in Picasso or Matisse with gorgeous laser-printed charts and then get flustered when Steve asked her a question. He lost confidence in her. He already had a likely replacement—Dave Barram, a long-time Hewlett-Packard controller who was now vice-president and chief financial officer of a start-up called Silicon Graphics. Before he fired her, he wanted to make sure Barram would take the job. But when he took Mike into his office and told him in confidence—he was always telling them things in confidence—what he was planning, Mike said, "Man, you can't do that!" Can this guy be trusted? he thought to himself. Out loud he told Steve he could fire Susan if he wanted to, but before he replaced her he had to tell her what the problem was. Steve immediately listed several reasons why he couldn't do that, but then he did it anyway. Susan told him he had to give her a chance to prove herself, and with Jay Elliot's encouragement he agreed. In the meantime, John developed an interest in Barram.

As for Mike, he became excited about the possibilities even as he grew more and more disillusioned about the reality. Steve and John were talking about making him the next president of Apple while they went off to run Xerox—but Apple was a mess. He didn't know what to think or how to feel. He just knew he didn't like the way they were operating or making decisions or representing reality to themselves and the world. Engineering was trying to do the undoable. Steve's staff was unable to work together. Marketing, split between two divisions, was sending out conflicting messages to the world. And he really got nervous when he tried to talk to Steve about what was wrong, because Steve thought the answer was for the Macintosh division to expand even further—to take over distribution and sales. So he started writing memos. He wrote memos to Campbell, to Jay Elliot, to Regis McKenna. He wrote awkward, sincere, very earnest memos, telling them that Macintosh—indeed, all of Apple—was broken.

Bob was too busy with engineering to worry if the organization was broken. The hardware for the FileServer was pretty much ready, but it might as well have been an empty box, because the only people he had to write software for it were tied up writing code for the network. As for the network, the software that would enable it to run electronic mail or send files from one Mac to another still existed only in prototype form. He'd probably have ignored the head-count restrictions he was under if the sales forecasts weren't so shaky, but it was pointless to hire engineers he might have to lay off in six months. And when he saw what was happening to the next-generation Macintosh—the one the committee was supposed to design to replace the TurboMac he'd scuttled—he got really depressed. He'd put Rich Page, Lisa's chief hardware architect, on the committee because Rich was working on a project—a large-screen, highly advanced, state-of-the-art Macintosh—that Bob thought he could scale down a little and put into production immediately. Instead, the committee machine had turned into Rich Page's machine and developed an incredible case of creeping elegance along the way. Big Mac—that was what they called it—had become a godawful minicomputer-class workstation. So he put together *another* team with directions to use the FileServer as the basis of a bigger Macintosh that was still something short of gargantuan.

Now they had Big Mac and this new Mid Mac and the FileServer and the network, all in various stages of development. But it was hard trying to plan for the future when the present was coming down around your ears. As Mac sales dwindled, inventory was piling up with the awful inevitability of cars on a rain-slick freeway. They had 250,000 Sony disk drives on hand, which at a 20,000-a-month run rate was a year's supply—but in January they'd be getting a new model that was smaller, cheaper, and more efficient. And when Bob called Sony to tell them to shut down production of the old drives, he was told politely but firmly that that would be impossible.

Sony had more than four hundred people assembling disk drives in a factory east of Tokyo, all young girls waiting to be married. They had to have something to do until they found a mate. To put them out of work would in the Japanese scheme of things be unthinkable. It would violate their entire sense of community, the spirit of mutual responsibility that holds the company and the country together. Far better to keep manufacturing drives and throw them in the ocean. So Bob and Debi flew to Tokyo for a day to work something out. They tried to get Mike to come because they wanted him to see firsthand how the decisions they made affected the lives of thousands of people all over the world, people who didn't speak English and never collected an Apple paycheck and weren't even represented by a number in the business plan. But Mike begged off, and Steve called a half-hour before the limo was supposed to take him to the airport and told them he couldn't go either. He was just too tired to deal with it.

■　■　■

All fall, Steve and Mike were flying back and forth to New York, offering previews of the Macintosh Office to stock analysts and business journalists. And all fall, the reception they were getting was unaccustomedly cool. Once Apple had been a darling of the Street, admired both for its spunky individualism and for its spectacular financial success—a success many early investors had been lucky enough to participate in. But the shakeout in the home market and IBM's dominance in business had changed the outlook. Twice Apple had blown it in the business market, and while no one on the outside was calling Macintosh a failure, it certainly wasn't having much impact in corporate America. Meanwhile, the gospel of entrepreneurship, the creed that Apple lived by, was undergoing a subtle transformation. The recent torrent of mergers and takeovers meant that Wall Street itself had gone entrepreneurial, and as money from all those deals and from the two-year-old bull market showered the Street, the focus of popular attention was shifting. America's heroes were no longer the whiz kids whose ideas the market financed—creative misfits like Wozniak and Jobs and Nolan Bushnell, the founder of Atari—but the business grinds who did the financing. The new heroes were the guys on the Street, sporting power ties and swinging deals.

Take Bruce Wasserstein, the pudgy thirty-six-year-old in the pinstriped suit whose exploits had just landed him in the pages of *Esquire*. Not a big name to the average Joe, perhaps, but if you were an M.B.A. in the Ivy League—and what college kid, in the wake of *The Preppy Handbook*, didn't aspire to *that?*—he was a superstar. As co-director of mergers and acquisitions—M&A, the glamour side of finance—at First Boston, he'd engineered four of the biggest deals of the century, including Texaco's $10-billion purchase of Getty Oil the previous January. He'd helped transform First Boston from a fading old-line investment bank to an aggressive and innovative institution. Nobody on his team sat around waiting for the phone to ring; they were buccaneers, scouring the horizon for possibilities. In the Getty deal, for example, he'd spent months trying to persuade Texaco to move, and in the final days he'd outmaneuvered a dozen other oil companies and investment bankers, slipped in with Texaco, and stolen the prize from an enraged Pennzoil, which thought it had already won control. *That* was entrepreneurship, postindustrial style.

Originally, in the wake of the sixties, entrepreneurship had come into vogue because of the neat way it reconciled the rebelliousness of the counterculture with the eternal verities of the American dream. Entrepreneurs wanted to change the world, they just had a different way of going about it. "Doing your own thing" came to mean making it on your own terms. But it was 1984 now; nobody cared about changing the world anymore. There was money to be made, and no end of things to spend it on. Apple had been right about one thing: 1984 wasn't like *1984* at all. It was like some speeded-up replay of the Gilded Age in crypto-fifties drag. It was a John Waters/Cecil B. De Mille spectacular starring Nancy Reagan as Carl Icahn's mom.

It was *Wall Street Babylon.* Why, in a single deal—the infamous Getty takeover, which would lead to a lawsuit from Pennzoil that would eventually drive Texaco into bankruptcy court—Ivan Boesky had raked in $100 million, or half of Steve Jobs's entire fortune. Profits like that meant the gospel of entrepreneurship was due for an update. The new gospel was the creed of greed. Greed was good—good for the greedy, good for the nation. Adam Smith said so. It had to be true.

It made Steve feel old to speak on college campuses and discover that the kids he met there cared less about his dreams and visions than about his net worth. The same kids were voting for Ronald Reagan that fall in overwhelming numbers, and why not? It was morning in America. The invisible hand was going to make them rich. The Gipper made them feel good—good about their country, good about themselves. If it feels good, do it—that was what they'd learned from the sixties. Self-absorption was taking a new turn.

The new ideology put people in touch not just with themselves but with their own selfishness. No one on Bandley Drive saw it coming. How could they acknowledge that time was passing them by—that this wasn't the moment to be pushing personal freedom and individual creativity, that there was no Apple Generation in corporate America? The new kids out of B school might like to think of themselves as entrepreneurial, but most of them were too stoked up on ambition and money-lust to go for the wrong label. They went for yellow ties, red suspenders, and Big Blue.

The hit movie of the moment was *Amadeus,* a Mozart for the new generation. Ostensibly it was a celebration of passion and genius, of a short life that yielded sublime beauty. In the prevailing current social climate, however, it became something quite different. It became a cautionary tale, a tragic fable set in a fairy-tale world of ermine and lace. The glittering rococorama of Hapsburg Vienna was a clear stand-in for the imperial Washington of the Reagan court, and the giggling, irrepressible little Mozart was—well, he was a young urban professional who was just too full of himself to fall into line. He was an arrogant genius who ignored the power structure and flouted the rules, and he paid for it. In a scene early on, impatient at being scolded by his patron, the prince/archbishop of Salzburg, for being tardy, he suddenly flung open the doors of the prince's chamber to the crowd that was cheering his performance. Bending low to receive their applause, he greeted the prince with his upturned rear and emitted a loud and heartfelt fart. Jobs too seemed driven to fart in the face of authority, and an unspoken consensus was beginning to build that he should pay for it.

One of the presentations Steve made that fall was in an executive dining room in the upper reaches of the Time-Life Building, for a small group of editors and reporters from *Time* and *Fortune* who'd been invited by Henry Anatole Grunwald, the editor-in-chief of Time Inc. There was no mistaking the corporate nature of the environment—a gleaming steel-and-glass tower on the Sixth Avenue side of Rockefeller Center, the postwar side, its vast concrete plazas and nearly identical modernist boxes presenting a sweeping, hard-edged vista meant to be enjoyed from the back of a black stretch limousine. High above the icy grandeur of the street, the dining room sat suspended in air like a beige power cube, its windows providing dramatic views of Central Park, the East River, and the towers of midtown Manhattan. A few blocks away on Madison Avenue, the art-deco crown of the Newsweek Building added a fanciful touch to the skyline. But there was no such frivolity here; Time Inc. was a more businesslike place, a repository of all the Protestant virtues.

Steve had met Grunwald in California a few months before, then phoned him at his office and asked breezily if he remembered telling him to come by the next time he was in New York. Grunwald didn't, but he'd found Jobs an intriguing young man, and he was pleased to have him to lunch. In the forty-fourth-floor dining room that afternoon, facing a portrait of the redoubtable Henry Luce, the Presbyterian missionary's son who'd founded this great Christian capitalist media empire, Steve switched on the field. He launched too quickly into a technical description of the office products Apple was about to introduce, losing most of his audience in a torrent of jargon. But he won them back when he moved on to the business side and demonstrated his impressive command of the numbers. He shocked them a little when he described IBM's PCjr as "tainted" and predicted that Apple would be shipping ten million computers a year by the end of the decade. Then someone asked him what he thought about *The Little Kingdom,* the recently published history of Apple by Michael Moritz, the *Time* reporter whose profile in the "Machine of the Year" issue had offended him so thoroughly.

Moritz, Steve said, had had the opportunity to write a very special book about a very different kind of company, but he'd chosen not to. Moritz could have written about Steve's philosophy of management, which involved running a company by vision rather than by rules. Instead of layering an organization with mid-level bureaucrats who stifle creativity and inhibit communication, Steve believed in running a flat organization and inspiring people by direct example. He contrasted Apple's attempts to foster innovation with IBM's history of stifling it once it had attained a monopoly in mainframes. But as he hit his stride, describing not Apple as it was but Apple as it might have been, he seemed to forget who his audience was.

Like IBM, Time Inc. was the product of an earlier era, a Calvinist, Republican institution so homogeneous and conservative that Grunwald had once had to worry that being Jewish might hold him back. It didn't have IBM's small-town roots, but it was every bit as boosterish and square. And naturally, as pillars of capitalism at the apogee of the American Century, the two companies hadn't remained strangers. J. Richard Munro, the president of Time Inc., sat on IBM's board. John Opel, the chairman of IBM, sat on Time Inc.'s board. So, however Grunwald and the other editors and reporters in the dining room that afternoon felt about the rather intense young man before them—and he was obviously newsworthy, no question about that—institutional loyalties and the Lucean legacy both suggested that Time Inc. would not become a Macintosh office anytime soon.

In the elevator going down, one of the editors—a middle manager, in effect—was asked what he thought. He wasn't too impressed. These young guys, he said, they sound great, they talk a real show. But you never know with a guy like that—he could be a big deal tomorrow, or he could be out of business.

III.
Over the Edge
January–May 1985

□□ **15** □□

Lemmings

It was the second week of January, 1985, and they were driving through a snowstorm without any wipers. That's how Steve saw it. Nobody knew what the hell was going on. Nobody could see a thing. They were all getting panicky. It had been like this ever since they got back from Christmas, when Bill Campbell and Joe Graziano had discovered that the figures that looked so promising at first in fact provided a dangerously blurry picture. During the Christmas quarter they'd shipped something like $700 million in product—more than the entire year of 1982, though still well shy of the $1 billion they'd geared up for. But now, for some reason, the dealers had stopped reordering. Then Campbell started making calls, and they began to find out why.

The dealers weren't reordering because they were already sitting on more unsold inventory than they could handle. Macs and IIc's were backed up everywhere, clogging the distribution channels, piling up on store shelves, unsold and unwanted. Only the IIe was continuing to move. Because Apple lacked a data-processing system sophisticated enough to track the dealers' inventory closely, it took them a while to discover how bad the situation was. But as Graziano added the dealers' totals to the machines that were piling up in Apple's warehouses, he began to show an inventory backlog of incredible proportions—tens of millions, maybe even hundreds of millions of dollars. The gamble they'd made in the fall, the decision to rev up production, to go soaring out over the edge to meet runaway demand, had backfired completely. There was no runaway demand. They were going to crash and burn.

And here was Sculley talking about *potato chips*. The whole exec staff had come down to Pajaro Dunes for a strategy session, and since Steve had been after him to fix the shortcomings in their inventory-control system, John had prepared an elaborate presentation on Frito-Lay. He handed out a thick sheaf of charts and diagrams to show how Frito-Lay's system worked. He put on a slide show with photographs of store shelves and potato-chip bags. Steve had heard a lot about Frito-Lay over the past two years, about how its ten thousand route salesmen gave it the edge in the battle for shelf space, but the lesson he'd gleaned wasn't quite what John had in mind. Steve had concluded that Frito-Lay didn't have to innovate because it controlled the shelf space so absolutely that no one else could muscle in. Several times over the past few months—at his Montgomery Securities speech in San Francisco, at his Time Inc. luncheon in New York—he'd asserted that Frito-Lay, with its army of service and support personnel, was just like IBM. Now John was holding up Frito-Lay as a model for Apple. John was explaining how Frito-Lay, with its sophisticated inventory-management system, knew exactly how many bags of corn chips and potato chips and the like it had on every dealer's shelf at every moment and could even break down sell-through by region and demographic profile. If someone at PepsiCo wanted to know how Chee-tos were selling last week to teenagers in Topeka, Kansas, compared with Albuquerque, New Mexico, he could find out in a snap. But at Apple they knew very little about sell-through, about customer satisfaction, about what was happening in the stores. They were driving blind.

Campbell wasn't exactly thrilled, since it was his organization that was being compared with Frito-Lay and found wanting. What's more, it was hard for him to see how his management of shelf space was more of a problem than Mac's lack of functionality. Macintosh might be easy to use, but what could you use it *for*? And Graziano wasn't much happier, because John's criticism was also directed at finance. Frito-Lay was a company that had figured out how to succeed on incredibly slim margins by paying attention to mouse-nuts numbers— the kinds of numbers Apple lost rounding off. Steve was already riding his ass about the numbers anyway. They never knew the real cost of anything, Steve claimed, because Graziano reported average costs rather than real costs. At every exec staff meeting now, Graziano would report one set of numbers and Susan Barnes would show up with another set and Joe and Steve would argue about what they meant and finally Steve would come unglued. He wanted specifics. He wanted precise data. He wanted to know *exactly* what Mac's profit margin was.

To follow his Frito-Lay presentation, John—at Steve's insistence—had scheduled a presentation by Debi Coleman on the distribution question. Bill was even angrier about this, since the distribution network she was proposing to dismantle was his. Demand for Macintosh was so light that Debi and her staff had had time on their hands for months, so they'd put together an impressive proposal for a just-in-time distribution system that would eliminate the need for warehouses and inventory and rely instead on overnight delivery by Federal Express. The distribution organization, on the other hand, had been taxed to its limits; over the Christmas quarter it had shipped more product than ever before in Apple's history. Roy Weaver and his staff had learned about Debi's appearance only a few days before, and the last-minute presentation they'd pulled together was embarrassingly inferior to hers. In the ensuing uproar, however, distribution itself was all but forgotten. Instead, everybody started yelling about the way Steve was interfering with the rest of the company—with sales, distribution, finance—and how John seemed unable to do anything about it.

Finally, at Jay Elliot's suggestion, they set up a task force to settle the distribution question. Jay saw the whole issue as an example of "top-down management," which was how he put it in *his* presentation, which he gave at the close of the retreat. Apple's middle managers—people like Peter Quinn, who'd left, and Dave Larson, who was about to—had come to feel that all the important decisions were being dictated from above. Because market research showed that consumers thought the IIc was too small to be very powerful, for example, Larson had been forced to run ads that showed it controlling the lights in the World Trade Center—as if that were something ordinary people might want to use it for. Jay pulled out a drawing of a hulking gorilla to make his point. And it wasn't just that all the decisions were coming from the top but that most of them were coming from Steve and John. The way the middle managers saw it, Steve was making all the decisions and John was in his shadow. Steve was being favored over all the other vice-presidents, and John wasn't taking the action he needed to run the company.

Jay's talk, coming after all the angry exchanges of the past three days, had an almost cathartic effect. As they prepared to return to Bandley Drive, Steve apologized for his misdeeds. He pledged to step back and not step on everyone's toes. And John made a pledge as well. From now on, he said, he was going to step forward and lead the company.

■ ■ ■

Monday night, Matisse and Picasso were in crisis. On the left side of Bandley 3's atrium, in Matisse, Steve and John were holed up with Susan Barnes, Joe Graziano, Del Yocam, Mike Murray, and Bill Campbell, arguing about Steve's new plan to get Macintosh moving again. On the right-hand side, in Picasso, Jay Chiat, Lee Clow, and two vice-presidents from Chiat/Day were fidgeting as they waited to make a final, desperate pitch for their own scheme—the "Lemmings" ad, which Apple had decided not to air. Already it was seven in the evening, and the pricing meeting—originally scheduled for three that afternoon—had barely begun. They had a long night ahead of them.

Over Christmas, Steve had gone skiing at Aspen, something he did often—Arthur Rock had a condo there, and so did Billy Ladin, the millionaire owner of ComputerCraft, a sixty-store chain based in Houston. Ladin had been selling Apple computers since the Good Earth days, and he'd always been a volume player. He believed in the fishbowl routine—give away the goldfish so they'll come back to buy the fishbowl. His success and ebullience made him one of Apple's most influential dealers; he spoke with Steve or John or Bill an average of once a day and was consulted on most major sales and marketing decisions—the "Test Drive" program, for instance. During Christmas vacation he'd told Steve that the real reason Macintosh wasn't selling was because it cost too much. So Steve had come back with the idea—the vision, if you will—that they should cut the retail price by $1,000.

It was a risky scheme; if it failed—if they cut the price and sales *didn't* go up—their profits would escape like air out of a balloon. Only if they sold enough to make that money back in volume would the strategy work. But Steve thought they could do it, and one day the week before, he'd grabbed Susan in the hall and said, "Got a minute?" That was how he always sprang his ideas. He'd been talking to Billy Ladin and he had this great idea, and what did she think? That was the end of her weekend.

Susan and Steve and Mike spent all day Saturday and Sunday brainstorming in Bandley 3 as Susan's staff sat nearby, crunching numbers on their Macs. Could it really work? Could the added volume offset the lost revenue? How could they structure the pricing in all the different sales channels—retail, university, and so forth—to get the best effect? Should they offer a rebate instead of cutting the price? They rolled numbers and rerolled them and rerolled them again. Mike brought his wife in so she could understand the kind of pressure he was under. On Sunday evening they made a presentation to Bill Campbell, who was having trouble buying into the vision: If they dropped the price too low, people might think the machine was just a toy. It was a funny company, he told them, where marketing wanted to cut the price and sales wanted to keep it high. But finally they won him over, and on Monday at three they were scheduled to make their pitch to Sculley.

John liked to run the numbers all the way through, to try several different scenarios and see what their impact on the company's earnings per share would be before making his decision. That required some fairly complex financial modeling, and as Susan and her staff went to work on Monday, they had to keep making revisions that threw them off schedule. The meeting didn't get started until well after six. Now it was seven o'clock, and John was coming at them with all kinds of what-ifs—what if they tried this, what if they tried that. For each one they had to roll the numbers all the way to the bottom line, which took forty-five minutes to an hour. And there was always the danger that they'd mess up—that they'd forget some obscure factor in the rush to make an instant analysis and come back with the wrong answer. They were under pressure. They were getting hysterical. They couldn't panic. Finally, as one of Susan's staff members was about to jump out of the room to run some more figures, Steve told her to sit down. They weren't going to roll ten different options, he told John. They were going to make some management decisions about which ones made the most sense, and then they'd roll those.

On the other side of the atrium, in Picasso, the Chiat/Day contingent ate carry-out pizza and paced the floor as they waited for the meeting in Matisse to end. Seven o'clock passed, then eight. Jay had flown in from New York; Lee and Steve Hayden and Greg Helm, the management supervisor on the account, had flown up from Los Angeles. Obviously they weren't going to make their return flights.

Finally Steve and John burst into the room, with Mike and Bill right behind them. The pricing meeting had just gone into a lull while more figures were rolled. They were eager to start.

Lee made the pitch. Yes, he admitted, "Lemmings" would not be received as well as "1984," because "1984" was a once-in-a-lifetime event. They were all agreed on that. But they had to do what was right for this moment in time, and "Lemmings," he declared, was what this moment required. It was Apple against IBM, and Apple needed to make a forceful statement, a strong emotional play to win people over to their point of view. To follow it up, they'd have some very straightforward, businesslike advertising for TV and the business magazines and *The Wall Street Journal*. They'd have—

The numbers were back. Steve and John disappeared into Matisse. For the next four hours they ricocheted back and forth, half an hour on pricing, twenty minutes on advertising, fifteen, ten, bouncing off the walls like Ping-Pong balls, *thwack–thwack–thwack*. "Lemmings" kept appearing on the TV screen, the funereal dirge of its soundtrack permeating the atrium, sinking into their brains like lead. Jay Chiat and Greg Helm ventured out into the atrium and got sucked into the pricing meeting. One after another the same dressed-for-success middle-management types toppled blindfolded over the cliff. One after another new pricing scenarios were proposed and new numbers were rolled. Finally Jay and Greg suggested that instead of cutting the price, they offer a rebate to the buyer and an incentive to the salesperson—a check for, say, $200. It was an interesting idea. They liked it. They liked it a lot. They even liked it after they got the numbers back.

But they still weren't sure about "Lemmings." Dealers and their own sales people were telling them it was insulting to their target audience—middle managers. Air time on the Super Bowl cost $1 million a minute, and Apple's financial picture was getting bleaker by the day. And the bottom line was, John felt it didn't communicate as well as "1984." It was too downbeat. It lacked the sense of hope and the message of good-versus-evil that made "1984" so remarkable. Jay was telling them it was the greatest piece of advertising anybody would see the entire year and it was right-on strategically and they should run it. But neither John nor Steve was convinced.

The issue put John on the spot. The month before, *Advertising Age,* the bible of Madison Avenue, had named him its "adman of the year," putting him in a pantheon with Lee Iacocca of Chrysler, Steve Ross of Warner, Barry Diller of Paramount, and Richard Wirthlin, the chief strategist of Ronald Reagan's 1980 campaign. He was the marketing guru of Apple Computer—indeed, of the whole personal-computer industry. He was supposed to know what he was doing. And yet, from the inside, many of the splashy marketing moves Apple had made since his arrival—the lifestyle ads, the Apple IIc campaign, the "Test Drive" promotion—had the distinct aroma of failure. The only unqualified success was "1984"—another Chiat/Day creation that almost hadn't run. It was awkward to say no to them after that ad's success; and yet if this spot backfired, it would be even more awkward to have said yes. Finally, sometime after midnight, he and Steve arrived at a solution. They decided to turn the whole thing over to Mike.

And so Mike Murray, at the age of twenty-nine, with no real-world product-marketing experience outside Apple, found himself with a million-dollar decision in his lap. Perhaps if he'd been more political about it—more of a lemming, in other words—he would simply have gauged his bosses' desires and acted accordingly. Certainly his gut response was that the ad was too negative. He thought it would leave people with a bad feeling. But after the meeting broke up, Lee walked him around the deserted parking lot and made a personal appeal. Lee was a good friend. As much as anyone he knew what Macintosh could do for people in business, and he thought "Lemmings" would help communicate that. It wasn't negative, he insisted. And by refusing to show it, they were cowering away from IBM when they should be out there pounding on their chests, showing everybody what winners they were. Now, when the momentum was against them, they had to be bold. And with "Lemmings," they could turn that momentum around.

Gradually Lee's words began to click in. This momentum thing, Mike thought—this momentum thing was real. Apple hadn't yet announced its quarterly results—Graziano and his people were still desperately trying to compute them—but word was already getting out that Apple's dealers were clogged with inventory. Everybody knew Apple had bought airtime on the Super Bowl to launch the Macintosh Office with another "1984"-style spectacular. What would people say if it didn't run? That Apple was in trouble? That Mac was running out of gas?

At six the next morning, Mike called Chiat/Day in New York and told them to buy back the airtime from ABC. Then he called John and told him he'd decided to run the ad.

■ ■ ■

Jay Elliot knew they were in for it when he opened the *San Francisco Chronicle* on Super Bowl Sunday morning. Huge letters jumped out at him from an otherwise empty page:

IF YOU GO TO THE BATHROOM

DURING THE FOURTH QUARTER,

YOU'LL BE SORRY.

At the bottom of the page sat the Apple logo, perky and alone. "Oh, shit," he muttered as he reached for his coffee. They were going to show it after all.

Super Bowl XIX was being played in Stanford Stadium, which sat in the midst of a vast eucalyptus grove on El Camino Real about a mile from Elliot's modest Palo Alto house. This year it was the San Francisco '49ers versus the Miami Dolphins, and the hometown frenzy added an extra edge to what was normally a made-for-TV spectacular. All week the Super madness had permeated San Francisco—sixty thousand tourists jamming hotels and restaurants, hanging onto cable cars, guzzling beer, buying stupid T-shirts, trying to crash the huge party at Moscone Center—and now it was spilling willy-nilly down the Peninsula. Stanford Stadium had been surrounded by RVs all weekend. The entire eucalyptus grove had been given over to a giant electronic tailgate party, with corporate tents surrounded by chain-link fences and rolling living rooms equipped with TV sets, video-cassette recorders, even satellite dishes. One group was barbecueing a forty-nine-pound pig named Danny, after Dolphins quarterback Dan Marino. "Nuke Flipper," read a banner in the trees.

Jay worked his way through the throng and took his place in the stadium. Each one of the 84,000 seats was covered with a cushion bearing the Apple logo, which made quite a display for the 120 million viewers as the TV cameras panned the stadium while waiting for the game to begin. The man in front of him turned around and noticed the Apple logo on his jacket. He turned out to be the marketing vice-president at Ford. "You realize that every marketing executive in America is eating his heart out because Apple did this," he said. Jay smiled wanly and waited for the game to begin.

As the team captains stood at the fifty-yard line, Ronald Reagan materialized on the electronic scoreboard, fresh from his inauguration earlier in the day, and flipped a commemorative medal. The 49ers won the toss. By the end of the first half they'd all but won the game, having scored three touchdowns in a nine-and-a-half-minute stretch of the second quarter to pull ahead, 28–13. Miami never recovered. But because it was supposed to be a tight game—the 49ers had been favored to win by only a field goal—Apple had bought the last time slot available. "Lemmings" was aired with one minute to go. The fans were totally silent as it ran on the electronic scoreboard. They remained silent for a moment or two afterwards, and then all the talking and shuffling and noise resumed as if nothing had happened. The Ford VP, whose ad had run earlier, turned around again and gave Jay a consoling look. "Well," he said, "one out of two isn't bad."

■ ■ ■

W-H-A-T -A- C-O-N-C-E-P-T-!

And what a display! It was Wednesday morning, the morning of the annual meeting, and the Mac crew had taken over most of the front rows at Flint Center, much the way they'd taken over Bandley Drive. A whole group of them had painted letters on their T-shirts so that when they stood up, *this* was what they conveyed to the eyes of the multitude. The concept was connectibility. The concept was event marketing. They were a high-technology, high-concept operation. They were Macintosh.

Flint Center had filled up faster than ever this year. Hundreds of people were standing outside at nine, waiting for the doors to open. By ten every seat was taken. But while the Mac division had been warned to get there early, the II division hadn't. Most of them ended up watching on closed-circuit television at a movie theater a couple of blocks down Stevens Creek Boulevard, and they weren't thrilled. But inside Flint Center, more people seemed more excited than ever before. They were doing it again. They were going to top last year. They *had* to be excited, although in fact they were feeling other emotions as well.

Mike Murray was depressed and angry. He knew the products weren't ready, he thought they were kidding themselves, he thought the whole thing was a farce. Bob Belleville felt nothing. As he sat behind the rows of the faithful, watching the whole thing unfold, he felt a vast emotional void, as if his feelings simply weren't there. Even some of the faithful weren't excited in the way they appeared to be. Threats had been phoned in against Steve, and as they sat in the front rows they were making macabre jokes about their role as "bullet blockers." A few were wearing T-shirts with targets painted on the back. Security men were roaming around backstage, their ears jammed with electronics. The air was crackling with paranoia and expectancy.

The reaction to "Lemmings" was enough to send them all scrambling for cover. Chiat/Day had hired Burke Marketing Research to do its standard day-after recall test on Monday, and while the ad Burked high, the fact that it was supposed to be about something called the Macintosh Office had barely registered at all. Meanwhile, Apple's switchboards were jammed with calls from irate consumers and harried dealers. Parents' groups were upset about the violence. School superintendents were saying they might get rid of their Apple computers because Apple was encouraging teenage suicide. A concentration-camp survivor in Florida wrote in to say he'd never buy an Apple computer because Apple was killing Jews. "Lemmings" was accelerating Macintosh's momentum, all right; it just wasn't reversing its direction.

Steve, his hair impeccably styled in an over-the-ears cut, took the stage in a double-breasted gray-flannel suit with a white shirt and a gray-and-white striped bow tie. He stood at the extreme left side of the stage; overhead his image was projected on two enormous screens. He was the picture of the New Age executive, fully electronic and larger than life. But as he spoke, there was little hint of the Bluebusters mentality that had reigned at the sales conference, no suggestion that middle managers who chose the IBM label were in fact lemmings marching blindly toward their doom. "Lemmings" was screened, but after it Steve himself came out blindfolded. Then he held out "a hand of peace" to their rival, promising an attitude of competitive coexistence, a dialogue between alien data environments.

"When we spoke of a two-horse race in personal computers in 1984," he said, "it might have seemed like we were on a collision course with IBM. But in 1985, as the smoke clears from the '84 shakeout, many of these large corporations are telling us that they're going to use both Apple and IBM workstations, or that they want to use Macintoshes to talk with their IBM mainframes. It's imperative that we talk with the IBM part of the world, that we exchange information and have frequent discourse. So for 1985, Apple proposes détente with IBM." A mock-up of *The Wall Street Journal* appeared onscreen above him with a headline that read, APPLE DECLARES DÉTENTE WITH IBM.

The concept he outlined—the concept of a Macintosh Office, linking small groups of workers electronically to each other and to the outside world—was, he declared, part of a transition between the first decade of the personal-computer revolution, in which the computer was transformed into a personal servant, and the second, in which it became a communications tool as well. He neatly summarized Apple's contribution to the first decade with a heartwarming little story. "I got a letter from a six-and-a-half-year-old boy a couple of months ago," he declared with a grin, "which to me completely sums up what we've accomplished in the last few years. It reads, 'Dear Mr. Jobs: I was doing a crossword puzzle and the clue was "As American as Apple——." I thought the answer was "computer," but my mom said it was "pie." ' "

But Apple's contribution to the second decade was going to be more problematical. The only new products Steve had to unveil were the AppleTalk network, the LaserWriter printer, and the Macintosh XL, which was simply Lisa with a hard disk and a new name. The products that would complete the concept—the FileServer to store everyone's computer files, software to send electronic mail over the network, a plug-in circuit board to allow IBM PCs to be hooked up to it as well—were promised for some time in the fall.

Bob felt nothing as he watched all this, null, nada. A few minutes later, as the crowd was dispersing, Steve came out to greet his team. Suddenly, as if from nowhere, huge tears welled up in Bob's eyes. All these expectations, all the work still in front of them—"We've got so much to do!" he cried. "And it's all such a mess!" Then he started sobbing and was unable to speak at all.

■ ■ ■

The stockholders' meeting, and the press conference that followed it, made for a brief hurrah. The board met that afternoon, as it did after every stockholders' meeting by dint of corporate charter, and this time its deliberations were not quite so perfunctory as usual. The board members were unhappy—with Steve, with John, with the way the two of them were behaving. It wasn't so much the unsold computers that were piling up in stores and warehouses; John was keeping them informed about that, and as long as they didn't get any surprises, they could take the philosophical view. They'd all been through downturns, and they'd get through this one. But they weren't at all happy about the way John and Steve were running the company together. Mike Markkula, who still had an office at Apple, had been getting calls from people who were upset at what was happening, and he and the other board members had decided to put the two of them on notice.

So the meeting ended with a sternly parental lecture in which the two errant youngsters were told to mend their ways. John was told he was being paid a lot of money to run the company and that's what they wanted him to do—run the company. Steve was told that he was *not* supposed to be running the company—he was supposed to run the Macintosh division, which, by the way, he wasn't doing such a great job at. He was told to mind his own shop and leave the rest of the company alone. He left the boardroom that afternoon in an uncharacteristic state—quiet, withdrawn. He walked across a couple of parking lots to Bandley 3, disappeared into his office, and sat down in front of his Macintosh. "I will not criticize the rest of the organization," he typed. "I will not criticize the rest of the organization. I will not criticize . . ."

The next morning, at the Red Lion Inn in San Jose, he and John had to face the stock analysts. The quarterly financial results had been announced the week before, and they were clearly problematical. On the one hand, sales for the Christmas quarter were spectacular—$698 million, more than double what they'd been the previous Christmas. On the other hand, as John had pointed out when the figures were released, the dealers were burdened with inventory and sales were already dropping off. The second quarter would be distinctly less spectacular, not just for Apple but for the whole industry.

Apple stock fell more than two points on the day he made his announcement. Even so, most analysts were less concerned about the excess inventory than about the shortcomings of the Macintosh Office. Michele Preston of L. F. Rothschild was calling the Mac Office a critical product and 1985 a critical year, and a lot of other people on Wall Street shared her view. They were clearly unhappy that the announcements at Flint Center did not include a file server.

But the big news at the Red Lion wasn't the Mac Office, it was

Macintosh itself. In the earnings announcement the week before, Apple had declined to break out the results by product line. Now Steve finally had to admit that Macintosh sales were disappointing. He told the analysts that Mac had been "left out in the cold" over the Christmas season. Of the totals for the quarter, the Apple II had contributed nearly $500 million; Macintosh had brought in only $200 million. John predicted that Mac sales for the current quarter would come to $200 million as well. Yet despite the poor sales and the strains they were causing, the two of them still seemed to be on the same wavelength. They still looked like a dynamic duo. Some thought it uncanny.

In the middle of the meeting, however, John was interrupted by a phone call. He disappeared for about ten minutes; the analysts barely noticed he was gone.

It was Wozniak on the line—hardly someone John heard from often—and he was mad. Woz had gone to work at the Triangle Building that morning and found the engineers in a bad state because they'd been left out of the stockholders' meeting the day before. They'd wanted to show that an Apple II could run a LaserWriter as well as Macintosh, but the demonstration had been yanked at the last moment. Instead, the II had barely been mentioned all morning. Woz himself was used to this kind of treatment—the II had been shoved aside for years, first in favor of the III, then for Lisa, now for Macintosh. But the others weren't, and it made him angry to see them so demoralized. Some of them were saying they were going to write a protest letter to Sculley. When he heard that, he went straight for the phone, because he knew his voice would be heard.

When John got on the line, Woz said, "As Apple's third-largest stockholder for the past eight years . . ." He knew that would get the guy's attention. And he knew that the thing the board of directors—any board of directors—feared most was a lawsuit alleging deceptive actions. So he told Sculley that the stockholders' meeting had presented a deceptive and fraudulent portrayal of the company's earnings. He told him that the people who own the company ought to be given an accurate picture of where their earnings were coming from. John tried to tell him it was just event marketing—that the Apple II had gotten its day in April at Moscone Center and this new product announcement just happened to coincide with the annual meeting. Woz pointed out that Steve had had plenty of time to talk about Macintosh at the Moscone event, and besides, the II wasn't even mentioned during the formal business session, when the officers got up to report on the state of the company. John tried to argue; Woz wouldn't have it. John tried to tell him they were providing the analysts with all the numbers: There, at least, the II was getting fair credit. But he found himself talking to a dial tone.

Woz had hung up on him.

16

Birthday

Every year around the end of January, most of the top executives in the business dropped whatever they were doing and boarded planes that would take them to Esther Dyson's Personal Computer Forum. There were workshops and panel discussions and speeches, including one this year by MIT's Marvin Minksy, the dean of artificial intelligence researchers. (Dyson had recently become taken with the potential of artificially intelligent personal computers.) But nobody went for the educational offerings. They went because it gave them all a chance to get together. At the sun-drenched tennis courts and desert swimming pools of the Pointe Tapatio Resort Hotel, far from the hubbub of trade shows, they could relax and talk deals—assuming, of course, that they liked to talk deals in a fishbowl.

The Pointe Tapatio was, in fact, the one spot in America where Silicon Valley, Route 128, Wall Street, Madison Avenue, and the corporate suburbs of New York all converged. Heavyweights from every corner of the industry were there: Rod Canion of Compaq, Bill Gates of Microsoft, Mitch Kapor of Lotus, Billy Ladin of ComputerCraft, Michele Preston of L. F. Rothschild, Floyd Kvamme of Kleiner Perkins. Apple sent twenty people, including Jobs and Sculley and three vice-presidents. IBM was amply represented, as were AT&T, Texas Instruments, and Hewlett-Packard. Data General, Digital Equipment, and Xerox were there; so were Morgan Stanley, Dean Witter, and Shearson Lehman; so were Chiat/Day, Burson-Marsteller, and Lord, Geller; so were *Business Week*, *Fortune*, and *The Wall Street Journal*. Most of the speakers this year took on the issue of innovation: John Sculley said there ought to be more of it, Ben Rosen accused IBM of stifling it, and Billy Ladin said he'd had about all he could handle. A couple of dozen software entrepreneurs tried to get Lotus to buy them out over drinks. Everybody was worried about their ideas being stolen, although, as Dyson pointed out, the real problem is usually getting them accepted.

Esther Dyson occupied a unique position in the industry. Raised in Princeton and educated at Harvard, she'd worked first as a reporter at *Forbes* and later as an analyst on Wall Street, where she fell in love with the Federal Express story and then with the personal-computer industry. Having left *Forbes* to get closer to the action, she left the Street to get closer still. She went to work for Ben Rosen, who'd recently decided to take advantage of his apparent clairvoyance by going into business as a venture capitalist, offering funding to promising start-ups. But Rosen was finding it awkward to put out a newsletter that covered the same industry he was investing in, so Dyson soon took over his *Rosen Electronics Letter* (which she renamed *RELease 1.0*) and his Personal Computer Forum as well. Working out of a cluttered office in the Seagram Building, she became the consummate insider, jetting ceaselessly around the country to dine with the movers and shakers, always ready with a quip when reporters called. The Personal Computer Forum hadn't become a fishbowl by accident; it was *her* fishbowl, and she made sure it was well stocked.

Mike Murray came this year with his own agenda. He wanted to get John in a room with Regis McKenna, whose opinions he knew John would take seriously, and tell him what desperate shape Apple seemed to be in. He'd prepared for this moment carefully. He'd planned his presentation. He'd written a memo that contained a ten-point strategy for turning the company around in the next ninety days. He'd rounded up Regis and John and was walking across a parking lot with them when they came across Steve. Steve said hi and asked what they were doing. Mike had to make up something fast, so he said they were just going to talk about some advertising stuff. Steve's face brightened and he offered to come along. Mike said no, he just wanted to try something out on these guys.

When they arrived at John's suite, he handed John the memo. As the three of them settled into easy chairs, he told John that he thought Apple was acting more like two companies than one. Instead of competing with IBM, the two product divisions were fighting with each other. It wasn't the personalities, he went on; it was the structure. He thought they ought to have one engineering organization, one marketing organization, one manufacturing operation. And he thought Steve should be removed as general manager of the Mac division. Management was obviously not his strong point, so they should find another role for him, something entrepreneurial and visionary and critical to the company's future.

John looked at the memo with its ten points and put it aside. Interesting, he said. But he couldn't do anything that radical; if he tried, it would break Apple. Mike said that if he *didn't* do something, it would break Apple. John returned his memo and thanked him for his concern.

■ ■ ■

Steve had his own plans. On January 31, the day after they got back from Phoenix, he took his staff off to Pajaro Dunes for an overnight retreat, and there he set out some ideas. The brief brush with humility he'd experienced after the board meeting was now forgotten. Massive growth seemed just around the corner, and he saw no better time to prepare for it than the present. He envisioned a huge Macintosh division with multiple engineering departments and multiple marketing departments and an entire galaxy of products. There were companies he wanted to acquire, not just dinosaurs like Xerox but fledgling operations barely out of the garage—techie outfits like Woodside Design, whose owner had just brought him a flat-panel display that was so crisp and efficient, so much better than anything on the market, that it could make "Mac in a book by 1986" a reality. He'd found another little start-up in Ohio that made a touch-screen—a pressure-sensitive display that would obviate the need for a mouse. With a flat-panel touch-screen you could build a notebook-sized Macintosh with a hard disk inside—perfect for, say, a college kid trying to take notes. Frogdesign was already busy designing models of BookMac, the first prototype for Alan Kay's long-sought Dynabook. Steve wanted to build a brand-new factory in Fremont to produce displays. He wanted to turn Woodside Design into an incredibly great research-and-development facility where brilliant individuals could work in isolation from the corporate environment. Macintosh, Apple Displays, AppleLabs—maybe he'd run them all.

This was Steve's management approach, to state a future no rational person would even dream of and try to make it real. Now he'd gathered them all in a room by the Pacific to draw his empire on the board. Debi and Susan and Mike seemed involved in what he was saying, and Jay Elliot was listening attentively, but Bob—what was Bob doing? Looking at tide tables? Bob was studying *tide tables* while he was rearticulating the vision?

"Bob," he said sharply, "could you join this meeting, please?"

Bob looked up, his exasperation masked by an expression of utter impassivity. Bob was not impressed with Steve's dreams of expansion, and as for the display, he figured they'd have to invest $30 million and who-knew-how-many years to get it rolling. As far as he was concerned, this was just another example of Steve getting lost in his reality-distortion field. Steve was silly. Tides were real. "No," he replied blandly. "The tide tables are more interesting."

What Bob thought they should be talking about was why they were failing. They *were* failing, he reminded them. There was no point in planning this big company Steve was dreaming up, because (1) Steve wasn't running it, and (2) they ought to be worrying about how they were going to be not failing. Why didn't they talk about that?

So they did, and that really got them into trouble. Soon Bob and Mike and Steve were standing on their knees on a sofa fighting about *Inside Macintosh,* the promotional publication Apple was selling to software developers. A three-volume set as thick as a phone book, it contained everything a programmer needed to know about the system; but because it was professionally typeset and printed on glossy paper, it cost nearly eighty dollars. Bob wanted something like the catalogs that electronics companies put out—loose-leaf binders crammed with typewritten pages and selling for two or three bucks apiece. He wanted every college student in America to be developing software for Macintosh. But when he'd complained, the people in publications got upset, and since publications was part of marketing, Mike got upset too. So they stood there on their knees and argued about it, and Steve decided that Bob was acting weird.

A couple of days later, Jay Elliot came around the engineering lab to speak to Bob about this. Apple's human-resources department was far more than the paper-shuffling personnel bureaucracy of most corporations; it was the guardian of Apple culture, and one of its jobs was to work these personality clashes out. For every senior manager in the company there was a corresponding human-resources manager, usually female, forming a sort of shadow management team whose job was to find out what the real management and the people who worked for them were feeling. Bob and Mike and Debi and Susan all had their own HR directors, as did their counterparts in the Apple II division. Steve had little use for Mary Fortney, the HR manager for the Macintosh division—she was a holdover from the Lisa group—so Jay acted as a personal facilitator for him and John in addition to his official duties as the HR vice-president. The combination of HR's confessional role and Steve's emotionally childlike nature gave a let-it-all-hang-out air to the Macintosh division that people in the rest of the company found unnerving—especially John, who'd been schooled to think of emotional sincerity as something akin to suicide. Bob, who was a little too Midwestern and Protestant himself for this brand of California pop-psych experience, referred to Jay's HR operatives as the Bene Gesserit, after the witches in *Dune* who actually ran the planet. They took it as a compliment.

It was about this time that the HR director for Macintosh engineering came to Bob's office and threatened to quit because she could never get in to see him. Bob was a busy man, but he didn't want her to quit—he was learning too much from her—so he responded in a way that was almost breathtaking. He told her that for the next two weeks, she could go everywhere he went. They dubbed it the "Velcro experience." She sat in on all his meetings, joined him for lunch with Steve, followed him everywhere except the bathroom. At the end of every day they discussed all his interactions to see how they could repair his relationships with people. It went so well that by the second week a dozen other executives around the company were having their own Velcro experiences, Jay Elliot among them. Bob was proud of himself. He'd invented a whole new management technique. He felt great.

During their two weeks, the two of them uncovered a number of personality traits that fed the distrust between him and Mike. For example, the way Bob spoke—slowly and deliberately, and sometimes with excruciatingly long pauses between sentences while he tried to find exactly the right wording for his thoughts. Mike interpreted this as a sign of deviousness, as if he were striving for the right effect. But there were deeper problems as well, like the fact that neither Mike nor Bob had much respect for each other's abilities. Bob thought Mike was a dismal failure—great at advertising, but what they needed now was someone who could get on top of sales. And every time Mike went over to the engineering lab, the only thing he saw was a black hole where the FileServer should be. The LaserWriter was obviously going to appeal to just a small number of people; without the FileServer, the Macintosh Office was a joke.

The FileServer really was in trouble now. After the Mac Office introduction, when the sales people started talking to corporate data-processing professionals, they ran head-on into all the "sociological" issues that Bob and Bud Tribble had been hoping to avoid. Corporate data-processing managers weren't very interested in networking three or four people; they wanted to network whole departments, and they were well aware of the issues involved, even if Apple's sales and marketing people weren't. Passwords and file protection and system administration were issues the ARPA researchers who'd invented time sharing had grappled with twenty years before. Anyone who studied computer science in college was bound to encounter them. But they were unfamiliar concepts at Apple, because Apple was still a "One person—one computer" company. Asking it to develop a network was like trying to get Nissan to develop a subway system.

So marketing came back to engineering and announced that the FileServer that had been promised didn't meet the needs of the market. But when they defined a product that met the needs of the market, engineering said they didn't have the resources to do it. Things continued like this, back and forth, back and forth, for meeting after meeting. It didn't help that the people who did understand the trade-offs involved, like Bud Tribble and Bob, were so lousy at explaining them. They tended to rely on phrases like "Well, Mike, you don't know how technical this really is." At this point Mike didn't *care* how technical it was, he just wanted the FileServer. Already the sales force was demotivated, the dealers didn't believe anything they were told anymore, the marketing department was so demoralized it was ready to quit, and they'd all made a joke of themselves. Marketing operated in long pipelines, just like engineering: It took months to prepare a sales-training video, and if you learned today that a product would be late, tomorrow you had to redo all your marketing plans. That meant they were operating in fire-drill mode all the time. Mike was getting increasingly disillusioned and detached. As he did so, he began to gravitate toward the Pink Palace.

Of Steve's four staff members, Mike was the only one whose job put him in regular contact with Sculley. They'd worked closely on advertising; they'd traveled together to trade shows and product rollouts. Mike seemed to look up to Sculley, to view him as a role model. As he began to spend more and more time in Sculley's office, however, Bob and Debi began to worry. Steve was becoming increasingly erratic, and as Sculley turned up the pressure on him to perform, Steve started blaming Sculley for Mac's failure: The salesmen were bozos, distribution ate up too much margin, finance wasn't reporting the numbers right, and he was doing nothing. He wasn't providing leadership. Bob and Debi got snippets of this, and as the mood grew worse, they went to Bill and Del and Jay, trying to figure out what was going on and how to make things right. They even talked with Jay about the possibility that he might take over the division on an interim basis. But they knew where their ultimate loyalties lay, and they weren't so sure about Mike's. Was he trying to pull something? Was Sculley, the master marketer, simply taking a promising young guy under his wing, or was Mike trying to plant a foot in both camps?

Finally Bob went to Sculley himself. It was a rare encounter; certainly Sculley didn't make a habit of dropping by the engineering lab. Bob showed up at his glass-walled office at the appointed hour, and Sculley ushered him in and offered him a Pepsi. After a little nervous chitchat, Bob asked if he and Mike were plotting something. John said no, there was no possible way he'd be plotting anything with Mike. In fact, he went on, he didn't even think Mike had the wherewithal to be running Mac marketing. Bob was shocked. Well, he asked, what the heck were they going to do? They couldn't bring in anybody from outside to take over Mike's job; the situation was too delicate for that. Sculley mentioned Jean-Louis Gassée, the general manager of Apple France. Bob didn't know Gassée, so all he said was, "Oh."

Then one day Mike went into Steve's office and told him he wanted out of his job as marketing director. He was turned off by all of it— by the people he was working with, the things they were doing to each other, their inability to deal with reality. He was a little surprised that Steve didn't beg him to stay. In fact, Steve wasn't averse to the idea of his leaving at all. If Mac was failing, Mike had to be part of the problem—witness "Test Drive," which had flopped because the last thing dealers wanted at Christmas was a lot of people coming in to check out a free Macintosh. So Steve asked Mike why he wanted to leave, and Mike said it was because he wasn't enjoying himself anymore—he was spending all his time as an administrator, he wasn't doing the creative stuff, and Steve should have somebody who enjoyed being a manager. (What he meant was somebody who enjoyed mixing it up with Steve and Bob.) When Steve asked who, Mike suggested Jean-Louis Gassée.

Gassée—yes, there was an interesting idea. Gassée was the head of Apple France, the most successful of Apple's international operations. Apple was so popular in France it outsold IBM. This might solve the problem. Did Mike mind if Steve gave him a call?

■ ■ ■

If the Macintosh organization was coming unglued, one reason was that Steve was so distracted. Lagging sales, the Macintosh Office, strategic alliances, technology acquisitions, the distribution issue, John's lack of leadership—it was all beginning to pile up, and as it did so Steve had less and less time for the routine business of running the division. And then, of course, there were the demands that came simply from being Steve Jobs. On a Tuesday afternoon in the middle of February, for example, he had a date at the White House. He and Wozniak and a dozen other people—the president and the chairman of Bell Labs, the designers of IBM's System 360 mainframes in the sixties, oil men and robotics experts and engineers from Boeing— were being presented a National Technology Award, a nicely polished chunk of wood and brass which would symbolize their contribution to the American economy. For the White House it was a thoroughly routine event, half an hour in the East Room sandwiched in between the proclamation of Lithuanian Independence Day and a reunion of the Marine Corps regiment that took Iwo Jima. For the honorees, however, it was something special—the President of the United States standing at a podium and calling them heroes on a par with Thomas Edison and Alexander Graham Bell.

Actually, the president was standing at a podium telling one of his jokes; it compared favorably to Wozniak's. "One of the last times this grand old mansion played host to an event that concerned technology was back in '76," he said. "1876." Reagan paused, flashed an absentminded smile, and waited until there was no more laughter from the audience. "President Rutherford B. Hayes was shown a recently invented device. 'That's an amazing invention,' he said, 'but who would ever want to use one?' He was talking about the telephone." Pause, smile, more laughter; only a couple of reporters noted that in 1876 Ulysses Grant was still president and Rutherford Hayes was running for office. No matter. "I thought at the time that he might be mistaken," Reagan continued. Pause, smile, uproarious laughter and applause.

Steve couldn't believe he and Woz were standing there all alone in the East Room like little boys, lost among all these people. The other twelve all had friends and relatives and company representatives in the audience and would be fêted that evening with celebratory banquets. Woz had just his wife, Candi—not that he minded—and Steve had no one at all. Why hadn't John done something for him? "The story of American technology is long and proud," Reagan was saying. "It might be said to have begun with a blacksmith at his bellows, hammering out fine tools, and the Yankee craftsman using simple wood planes, saws, and mallets to fashion the fastest-sailing ships on the ocean. And then came the railroad men, driving spikes across our country." If Leland Stanford had been honored at the White House, the Southern Pacific would certainly have taken notice. Yet after it was over there was nothing for Steve and Woz to do but take a walk and duck into a sandwich shop.

Steve wasn't so happy with Wozniak these days either. Two weeks earlier Woz had left Apple to start a new venture, and his departure had been accompanied by an angry blast in *The Wall Street Journal.* "Apple's direction has been horrendously wrong for five years," he was quoted as saying, amid accusations that Apple had refused to continue development on the II and hoped it would go away and die. But that wasn't why he was leaving; he was leaving to start a new venture.

Over the past few months he'd been spending a lot of time with Joe Ennis, an eccentric young engineer in the Apple II division who had some visionary ideas for the old machine. Ennis was working on voice recognition and synthesis for a new version of the II that Wayne Rosing had started work on, a successor to the ill-fated IIx that would feature improved color graphics and sound. (In fact, Apple was continuing to update the II, although it wasn't getting any encouragement from Jobs.) Ennis's dream, however, was to take the II to the outer limits of technology by reducing the entire machine to a single chip. In that form they could take it out of its box and pop it into anything—TV sets, appliances, wall sockets, phone lines. Instead of a computer that was used in the home, it could be the computer that controlled the home, and everything in it.

Years earlier, when the Apple II was still new, Woz had sponsored the design of a phone-line controller, a circuit board that, when plugged into a II that was connected to the phone lines with a modem, could enable it to do such chores as automatic dialing. To do the job he'd hired John Draper, the infamous Captain Crunch whose phone-breaking exploits had inspired him and Jobs to build blue boxes at Berkeley. Draper designed a board that could also crack "WATS-line extenders," the four-digit codes that callers to certain 800 numbers could use to get on an outgoing WATS line and dial long distance for free; as a result, Apple refused to market it, much to Woz's displeasure. In the years since, phones themselves had been equipped with microchips, enabling them to perform the automatic dialing functions—the legal ones, at any rate—that once required a computer and a whole battery of special equipment. And Woz had come to realize that anytime a special function could be pulled out of the computer and put into a smaller and more convenient device (a pocket calculator, for instance), that's what people would want.

He and Ennis were sitting in the lab one day when they got an idea. What if you built a little gadget that could operate not just one remote-controlled home electronics device—the TV, the VCR, the CD player—but all of them? Woz was skeptical at first. He pointed out that each piece of equipment is controlled by a different code; Ennis showed him that owners could easily "train" their controllers by playing different infrared signals into them. Suddenly he realized that this was a product people could use. With twenty or so remote-controlled devices in his own home, he certainly realized it was a product *he* could use. It didn't seem right for Apple—Apple was a computer company, and this wasn't a computer—so he decided to start a new company. First, because he didn't want any trouble, they showed the idea to Del Yocam and Wayne Rosing, who passed on it just as Hewlett-Packard had passed on the Apple I a decade earlier. But Del and Wayne both said they'd buy one, and that was all the encouragement Woz and Ennis needed.

Woz decided to call his new company CL9 after the Cloud 9 Restaurant on the highway over the Hill to Santa Cruz, just down the road from his house. The product he called MBF, short for "Man's Best Friend." That's what their product would be, a faithful electronic servant. He hired frogdesign to give it a friendly look. He would provide most of the funding himself. Already he'd begun selling his Apple stock—at $30 a share, his 4 percent of the company was worth about $70 million—and putting it in municipal bonds. Now he could invest it in his own company.

To the outside world, news of Woz's defection could only mean something was dramatically wrong at Apple. Word was out that the II division, the backbone of the company, was dispirited at being treated like second-class citizens; that middle managers and key engineers were heading for the exits; that officers and directors were selling their stock in the company. Mike Markkula had sold $15 million worth of stock since the stockholders' meeting, Ken Zerbe $6 million, Joe Graziano and Del Yocam about $1 million each. Dave Larson had quit, as had the advertising director and the retail sales director. "Apple is a big business now," Sculley explained to the *Journal*. "Some people can't adjust." To replace them, he was bringing in people who could—people like Tom Marano, the new vice-president of sales, a onetime Procter & Gamble zone manager who'd been hired from PepsiCo to report to Bill Campbell. Analysts on the Street, uneasy at the signs, began saying Apple was in trouble.

Later that week, after a stormy executive staff meeting that Jobs failed to attend, Graziano turned in his resignation as well. The exec staff was meeting almost every day, trying to figure out what to do about the losses that were piling up. Their budget was based on sales of $600 million a quarter, but Joe's analysis showed that sales were going to be more like $400 million a quarter. What were they going to do—close the Singapore plant? close Dallas? have layoffs on Bandley Drive? Neither Steve nor Del wanted to take drastic cuts in his organization. Steve was still on Joe's back about the way he presented the numbers, and John wasn't exactly pleased to be running a company whose finance officers couldn't report balance sheets that were compatible with each other. Joe was as frustrated by them as they were with him. So when Steve didn't come to the exec staff meeting at which they were supposed to agree on the cuts, he decided he'd had enough. He went into John's office and asked if John had confidence in his performance. When John said no, he resigned.

John already had his replacement picked out: Dave Barram, the former Hewlett-Packard controller whom Steve had wanted to put in Susan's job in December. HP finance people were a hot commodity in the computer business. They knew how to keep track of inventory, they knew how to run things lean and mean, they knew how to show a good balance sheet, and they were always popular on Wall Street. With Barram in place, he could take inventory control out from under Campbell and put it in finance and feel confident it would be managed closely. That was the key to profitability, because the less cash they had tied up in inventory, the more you could see on the bottom line. He'd make an offer soon.

■ ■ ■

Steve's thirtieth birthday was on Sunday, February 24. He was celebrating in grand style—a formal dinner-dance for three hundred at the St. Francis Hotel, entertainment by Ella Fitzgerald. But the graciousness, the fairy-tale quality of the first Macintosh Christmas party two years ago, was gone. He was beginning to think of parties like this as a civic obligation: Somebody had to give them, so he did. And as a milestone, this one did not come at a propitious moment. Macintosh wasn't selling. Apple wasn't working. He was beginning to think he'd made a mistake hiring Sculley. He couldn't understand why John wasn't doing more about sales, about distribution, about enabling Mac to succeed. He was beginning to think John was just a manager, someone who lacked vision. He was feeling morose, and having three hundred people to entertain didn't cheer him up.

All his former girlfriends were there, and so was his new one, a gorgeous blonde who worked at Hewlett-Packard. All the key Macintosh engineers had come, even those who'd left Apple. Burrell Smith was all decked out in white—white tuxedo, white shoes, white tie. Several wore their tuxes with sneakers. Naturally, they all brought presents. Steve hated presents. Every time he went to Japan people showered him with presents; often he just left them in his hotel room. He already had everything he wanted, and he didn't want much. But people had chosen marvelous gifts for this occasion—Steuben crystal, cases of fine wine, a framed share of IBM stock from Regis McKenna—and they were naturally dismayed when he just left them there in a heap.

Dinner consisted of things like goat cheese and salmon mousse, stuff none of the engineers would touch. Woz went around the room, putting together a party to rendezvous later at Denny's for some real food. That was easy. It proved harder to find someone to propose a toast. One of the Mac crew suggested to Bob Belleville that he do it, but Bob pointed out that it was really John Sculley who should do the honors. So a couple of people went to John's table, and when they asked him he declined. Eventually he relented and made a toast to the guiding light, to the man who sees the future. Steve beamed. Then Ella came out to sing and got his name mixed up with Wozniak's.

The next day, Steve sent out a memo to all Macintosh employees entitled "Rough Sailing Ahead." It cited depressing business conditions and then asked what they could do. Well, for starters, they could get rid of the free juice. They could stop ordering in catered lunches, and they could fly business class instead of first class, and they could stop holding off-site retreats (unless they felt like bringing sleeping bags into an empty grade school or a church basement). They could also stop paying overtime and cut down on consultants. If the consultants they'd hired last year were so smart, Steve pointed out, they wouldn't be in this mess.

17

King of France

The beginning of the end came on a rainy night in March, the night John finally confronted Steve. He wasn't eager to go through with it. But Jay Elliot had been pushing for a meeting, because he thought it was time the two of them shared their feelings about each other. For John, that meant telling Steve he was dissatisfied with the way he was running Macintosh, telling him they were going to have to find something else for him to do. And yet John seemed almost afraid of Steve—afraid of his power, his eyes, his hold over him. Steve and his minions had grown openly contemptuous, not just of the II division but of corporate Apple as well—"Corportino," Debi called it. More and more, Corportino was being challenged to justify its own existence. This meeting was considerably overdue.

Sometime after six, John and Jay left the mauve confines of the Pink Palace and walked through the parking lot and around the corner to Bandley 3. Though the distance was only half a block, it was as if they'd left a glitzy suburban office park and entered a student union. Ever since '83, when all the other corporate execs had moved into the new headquarters building, Steve had kept his office here, preferring the company of his little band of pirates to that of the men who ran the company. It was a cramped little office, more appropriate for a student activities director than for the chairman of the board of a Fortune 500 corporation: a featureless cube with a round table in the middle and one small window overlooking a parking lot. John and Jay took a seat at the table. Steve joined them.

John announced that he was concerned about the Macintosh division and Steve's ability to manage it. He felt the company needed a different kind of leadership in that organization, and he wanted Steve to think about finding a new role for himself. He was also upset because he'd heard that Steve had been talking about him behind his back, and he couldn't tolerate that kind of assault on their friendship.

Steve listened to all this and then unloaded. He couldn't believe what he was hearing. Business was down, costs needed to be cut, things needed to be cleaned up, and John wasn't doing anything—he'd simply retreated. It was as if he'd gone on vacation starting in December. So he told John that *he* was the one with the problem. He was the one who wasn't doing his job. As his voice grew louder and angrier, he accused John of not helping him, not managing him, not leading him. He told John he was doing a terrible job of leading the company. He was disappointed with what John had brought to Apple. He started to cry. John bit his fingernails and looked at the wall.

John was willing to acknowledge that he hadn't been running things as aggressively as he might have, but he also had to say that Steve hadn't given him the opportunity. Steve was always interfering. That's how the finger-pointing began. Why was Mac in such trouble? Steve claimed it was because John wasn't keeping on top of the inventory situation, wasn't taking care of the distribution issue, wasn't taking charge of finance, wasn't providing the leadership to run the company. John said it was because the product wasn't right, because they didn't have the software and the office products to make it work. Maybe he had been too far removed from operations, but now he was going to take charge, and he wanted somebody else to run Macintosh. He mentioned Jean-Louis Gassée as a possibility. Finally, about one in the morning, the meeting broke up. Steve said he'd think about it.

This man Gassée was turning up more and more. First John had brought him to Cupertino in September to talk about heading up a new software division. They'd discarded that idea, but then he'd come back in February to interview for Mike's job as director of marketing for Macintosh. He'd gotten mixed marks from Steve's staff—Susan got along with him okay, but Debi found him arrogant and sexist and Bob didn't trust him. He wasn't beige, that was for sure; he was as French as a glass of Pernod, all black leather and filthy jokes. On Bandley Drive he was known as "the King of France." A wry, quasi-intellectual figure who'd once been on a list of France's ten best-dressed men, he was the technocrat as café revolutionary, spouting existential mumbo-jumbo about personal computers and the future. After a student fascination with poetry and mathematics, he'd worked for Hewlett-Packard and Data General before taking over Apple France in 1981. His success in that job made him one of the few people in the company who looked ready to move up.

But into Steve's position? Steve was of two minds about that. He'd already been thinking about eventually turning over the Macintosh division to someone like Debi or Bob while he went off to run AppleLabs or formed a group to develop the MacPhone and explore other possibilities in telecommunications. Jean-Louis was a promising candidate to run the division, and putting him in Mike's job for a while would be a good test. But Jean-Louis didn't trust Steve—or, more precisely, he didn't trust his own ability to withstand Steve's seductive powers. Steve was the most magnetic person he'd ever met; if he wasn't careful he might end up mesmerized, a vegetable. So before he'd move to California, Jean-Louis wanted a formal commitment—a letter from Steve guaranteeing that he'd take over the division within a year. Steve was furious at the idea. He thought it a bad joke. Jean-Louis stayed in Paris.

■ ■ ■

In the midst of all this—the chaos, the confusion, the accusations, the tears—came a reminder of who they were and what they were supposed to be doing. It was brought by two consultants, Pat Caddell and Scott Miller. Back in November, when Apple's election-week edition of *Newsweek* came out, Mike Murray had read a lot about Caddell, the *enfant terrible* of Washington pollsters. Caddell had recently joined forces with Miller, the former creative director on the Coke account at the McCann-Erickson advertising agency, to form a think tank they called Flying Fortress, because they spent most of their time on planes. Other clients included Sadruddin Aga Khan, whose nuclear nonproliferation conference was coming up in Monte Carlo, and Coca-Cola, which was about to bring out "new" Coke. So Mike called Caddell in Washington and invited them out for lunch with him and Steve, and they flew out and ate sprouts and talked about stuff—politics, business, what was going on in the world. They'd gotten together a few other times since then, and now, in March, Caddell and Miller were delivering their report, which was called "The Dolphin versus the Shark." They'd fallen for the vision just as thoroughly as Jay Chiat and Lee Clow had before them, and what they considered in their report was Apple's positioning in comparison with IBM's—not its product positioning (they didn't know that much about the products) but its corporate image in the marketplace of ideas.

IBM had been all but forgotten on Bandley Drive, what with all the fighting over sales and distribution and how to report the numbers. But now Caddell and Miller—the Young Turks of Washington and Madison Avenue, respectively—were telling them that Jobs had created in Apple a machine and a business and a philosophy of life that was in such direct contrast to IBM's that they didn't see how it could fail. They saw IBM in terms of people wired into the central machine, learning its syntax, adjusting to its dictates, being judged by its measure of efficiency ("Do Not Fold, Bend, Spindle, or Mutilate"). They saw Apple in terms of machines serving people, fitting their needs, enhancing their creativity. They saw not just a market competition between Apple and IBM but a conflict between two radically different visions of the individual, of the institution, and of the nation. And they didn't think much of measures like ending the free juices—"going for the capillaries," they called it. The real problem was the constant shifts in Apple's business strategies, shifts dictated by Jobs's highly unrealistic, almost childlike sense of time—his habit of saying if the world doesn't change by next Wednesday, scrap it and do another world which will change on Saturday, all the contents of which will be different by Monday.

Caddell thought Macintosh was perfect for the generation of people who want choices, options, who want the constant and inalienable right to reinvent themselves—for the people who are just like Apple people. In "The Dolphin versus the Shark," he and Miller urged them simply to let IBM be IBM. They called for "marketing jiujitsu" to turn IBM's strengths into weaknesses while transforming Apple's weaknesses into strengths. Large, menacing, and single-minded, the sharklike IBM could be surrounded and confused by a smart and agile foe. And one way Apple could be smart was to recognize that it was more than a company, it was an idea, and it should be selling that idea to the American public.

At this point, Apple was an idea in trouble; yet IBM was having problems of its own. A few days after "The Dolphin versus the Shark" was delivered to Cupertino, Don Estridge, the man who'd led the development of the PC, was declared a "hero of the IBM Corporation" and elevated to a vice-presidential job at corporate headquarters in Armonk. While Estridge's reassignment was actually very much in line with IBM's corporate policy of rotating its executives to give them the breadth of experience they needed to lead the company, the trade press interpreted it to mean he was being kicked upstairs. Clearly Armonk had decided to rein in its freewheeling PC operation in Boca Raton; not long before, sales had been taken away from Boca and given to the corporate distribution arm. And Estridge's replacement was a pin-striped corporate type named William Lowe.

Much to Armonk's surprise, the PC had evolved into IBM's basic corporate workstation, which meant its PC strategy now had to be tied into its whole office strategy. And while Boca was responsible for $5 billion of IBM's $46 billion in annual sales, it had also made some unfortunate mistakes. It couldn't meet demand for its powerful new PC AT because a California company couldn't deliver the hard disk drives it had promised—an apparent vindication of the long-standing IBM rule against relying on outside suppliers, a rule Boca had broken from the start. And the PCjr had been bungled because Boca misjudged the market. Estridge and his people expected the machine to be bought by computational naifs, but most purchasers, it turned out, knew exactly what they wanted. They wanted a computer big enough to run the programs they used at the office, and that's what Junior couldn't do.

About the time Estridge and his wife were moving into their new home in the Connecticut enclave of New Canaan, a short drive from Armonk, IBM made the magisterial announcement that it had "completed production" of the PCjr. In other words, the Junior was *fini, kaput,* gone. IBM wasn't going to build any more. Sales of the Junior had gone wild over Christmas, thanks to an ad blitz and price cuts that dropped it about two hundred dollars below the Apple IIc. Several people in the industry, Jobs among them, had suggested that Armonk was unloading Juniors at prices below what it cost to produce them—an invitation to a new antitrust suit, since dumping product in order to drive out competitors was illegal. Now, as one IBM watcher observed, Big Blue was declaring victory and pulling out. The major winner stood to be Apple.

Despite Wozniak's defection and all the others, no one yet realized that Bandley Drive was about to be the site of a crash-and-burn. At Apple, however, the signs were growing stronger. Jobs's behavior had become increasingly erratic. He'd always been subject to periodic mood swings; on a good day he was charming and companionable, but on a bad day he could turn nasty and hostile. Insiders who needed to see him generally called his assistant to find out which kind of day he was having. Now the swings were growing more and more severe. One day he was at frogdesign when he noticed some of the work the designers there were doing for Wozniak's new company. He flew into a rage and demanded that they stop immediately. He cited a clause in their contract that forbade them from working for competing companies and insisted they choose between Woz and Apple. He called Woz on the phone and announced that Apple would stomp anything that tried to compete with it.

Steve wasn't the only one acting strange. One day in the Pink Palace, Susan Barnes was with several other key finance people—the corporate treasurer, her opposite numbers in the II division and in distribution—giving a report to Sculley and his staff. John had named them all to a cost-cutting task force, a bipartisan effort to come up with a list of expenses to trim. One item that came up in the presentation caused John to remark offhandedly that she'd be covering it in the division review, right? The correct answer was "Right." But Susan said, "What division review?" And when that happened, John went nonlinear.

In engineering parlance, "to go nonlinear" means to make a discontinuous jump, to veer off the screen, to go suddenly over the edge. People were going nonlinear on Bandley Drive more and more these days, and now it was happening to John. After two years as an emotional cipher, he suddenly switched to an "on" state. He was screaming, cursing, pounding the table. He'd scheduled a formal performance review for all the different divisions of the company, and Steve had never even told his staff about it? He couldn't believe it. Well, there *was* going to be one, and if her boss didn't show up for it he'd be fired.

Susan, somewhat taken aback by all this, returned to Bandley 3 and asked Steve what was going on. Steve told her not to worry, there wasn't going to be any division review. John didn't know what he was talking about.

■ ■ ■

The April board meeting did not get off to a good start. It began, as most of them did, with a catered dinner in the boardroom on the third floor of the Pink Palace. The wall of windows above the treetops brought the Valley inside, flat green giving way to ragged mountains, the sky glowing pink and gold. But they weren't there to admire the view. The situation was worse than in January; they were in a downward spiral and accelerating fast. John wasn't managing Steve, even though several of them had told him that was his job from the beginning. Steve was doing a poor job with Macintosh. Wozniak, after returning to Apple through the back door, had left in a storm of bad publicity. The stock had gone into a nosedive. Inventories on the Macintosh and the IIc were so high they'd had to close the factories for a week. The resentment between the Macintosh and Apple II divisions had broken out into the open. Vice-presidents and middle managers were parading into Markkula's office, telling him how bad things were. The board wanted a way out, a plan.

Steve's presentation was set for the next day—Thursday, April 11. He was going to make a pitch for the technology he wanted to acquire—the technology that would make BookMac a reality. The star presentation was Woodside Design, with its flat-panel display. That morning the board members got off the elevators and found two computers set up on a table outside the boardroom—a IIc with the painfully inferior flat-panel screen that had been designed for it, and a IIe with a conventional monitor. On top of the IIe was a wire-wrap prototype of the Woodside display—a tiny screen with a blue escutcheon plate around it, dried glue oozing out around the edges, and blue wires sticking out the sides. On the screen was an animated picture of a figure running in front of a picket fence.

Woodside's proprietor was there, a thirty-three-year-old inventor named Steve Kitchen who'd come to California from New Jersey and struck it rich with a home-computer version of Donkey Kong, the popular video-arcade game. Kitchen was a wiry young man, thin and intense, with gold-rim glasses and straight black hair he wore long and behind his ears. He'd dropped out of college because he thought he knew more than his teachers, and this display suggested that he was probably right. He and Jobs had been talking since December, and in Steve's mind he'd already begun to assume the mantle of Woz and Burrell. This was the untutored genius who could lead him back to the garage—a return to Eden that promised to be a lot more luxurious than the trip out had been, if the resources that were turning up at Woodside's labs were any indication.

Jobs and Kitchen had settled on a purchase price for Woodside and its technologies of $15 million. They'd also picked out an empty building in Menlo Park, a twenty-minute drive from Cupertino, where AppleLabs' engineers could work undisturbed. Jobs was so certain the deal would go through that a few weeks earlier, when Al Eisenstat, Apple's chief legal officer, reminded him that they shouldn't hire new people until the venture had been approved by the board, he'd looked up and declared, "I *am* the board." All the same, Kitchen had decided to stage a knock-'em-dead presentation, and this was the script they were now following for the demonstration outside the boardroom.

As he stood there explaining how revolutionary the little wire-wrap display was, Jobs surreptitiously pressed the "tab" key of the IIe. Twenty seconds later, as he looked on in feigned astonishment, the monitor switched on of its own volition and a message appeared onscreen:

Excuse me, gentlemen—

I've seen dozens of one-inch-square flat panels, and everybody says the same thing:

"Just give me 10 million bucks and I'll make an Apple II-sized display."

Well . . .

Please remove my monitor and I'll show you how to save 10 million bucks—

So they did what the computer said, and underneath the monitor, where the top of the IIe should have been, they found a fully func-tioning four-by-five-inch display screen embedded in a molded plastic panel that bore the logos of Apple and Woodside Design. They flipped up the panel, which was less than an inch thick, and as they watched, a little Macintosh cartoon appeared onscreen. "Whimper," said the cartoon. "Gotta lose weight. How? Of course—Flat Mac!"

Well, that was certainly worth a chuckle or two and a slap on the back as they proceeded into the boardroom. Once inside, Kitchen and Jobs made an elaborate twenty-minute pitch for the labs and for the flat-panel factory, which they estimated could be producing 20,000 displays a month after an investment of eighteen months and $20 million. Impressed as they were with Kitchen's demonstration, however, the board members were not convinced that Jobs could get a factory up on time and on budget. Their experience with the Macintosh factory didn't make them any more sanguine. As Henry Singleton pointed out, this kind of manufacturing wasn't just a matter of stuffing chips into boards; it was basic materials processing, something no one at Apple had any experience with. They were already unhappy with the way Jobs was running the Macintosh division, and they certainly weren't ready to hand him another.

There was one final item on the agenda. It was John's. He wanted Steve to step down as general manager of the Macintosh division. He could stay on as chairman and he could continue to have a major voice in the company, but he couldn't stand over John in one capacity and serve under him in another. What's more, the partnership between them was over. From now on, Apple's "one leader" would have to be John alone. If the board didn't back him on this, it would have to find another president. John was no longer willing to stay with things as they were.

Steve was stunned. He couldn't believe John would do it. But the board wanted to meet privately with John. As he stepped out into the hall, Steve saw Del standing nearby. He went up to Del and told him he wouldn't believe what John was trying to do to him. Then he started to cry. Del put his arms around him and the two of them stood there, awkwardly, while the board members debated his fate.

Then they wanted to meet privately with Steve, and when they had him alone they roasted him. They told him he was a punk kid who didn't know what he was doing. They told him to shut up and let John run the company. They told him to find somebody else to head up Macintosh. As for the Woodside acquisition, they tabled it. The issue remained open, but before he could go ahead, Steve would have to satisfy their concerns.

■ ■ ■

The board meeting ended late that afternoon. Steve didn't return to Bandley 3 after it was over, and he didn't show up the next day either. Early the following week he flew to Tokyo with Bob Belleville for a ten-day trip to look at the latest research in flat-panel display technologies at companies like Epson and Sony. Steve was a morose presence, sullen and withdrawn; but a couple of engineers were traveling with them, so Bob had little chance to talk with him about what had happened on Thursday. He'd scheduled a brief respite in Kyoto in the middle of their visit, one day and two nights with nothing to do but visit Zen temples and gardens. They were staying at the Tawaraya, a three-hundred-year-old *ryokan* in which all the ancient traditions of Japanese inn-keeping were observed. Their room opened on two sides to an interior garden, a small and harmonious paradise from which all the clamor of modern Japan had been shut out. As soon as they had their baths and donned their robes and ate their meal, Steve fell back on his tatami mat and went to sleep. Bob rose early the next morning and went for a walk, and when he returned at nine he had to wake Steve up. He'd been sleeping for fourteen hours.

The next day they took the train to Matsumoto, a castle town high in the Japan Alps, to visit Epson. The cherry trees were in bloom, their delicate pink blossoms affording an exquisite contrast to the deep green forests and the snow-covered peaks. Steve ignored the view. Epson took them to an elaborate beef dinner, which embarrassed everyone because Steve, whose idea of junk food was chicken, wouldn't touch it. It wasn't until they were on the train back to Tokyo that Bob finally got a chance to talk with him alone about the board meeting. After hearing his story, Bob left no doubt where he stood. If Steve wanted to run the company, fine; he'd help any way he could. Otherwise, he was out. He didn't want to work for Gassée, and he certainly wasn't impressed by Sculley, who seemed totally uninterested in engineering and struck him as a cold fish besides.

This had a galvanizing effect on Steve. After they checked into the Okura, he went to his room and called John at home—it was the middle of the night in California—and told him what he thought of him and where he could go. The next morning, as if by magic, he woke up feeling delightfully refreshed. When he came down for breakfast he seemed to be floating on air. Wasn't it wonderful here in Tokyo? No, Bob groused, it wasn't wonderful at all. It's horribly expensive, you can't get coffee with your breakfast, and you could wait half an hour for your scrambled eggs. No, no, Steve insisted, it's *beautiful*. Bob wanted to know what he'd been drinking. But of course he hadn't been drinking anything; he'd simply had a long talk with Sculley, and now everything was going to be fine.

■ ■ ■

When Steve got to Norita for the flight back to San Francisco, he ran into Wayne Rosing in the JAL ticket line. Rosing had never been one of his favorite people—he was the minicomputer designer from Digital whom John Couch had hired to design Lisa, and now, as engineering director of the Apple II division, he was the sole remaining senior engineer whose vision diverged from Steve's. Wayne wasn't that fond of Steve, either. As they stood in the ticket line, Steve unloaded on one of Wayne's pet engineering projects. Later, when Wayne got back to Cupertino, John came to Del's staff meeting and made the same criticism. Wayne didn't believe in coincidences. He had no idea what had happened at the board meeting, so he simply read this as another example of top-down management, with Steve pulling Sculley's strings. Sun Microsystems, an ambitious computer start-up in Mountain View, was trying to lure him away to run its engineering operation, and he knew what would happen to him if Steve and John got into a power struggle and John lost. He called Sun and accepted.

Wayne's departure threw the II division even further into disarray, just as the chaos in Steve's camp was spilling out into public view. The situation was crystallized by the abrupt cancellation of the Macintosh XL, the refitted Lisa that was supposed to serve as the hard-disk machine for the Macintosh Office until they could re-engineer Mac itself to take a hard disk. Sales and engineering had sailed right past each other on that one. Bill Campbell wanted all the sales he could make; Bob Belleville was convinced they were losing money on every one. With Bob's encouragement, Steve had decided to build only as many as they had parts for. By the end of 1984, Lisa sales had dropped to just a few hundred a month, so it looked like they'd have plenty of parts to keep going until the Macintosh replacement was ready. But after the Macintosh Office introduction in January, with the machine repositioned as the Mac XL and the price cut to $3,995, sales suddenly took off. New parts couldn't be ordered in time to maintain production, and Campbell was afraid that word of the parts snafu would leak out to dealers. So while Steve and Bob were in Japan, Apple announced that the machine was being discontinued.

There were signs about this time that the Mac Office strategy might actually be working. Federal Express had recently placed a $5-million order, and orders of $2 to $3 million were coming in from companies like Honeywell, Motorola, and GTE. The sense of the industry, however, was that Macintosh would never really be accepted by corporate America until Apple delivered sophisticated business software and developed the networking capacity to tie Macintosh to the IBM world. Yet serious networking, like the FileServer, remained no more than a promise, and Lotus had just announced that Jazz wouldn't be out until May, two months late. The Mac XL was one of the few components of the Macintosh Office that was actually in place, and now, only three months after its introduction, it was being suddenly and inexplicably canceled. "People were beginning to think that Apple had its act together," one puzzled analyst told the *Journal*. Now they had to think again.

The erratic product announcements, the highly publicized defections, the surfeit of inventory, the week-long factory holiday—all were beginning to take their toll. Apple stock was trading around $20 a share, so low there was talk it would invite a hostile takeover. Wall Street and Silicon Valley both were rife with rumors, fueled by the recent procession of high-level visitors from AT&T, from GE, from GM. Xerox, Digital Equipment, and Wang were also frequently mentioned as suitors. Apple executives admitted trying to forge a "strategic relationship" that would help them penetrate the office market but insisted the company was not for sale. In fact, the reason it wasn't for sale was that no one was interested in buying it: In recent weeks, the talks Steve and John had been conducting with GM, GE, AT&T, and Wang had all fizzled out.

No one on the outside was yet aware of the fighting between Steve and John. But if the analysts were in a mood to be wary on May 1, when they gathered at Rickey's Hyatt House for Apple's spring analysts' meeting—and a lot of them were—they found nothing there to reassure them. Events at Rickey's suggested a company under siege. Reporters were barred from the room. Neither Steve nor Del was anywhere to be seen, and John was clearly nervous and on edge. His face looked haggard, so creased and drawn from tension and lack of sleep that he seemed to have aged ten years since January. Instead of giving his usual suave performance, he was short and snappish. He took a few questions and then cut out abruptly, without even staying for cocktails. People left with the feeling something big was about to blow.

They were right. John was now drawing new org charts on the board behind his office door, org charts which showed the company divided up by function rather than by product. With this scheme he could eliminate the competing product divisions with their duplicate functions—engineering, marketing, finance, manufacturing—and form a single product development group, a single marketing organization, and a single manufacturing operation. Steve was bitterly opposed to the idea; large functional organizations, he argued, never have the entrepreneurial flair of small groups committed to a single product vision. He was convinced that great products don't come into being because marketing decides what the market needs and engineering builds it to order; they come about through a constant series of interactions between marketing, engineering, and manufacturing, all of them working together in an environment where excellence is demanded. That's what he'd tried to create with Macintosh.

And he was no longer prepared to give it up, either. The dressing-down he'd gotten from the board on April 11 had had a catalytic effect. He'd trusted John, he'd trusted the board, and now they'd turned on him. If he let them shunt him off to the sidelines, the revolution would march by without him. John and the board were businessmen, not visionaries. They were going to screw it up. They didn't understand the consumers, they didn't understand the marketplace, and most of all they didn't understand the computer's potential—the opportunity it gave them to change the way people lived and worked and thought. He did. This was his chance to change the world, and he wasn't going to stand by and have it taken away from him by people who had eyes only for the bottom line.

And yet it wasn't entirely clear how much choice he'd have. He'd returned from Japan to find Jean-Louis Gassée in Cupertino, fresh from a ropes-on-the-beach experience Jay Elliot had been running at Pajaro Dunes. A few days later, still defiant, he sat down with John and Jay and Gassée at the round table in John's office to discuss the transition John wanted to effect. Gassée would come in as marketing director for Macintosh, but in fact he was going to run the division while Steve went off to do research and development, possibly as head of AppleLabs. The big question John had was, would Debi Coleman work with him? Jay had just thrown them together at Pajaro Dunes with precisely this question in mind. So they called her in from the factory in Fremont and asked her. She looked around the table at the somber faces, thought for five seconds, and said yes.

Nothing was settled that day; Gassée returned to France. A few days later, Jay flew to Paris to attend an HR conference for Apple

International—forty people meeting in the stately grandeur of the Hôtel Inter-Continental just off the Place de la Concorde, the vast ceremonial expanse where, not quite two centuries before, Louis XVI had been beheaded. Jean-Louis came in to meet him from Apple France, four miles down the Champs-Elysées in the harshly modern suburb of Neuilly. Jay was staying at the Hôtel Lotti, next door to the Inter-Continental and across the street from IBM. They had a drink downstairs, surrounded by tapestries and marble. It was late afternoon.

Jay was direct. He told Jean-Louis, whom he addressed always as John-Louie, that the relationship between John and Steve was getting worse. They needed some stability in Cupertino, someone who could provide leadership and make a difference. He wanted Jean-Louis to come in as marketing director for Macintosh. He couldn't promise what job he'd end up in; he just needed to go back there and have faith that it would work out. When Jean-Louis expressed some reluctance to move halfway across the world and risk being blown out of his job in a week, Jay told him he'd simply have to have faith that Apple—that is, Jay—wouldn't let that happen. Jean-Louis felt queasy, but he agreed.

Jay was playing his trump card. With John and Steve at an impasse, he was now the *de facto* leader of Apple, and he'd decided it was time to act. For months he'd been working in subtle ways to make Gassée—Gallic, quixotic, profane—seem less alien to people in Cupertino. He wanted them to think of Jean-Louis as he did, as John-Louie. He'd brought him over repeatedly, arranged lunch dates so Steve's staff could get acquainted with him, paired him with Debi at Pajaro Dunes. He didn't know what would happen between John and Steve, but he felt confident that somehow Steve would agree to take a different role. When that happened, they'd need somebody to take over Macintosh. And if the Macintosh division ceased to be— if they merged it with the II division to form a single product-development group—they'd need somebody to lead that effort. It was too late to bring in an outsider. Jean-Louis was no engineer, but with his visionary style and his reputation for savvy marketing, he was the only person inside the company who seemed capable of the task.

That night, in his room upstairs at the Lotti, Jay called Steve and told him what he'd done. Steve got angry; he didn't want Gassée around. But Jay insisted it was the right thing to do. Apple needed him, Jay said, and as the head of HR he'd decided to bring him over.

18

China Trip

Saturday, May 11, and yet another crisis had been penciled into Mike Murray's life. This time the trouble was Billy Ladin's. The ComputerCraft chain was in big trouble financially, and Billy and his management team were flying in from Houston to see what Apple could do to help them out. Bill Campbell had scheduled an early-morning meeting in the boardroom. Mike rolled out of bed a little after six and padded gingerly through the house so he wouldn't wake the kids. The trees were so thick it was still dark inside; he groped for the bathroom light and shut the door. Outside, the sun crept up on a prim if slightly exotic suburban streetscape, the low-slung ranches half-hidden behind their double garages, the tiny yards lush with bougainvillea and lemon trees. By seven he was dressed and ready.

The drive from Los Altos to Cupertino was easy—a short sprint down Foothill Expressway, arrow-straight through Los Altos along the route of the old Blossom Car streetcar line; then a curve and the on-ramp to Interstate 280, the Junipero Serra Freeway, just as it dropped into the Valley from the grass-covered hills. A scant half-mile to the west the Oriental tower of a Catholic seminary presided over a medieval landscape; in the other direction lay Cupertino, all condos and gas stations with the crackle of high-tension wires overhead. The Pit, as they called it in Santa Cruz, but it was a Pit that held a singular allure, a Pit that could suck you right in. Into the Pit, right at the De Anza exit, then a couple of blocks down the vine-shaded boulevard—*vroom! vroom!*—then right again and one block over to Bandley. The Mac Building faced due west, into its own parking lot.

Mike walked in and found Jean-Louis Gassée sitting outside Steve's office. That was strange—wasn't Gassée supposed to be in France?—but he was in too much of a hurry to give it much thought. He went to his own office, quickly reviewed his presentation, and headed over to the Pink Palace for the meeting. On his way out he stopped for a moment to chat with Jean-Louis. Naturally, the first thing he asked was what Jean-Louis was in town for.

Jean-Louis was at something of a loss. He was there to take Mike's job, and Jay had assured him that Steve would tell Mike all about it. Mike did *know* why he was there, didn't he? But no, Mike didn't know. So Jean-Louis, not knowing what else to say, simply said he was there to accept the job of marketing director for Macintosh.

Mike said, "Oh!" Immediately he saw his whole life pass in front of his eyes. He didn't mind if Gassée took over his job—it had been his idea in the first place, after all—but this wasn't how he wanted to find out. He wanted another job first. For three years they'd run him mercilessly, and now that he was exhausted (*crash and burn*) they were just going to toss him aside? He felt insulted. He felt used and thrown away. He couldn't believe Steve would do this. As soon as the meeting with Billy Ladin was over, he raced home and told his wife what had happened. Joyce was as shocked as he was. He decided to go back and confront Steve. As he slammed the car door, their four-year-old son turned to Joyce and in his little-boy voice said, "Life's tough, isn't it, Mom?"

Kids say the darnedest things, Mike thought as he sped down Foothill. Up the on-ramp, swoop down 280, hard right on De Anza, squealing halt in the parking lot. Steve was in his office with Jean-Louis. Mike walked in and told him they needed to talk about today.

"Sure," Steve said. "About what?"

"About this," Mike said, eyeing Jean-Louis.

"Really?" Now it was Steve's turn to be lost. After all, it was Mike who'd suggested bringing Gassée in for the job. And he was sure he'd told Mike that Gassée would be coming. Orchestrate Mike's next career move? Well, of course they'd figure out something else for him to do. The question was what, and when.

That evening, Sculley called Mike at home. He apologized for the way the whole thing had been handled and suggested they get together at Steve's the next day to find him a new job. So about two on Sunday afternoon—he was a bit early—Mike drove up 280 from Los Altos to Woodside, where Steve had bought a new house a couple of months before.

Thirty years ago, Los Altos had been the kind of town where people rode down Main Street on horseback and hitched their steeds to a rail. Woodside still was. The Sculleys lived in Woodside too, but on the east side of the freeway, the well-manicured side, in a safe executive Tudor with persimmon interiors and a view of the country club. Leezy had good taste—*Architectural Digest* taste. Steve's place was on the other, horsier side, where the houses were scattered apart and the landscape not so tamed. While the house he'd left in Los Gatos had been the black sheep of a suburban hillside paradise, this one took no note of conventional notions of respectability. This was the estate of someone who could afford to ignore them—a secluded rancho on the outskirts of a quiet country village much favored by semiconductor millionaires. Its hacienda, a rambling white stucco pile which could have been left over from a Rudolph Valentino fantasy about the life of the dons, had been built by a San Francisco inventor whose city home was the top floor of the St. Francis Hotel. La Casita Español, he and his wife had called it: the Spanish Cottage. Grand in scale, with an arched entrance loggia and vast, echoing chambers, it had fallen into disrepair and was all but devoid of furnishings. Steve was already having plans for a new house drawn up.

John wasn't yet there when Mike arrived, so Steve walked him around the grounds and they talked. Mike was his confidant, and Steve was agitated. Something had to change, Steve had decided. John had to go. He simply didn't know what was going on. He didn't understand how the business worked, or how complex it is to take products out, or what a leverage point distribution could be. If Apple closed down all its distribution centers and went with Federal Express, they'd realize not just financial economies but information-gathering economies as well. It could take weeks to discover that Macs were piling up in company warehouses and on dealers' shelves, but if they piled up in Fremont, someone would notice right away. If they could just get rid of the warehouses—

John's Mercedes pulled into the drive. Suddenly it was time to stop worrying about John and figure out what to do with Mike. Now it was Steve's turn to become the bad guy while Mike and John tried to come up with a new job. After talking it over for a while, they decided to make him "director of business development," a post in which he'd investigate acquisitions opportunities—start-up companies that Apple might want to buy. He'd report directly to John and have an office next to his in the Pink Palace. It sounded good. Mike liked it. They agreed to make the formal announcement the next morning.

■ ■ ■

Monday came and went and no announcement went out. Tuesday was the day John and Steve, after a great deal of rancor, had finally set for the division review. The II division had already had its review and passed handily. Of course, even with the huge inventories they had on the IIc, the II division's Christmas sales amounted to a large chunk of the total its business plan had predicted for the entire year. The situation with Macintosh was different.

The review was held in the boardroom, around the corner from John's office. On one side of the table, making the presentation, were Steve and his staff—Susan, Bob, Debi, and Mike, in his last official act as marketing director. Arrayed against them, or so it appeared, were John and his staff—Jay, Al Eisenstat, and the new chief financial officer, Dave Barram, all looking cold and inquisitorial. Jean-Louis watched, ostensibly part of the Macintosh contingent, yet not implicated in its misdeeds. For the others, it was almost as if they were being handed shovels and asked to dig their own graves.

Steve led off with an overview. He outlined the products under development—Mid Mac, Big Mac, the FileServer—and the schedules they were on. Where was the FileServer?, John wanted to know. Steve deflected him and went on. He expressed confidence that Mac sales would pick up and pointed out that the division would be more profitable once the rest of the company—distribution and finance, in particular—had been gotten into shape. Finance was still reporting average costs rather than real costs, which meant the divisions weren't getting the kind of information they needed. And there still wasn't any action on his distribution proposal, which would save them money on personnel, inventory, and real estate.

Susan followed with the financial report, which was grim. She laid the picture on the table—the numbers they were supposed to have made, the numbers they actually had made. What the business plan said they'd be doing versus what they were doing. The 1985 business plan called for sales of 50,000 Macs a month, 600,000 for the fiscal year that would end in September. By then they were supposed to have brought in $1.2 billion, half the company's revenues. By that measure, there was little denying that they were failing.

Mike's presentation followed. Even in a lame-duck role his enthusiasm was effervescent and undiminished, and today he'd chosen to propose that they completely retarget their market—that they forget about the Fortune 1000 and direct their marketing efforts at small businesses and professionals instead. Apple couldn't be all things to all people, he reasoned; and while it might not appeal to corporate America, it could appeal to individuals who empathized with Apple and what it represented. He'd spent the better part of a week on this, putting together an elaborate presentation with slide after slide showing the market neatly segmented into interlocking circles and triangles according to a complex scheme he'd worked out, but he hadn't gotten past the first one when John broke in, angrily demanding to know why there wasn't better marketing. Then Steve jumped in after him, and it was twenty minutes before Mike got to show his second slide.

Of the four of them, Bob was in the toughest spot politically, because engineering had failed to deliver the FileServer. (No one seemed to care about the LaserWriter.) He could have attacked them for putting engineering under hiring constraints so they'd have more money to buy advertising, or he could have simply admitted that the entire engineering lab had crashed and burned. Instead he delivered a lengthy tutorial on how the engineering process works. He outlined the three main elements of product development—the basic features of the product, its cost, and its schedule. At best, he said, you could control two out of the three. Just as everybody was beginning to wonder why he was giving them this college lecture, he flashed a slide that showed a new ship date for the FileServer—spring 1986. The response on John's side was shock and disbelief. This wasn't going to work! They'd been lied to, they knew it. Hadn't the exec staff been assured on a weekly basis that this product was on schedule?

At noon the meeting broke for lunch. Jay was in his office with John, talking about the products the division had under development, when Jean-Louis stormed in and announced he was going back to Paris. John got up and left. Jean-Louis was agitated. The presentation had confirmed his worst fears—that the division had no strategy, no methodology, that it was getting by on stream-of-consciousness planning. He was going back to France, he didn't want to get involved

272 ■ Over the Edge

in this mess, it wasn't going to work. But Jay was blessed with a calming voice and a reassuring presence, and just as he was always able to get through to Steve when no one else could, this time he talked Jean-Louis down. Yes, he admitted in his smooth, deep, even tones, things were screwed up—but that was why they needed him there. No one else could contribute what he could. Apple needed him. When the meeting resumed, he was in it.

Debi Coleman made the final presentation. She too had spent nearly a week preparing it, and unlike the others she had nothing unpleasant to disclose or live down. In twelve months, she'd transformed what once had looked like Steve's biggest folly into a model of high-tech manufacturing. While the others were missing their delivery dates and launching ill-conceived marketing schemes and totaling up a dismal set of numbers, she'd buried the company in Macintoshes. With professional-looking slides and an elaborate set of performance criteria she showed her accomplishments—higher yield, lower cost, greater capacity. Of the five of them, she was the only one who finished her presentation with more credibility than when she'd started it.

Steve ended the day with a personal plea to John. Speaking in impassioned tones, he told John that he felt he'd made a major contribution to the company, and that the skill set he'd acquired would allow him to contribute even more. And while he'd fought John's plan to reorganize the company along functional lines, he could see valid reasons for doing it. He was willing to buy into it. If they did do it—if the Macintosh group he'd taken over when Scotty divisionalized the company four years earlier was going to be subsumed in another reorganization now—he still wanted desperately to have a role. He wanted to run the product-development group. He wanted the chance to do it again. He wanted to keep the dream going.

There was nodding and murmuring from the other side of the table, polite but noncommittal. Steve was begging now, you could sense it, but he was getting no response. There was nothing to do but pack up and leave.

■　■　■

The division review was a rite of passage, a bar exam in hell, and getting through it alive was certainly cause for celebration. So Steve and his people got together that evening at Nina's Café in Woodside, a roadside gourmet restaurant not far from Steve's place. Nina's was a little wooden storefront that could have served as a Wild West stage set—a false-front building on the winding two-lane highway that passed through Woodside on its way up to La Honda and across to the Pacific at San Gregorio. Steve was there, and Bob and his new girlfriend, and Mike and Joyce, and Susan and Debi and Jean-Louis. That last was a bit of a problem, at least as far as some of them were concerned, but Steve wanted to make sure everybody was comfortable with the transition. In any event, Jean-Louis tried to busy himself being charming and French and ordering wines.

He also left early, and as soon as he did the others closed ranks around Steve. Bob proposed a toast "to those of us who really understand what the world according to Steve Jobs is all about"—"the world according to Steve Jobs" having become the putdown of choice for those at Apple who preferred to live outside the reality-distortion field. Mike and Joyce left early too, and when they did Bob got suddenly emotional and gave Mike a hug, for it was his last moment as part of the team, and while they'd had their differences, Bob thought no one should have been treated the way Mike had been. One by one the others left too, until finally it was just Steve and Bob in the parking lot.

They sat in Steve's Mercedes in the chill night air and mulled over their options. The division review had led Bob to conclude that this was the time to move. No more Mr. Nice Guy, he told Steve; this is a political fight to the death. They had to win. Anything was justified at this point, because it was them against Sculley. Steve said, "What do I do?"

For all his innate charisma, for all his conviviality with business leaders and celebrities, Steve's view of the world was startlingly naive. He was certainly capable of being manipulative, but in a way that was seductive and childlike; he was too self-centered to be cynical or calculating or scheming. He was incapable of viewing the world from anyone else's perspective. He had not, for example, bothered to mend his relationship with the board members who'd voted to slap him down in April. They were men he'd known and worked with since the garage days; several—Mike Markkula and Arthur Rock in particular—had become father figures to him, and he simply couldn't believe they wouldn't back him in a showdown. Bob told him to start talking to them, to stop behaving like a strange person, to show them that his plans were sane and reasonable and not the ravings of a madman. He told him to feel out the exec staff members, to talk to each one privately and get a sense of who could be brought over to his side at the right moment. Campbell was a possibility. Elliot he'd have to be careful with. Del would want to know what was in it for him, and with good reason—what *would* Del get if Steve won? Would he get to work for Debi Coleman? He might not think that was such a great idea.

Of course he'd work for Debi Coleman, Steve replied. Debi's the best.

Right, Bob said, in a voice edged with sarcasm and despair. Somewhere at home he had a battered copy of *The Prince* he'd picked up years earlier at a secondhand book store for ninety-nine cents. It was a volume he'd grown rather attached to, but he made a mental note to bring it to Steve the next day. It was time Steve read some Machiavelli.

■ ■ ■

In fact, Steve had the nucleus of a plan already, and over the next few days he and Bob spent hours talking it over. They walked across every parking lot on Bandley Drive, back and forth, racking up the miles. Steve explained his plan like this.

For months, Al Eisenstat and Ken Zerbe had been working on a deal to sell computers in China. It was a complicated proposition, not just because of difficulties of doing business in China but because the American government kept a tight hand on technology exports to less-than-friendly nations. Finally they'd won approval in Washington, and in April the deal had been set. As Apple's chairman, Steve had been invited to the deal-signing ceremony at the Great Hall in Beijing, and he'd casually let it drop to John that he might be going. As Steve had anticipated, John said he wanted to go, so Steve dropped out. John was set to leave on May 24, the Friday before Memorial Day—little more than a week away—and while he was gone, Steve would go to the board members and explain how John was failing to lead the company. He'd rally the exec staff members too; and then, when John got back, Steve would march into John's office with the top twenty people in the company and tell him he wasn't providing the leadership the company needed and it was time for him to leave.

It was less a plan than a fantasy, and about as Machiavellian as Sherman's march through Georgia. Not that anything about Steve was ever Machiavellian; he was used to asking for what he wanted and getting it. But it was all they had, Bob thought, and there was even a chance—a slim chance—it might work.

Of course, with the game they were in now, Bob realized, it would have been better to drop back twenty yards and punt, but there seemed little point in telling Steve that now. Nor did it seem productive to ask blunt questions, like why Campbell or Yocam would risk an executive-level position backing someone as dubious as Jobs. Instead, Bob tried to talk him through the process step by step, helping him strategize. How many people would they have to have? Which ones were likely to back them? And what would they do if they won? The company was such a wreck—largely thanks to Steve, Bob pointed out—that they'd have to change almost everything, including much of what Steve held sacred. Could he handle it? Yeah, Steve said, he could handle it. But he seemed to be getting the picture.

The following week, the week John was to leave, Steve started to feel out the key exec staff members. He was careful not to say what he was planning, just to talk about his vision for the company and John's failure to act and what they needed to do to turn things around. He went for a long walk around the parking lot with Del, and Del seemed to be agreeing with a lot of what he was saying. At a certain point, however, Steve was just unable to stop himself. He said he wanted to run operations, and he informed Del that he really was a much better operations person than Del was.

Del couldn't believe it. He wasn't much of a risk-taker himself, but he thought of himself as one and admired those who were, and he was totally enamored of Steve; he thought of Steve as the spiritual leader of Apple. But a better *operations* person? He stopped dead in the middle of the parking lot. Steve kept on walking, and when he'd taken a few steps and noticed Del was no longer with him he turned around. Del asked him to repeat what he'd just said, so he did. After all, he was just repeating what should have been plain to everyone. But it wasn't plain to Del. Del was upset. Del told him that obviously wasn't the case and walked away, leaving him standing on the asphalt alone.

■　■　■

Construction was supposed to begin on Mike Murray's new office soon. He was in an anomalous position, no longer working for Steve, ostensibly reporting to John, but in an ill-defined job, sitting in a corridor outside John's office at a desk that used to belong to a secretary. Neither Steve nor John had asked him to, but he'd decided to hold a conference to come up with a way to save the company. He was operating free-lance; it was as if he had this sick friend, Apple, and he had to help it get better. He'd invited Pat Caddell and Scott Miller, Regis McKenna and the chief Regette, Lee Clow and a few of the other key people Chiat/Day had on the Apple account. Regis didn't show, but the others did. They met in a little conference room at the back of Rickey's Hyatt on Wednesday, May 22, two days before John was to leave for China.

Mike didn't know about Steve's plan to seize control over the weekend, but mayhem could be read in the air. There were rumors that Steve wouldn't be heading the Macintosh division any longer, that John was about to centralize the company, that there wouldn't even *be* a Macintosh division. For their meeting at Rickey's they didn't have a formal agenda; the point was to generate ideas, and Caddell and Miller set the tone. They summarized the situation briskly: If Jobs threw Sculley out, it would look like the inmates had taken over the asylum; if Sculley threw Jobs out, it would look like he'd extinguished the eternal flame. Caddell sketched a formula on the board to demonstrate how to get from where they were now to where they wanted to be. They talked about how John needed to be decisive, to take control, to be a leader. They talked about what Apple represented and how they could leverage the value of its name. One thought gave rise to another in a random fashion until finally they hit upon the two-word phrase that captured the goal they needed to strive for: "One Apple." They had to unify. Mike wanted to print up T-shirts.

Steve's weekly staff meeting was at nine the next morning in Picasso, and though Mike no longer worked for the division, he'd been invited to attend. Gassée was at Pajaro Dunes for more ropes-on-the-beach—Jay was putting him through his paces—so the only person present who wasn't a hand-picked member of Steve's team was the Macintosh HR manager, Mary Fortney. Once they'd finished with the regular business, Steve asked Fortney to leave. She reminded him that nothing happened in the company that she didn't know about. He knew that, but he really needed to ask her to leave. Then he closed the door and drew the curtains tight and sketched an organizational chart on the board.

The chart showed Bob managing engineering, Debi in charge of manufacturing, Susan as corporate controller, Bill Campbell running sales, and Steve himself as president and CEO. Steve asked Mike if he'd like to take over human resources, since he cared so much about the things Apple stood for. Then he realized that Mike didn't yet know the plan, so he stopped the meeting abruptly to take him on a walk around the parking lot. There, while the others waited, he outlined the scenario he'd developed for John's overthrow. He began with the climactic moment—on the morning of John's first day back from China, when Steve, flanked by Bill on one side and Del on the other, would walk into John's office and announce that his services were no longer required. John would look at Del and Bill and they'd be nodding their heads in agreement. The phone would ring on his desk and it would be the board of directors saying yes, it was all true, just as Steve said. Defeated, John would have no choice but to accept the meaningless position of vice-chairman they were throwing him and slink off into well-deserved obscurity. Steve could see it all so clearly, this superbly orchestrated moment of triumph. But how was he going to get there? He'd have to go to the board. He'd have to convince Mike Markkula and Arthur Rock and Henry Singleton. He'd have to . . .

Mike went slightly numb at what he was hearing. He liked Steve and felt very close to him, but he didn't like the way Steve had been running the Macintosh division and he certainly wasn't happy about the prospect of Steve's taking over the whole company. But then, he wasn't much happier with the way John was running things. He was too confused even to know how he felt.

He got a lot more confused that afternoon, when he got up from his new desk in the Pink Palace to pop into John's office and found John with an org chart of his own—one that showed Bill running sales and marketing, Del in charge of product development and operations, and Steve in a little box at the bottom, doing advanced development. This was it, Mike thought. Either the inmates would take over the asylum, or the eternal flame would be extinguished. And in the meantime, he was in a pretty sticky situation himself.

■ ■ ■

Al Eisenstat was having a little dinner party that evening for John and Jean-Louis and their wives. For John, it was to be his last social event before leaving for China with Ken Zerbe the next afternoon. For Jean-Louis, it was the biggest survival test yet in this curious minefield that was Cupertino—for Jean-Louis now knew about Steve's scheme too. That afternoon, shortly after he'd gotten back from Pajaro Dunes, Steve had walked him around the parking lot and told him about the China trip—what they were going to do while John was away, how they'd march into John's office and tell him he wasn't needed anymore, the whole fantastic scenario. They ended up sitting on the grass next to Bandley Drive with Steve telling him how John was killing his company. "Steve," Jean-Louis said, "it's not *your* company, it's *our* company." If Steve had any sense, he went on, he'd retire and come back on a white horse after John had screwed up. But that wasn't the way Steve worked.

Steve hadn't been sure how Jean-Louis would respond, so he'd decided to wait until the last minute to tell him. But he didn't wait until John was gone—he was too impatient for that. He couldn't hold it in any longer. He couldn't wait to tell Del and Bill and Jay either. That evening, as John and Jean-Louis were chatting over cocktails at Al's, he was ringing them up at their homes to get their support. He was met with a stunned consternation, a Jesus-Christ-what-am-I-going-to-do-now? response. Del said he'd get back to him and got off the line and immediately phoned Jay. Steve was a true visionary, Del thought, but this time he'd gone over the edge. He'd reached a point where there seemed to be no rhyme or reason to anything he said. And while Del agreed with some of his criticisms, he had no desire to be part of any coup attempt. What the hell should he do?

Jay told him to do whatever he was going to do. Personally, Jay agreed with Steve—he thought John was a none-too-powerful person who acted like he was more interested in selling the company than in leading it. But when Steve asked for a commitment, Jay told him no, he wasn't the person to run Apple. The person to run Apple, Jay thought, was John—not because he was the right person, but because he was the only person.

Because he was with John that evening, however, the first move was Gassée's, and he elected to spill. They were all sitting in Al's den, a cozy, book-lined room with a view of the driveway and the tree-shaded streets of Atherton, sipping drinks before dinner. Don't go to China, Jean-Louis said. Naturally, John asked why. Because if he went, Jean-Louis said, he might not have a job when he got back.

19

Jonestown

It was a nattier-than-usual Steve who bounced into the boardroom on Friday morning, a model young executive in a hand-tailored gray-striped Wilkes-Bashford suit. The other exec staff members were already seated, and since Jay had taken Steve's usual place—just to the right of John, who sat as always at the head of the table—Steve took a seat at the far end. They were meeting that morning to discuss what John would say to the two-dozen middle managers who'd be gathering downstairs in a couple of hours to hear a reassessment of their basic strategies. But the air of expectancy and dread that greeted Steve as he entered the room was caused by more than the fear that they were focusing on the wrong markets; after Thursday night's phone calls, anything could happen. It didn't take long to find out what.

John looked like a man who was trying to summon up his last iota of energy. Gone was the runner's edge; in the past couple of weeks he'd turned into a sack of parsnips, thin, pale, and misshapen. But as Steve started to sit down, John looked at him head-on across the long expanse of polished hardwood and made an announcement that hit the other end like a bowling ball. He said he'd heard Steve was going behind his back to try to kick him out of the company.

Steve's pupils narrowed to the size of pin pricks and honed in on John with a stare of laserlike intensity. This wasn't on his agenda until John got back from China next week; but as long as it was out on the table, he was ready to take up the challenge. That's right, he said. John should leave. He didn't know how to run the company.

And while he was accusing Steve of sneaking around behind his back, he himself had gone to the board in April to have Steve removed as head of the Macintosh division. He was supposed to be Steve's mentor, supposed to help him learn to manage a big organization, and instead he was trying to kick him out. He was a sleazeball.

John started to stammer, a childhood trait he thought he'd outgrown years ago. Slowly, shakily, he forced the words out. He hadn't been able to help Steve because the company was in too much of a crisis. He'd tried to save their friendship, but now it wouldn't work any longer. He couldn't tolerate this. He couldn't trust him.

John had to go, Steve repeated. He looked around the room. They all agreed, he went on. John wasn't providing leadership, the company was a wreck, they wanted him out.

God, John thought, what if he's right? He couldn't go on without the others' support. He'd have to see who they backed. So now, one by one, clockwise around the table, he called on them to declare their loyalties—starting with Del, who was seated to John's left, his back to the window.

Suddenly it was their turn to squirm. They'd been expecting something, but not this. As a group they were as unhappy with John as Steve was, but for opposite reasons. No, he wasn't providing leadership; he was constantly deferring to Steve. They didn't want either one kicked out of the company; they wanted John to stop Steve from riding roughshod over it.

Del was torn. He felt so attached to Steve, to Woz, to all that they'd accomplished together, and John clearly represented something else, something less personal, something corporate. This was the turning point. Having no choice, he plunged ahead unrehearsed. He loved Steve, he said, loved him for making them what they were today, and he wanted him to play an active role in the company. But he respected John for his experience and capability, for the knowledge and expertise he'd brought to the company, and he'd support him in whatever decision he made.

Al Eisenstat was sitting farther down the table, closer to Steve. Like Del, he turned to Steve as he began to speak. He said he cared about Steve and John both a great deal and he wanted Steve's contribution to the company, but he'd have to go along with whatever John's decision was. Then he told Steve how sorry he was.

Across from Al, facing the window, was Bill Campbell, the chief coach of sales. He turned to Steve and spoke in a voice that almost quavered. He said he really wanted Steve to have a role. He said it would be a real shame, not just for John and Steve but for Apple, if the two of them didn't work out their differences.

Next to Bill was Regis McKenna, who sat in on their meetings as an *ex officio* member. He'd told Steve before he couldn't run the company, and he told him again now. He felt John had to be given the opportunity to run Apple, and he'd support him.

Dave Barram was sitting between Regis and Jay, looking a little like Dabney Coleman with his bushy moustache, receding hairline, and homespun features. He'd been there less than two months; he echoed the others.

Jay spoke last. He thought they were both being self-indulgent with their little power struggle. They were too wrapped up in themselves to care about the five thousand people who worked for the company. It was ridiculous, he told them, that they couldn't work this thing out. He wouldn't pledge his loyalty to either one of them; he was pledging it to Apple.

Steve sat listening with his head down. When the litany finally ended, he looked up and in a quiet voice, not quite tremulous, said he wasn't sure what he was going to do. His face was a mask of utter devastation. There was no trace of the sparks he'd fired earlier; in their place was the uncomprehending stare of a little kid whose world has just been shattered. John, crumpled into his chair at the other end of the table, looked scarcely better. Bill and Jay pleaded with them to keep it together, to work it out, not to blow up Apple in their spat, but it was too late. Finally Jay reminded them that they had a lot of people downstairs and they had to tell them something.

■ ■ ■

Two floors below, twenty-four people from across the company—engineering directors, marketing directors, sales executives, HR managers—were crowded into a long, narrow, L-shaped meeting room to hear John's pronouncements on the crisis they were facing in the marketplace. Alan Kay was there, and Tom Marano, the sales director who'd just been hired from Pepsi, and all of Steve's and Del's staff members, including Jean-Louis and Mike Lorelli, the marketing whiz from International Playtex whom Del had just hired to replace Dave Larson in the II division. The audience seemed sorted by order of knowledge, with those least aware of the true crisis at the front of the room and those most aware in the rear, as far away as possible.

The Macintosh staff was sitting at the very back, and when the exec staff members came down they sat alongside them. Steve came in last, looking like a dead man, and took the backmost seat of all, in a corner.

It was with a noticeable absence of enthusiasm that John took his assigned place at the front of the room. He made no mention of what had just happened upstairs. Instead he spoke in vague and general terms about Apple's future and the hard times ahead. John had a mind like an outline processor, able to tick off points and subpoints and sub-subpoints for hours without recourse to notes, and as he addressed them all in his dull, dry monotone, this outline processor clicked on. He started to lean against a pillar for support. For an hour and a half he droned on about expense reduction and new products and accountability and communication. He sketched out seven goals and announced the creation of "study teams" to investigate their problems and come up with solutions. As he spoke, he moved more and more behind the pillar. Finally, almost hidden, he asked for questions.

Study teams. These were pirates, or had been, and now they were being asked to submit written reports in triplicate. They were taking the committee response. They wouldn't have to *meet* the crisis, they could just study it to death. Bill and Del looked disgusted. Steve sat in the corner with his arms folded and his head down. Alan Kay asked why they didn't give money to universities to fund basic research. Finally, without another word, everyone filed out.

■　■　■

As the room emptied, Steve pulled Mike and Debi and Susan aside and said he wanted to see them back at Bandley 3. He was trying to find Bob too, but Bob had already disappeared. Then Steve saw him in the parking lot, heading for his Ford camper at a trot. Bob was getting out of there. It was Friday of Memorial Day weekend, and he had two weeks of vacation coming up and tickets to see Wagner's *Ring* cycle at the San Francisco Opera. He was tired, very tired, and he needed some time off. But Steve ran out after him and yelled his name as loud as he could and kept yelling until Bob had no choice but to turn around. Reluctantly, he went with them.

They got to Picasso and Steve collapsed in a chair, fighting back sobs. He'd just been asked to step down, he told them. He wanted them to stay and help Apple. Apple really needed them now. Soon they were all in tears—Steve, Bob, Debi, Susan, everyone except Mike. Mike felt emotionally disconnected, more like a spectator than a participant. He was saying they could still solve this problem. Bob wanted to slug him.

Steve was talking now. He was telling them that working with them had been one of the best times of his life, and now he was going to resign. Bob thought that was the right thing to do, and he was prepared to do the right thing too. A gentleman does what a gentleman has to do. That's it, we lost, I'm out, he said. He stood up to shake Steve's hand, but Steve wouldn't shake.

Bob went out the door and headed for his office to pack up his things. Steve turned to follow him, but Susan and Debi blocked his way. "Don't go out that door," Mike cried.

Steve paused and asked why.

"Because the minute you do, everything will be changed."

Fighting back tears, Susan and Debi led him back to the table. They had to reason their way out of this. They had to salvage something. A few minutes ago they'd been people with a mission—they were bringing high-level technology to individuals rather than corporate data centers, forming a new paradigm for Apple, for the industry, for information. That sense of mission was what Steve had given them. He'd put them in an environment where they could challenge all standard procedures, all assumptions, even their own. He'd told them Macintosh could change the world and they believed it, because *they* were changing the world.

But now it was beyond all salvaging. Bob could see that right away. He tossed his belongings into a box—there wasn't much, he'd never felt comfortable enough at Apple even to move in properly—and headed for the door. On his way out he left a hastily scrawled letter of resignation on his HR woman's desk, a final missive to the Bene Gesserit. He felt relief, exhilaration almost. He was so tired, and now it was over. His mind kicked back to the November staff meeting when Steve walked in and asked what price he'd have to pay for failure. This was the price, Bob thought. They were paying it now. They'd be paying it for a long time to come.

■ ■ ■

Leezy was livid when she heard the news. Not for a moment had she shared John's fascination with Steve; for two years now she'd resented his intrusions and demands—the endless meetings, the phone calls in the middle of the night, the rapport that they and they alone shared. Steve was evil, Steve had the devil in him, she could see it. Now at last her true feelings could spring forth, fury uncaged. And yet she remained controlled . . . so controlled. She'd never felt so controlled in her life. She drove off in search of Steve. Finally she could tell him what she thought.

She caught up with him in the parking lot of the Sun & Soil Restaurant, a natural-foods joint near the Mervyns discount store in the little shopping center where Bandley Drive hits Stevens Creek Boulevard. Susan and Debi were with him. She stepped out of her Mercedes and called him over. As he came closer she started to let it out. He was *ruining her husband* . . . John was his *friend* . . . but Steve would never know it because he was *empty inside*. It made her feel good to say these things. She didn't believe in holding back. She swept away in triumph.

A few minutes later she joined Al and a crowd of other execs as they stood outside John's office on the third floor of the Pink Palace. Everyone was frantic. No one knew what to think. Events were going past in a blur. John was on the phone to Gerry Roche, the headhunter who'd put him in touch with Steve in the first place. Even though the poll in the boardroom had gone his way, he didn't think he had the support he needed. He didn't think he was ready for the challenge. He didn't have the strength to carry on. When Jay Elliot came back from lunch, Leezy was almost breathless. "Have you heard? Have you heard?"

Heard what?

John was resigning.

Jay just stood there with his mouth agape. They'd all made this excruciating commitment to John in the boardroom, and now he was *resigning?*

Yeah, Al said, it was true.

Fuck this, Jay said. What a bunch of assholes. He packed up his desk and left. His marriage was a shambles, he was in the midst of a divorce, he was fighting to save the company, and now John was resigning? Fuck it. He was going to drive to Sausalito and have a drink at some nice little outdoor café and watch the sailboats on San Francisco Bay.

John came out and asked Al if he wanted to go for a ride. They climbed into Al's Porsche and headed up 280, into the hills above Palo Alto. He couldn't go on like this, he told Al as they sped up the highway. He didn't have the stamina. He'd failed. Then they were in Woodside, pulling into his driveway, and he realized that what he wanted most of all was sleep.

■ ■ ■

Steve spent most of the day Saturday at home. He was listless and depressed, but he stayed on the phone. The reality-distortion field was functioning smoothly. He phoned Al and heard him say that John wasn't providing leadership. He phoned John and suggested they go for a walk the next day in the hills above Stanford. He phoned Mike Markkula and tried to set up a meeting at Markkula's ranch in Carmel Valley, on the edge of the Ventana Wilderness just over the mountains from Big Sur. He wanted to come down with his staff and tell Markkula what was really wrong at Apple. As the second-largest stockholder and former president of the company, Markkula carried a lot of weight with the other members of the board. And Steve was certain that once Markkula heard the real story of how John wasn't providing leadership, everything would change.

Mike Murray called after dinner to ask how Steve was doing and see if he wanted to go out to a movie or something. Steve wanted to watch *Patton;* he thought it might be instructive. He asked if Mike had a video-disk player at home. No, Mike said, but they had a videocassette recorder. That wouldn't do. Videocassettes were second-rate technology. Steve offered to bring over his video-disk player and his *Patton* video disk. But then he remembered he'd lent his *Patton* disk to his dad, so he and Mike ended up driving to his parents' house to get it.

Paul and Clara Jobs still lived in the modest Los Altos ranch house where Steve had grown up. It was a short ride from Mike's place, just a mile or two down Foothill Expressway and off on a couple of side roads. But when Steve and Mike got to the house, no one was home. They hadn't thought to call, and Steve didn't have a key. They walked around the house, tried all the doors, stood on the lawn. No way in. Finally they went to a video store. But the video store didn't have *Patton* on disk, so they had to settle for something else. Steve opted for Hitchcock instead.

■ ■ ■

John had his self-confidence back when he and Steve took their Sunday afternoon walk. The air was dry and hot, with a pungent, grassy smell that almost made the nostrils flare. They strolled for hours across the straw-colored hills between Woodside and the Stanford campus, trying to find a role for Steve they could both live with. Steve had plenty of ideas. He wanted John to put him in charge of the product development organization John wanted to set up, the group that would combine the engineering labs from the Macintosh and Apple II divisions. John could be in charge of sales and marketing and together they could report to the board of directors. Or if John didn't like that, maybe he'd rather relinquish control, step up to the post of chairman, and let Steve run the company as president and CEO. John argued, but Steve could sense him wavering. They drove away without agreeing on anything.

As Sunday turned into Monday and the long Memorial Day weekend waned, Steve continued to nurse the hope that things would somehow be made right—that John would still be fired, that John would step aside and let him run the company, at the very least that John would relent and put him in charge of product development. Markkula didn't express much enthusiasm about having everybody come down to Carmel Valley, so Steve asked them all to hang on until he could set something up. Finally Markkula agreed to meet with them on Monday evening at Steve's house in Woodside.

Like everything else, the meeting with Markkula didn't go the way Steve thought it would. Markkula set the ground rules. The main rule was, Steve couldn't say anything. Markkula wanted to hear from Steve's staff members directly; he didn't want Steve prompting them.

It was chilly that evening, and there was a draft inside the echoing chambers of Steve's empty San Simeon. A fire was burning in the living-room fireplace. The room was vast, close to two thousand square feet, and bare except for the fire and a single Oriental carpet that covered a fraction of the floor. A large box of cherries provided refreshment. Markkula listened quietly as the four lieutenants gave their views of what had gone wrong, of how they'd come to be in this state, of what they could do to get out of it. There was no banter, no chit-chat, no comic relief. He wanted to know about the FileServer. He wanted to know about the distribution issue. They moved into the dining room, nearly as vast, nearly as empty. They pulled some folding chairs up to a card table and ate vegetarian whole-wheat pizzas. Steve had a new live-in couple; they did organic gardening and natural-foods cooking and had degrees in environmental studies from Berkeley. The pizzas were theirs.

Bob spoke last, and of the four staff members he seemed beyond doubt the hardest hit. He looked devastated. In three years at Apple he'd turned Steve's product vision into a reality, and now his marriage and his career were in shambles. The only coping mechanism he had left was withdrawal. Apple, he told them in a voice that barely rose above a whisper, had broken his heart.

Markkula told Bob, don't quit. Otherwise he said almost nothing. When it was all over, he stood up. The matter would be resolved soon, he said, and it wouldn't be to everyone's liking. Then he got in his car and drove off.

■ ■ ■

On Monday, while Steve was setting up the session with Markkula and Ken Zerbe was off in Beijing signing the deal with the Chinese, John held a series of closed-door meetings with some of his key vice-presidents. One by one he pulled them into his office to see what they thought about keeping Steve on in some capacity—maybe as head of product development, maybe in some other role. He was worried about how it would look to outsiders if Steve was fired, and how it would affect the company. After all, as far as the world was concerned, Steve Jobs *was* Apple. But the people he consulted couldn't believe he'd even consider keeping Steve in any day-to-day operating role after all that had happened between them. So on Tuesday morning, he had breakfast with Steve and told him he didn't think there'd be a role for him at Apple. Then he drove to Mike Markkula's house in Portola Valley, a secluded enclave nestled in the foothills above Stanford, to have his own audience with Markkula and seek his blessing for the step he was about to take.

Steve was right about one thing: Markkula's was the vote to swing. As a co-founder and former president he held an exalted status on the board; his was the voice of reason. And Steve, by so ineptly forcing the board to choose between John and himself, had in his desperation reduced the issue to a stark and simple choice. They could back John, who might be able to staunch the flow of red ink and lead them back to profitability; or they could back Steve, whose only visible talent was his ability to articulate a vision they'd never fully shared in the first place. The dichotomy was an old and familiar one, the one everything in California seemed to revolve around from the days of the Gold Rush on: between the lure of gold and the vision of a golden land, between the bonanza and the dream, between two views of Eldorado. As a member of the board, Markkula was charged with maximizing Apple's value for the shareholders—chief among whom he had to include himself, since he owned 5.5 million shares amounting to some 9 percent of the company. Beyond that, he was a semiconductor man, a veteran of Fairchild and Intel; and as with most semiconductor men, his natural instinct was to go for the gold.

Hours later, after a lengthy presentation and a grueling cross-examination, John drove away with Markkula's support. When he got back to his office, he polled the other board members on the phone and got their backing as well. The matter was settled. He was in command.

So on Tuesday evening, less than twenty-four hours after the whole-wheat pizza dinner, John phoned Steve at home. The call was brief and direct. It was official now: Steve was being removed as general manager of the Macintosh division, and he wouldn't be getting any other operational role in the company. In a few minutes it was over, and Steve was left alone with the realization that he'd lost—lost the company, lost his dream, lost his chance to change the world.

Over the next few hours, sobbing and nearly hysterical, he called around to say good-bye. He called Bill. He called Al. He called Susan, who was out swimming; he left a message on her machine. He called Mike Murray. Mike's phone was busy, so he called an operator, told her it was an emergency, and broke in on the line.

Joyce was talking to her sister long-distance. She was irked; this wasn't the first time Steve had pulled this stunt. "This better really be important," she said when Steve got on the line.

"It is," Steve said, in a voice so strangled it sounded like death. Mike was reading in a chair nearby. Joyce handed him the phone and said, "Uh-oh."

Mike took the receiver. Steve stayed on for just a moment. Choking back tears, he said he just wanted Mike to know that the past few years had been one of the best times of his life. He wanted to say good-bye, and the phone clicked dead.

Mike hung up and thought, This guy sounds terrible. He decided he'd better go up there and see what was happening. He jumped in his car and sped up El Monte to the freeway. It was a ten-minute drive up 280 to Steve's house—past the glitzy hillside villas of Los Altos Hills and the scattered oaks of the Stanford lands, then back roads to Steve's gate, still open as usual. The past three years spun willy-nilly through Mike's mind as he drove, the whole incredible trip. He imagined finding Steve sprawled on the floor, a suicide. He'd have to call the police. Ambulances would come, and then the press. It would be all over the papers in the morning. What would the headlines say? How would Sculley feel? Couldn't they have talked just one more time?

The hacienda was completely dark, its white walls gleaming in the moonlight, the live oaks casting deep shadows across the grounds. The front door was open, a massive slab of oak. The house was creaky and forbidding. Mike dashed frantically through the empty rooms. He couldn't find Steve anywhere. He ran out a back door to the courtyard, then sprinted up an outside stairway to Steve's bedroom and knocked on the door. A light was on inside. "Steve?"

It was a spartan little room, just a mattress and some blankets on the floor and a single light overhead. A metal bread rack against one wall was stacked high with television and stereo equipment; clothes were piled on the floor. Steve was sprawled across the mattress. "Oh, hi," he said as he looked up, bleary-eyed from crying. Mike lay down and put his arms around him, and they cried together. No, Steve assured him, he hadn't been thinking about anything stupid at all. He'd just been wondering why everything had to be this way.

■ ■ ■

The reorganization began first thing Wednesday morning. For the next two days, John and the remaining exec staff members—Del, Bill, Jay, Al Eisenstat, Dave Barram, and Mike Spindler, the head of international—met in the boardroom, arguing about how to structure the company. John, whose paramount concern had become instituting controls, wanted it split along functional lines. He saw a company divided not between two competing division managers but between two powerful executive vice-presidents, one in charge of sales and marketing, the other running operations—product development, manufacturing, and distribution. Other people had other ideas. Markkula liked the idea of returning to a functional organization, but he thought they ought to have another executive vice-president to handle the administrative chores—finance, legal, and human resources. Jay disliked a functional organization for the same reason Steve did—because having everybody on the same team made it hard to foster any kind of entrepreneurial zeal or drive for greatness. But if they had to go functional, he at least wanted to maintain a heavy product emphasis. The thought of smashing the two engineering departments together was a tough one for him.

Then there was the question of who was going to get what. There were only two possibilities for the two top jobs John was proposing. Bill had been hired to handle marketing before he was given sales; obviously he'd get the sales-and-marketing job. And if the operations post didn't go to Steve—a possibility that was now utterly out of the question—the only choice was Del. That was a wry twist of fate, for Del's plodding managerial style was the antithesis of Steve's anarchic creativity. Del was the soul of control. To Steve, his very name rang of mediocrity—no forward thinking, no attempt to do anything great, just stamp it out on schedule. Putting him in charge of operations would be a signal that henceforth Apple would be a radically different company.

Below the top level, it was a free-for-all. Gassée seemed right for the product-development role, but should he report to Del or directly to John? Should they put Debi in charge of manufacturing, as Bill and Jay wanted, or give it to Del's guy from Dallas? The sales half of Bill's domain would go to Tom Marano, but should they give marketing to Mike Lorelli, the new guy from Playtex, or hire from outside? And what were they going to do with Mike Murray?

While these issues were being thrashed out in the boardroom, the Macintosh staff, now leaderless, was running a vendor conference at the Red Lion in San Jose, a followup to the Team #1 conference of August 1983. They were honing the vendor base, cutting the list of suppliers, rewarding the good ones and eliminating the rest. Steve was at home, not even answering his phone. But John gave a speech in his place, Susan and Debi tried to carry on as if nothing were amiss, and even Bob was there, having torn up his resignation letter. The suppliers never suspected that in a few days there'd be no more Macintosh division. Susan handed one of them her business card and heard him cry facetiously, "Wow! A Macintosh division business card! This is a rare memento." You don't know how rare it is, she thought.

Most of the names had been penciled in by late Thursday afternoon. Susan and Debi got word at the Red Lion to report to Cupertino. They'd been sitting on a couch with Bob, trying to guess what was happening. Maybe they'd be put in charge of the company store? Debi could run the cash drawer, Susan could do inventory, and Bob could be the fix-it man. But when they got to Bandley Drive, Debi was directed to Del's office and offered manufacturing, while Susan was met by Dave Barram and urged to take the controller slot in sales and marketing. Steve saw her go in—he'd finally come in, late in the afternoon—so he called her in Barram's office. Just remember, he told her, for every Mac they ship it's our success, and they can never take that away from us. When she came out, he was gone.

Bob wasn't called, so he sat at the Red Lion, sweating it out. The next day—Friday, a week after John was to have left on his China trip—he went in early, about five-thirty or six, and ran into John in the parking lot. John asked him up to his office and sketched out what seemed to Bob like a cockamamie organization with a technology slot reporting to Gassée. Would Bob like to work for Gassée? No, but he'd talk to him. When he did, Jean-Louis asked him to continue running Macintosh engineering, but not to take over the Apple II; he was going to run that himself for a while. In that case, Bob said, he wanted to go ahead with his vacation. He thought he deserved it.

Meanwhile, Mike Murray was sitting at his little desk outside John's office, talking to Steve on the phone and wondering why he wasn't being called into the boardroom. Steve was asking what he should do. Mike said he could do one of two things. He could take Apple down with him and be a real jerk about the whole thing, which was probably what he felt like doing, right? *Right!* Or he could be a statesman. What's that mean? A statesman, Mike explained, is someone who behaves like a gentleman no matter how much it hurts. A statesman was what Steve ought to be. He might want to come back to Apple someday, and he shouldn't burn his bridges now.

So on Friday morning, when John called a meeting in the Pink Palace to announce the new regime, Steve was there. It was the last day in May. The meeting was almost a replay of the one the Friday before—same people, different room, new message. John showed the new org charts and announced the new assignments. Neither Mike's name nor Bob's appeared; Steve's occupied a box labeled "chairman" that had no lines connecting it to John or anyone else. John described his role as that of a "global visionary" but took no notice of him sitting there. People clapped, but it was awkward and stiff. As soon as it was over, Mike drove high up onto the ridge above Stevens Creek and got nauseous. He had to stop the car and get out and sit on the pavement, gasping for air like any other crash-and-burn victim. It was his thirtieth birthday.

Down below, Bandley Drive was awash in rumor—that Steve had been forced out, that the Macintosh division was being eliminated, that the whole company was in for a shake-up, that everybody would lose his job. All afternoon, the heads of the company—Jean-Louis played the role for the Macintosh division—gathered their people and told them what they could. As the news spread, people seemed to look at Bandley 3 with a mingling of fascination and dread, as if it were the scene of some experiment gone horribly wrong. Already people in the II division had taken to likening Steve and his band of pirates to that other group of Bay Area visionaries, Jim Jones and his People's Temple. Now you could all but see the bodies inside, bloating in the heat. No more free juices here: Bandley 3 was Jonestown.

IV.

Joining the Navy

June 1985–January 1986

20

Rule of
the Bene Gesserit

It was time to throw open the windows. Jean-Louis Gassée was ordering vanity plates for his new Mercedes—OPEN MAC, they were going to read, and that was exactly what he and Mary Fortney were trying to do. As HR director for Macintosh, she'd long been frustrated by the way Steve treated her, with an indifference that frequently crossed the line into hostility. It wasn't just that she was a holdover from the Lisa division; it was her style as well—the long red fingernails and the dramatic black eyelashes and the tight black dresses, all of which added up to a kind of flair that seemed more suited to "Dynasty" than to Bandley Drive. But now, with Steve gone, she had the chance to remake his organization the way she saw fit. She wanted to open it up, to bring it together with the rest of the company. Jean-Louis wanted to do the same with Macintosh itself—to open it up to outside developers who could build add-on boards that would make it as flexible as the Apple II. For years Del had told Steve that by closing Macintosh he was losing the one thing that had made the Apple II so successful, and now they were going to open it up. An open Macintosh, an open culture. It was unbelievably exhilarating. Suddenly she was having the time of her life.

The same kind of restructuring was taking place all across the company. Managers in every division had to reshuffle their employees and reorganize their departments, and invariably they did it with HR at their sides. Bill Campbell's new sales-and-marketing division had to absorb marketing people from both Apple II and Macintosh. Gassée's product development group had to do the same with engineering. Because they headed a network that extended into every crevice of the organization, Jay Elliot and Mary Fortney and her counterparts in the II and sales divisions knew everything that was going on—who was unhappy, who was jealous, who was saying what to whom. They were able to hold the place together even as they tore it apart and reassembled it in a different order. Bill and Jean-Louis played their parts, but it was HR that held the meetings, HR that shaped the org charts, HR that decided what names would go in which slots.

With two engineering departments to run, Gassée was under something of a handicap. He hadn't yet been there a month, and he wasn't even an engineer; like Steve, he was really a product-marketing person. He could say what a product should look like, what features it should have, but he couldn't provide day-to-day decisions on its technical details. And with Wayne Rosing gone to Sun and Bob on vacation, he didn't even have any engineers to call on. All he had was the Bene Gesserit—Mary Fortney and the HR managers for the engineering labs of the two product divisions. He was unpopular with many people, but Fortney liked him a lot—he was smart, he could talk about something other than diodes, and he had the same ideas she did about what was wrong with Macintosh and the people in it. They didn't want a spoiled-kid type of operation anymore. They wanted people who were not just technologically bright but human beings as well. So she'd meet with him to discuss the kind of organization they wanted and tell him what was going to happen next. She'd meet with her HR people to decide who should report to whom. Then they'd meet with the engineers themselves to hand out the assignments.

To the engineering managers—the people who were running the projects in the lab—the whole thing seemed a little strange, especially since the meetings all felt like group therapy sessions. Jean-Louis never stood up and told them what was going to happen; instead, he and Mary would call meetings at which they were all supposed to decide how to put things together. Before the meetings were held, however, Mary and her people had already made the important decisions and approached the people they were going to ask to run things. The meetings were thoroughly scripted, and HR had the script. Mary was a facilitator, making suggestions, guiding the process, like the psychologist who stays in the background but exerts control with the subtle and well-timed remark.

Bob hadn't been home more than a few days when he got word

that he was being ousted. He went to see Jean-Louis, who equivocated at first and finally told him he had to decide if he was in or out. So Bob went for a long walk to the top of Black Mountain, to sit on the transformer and get the information buzz, and on the way down he realized that he wanted out. He had no confidence in the people running the company. They'd run it into the ground and nobody on the outside would realize it for years and he'd have to stand by and watch it all. Anything was better than that. So he resigned for the second and final time, and the company was left with no one to run engineering.

Then there was marketing. The HR woman in charge was bright, down-to-earth, and aggressive, and she had as good a relationship with Bill as Mary did with Jean-Louis. The meetings followed the same pattern, with HR deciding who the key players would be. But there was one human resource the Bene Gesserit couldn't deal with. The Mike Murray issue, as it came to be known, had to be settled at the exec staff level. The business development job they'd given him wouldn't work, because John had to focus all his attention on re-building the company; so they tried to find him a job in marketing. Unfortunately, Mike hadn't always been too diplomatic during Macintosh's headier days, and one of the people he'd gone up against was Bill. Mike was a Mac maverick, and that didn't square with Bill's idea of team play.

Then one night, just before the new org charts were to be published, Bill and Mike went out for a drink at a Palo Alto bar. They stayed there until one in the morning; and the next day, when the new organization was announced, Mike had a job reporting to Mike Lorelli, the new marketing director from Playtex. Lorelli had seven marketing managers reporting to him, except that now two of them—the one in charge of advertising and promotion and the one in charge of public relations—found themselves reporting to Murray instead. No one was fooled; this time too, Mike was in a made-up job.

A lot of other people weren't even that lucky. On Friday, June 14—three weeks after the boardroom confrontation that set the whole thing in motion—HR announced layoffs that totaled a fifth of the work force. The Dallas factory was closed, and two smaller factories in Los Angeles and Ireland were shut down as well. Production of the IIe was shifted to Singapore, production of the IIc to Fremont. Some twelve hundred people lost their jobs, most of them factory workers. Even in Cupertino, nearly two hundred and fifty people were let go—called into their manager's office to get the word, then sent down the hall to HR for counseling and outplacement. HR tried to do it all humanely—there were generous severance payments and special crisis centers in case anyone got distraught—but there was no arguing about whether the cuts were needed. That same day, as the laid-off engineers and marketing people from Bandley Drive were getting drunk at Eli McFly, the public-relations office announced that Apple would soon post its first quarterly loss in history.

■ ■ ■

There was one problem no one knew how to deal with—not HR, not the exec staff, not John or the board. What were they going to do with Steve? As the chairman and largest stockholder, he hardly seemed in line for outplacement counseling; and yet they didn't exactly want him around, either. For a while there was talk of sending him to outer space. Several months earlier, NASA had approached him to take part in its civilian astronaut program—the one that was scheduled to begin in 1986 with the voyage of the *Challenger*. That would keep him busy; he'd have to spend at least six months training and getting in shape. He was intrigued by the idea, even though his friends from Macintosh pointed out that he wouldn't like it because he couldn't go first class.

On the other hand, he could fly first class to Russia. Al Eisenstat had been having discussions with a number of high Soviet officials who were trying to respond to Mikhail Gorbachev's desire to make the Soviet Union computer-literate, starting with children in school. So Steve and Al spent a week in Moscow, talking with various officials about computers in education—in particular, the Apple II. Steve was shocked at their technological backwardness, which he attributed to the lack of a consumer culture which would create demand. At the same time, it didn't take him long to realize that part of the official strategy was to limit communication: Photocopying machines were kept under lock and key, and over and over the people they were meeting with stressed that they wanted computers but not printers or modems. And while the television in his room worked fine, repairmen came in to fix it on three different occasions.

While he was in Moscow, it occurred to him that maybe he should volunteer to move over there and set up the entire educational computer system. He thought he could do a good job, and he'd always thought of school as a good place to introduce social change—it caught people when they were still receptive to new ways of doing things, and it gave them tools they'd use all their lives. He quickly realized that this wasn't what he really wanted to do; you couldn't even get good pasta in the Soviet Union. But what *did* he want to do? And why had Apple done this to him? That's what he couldn't understand.

Steve spent a lot of time alone at his Woodside estate, trying to figure it out. Sometimes he'd sit outside at night with his feet in the hot tub, gazing at the stars, wondering about life on other planets. Then he'd play it all back in his mind, hoping to see what had hit him. It took him a while to focus the blame. Was it Sculley? Was it Markkula? Was it the venture capitalists on the board? He couldn't believe what had happened with Sculley. He'd coaxed him on board, given him his trust, made him his right-hand man, and now the guy had stabbed him in the back. It was exactly what he'd feared in the first place. He should have kept it all for himself. And Markkula— Markkula hadn't stood up for him. He'd given Markkula the opportunity of a lifetime when he'd brought him into Apple, and Markkula hadn't returned the favor. Markkula was just like all the rest of them—the vulture capitalists.

One thing Steve knew: He couldn't leave Apple. Apple was his, Apple was him, Apple was all he'd ever known. But what was he going to do there? He was still chairman of the board. What was a chairman supposed to do?

That was precisely the question John and the exec staff were wrestling with. According to the corporate bylaws, the sole function of the chairman of the board was to chair the board meetings. Since the board met only a few times a year, that would leave Steve with a great deal of time on his hands. Bill wanted him to speak at the sales conference in October, and there was an endless number of personal appearances he could make. But Steve didn't want to become another Woz—someone to be trotted out for public occasions. He didn't want to be a figurehead. He wanted to do something.

Yet it was too late for that now. There was no role for him at Apple anymore, and more than anything else it was the move that made that clear. In the six weeks that followed the layoffs, as the reorganization took hold, nearly everyone at Apple was moved to a new location. As chairman of the board, Steve should have rated an office in the Pink Palace. He wanted the office he was supposed to have had when they moved into the building in 1983—the one Floyd

Kvamme took then and Al Eisenstat had now, directly opposite John's on the third-floor executive suite. But John didn't want him around. John wanted him somewhere else, so he was moved to the annex to Bandley 4, a small white stucco building with a red tile roof across the street from what a few weeks before had been the Macintosh building. Aside from his secretary and the security guard, he was the only person in the building. He called it Siberia.

■   ■   ■

The exec staff by this point was meeting once a day. Every morning at seven or seven-thirty they'd get together to review the issues—to see where they were on schedules, on dollar commitments, on cash flow, on people issues. At nine or ten they'd break, each one going off and doing his bit to keep the company afloat. Faced with a state of perpetual crisis, they were pulling together, figuring out what had to be done and doing it. John's contribution, at least as some of them saw it, was to stay the hell out of the way and let it happen. A more charitable reading would be that he provided the overview, the glue that held their efforts together. Either way, it was rule by committee, with everyone scrambling to make it work. In their desperation they often ended up falling all over themselves.

The biggest problem was sales, which had to pick up soon or they'd really be in trouble. John spent a week talking to dealers, trying to find out what would make the products move. He spent one day with national chains, one day with regional chains, one day with independents, one day with multiple stores. Each morning he came in with a new strategy. And Lorelli's approach to marketing was essentially what worked at Playtex—Sunday newspaper inserts, that kind of thing. At age thirty-four, he considered himself something of a stud buffalo brought in to increase of the level of sophistication and teach people some of the traditional skills you need in business. He'd been in charge of marketing for the family-products division of Playtex—tampons and the like—and the formula there for rescuing a sagging product called for color flyers stuck between the drugstore and the pantyhose inserts. So Apple and Chiat/Day prepared a promotion, the "American Dream Sweepstakes," that was built around a scratch-off coupon people could take to a computer dealer to see if they'd won a Mac. It became known around Apple as the "scratch 'n' sniff" promotion.

Mike Murray played along with the new regime—"great theme,"

he wrote in a memo on the scratch 'n' sniff to Tom Marano, the sales director. Everybody was playing along—who wouldn't, after all that had just happened? A fifth of the company had just been laid off, and those who were left were more interested in protecting their jobs than in taking risks. The place was becoming less entrepreneurial by the week, and Lorelli, schooled in buttoned-down East Coast corporate management techniques, was a catalyst for the new order. His staff members noted a concern for status issues, like whether Bill Campbell should be talking directly to people a couple of levels down. He'd pass people in the hall without stopping to chat and make them feel part of things. When he did want to talk to someone and other people were around, he'd ask them to leave. He seemed more interested in withholding information than spreading it.

Mike tried to join the team, but his heart wasn't in it. He couldn't respect Lorelli. He had an important-sounding title and an important-looking office in the executive suite, and yet by mid-afternoon he'd be sitting at his desk doing nothing and hating himself for it. Then one day he was talking with Steve on the phone. He was telling him what a tough time he was having when Steve pointed out that there was plenty of empty space where he was. Why didn't he just come over? So without telling anyone, Mike packed up his Macintosh and his papers and some books and walked across the street to Siberia. His secretary looked for three days before she found him.

■ ■ ■

What was Steve doing? That was the big question in the Pink Palace. He was making them all nervous. Everything was making them nervous. The stock was trading between $15 and $16 a share, after hitting a low of $14.75 in June. The Street was rife with speculation about a takeover: Apple's deflated stock price and continuing freedom from debt made it a tempting target financially, though there were analysts who looked at its product line and asked who'd want it. In mid-July the public-relations office announced the quarterly results, which included a loss of $17 million. There was actually a small profit on sales, but the cost of the reorganization was put at more than $40 million. This "unusual item," as it was listed on the financial statement, included plant and equipment write-offs, lease-canceling fees, severance pay, and other charges. Like other companies facing a loss, Apple wanted any subsequent improvements to appear as dramatic as possible. So the financial people had taken a hit on everything they could find, including a large number of Apple IIc's that looked as if they might sit in the warehouses indefinitely.

The analysts' meeting, which was held at Rickey's a week later, was so downbeat that one observer described it as "funereal." John made no mention in his speech of the Macintosh Office, though he did describe Apple's interest in the consumer market as little more than a by-product of its focus on the education and business markets. He outlined the new organization ("One Apple") and promised not to take the kind of risks with inventory that they'd taken last fall. During the question-and-answer session, he said bluntly that as far as the operations of the company were concerned, Steve Jobs would have no role, now or in the future. Then he introduced Jean-Louis Gassée as Apple's inspirational new leader of product development.

Steve didn't read the news accounts the next day, but his friends from Macintosh did, and they were horrified at what John had said. No operating role for Steve, now or ever? It was inconceivable. Steve could be nothing if he wasn't in operations. Even if all they did was send him out to talk at trade shows, he'd take an operational role, reinventing products on the fly. (Belleville used to take notes whenever Steve gave a speech so he'd know what they were supposed to be developing.) Now Sculley was saying that he was out, period—and that was unthinkable, to Steve more than anyone else. When people started calling to ask him if what John said was true, he got so upset he burst into tears.

That same week, he filed papers with the Securities and Exchange Commission announcing his intention to sell a large chunk of his Apple stock—850,000 shares, worth about $14 million at current prices. There'd been reports he'd tried to stage a leveraged buyout, lining up backing from Morgan Stanley to borrow enough money to seize control of the company. With an 11 percent stake, Steve was obviously a potential threat. Even with only 9 percent, he'd still be the largest shareholder by far—and while the sale made it clear he wasn't contemplating an attack, it didn't leave Apple any more secure financially because the natural expectation was that he'd keep selling. The six million shares he had left would keep the stock price down like a rock, and that would leave them vulnerable to a takeover bid from some other quarter.

Steve was selling for the same reason many people sell their stock: He didn't have any faith in the people who were running the company. First they'd sent him into exile, and now, despite Sculley's initial statements that he would serve in some vaguely defined role as a corporate visionary, it was being made clear that his ideas were no more welcome than his presence was. A taste of the new order came when one of his former associates tried to find him in Siberia. She didn't know where his new office was, so she went to the receptionist in Bandley 4 and asked. The response was crisp and to the point: "Steve Jobs doesn't work here anymore," the receptionist informed her. Yes, she said, but he has an office here and I need to talk to him. At that point the receptionist echoed Sculley's words to the analysts as if by rote. "Steve Jobs," she said, firmly and with great finality, "does not have any operating responsibility in this company."

The transition was being made.

21

Next

Steve didn't spend much time in Siberia. It was too depressing, and there was no reason for him to go anyway. He had no job to do there, no role to play, and only Mike Murray to talk to. Instead he flew to Italy with his girlfriend. He wanted to wander the hill towns of Tuscany—timeworn villages like San Gimignano and Montepulciano, with their medieval towers and their Renaissance palazzi set amid vineyards and olive groves and straw-colored hills. It was a little like the San Francisco Peninsula, only with abbeys instead of shopping centers. Anyway, he liked it there. He wanted to look at the architecture. Maybe it would offer some inspiration. He could use some: His apartment in the San Remo was still a cavernous, rubble-filled shell, and the hacienda in Woodside was crumbling around his ears. More than that, he needed to fill his time.

After Tuscany there was Paris. Even in August, Paris was better than Cupertino. He began to think about not going back. This was like a vacation from figuring out how to get on with his life. Maybe he could make it a permanent one. He was young. He had money. He could become an expatriate. Then he remembered he had a dinner date with Susan Barnes, so he called to tell her he couldn't make it. He was in Paris, he explained, and he'd decided to spend the rest of his life abroad. He hadn't expected her to start crying into the phone.

That's great news for you, Susan said between sobs. She was really happy for him, but this wasn't a day she could take it. Steve asked what was wrong. All she would say was, if he ever decided to do something else with his life, he should let her know. Because right now she was ready to leave.

There'd been a lot of back-and-forth among the exec staff about whether Susan should even be talking with Steve, let alone having dinner with him. Del thought it improper for her to take his calls. Could some sort of conspiracy be taking place? Her boss, Bill Campbell, came to her defense. He told the other vice-presidents it was none of their business. She went to Dave Barram and asked what to say when Steve asked questions like "How are things going?" or "How's Macintosh selling?" Barram said he was chairman of the board; she could tell him. But *how much* could she tell him? Finally she got word that John would keep him up to date on those issues and she should talk to him about other things.

Steve's expatriate phase didn't last long; a week after his phone call to Susan, he was back in California. He still had no idea what to do next. For a while he thought about politics. He talked with Pat Caddell and Scott Miller about running for the Senate. (Having finished up the Monte Carlo nuclear nonproliferation conference, they were now plotting the reintroduction of "old Coke" as Coca-Cola Classic.) Steve had long fantasized about entering politics on the John Kennedy model, taking over the government, straightening out the bureaucracy. They saw in him the charisma, the larger-than-life quality of men like Kennedy and Reagan, the messianic appeal of one who has the answer and wants to share it with the world. It was too bad he'd never registered to vote. But Steve was able to look beyond that as a problem. Susan warned him that he'd be ripped to shreds in the press, but he figured there was nothing they could print about him that they hadn't already. A bigger difficulty was that he didn't know which party to run under. Maybe he could offer himself to both.

Then there was biology. The year before, when François Mitterand of France had paid a visit to Silicon Valley, Steve had called Donald Kennedy, the president of Stanford, to suggest that Stanford hold a luncheon in his honor. Kennedy liked the idea, and at the lunch that ensued Steve had found himself seated next to Paul Berg, a Stanford biochemist and Nobel laureate. Steve came away from lunch with the impression that, in essence, life is soup. After countless millennia of inquiry, through witchcraft, theology, philosophy, and science, mankind was finally on the verge of discovering the secret of life, and what was it? A chemical stew in which information is encoded algorithmically, just as it is in computers. Biology and electronics were one—they just used a different delivery vehicle. A different encoding system. It was too much! You throw elements in a pot and electrostatic charges randomly occur and things happen and intelligent life emerges. It sounded so trivial, and yet the implications were so enormous.

So he called up Paul Berg and made a date for lunch. He thought it was time to educate himself a bit. Maybe he'd even go back to school and catch up on the new biology—spend a few years and try to figure it out for himself. They met at Stanford and talked about how biology works and how it might be simulated on a computer. When Steve asked why college professors didn't run simulations of Berg's experiments for their students, Berg told him most classrooms didn't have computers powerful enough to do the job. Steve started thinking about what teachers might be able to do if they had the right tools—tools it apparently hadn't occurred to them to ask for.

After his return from Europe, Steve had started a list of the things he'd done over the past ten years that meant a lot to him. As he kept writing things down, three items began to pop out, each of them having to do with school. There was the Apple Education Foundation, which the company had set up after getting an appeal from the United Way: Figuring that it could get more leverage out of its donations than the United Way could, Apple had started dispensing grants of money and computers to schools and community groups. Then there was "Kids Can't Wait," which saw thousands of Apple II's donated to California public schools in exchange for a tax write-off. And there was the Apple University Consortium, which made Macintosh available to colleges and universities at below-retail prices.

By this time, life for Steve had boiled down to a series of one-event days. He'd take an entire day to buy a new 35-millimeter camera. The Macintosh crowd had been after him all summer to start a new venture, but he couldn't muster any enthusiasm. At one point, Andy Hertzfeld and Bud Tribble and a couple of other engineers from the core crew had gotten together to try to goad him into it over dinner. Bud was particularly eager to do something new; he'd just come back from medical school a year ago, and now he was in charge of a hundred and fifty people—not the kind of role he'd fancied himself in. Susan told him how unhappy she was in finance; Steve told her to stay, make it work, Bill needed her. Bob Belleville wanted to do some work in telecommunications; Steve wasn't interested. But then, not long after his lunch with Berg, Rich Page called, totally distraught. Jean-Louis had just canceled Big Mac.

Big Mac was one of those engineering projects that collapse of their own weight. Originally the committee project that was supposed to replace Burrell Smith's TurboMac, it had been nurtured by Page into an almost minicomputer-class Macintosh. Bob thought it suffered from creeping elegance—no, galloping elegance, absolute runaway foaming-at-the-bit elegance. Thoroughly disheartened, he'd started Mid Mac as an alternative—a modular Macintosh with a twelve-inch screen and expansion slots inside. When Jean-Louis took over, Mid Mac got the resources while the Big Mac prototypes sat on a shelf. Then Mid Mac got Big Mac's microprocessor—the new Motorola 68020, the most advanced version yet of the 68000 that lay at the heart of the original Macintosh. That made Big Mac superfluous: Mid Mac was a smaller, less expensive, more flexible machine that could be upgraded to Big Mac's capabilities with ease.

Shortly after Rich's call, Steve heard from George Crow, an analog engineer who'd worked with Bob Belleville to make the Sony disk drive work on Macintosh. Crow was a very level-headed guy, older and more experienced than most of the Mac team, but right now he was furious. One of his projects was being buffeted about by a group that had reported to Del before the reorg, and when George went to Jean-Louis he couldn't get in to see him. When Jean-Louis didn't call that evening, George phoned Steve and then Bob. He told them he was going to quit and asked what they were doing. Bob said he wasn't doing much and hadn't had much luck finding work himself. Steve urged him to hang in there. He didn't have any immediate plans, but he did have a couple of things on the back burner.

Lunch with Paul Berg had helped crystallize a few ideas in Steve's mind. He was beginning to think there was a need for a computer that would be powerful enough to simulate complex biochemistry experiments and yet inexpensive enough for colleges and college students to afford. The education efforts—the Education Foundation, "Kids Can't Wait," the University Consortium—were staring out at him from the list he'd made. And people were calling, telling him they wanted out—first Bud, then Susan, then Rich, and now George. With Rich to design the digital boards, George to design the monitor and the power supply, Bud to do the software, and Susan to run finance, he'd have the nucleus of a computer company. All he lacked was marketing.

The obvious candidate for a company that would sell computers to universities was Dan'l Lewin, the young marketing guy who'd put together the University Consortium for Apple. Lewin was tall and young and well spoken, with a chiseled jaw and movie-star looks and a disarming sincerity of manner, and he knew the university market better than anyone. On the day after Labor Day, Steve picked up the phone.

He happened to call at a good moment. The University Consortium, while extremely profitable for Apple, had nearly been killed in the confusion of the June reorg because a lot of retailers—the lazy ones, Lewin thought—claimed it was taking business away from them. Lewin had helped fight that off, but during the reorg he'd been taken out of college sales and put in charge of marketing for all of education, and he didn't like the way the new marketing organization was shaping up. He respected Campbell, but he was frustrated by Lorelli's consumer-goods management techniques—the secretiveness, the constant status worries—and burnt out from the long hours and constant traveling. Then, the week before Labor Day, he'd gone on vacation in Los Angeles, and while he was there he'd run into an old friend who'd been reading about Apple in the papers and wanted to know if Dan'l was kicking Steve like everyone else. He wasn't, but he hadn't talked to him all summer, so he made a note to call when he got back to work on Tuesday.

He was a little surprised when Steve called him first. They laughed for a moment about the coincidence, and then Steve asked if he wanted to talk. He said sure, and they made a date for the end of the day.

It was sometime after five when Dan'l drove through the open gates and up to Steve's house. They spent a couple of hours walking around the grounds. Steve told him he was thinking about starting a new company that would do something for the higher-education market. Did Dan'l think that was an interesting idea? He thought it was extremely interesting. He'd wanted to teach high school himself when he'd moved to California in 1976, fresh out of Princeton with a degree in politics; but there weren't any jobs, so he'd gone into sales and marketing, first for Sony and then at Apple. Still, he had some reservations about what Steve wanted to do, and he left without making any commitment.

The other four arrived for dinner a short while later—George, Rich, and Susan and Bud, who were going together. They sat in the dining room and drank California wine and ate vegetarian pizza. At first it seemed the gripe session would go on forever: All of them wanted to get out of Apple. Then Steve announced that he was thinking of starting a new company that would make the next great computer for higher education. The others weren't all convinced it would be successful, but they didn't like what Apple was becoming and they did like working with Steve—the ideas, the excitement, the risk. After all, this was still Silicon Valley, and joining a start-up was what you did. It wasn't long before they were talking about salaries and engineering features and what kind of company they wanted to build.

Steve called Dan'l on Friday evening to tell him it looked as if he'd definitely be starting a new company. He named three of the people who'd be leaving with him—Susan, Rich, and George—and said there was another person in software who didn't want his name used. Dan'l was leaving Sunday for a meeting in Minneapolis; on Monday night he was flying to Austin to meet Campbell, who was scheduled to give a speech at the University of Texas. He promised to call Steve from his hotel Tuesday night to let him know if he'd be joining them. The September board meeting was scheduled to begin Thursday evening, and Steve wanted to use the occasion to announce his plans.

■ ■ ■

September was not a good time for Apple. The company was split down the middle on the Steve issue: Some people were glad to be rid of him, others were wearing T-shirts that read WE WANT OUR JOBS BACK, most felt a mix of both impulses. People at every level were nervous, insecure, fearful of the future. At the top there was a rudderless sensation. Even with Steve gone, John seemed unable to give coherent direction to their efforts. Marketing programs were being blown, money was being wasted, there didn't seem to be any accountability, there wasn't any leadership in meetings, John just seemed to sit there as events swirled around him. They all seemed to be on their own. Jay Elliot grew queasy enough to go to Mike Markkula and Arthur Rock; others did likewise. If the board didn't intervene, it looked as if the company might sink into oblivion.

So the September board meeting came at a particularly awkward moment—dangerous for John, difficult for the exec staff, tricky for Steve, troublesome for the board. John seemed visibly nervous; having Steve in the same room was a stress test he didn't enjoy. He and

Al Eisenstat had put together the agenda, which consisted mainly of a series of presentations on the turnaround they'd accomplished since June. John made a presentation about the layoffs and the reorganization and the status of the company. Del made a presentation on the product strategy, Bill on sales and marketing, Dave Barram on the financials. The board members seemed to greet them all coolly.

The final item on the agenda was something labeled "chairman's report." Neither John nor Al knew what it was. Speaking from a prepared script, Steve quickly outlined his plans. He'd decided to get on with his life, he told them; he was thirty years old, and it was obvious he had to do something. Over the summer, he'd thought about doing a number of things—going into politics, maybe going back to school, or starting a company of his own. He'd decided on the last. As he looked back on his years at Apple, he realized that it was bringing the computer into schools that had meant the most to him, and the company he wanted to start was one that would build computers for the higher-education market. He didn't offer any details—at that point, he didn't have any—but he did say that his new venture would be complementary to Apple, not competitive with it. He added that he'd be taking a handful of people with him, and that he thought he should resign from Apple's board.

Once he'd finished, the board members asked him to leave the room while they discussed the matter in private. Some of them were surprised he'd moved so fast; on Saturday night, when he and his girlfriend had driven up to San Francisco for dinner at Arthur Rock's mansion in Pacific Heights, he'd said he still hadn't made up his mind what to do. Nonetheless, his plans sounded interesting, and if this new venture really wasn't going to compete with Apple, they might even want to invest in it. After half an hour of discussion, they invited Steve back into the boardroom.

John spoke for the board. They didn't want him to resign, he said, but they didn't want him to raid the company either. If indeed his company was not going to compete with Apple, they might be interested in buying a stake in it—perhaps as much as 10 percent. Steve still thought he should resign, but he agreed to hold off for a week while he thought about it. As for the possibility of Apple investing, he'd have to think that over as well. Markkula suggested he talk it over with John the next week.

As soon as the meeting was over, Steve drove home to Woodside. It was early evening, and the other five—George, Rich, Susan, Bud, and Dan'l—were already waiting at his house. So was Larry Sonsini, a Palo Alto lawyer who'd been Apple's corporate counsel since it went public in 1980. A trim, middle-aged man whose rapidly growing firm specialized in securities law and corporate mergers for high-tech companies in the Valley, Sonsini had been called in by Steve to advise him on how he should behave as chairman of Apple's board. Apple hadn't had much call for outside legal advice in the past couple of years—client and customer relationships and tax matters were all handled internally, by Al—so Sonsini was perhaps not as clued into the emotional tenor of the third-floor executive suite as he might have been. But he had a calming manner and an authoritative voice, and there was no reason to think his legal advice was anything less than expert.

This was the first time the other five had met with Steve as a group, and there was a definite charge in the air, a tingle of apprehension and excitement. Joining him was an act of blind faith, like stepping over a cliff, for regardless of how they felt about Apple—and their feelings ranged from a sense of betrayal on Rich's part to a twinge of nostalgia on George's—there was no question that it offered more security than Steve could. They were starting out with no business plan or stock plan or company charter or product definition; they hadn't even agreed on their salaries. Still, there was no turning back now.

They sat up expectantly as Steve read them the script he'd used at the board meeting, and when he'd finished they all told him it was great. Then, over a dinner of fresh pasta in the dining room, they started debating what they should do next. Both Steve and George were intrigued by the idea that Apple might invest in them. They could build the product they thought was right, sell it directly to the college market, and maybe offer it to Apple to sell as a business machine. But Susan went crazy at the thought. She was the only one there, she reminded them, who worked on the third floor; she knew the guys on the exec staff, and they weren't going to sit still for this. They were totally paranoid about Steve and what he was going to do to Apple. They'd kill.

The other big question was how they'd go about making their exit. To avoid creating a panic, George suggested they resign separately over a period of several weeks; if they all left at once, it might look like some kind of conspiracy. But Steve didn't like that idea, and neither did Sonsini. If they went in and resigned one by one, Sonsini argued, it would look awful, because John and the exec staff would have no idea when it was going to stop. They might think Steve was going to take half the company with him. It would be much cleaner if Steve wrote John a letter saying these five people would be leaving. In any case, he didn't think Apple would take action against them. Probably it would do what most other companies in the Valley did when a founder took off—let him go quietly.

With the resignation issue decided, the new company's founders could start talking about what they were going to pay themselves—less than they were making at Apple, and of course Steve would be footing the bill—and what percentage of the company they'd each get. At that point it was time for Sonsini to leave. As they stood up to shake his hand, there was talk that maybe he'd be their corporate lawyer.

■ ■ ■

At 7:30 the next morning—Friday, September 13—the executive staff was scheduled to convene in the boardroom to deal with issues from the board meeting. At 7:25 or so, Steve went to John's office and handed him the letter he'd written. "Dear John," the letter began. It listed the five people who were planning to leave and asked that their exodus be "as smooth and unharassed" as possible. John scanned it briefly and asked about the other two things. The other two things? Yes—could Apple invest in Steve's company, and what about his staying on the board? Steve suggested they talk about that next week.

A couple of minutes later, John walked into the boardroom and took his place at the head of the table. Then, in matter-of-fact tones, he gave the six exec staff members the news: Steve was leaving to form a new company that would be noncompetitive with Apple; the board was thinking of investing in it; and the following five people would be leaving with him. He read off the names, and almost immediately the meeting dissolved into pandemonium and outrage. Steve was taking Bud Tribble—their head of software, whom Jean-Louis had thought was solidly with them? He was taking Dan'l Lewin—their head of education marketing, who knew the field better than anyone else? Jean-Louis and Bill were beside themselves. Del and Jay went berserk. Steve was going to destroy the company he'd built—and John and the board were going to let him do it? This was what they'd feared most.

Fueling their resentment was the ho-hum way the board had received their presentations on the turnaround the day before. As far as the exec staff members were concerned, *they* were the ones who'd kept Apple going all this time, not John or the board, and they weren't about to let Steve wreck it now. He knew everything about Apple, and they had no idea what he was planning. He could take their technology; he could take their people. There was no telling where it would end—he could empty half of Bandley Drive if he wanted to. And he'd planned the whole thing while serving as chairman of the board. Chairmen don't do that, they were convinced of it, and boards don't act that way in response.

John and Al Eisenstat looked a little nonplussed, as if they didn't quite see the problem. The outburst swirled around them regardless. How could Steve do this to Apple? How could John and the board be so naive? How could any of them say this new company would be noncompetitive? It wasn't lingerie Steve would be selling. Then Jay and Jean-Louis took up the leadership issue—the leadership that needed to occur and hadn't. John sat slouched in his chair, biting his nails and fixing one or another of them with his cold, penetrating stare. Finally he said he'd have to think about it some more. He went to his office and tried to get a couple of board members on the phone—Arthur Rock, Henry Singleton, Mike Markkula. He wanted to hear what they thought. But he couldn't reach any of them, and by the time he got back to the boardroom, the exec staff had reached a consensus. One by one they told him: What Steve had done was wrong, and John had to take action against him.

■ ■ ■

Dan'l Lewin had decided this would be a good day to go in late. He was still in the shower when the phone rang. It was Campbell; he'd just run out of the exec staff meeting. Dan'l grabbed a towel and took the receiver from his wife. Bill couldn't believe that Dan'l was going to go with Steve. Well, Dan'l said, he wanted to come in and talk about that. Bill just had to know if it was true. It was.

George Crow tried to find Jean-Louis to resign, but he was nowhere to be seen, so George taped a resignation letter to his chair. Susan Phalen, his HR woman, didn't seem to be around either, so he left a copy on her desk. Then he went back to his desk and waited for something to happen. Nothing did.

Susan Barnes went into the corporate controller's office and handed him her resignation letter. He looked it over and said he wasn't surprised. It was obvious she'd been unhappy; they had a nice talk. She explained that she wanted to give her two weeks' notice. The phone rang. It was Dave Barram, who'd just bolted out of the exec staff meeting and wanted to know if her boss knew what the hell was going on. Well, yes; as a matter of fact, Susan was right there in his office. A few minutes later she went over to look for Bill. She tried to stop him as he ran out of the boardroom; he shook her hand and wished her good luck and hurried off.

That afternoon, one of the Bene Gesserit appeared at Lewin's desk and very courteously escorted him over to Mike Lorelli's office and then upstairs to Bill's. They all seemed to wish they didn't have to do any of this, but it was clear they didn't have any say in the matter. Bill congratulated Dan'l on the contributions he'd made to Apple and assured him they'd never go away. Dan'l was too choked up to speak. He valued Bill's guidance, his friendship, his leadership. He hadn't wanted to leave that way, without giving any hint of his plans, but he'd had no choice. Bill was an officer of the company. Anything he knew he'd be obligated to reveal.

By this time it was apparent that Steve needed a new lawyer. Sonsini recommended he get in touch with David Balabanian of McCutchen, Doyle, Brown & Enersen in San Francisco. McCutchen, Doyle was one of the biggest firms in the city; Sonsini's partner had been a McCutchen person and had a high opinion of Balabanian. The next morning, as Balabanian was eating his breakfast and scanning the morning paper at his white stucco home in the Berkeley hills, he noticed a story about Steve Jobs's stormy departure from Apple Computer. He'd just started to read it when the phone rang. "Hi!" said the voice on the receiver in a high-pitched, energetic burst. "This is Steve Jobs." He was calling Balabanian, Jobs explained, because he thought he needed to meet him. "I think you're right," Balabanian replied.

■ ■ ■

As Balabanian was cruising across the Bay Bridge and down the Peninsula to Woodside, Apple's exec staff was meeting in emergency session in the boardroom. They wanted to know what the board was planning to do—what action would be taken against Steve, what would happen to Apple, what they should tell their people. It seemed obvious that Steve was violating his fiduciary responsibility in hiring away critical employees while he was chairman of the board. By the end of the morning, John and Al were beginning to see their point. The board members John had managed to reach on the phone were becoming upset as well. They knew how Steve would have reacted if someone else had left the company this way; Arthur Rock was beginning to think he felt the rules were made for someone else. And while they had no way of knowing if he were taking any secrets or not, they intended to make sure he didn't.

The exec staff met again on Sunday—not a popular move, since the '49ers were playing the Atlanta Falcons that afternoon, and some of the vice-presidents were eager to see the game. But Markkula came in that day, and John made the case against Steve. The doubts the others had had about John were forgotten now; he was their champion, thrust to the fore to redress the wrongs they'd suffered. Far from having vague intentions to start a complementary venture, John declared, Steve had actually planned and executed a raid on Apple. He'd breached his fiduciary responsibility as chairman, and the board needed to do something—to send a message that people couldn't just steal away Apple's employees and trade secrets at will. Markkula listened carefully, and as he did so he became more and more incensed. He'd been Steve's mentor, his father-figure, his sanity check, and now Steve had crossed the line. Steve was uncontrollable. They'd have to take action.

Once Markkula had gone, they began to plan their strategy. They talked about how Steve was viewed as some kind of messiah at Apple, and how they needed to expose him for the fraud he really was. But you don't just demote a messiah or shunt him upstairs; you have to kill him in eyes of his followers. They couldn't kill Steve literally, of course, but they could replace him. They could bring in a new messiah. And fortunately, as Jay pointed out, they had a ready-made candidate waiting in the wings: Steve Wozniak. Like Jobs, Woz was a founder who'd come and gone from Apple, and he'd left this last time, it seemed, only because of the treatment John and Steve had given the Apple II at the annual meeting. He lacked Jobs's charisma and power, but he had a certain inimitable style of his own, an ingenuous charm that could be enormously appealing. Best of all, he could bring continuity and stability to a rocky transition; he could offer them a founder's blessing. He was the ultimate human resource. Not everyone agreed, but John thought the idea was terrific. He even volunteered to make the call.

■ ■ ■

All weekend the reporters were calling—calling John, calling Regis, calling the Regettes, the board members, the exec staff, the defecting employees, Steve, anybody who could tell them what the hell was going on. A couple of exec staff members gave blind quotes that offered tantalizing suggestions of a boardroom aflame, but most people stayed quiet. Steve's housekeeper spoke in a bouncy, youthful voice that sounded exactly like Steve's, so he had something of a credibility problem when he answered the phone. He'd say Steve wasn't in and the reporters would say, "This is Steve, right? I know it's Steve!" and he'd say, "No, it's Mark," and they wouldn't believe him. On Monday, however, Steve suddenly relented.

First he called a number of reporters he'd met—reporters from *The New York Times, The Wall Street Journal, Business Week, USA Today,* the *San Francisco Chronicle,* the *San Jose Mercury-News*— and told them to come to his house at different times the next day. Then he realized he hadn't the slightest idea how to stage a press conference, so he called Andrea Cunningham, a former Regette who'd recently left to set up her own public-relations firm, to ask for help. She wasn't home, so he blurted a frantic message into her answering machine and hung up.

As it happened, Andy Cunningham didn't get home until late that night, and she left early the next morning without listening to her machine. It was early afternoon before she called Steve's house. She got Dan'l. They really needed her, he said—could she please come over right away? She drove up just as Deborah Wise of *Business Week* was coming out the door. Steve had already walked her around the grounds and given her his story; a short while before, he'd done the same with Patricia Bellew of the *Journal.* The Jolly Roger was flying overhead—the same skull-and-crossbones that had flown over Bandley 3 in Macintosh days. Andy ran inside and found Steve in the dining room. He told her they were having a press conference next. Just as she started to beg him not to, Kathy Rebello of *USA Today* walked in. He asked Rebello to wait outside and began to argue with Andy about whether he should be talking to the press. Three more reporters came to the door while they were talking.

There was no way they could call off the press conference now, with four reporters standing in the driveway. Andy came out and suggested they do a series of one-on-one interviews instead, but they didn't go for that. They were all facing deadlines, and they all wanted to go in together. So they were ushered into the living room, its vast expanse punctuated only by a leather sofa and chairs, an awesome stereo system, and a scale model of what the estate would look like once Steve had torn the house down and built a new one in its place. None of them could quite believe how empty the place was. This wasn't how a chairman of the board was supposed to live. It looked more like a rock star's house—like an adolescent fantasy of what fame and money could buy. Either that or he'd just moved in.

Suddenly Steve appeared. He was charming, conciliatory, magnanimous. But he thought some of the things that were being said about him were unfair; he wanted to tell his story. For the next half-hour he did, trying not to sound immature or self-pitying and very nearly succeeding. This was the "new" Steve Jobs, the Steve who'd used his summer exile for self-examination and growth, the Steve who'd grown up. Later the *Mercury-News* reporter arrived, and later still Steve sent a messenger to the *Mercury-News* building in San Jose to deliver his letter of resignation from Apple. "The company's recent reorganization left me with no work to do," it complained. "I am but thirty and want still to contribute and achieve."

Steve and his followers had chosen Next, Inc. as the name of their new venture, and that afternoon they sent in a form to register it with the California Secretary of State. Steve was going to put his letter of resignation to Apple into a mailbox along with it, but Susan Barnes reminded him that he'd gone a long way with Mike Markkula over the past ten years and he might want to deliver this item personally. So she and Bud got in the car with him and drove to Mike's house in Portola Valley, a few minutes away by back roads. Steve went to the door; if he didn't come out in fifteen minutes, Susan was going in after him.

Mike ushered him inside. There he met Al Eisenstat and the attorney Apple had just hired to handle the case against him—Jack Brown of the Phoenix firm of Brown & Bain. Brown was high tech's heavy hitter, a trial lawyer who specialized in intellectual property cases. He'd done a lot of litigation for IBM, and he'd represented Apple in its suit against Franklin Computer, a manufacturer of Apple II clones which Apple had sued for infringement of copyright, resulting in a landmark ruling which established that operating systems could be copyrighted as if they were novels or songs or plays, and also resulting in the bankruptcy of Franklin Computer. Brown was a heavy-set man with bushy eyebrows and a downturned mouth and a thick thatch of shiny black hair. Steve was surprised to find him there. The four of them started arguing. Mike was telling Steve, if he'd just been willing to stand in a corner for a year . . .

Steve's fifteen minutes were up. Balabanian had given them strict orders not to talk to these people without him present. Susan made Bud promise to come in after her if *she* didn't come out in fifteen minutes. She could see them arguing inside as she walked up to the door. Mike answered it, feigning surprise. Susan Barnes! Fancy seeing her there! She grabbed Steve's arm and told him it was time to go.

Steve was livid as they sped back to Woodside. Stand in a corner for a year! They'd already sent him to stand in a corner once and he'd come back with Macintosh. He wasn't ready to do it again.

That evening, Markkula issued a statement from his house reviewing the events of the past few days. "As chairman of the board, Steve Jobs is responsible for protecting Apple and acting in the best interests of the company," the statement concluded. "In light of recent events, the board of directors continues to evaluate what possible actions should be taken to assure protection of Apple's technology and assets."

After this rather thinly veiled threat, the dispute became a matter for the lawyers to handle. Negotiations continued through the week at Brown & Bain's offices in Palo Alto. Steve alternated between meeting with his lawyers and meeting with the *Newsweek* reporter he'd chosen to get the in-depth story of his departure from Apple. By Friday it looked as if the lawyers had reached a settlement. Balabanian's office put together a draft agreement on Saturday, and on Sunday it was telecopied to Palo Alto. On Monday morning, however—the day the *Newsweek* article appeared—one of Brown's partners called Balabanian with different news: A messenger was on his way to the Santa Clara County Courthouse in San Jose to file a civil complaint against Steve Jobs and Rich Page. The suit accused Jobs of secretly planning a "nefarious scheme" to form a company that would use several of Apple's key employees and its "next generation" technology to compete with Apple. The phrase "nefarious scheme" appeared repeatedly in the complaint, as though it were some kind of mantra, some hypnotic chant to break the fraud-messiah's spell.

22

Apple Classic

"New Attitude!"

That's what they had, a whole new attitude. They were holding the sales conference in San Diego this year because they couldn't afford Hawaii—the board had ordered them to go somewhere cheaper last spring, when the inventory pile-up made it clear they were spending more money than they were taking in. Now they were all set up at the Sheraton Harbor Island, eleven hundred Apple folks in a concrete slab at the edge of San Diego Bay, with sailboats on one side and destroyers on the other and jetliners screaming overhead. It wasn't exactly Waikiki, but it was warm. And anyway, they had a new attitude, as the Patti LaBelle sound-alike who'd recorded a specially rewritten version of her hit song kept reminding them. They were the new Apple. It was time they got Back to the Future.

"Back to the Future" was their theme this year. They were putting the past behind them, getting back to business; and that's what Apple's business was—the future. But what kind of future would it be? The sales conference's organizers had had only a couple of months to put the whole thing together, and that wasn't much time if you were going to invent an entire future and mount it onstage. So they opted for a fifties sci-fi version of the future, which made for a nice tie-in with the movie—the Steven Spielberg production, starring Michael J. Fox as the teenager who time-travels back to the fifties and gets mixed up in his own parents' adolescence. It was also cheap. So at eight in the morning of Monday, October 28, the sales people who'd filled the Champagne Ballroom for the opening session were greeted by an Apple "salesman from the future" wearing black tights, a silver-lamé cape, a metal breastplate, and a helmet with sparkplugs sticking out of it.

So what was it like in the future? Well, the salesman and his two sidekicks (one of them a robot) had gotten onstage to tell them. For one thing, there were no longer any computer stores—that had been changed by a man named John Sculley. Instead there were vending machines—two kinds, regular and commission-free. Lisa had been brought back as "Lisa Classic." And John Sculley had been deified. In the future, whenever you spoke his name, you bit into an Apple and flung your right arm out in salute.

But the deification of John Sculley was minor compared to the transformation that was wrought on Del Yocam a few days later. It happened on Thursday morning, when Del came out to give the opening speech for the final day's session. He walked onstage in an outfit straight out of "Miami Vice"—blue blazer, fuchsia T-shirt, aviator shades—and right away it was clear that the old, dowdy Del was a thing of the past. The new Del was famous. He was a celebrity. He had more charisma than Steve Jobs ever imagined. The stage was lined with pictures of his face that had been blown up and dropped into oversized magazine covers—in many cases, where Steve's face had once been. There he was on the cover of *Business Week,* as *Time*'s Man of the Year, with Linda Evans, with Bo Derek. As he made his way to the podium, flanked by a pair of statuesque models in black cocktail dresses, the loudspeakers blared out the chorus of "Fame," David Bowie's funky, brassy strut, lending an edge of almost surrealist irony to what was already a wrenching scenario.

Del loved it. It was his moment of vindication—the long-neglected hero getting his due at last. It was the new Apple.

■　■　■

"The new Apple," Sculley declared the following Monday, "is working." He gazed out at his audience—row upon row of Wall Street analysts seated in powder-blue chairs amid the freeze-dried rococo of the Versailles Room of the Helmsley Palace Hotel in New York. If in fact the new Apple was going to work, these people would have to be convinced of it first. Right now the stock was still stumbling along in the basement at about $19 a share, up slightly from its summer low but not enough to demonstrate much in the way of renewed confidence. Yet it had gone up $1 the day after Jobs resigned, and his departure had been cheered by most of the money men who funded the industry. Too brash, that was the consensus—arrogant, self-aggrandizing, immature. Some had even seized his demise as an occasion to take public potshots. "It's good news for Apple that he's out of their hair," proclaimed a Palo Alto venture capitalist in *Time*. "He ruffled a lot of feathers on Wall Street," explained a New York broker in *Newsweek*. If Sculley was to find a sympathetic audience anywhere, it would be here, in a room full of pinstripes and braces.

Not that sympathy was liable to translate into action. The palpable hostility that had marked the last meeting at Rickey's was gone, but the skepticism that had taken its place wasn't much better. You could almost hear it, just below the hiss of canned air as it was blown into the windowless room. In the past few weeks, a handful of analysts— Charles Wolf of First Boston, Tom Rooney of Donaldson, Lufkin & Jenrette—had put Apple back on their recommended lists. Yet few if any of their clients among the big institutional investors seemed inclined to follow them in. Analysts at the institutions were talking about Apple disappearing within twelve months. The last thing they wanted to do was own its stock.

"Fiscal 1985 certainly *was* a turbulent period for Apple and our industry," Sculley admitted, warming toward his theme. "That fact was well chronicled by you and other industry watchers." He drew a breath. "From my perspective, fiscal 1985 was also *the year Apple grew up*."

He'd flown to New York to make a year-end report, and he had a difficult year to explain. In the past twelve months, Apple had suffered its first quarterly loss, laid off a fifth of its work force, lost both its famous co-founders, and stumbled for a third and perhaps final time in the office market it had made such a show of targeting. It had come to the brink of disaster, and in an IBM-dominated world it seemed well-positioned to fall over the edge, just like Osborne and Atari before it. Sculley's task was to reposition it for success.

His strategy was to invoke the myth of "the new Apple"—the post-Jobs Apple. It was the other Apple those things had happened to. The new Apple had grown up. Sales were rebounding, and profits were going to be significantly higher in the year to come, even though price cuts would keep their revenues about the same. They were a $1.9-billion corporation now, with more cash on hand than ever before. And no longer were their sales channels clogged with inventory; after closing three factories, the challenge would be to keep up with demand.

"The bottom line here is that we are becoming more market-driven and more customer-oriented," Sculley declared, "which are extremely important steps for us to take as the industry becomes more competitive. Apple *is* growing up."

It was the perfect message for his audience, for if there was one thing the young professionals of Wall Street admired it was grownups. That was Steve's problem—he wasn't a grown-up. His boundless enthusiasm and uncensored creativity came in a package with impatience, self-centeredness, and guileless naiveté. When all was said and done he was just a kid; and as with any kid, you didn't get the good side without the bad. From now on, Apple's success would depend on its ability to keep those qualities in check. What Apple needed now, everyone seemed to agree, was steadiness, maturity, discipline—not qualities Steve was known for.

The Street's distaste for Steve extended beyond any personal traits, however. The Street disliked him for the same reason corporate America did: He was too radical, too much the maverick. He wasn't *safe*. As the guru of personal computing—a technology that promised to alter the balance of power between the individual and society—he'd become the leader of a technological youth cult that was out to change the world. A decade earlier, when Apple had blossomed forth from the mysterious electronic wonderland of Silicon Valley, this may have seemed like a good idea. It didn't anymore. Not only was no one interested in changing the world; the promise of computer power for the individual had given way to a future in which everyone would be wired to everyone else. Computers seemed destined to be nodes on a network, not bastions of individual creativity. The times had changed faster than Steve had, and as much as he was Sculley's victim or the market's or his own, he was theirs.

The fact is that by 1985, the fifth and most triumphant year of the Reagan administration, Steve Jobs was looking not just immature but dated, like a laid-back California singer-songwriter whose million-selling albums carried too many references to pot. Personal-computer revolution? *Just say no.* Entrepreneurship made good ideology, but like most ideology it worked better in theory than in practice. That's why Steve could get a medal in the White House in February and be a washout on Wall Street a few months later. But his cardinal sin in the eyes of the Street—worse than his youth, worse than his arrogance, worse even than the poor performance of his company—was his decision to start selling his stock when it was clear that nobody wanted to buy. That was the ultimate in uncool acts: Steve Jobs, party animal, throwing away money. They couldn't believe it was happening.

No, they didn't much care for Steve in the pink-and-blue confines of the Versailles Room that day. What they thought of John would depend on what kind of numbers he turned in.

■ ■ ■

If Apple was to convince the analysts, it would first have to motivate its employees. That was HR's responsibility. So on Tuesday, the day after he briefed the analysts, John spoke to the troops at a half-day "worldwide communications meeting" in Flint Center. The entire population of Bandley Drive—more than fifteen hundred people—turned out. The event was transmitted live by satellite across the bay to Fremont and sent out on videotape to Apple's distribution centers and international facilities. John gave a talk and the exec staff members spoke and then Jay Elliot did a Phil Donahue–type interview with them, asking them questions people wanted answered. It was the "Re-Orient Express," part of a plan Jay had devised to get them through the healing process.

At an exec staff meeting a month earlier, Jay had delivered an "Apple 'Stock' Report" that dealt with the HR issues facing the new Apple. His presentation started off with a chart that showed the employees' "stock"—their faith in the company—declining drastically over the past nine months. The big issue was whether Camelot had died. The goal was to bring the company together, make it "one Apple." To do that, Jay wanted to "market" the company to its own employees—to develop a campaign promoting the qualities that made Apple unique. He wanted to open up communications with a quarterly video magazine and a monthly print magazine and an electronic bulletin board and a series of weekly lunches between senior managers and small groups of employees—a program he dubbed "the Hearsay Café." He wanted to offer day care and sabbaticals, revamp the profit-sharing program, and institute a worldwide no-layoff policy. He wanted to get people back in high spirits within the year.

They certainly weren't in high spirits now. Jay had led a series of focus groups at the Red Lion with about eighty key people in the middle and lower levels of the company, and what he heard was that they were all worried about where Apple was going. Even the people who resented Steve's behavior were upset that he was gone, because he was the visionary and nobody else seemed to know where they were headed. John was barely visible outside the Pink Palace; the technical leaders—Bob Belleville and Wayne Rosing—were gone; nobody seemed to know what was happening. The only news people got was what they read in the *San Jose Mercury-News* and *The Wall Street Journal*. They didn't know if things were under control or not. But if they didn't know what was happening, maybe nobody else did either.

The Re-Orient Express was supposed to allay those fears, and to help get the message across, Steve Wozniak had been persuaded to utter a few benedictory remarks. Woz liked the new Apple. You could say all you want about dreams and your own ego, he'd come to realize, but if your company doesn't make money you aren't doing the world any service. You couldn't just create new technologies to thrill the purists; you had to run a business as well. You had to meet the needs of your customers and create value for your shareholders, and that looked like the kind of thing Sculley could do.

Woz had been pleased when John called him up. In the past few months they'd chatted a couple of times about products, particularly the Apple II line, but Woz had never mentioned any of the stuff he read in the papers—the lawsuit against Steve, for example. He'd had lunch with Gassée, too. Gassée, with his talk of open systems and expandability, was his favorite person at Apple. Woz didn't want to take up too much of their time because he didn't have that much to contribute, but he was happy to get onstage at Flint Center and tell a couple of jokes if it would boost morale. So when John picked him out of the crowd, he made his way to the podium, a Hobbit figure in his beard and jeans, as the entire audience stood and cheered. "I've been hearing a lot about the new Apple," he quipped when he got to the mike. "Is that anything like Apple Classic?"

Well, yes, it was. As the raw wounds began to heal and the angry memories began their slow fade, Bandley Drive was becoming a different place. The new Apple liked to think of itself as entrepreneurial, but it also called for more structure, more obedience, more discipline, less pushing back. Smart kids with little or no qualification for their jobs had been replaced by M.B.A.s who did things by the book. The visionary who spun out more ideas than he could keep track of had been supplanted by the bean counter who carried a stack of notebooks and wrote down every detail. Bandley Drive was becoming an entrepreneurial theme park, fastidiously preserving the trappings of entrepreneurial zeal while the essence—passion, excitement, risk—was quietly shunted aside. As a Formica-clad Pizza Hut was to a little mom-and-pop pizzeria, as an air-conditioned Taco Bell was to a dusty Mexican *taquería,* the new Apple was to the old. The word people used was "Scullification."

Woz liked to think that John had gotten so sold on Steve Jobs's dream of changing the world through personal computers that he wouldn't let anything stand in his way, not even Steve Jobs; but with Steve gone, it became a different dream. Sculley was a systems man, and as he began to assert himself, Apple's focus began to shift more and more from the individual to the group. "One man—one computer" was an idea whose time had passed. The new watchword was "networking," and the guru of networking was Alan Kay.

During the summer, when Apple was at its nadir, Kay had discovered a prior engagement at a chamber-music camp in New Hampshire. But on his return he started having long chats with Sculley. The more Kay and Sculley talked, the more their admiration for each other intensified. Sculley started to think of Kay as a Renaissance man; Kay began to liken Sculley to Lorenzo de' Medici. Sculley was fascinated by what had happened at PARC. He discovered that the ideas PARC had become famous for—the ideas behind Lisa and Macintosh and the LaserWriter—were in fact just a by-product of the research that had gone into the Dynabook. The Dynabook still didn't exist, but the spinoffs for Apple alone were bringing in hundreds of millions of dollars a year. Sculley concluded that Apple would get a good return on its investment in Kay's research, even though it was unlikely to accomplish anything close to its goals by the end of the century. The thing was, not even Kay knew where his work was going to lead. It was like he just homed in on a magnetic field so strong it dragged him out into the future with it. So that fall, Sculley gave him the go-ahead on a blue-sky research project that was modeled after the Smalltalk project Kay had run at Xerox PARC.

Like most computer scientists, Kay had come to think that before too many years, computer networks would offer people access to anything from the branch bank around the corner to a business meeting on the other side of the world. Networks would offer so many options that to take advantage of them, people would need to equip their Dynabooks with artificially intelligent "agents"—little computer programs that would work the networks, gathering information and answering the phone and doing whatever their human masters required. He wanted to try building these agents; and the best way to do that, he'd decided, was to give the kids in a West Hollywood elementary school he'd picked out the tools to create a simulated plant-and-animal environment—a computer-generated "vivarium" filled with animated and artifically intelligent fish. In a few years, if everything went well, the fish would begin to act as personal electronic servants for the kids, running errands inside their computers, assembling information from a data base that would resemble an underwater "cave of knowledge." The teachers had already agreed to give an A to any paper a kid could get a fish to put together.

So they were going back to the future—but the future they were aiming for was as different from what Jobs had envisioned as the company that was going there. There was still room for childlike creativity and wonder at Apple, but in the research labs, cardoned off from the rest of the company. What the rest of the new Apple was coming to resemble—and from the point of view of countless thousands of stockholders, employees, and consumers, it could have been a lot worse—was the old Hewlett-Packard: a sane, dull, but blessedly predictable place where people did their work every day and then went home. Where all the rules were written down and things seldom happened by surprise. The new Apple would make money for its shareholders and provide security for its employees and try to anticipate the technological needs of its customers, and it would even issue statements about the need to change the world. But never again would it shock anyone or challenge every assumption or cause heads to spin with its brilliance and self-absorption. It was here to sell computers. That was what being grown up was all about.

□□ 23 □□

Perfect World

That same Monday, as Sculley was in New York addressing the analysts, Apple made a dramatic announcement: It was going to file a court order against Steve, seeking an injunction to bar Next from using any of its proprietary technology. Widely interpreted as a sign that Apple was serious about the lawsuit, this announcement came at a time when the suit, indeed the whole affair between Steve and John, was becoming an embarrassment. Prominent analysts were calling it ridiculous, immature, the kind of thing most companies would settle in the boardroom. Instead, it had moved into the courts and onto the front pages of newspapers across the country.

There were two legal bases for Apple's complaint. The first was that Jobs had violated his fiduciary duty—the trust he held as chairman of Apple's board—by scheming to lure away key Apple employees for a competing venture. The second was that Jobs and Page were planning to use Apple's trade secrets in the product they were developing. Most of October had been taken up with legal skirmishes—discovery motions, protective orders, memoranda in support of proposed protective orders, that kind of thing. On October 23, however, Balabanian had filed a demurrer, a motion challenging Apple's theft-of-trade-secrets claim as legally insufficient. In its suit, Apple had failed to identify the secrets Jobs and Page were supposed to have stolen; when Balabanian cited a newly passed California law that required it to do so, Apple had responded with a list of secrets that he considered vague and all-encompassing. The demurrer was, in effect, a "so what" motion: Even if we've taken these things you call secrets, so what? A hearing date was set for Thursday, November 7, three days after Sculley's appearance before the analysts.

That morning, the two sets of lawyers converged on the Santa Clara County Courthouse in downtown San Jose. Steve was with them; John, having delegated the legal issues to Al Eisenstat, was not. Except for the cases that passed through it, the courthouse in its little palm-shaded square could have been in Bakersfield. Downtown San Jose was a flat, half-deserted grid that still had the dusty air of a small farm city, even though the farmland that once surrounded it had filled up with shiny new office parks. But Judge Peter Stone, who was hearing their motions, ruled on one or two trade-secrets cases a day. He had a crisp, no-nonsense style and a quick sense of humor that helped keep things moving. He also had a lot of motions to hear that day; *Apple* v. *Jobs* would get just a few minutes.

In addition to the demurrer, Judge Stone faced a flurry of motions asking him to referee the latest in a series of disputes over how to go about pretrial discovery—the lengthy process in which the two sides disclose to each other the basic elements of their cases. This time it was a wrangle over what documents Jobs and Page should have to produce and which side should take depositions first. This kind of thing could go on forever, and there was no particular reason the taxpayers of Santa Clara County should have to pay for it. So Judge Stone named a "special master"—Judge Barton Phelps, a distinguished-looking gentleman, tall and silver-haired and recently retired from the same court—to hear any future discovery disputes. His fee would be paid by the litigants. That settled, it was time to move on to the demurrer.

Apple didn't want its secrets discussed in an open courtroom, so they took up this issue in the judge's chambers. Steve walked in, apologizing for his blue jeans; he'd expected to be able to sit in the back of the courtroom unnoticed. Judge Stone listened to the lawyers for a few minutes and then granted the motion. Apple had five days to file a revised list of trade secrets.

■ ■ ■

While the lawyers were jockeying for position, Steve and his followers had to set up a company. They were six crash-and-burn victims on an emotional roller-coaster ride, and no one had bothered to strap them in. One day they'd be doing great; then they'd hear a rumor the board had gotten mad again and pitch headlong into the abyss. But being sued had one good effect: It gave them an instant bond. Suddenly they were all in this together. There was no looking back, no second-guessing their decision to leave Apple. It was one for all and all for one.

Even allowing for the disruption of the lawsuit, Next could hardly be considered a conventional start-up. The standard procedure was to start with a business plan and a product definition, secure capital from a couple of venture partnerships, rush a product to market as quickly as possible, and then go public at the earliest opportunity so the founders could get rich. But Steve had learned a lesson at Apple. He was determined to maintain control this time, to keep the company private and not seek funds from the "vulture capitalists"—the men who'd failed to back him in the showdown at Apple. In return for 70 percent of the company, he committed $7 million to bankroll their efforts. They devised a financial structure that would allow the others to cash in their equity while the company remained private.

Steve was also determined that Next, like Macintosh, should be a model work environment. He got a health-insurance plan that offered spousal benefits to people of either sex who were living together. Rather than rent space where it was cheap, such as in the hot, flat, overdeveloped office corridor along U.S. 101 in Sunnyvale and Santa Clara, he decided to set up shop in Palo Alto, close to Stanford. They found a little two-story concrete office building in the Stanford hills, nestled into a hillside behind a larger building and half-surrounded by open land. They camped out on the first floor while the second-floor office space was under construction, then moved to the second floor while the engineering lab and conference rooms were being built downstairs. To make sure it was done right, Steve hired another person from Apple—the interior designer who'd overseen the renovation of Bandley 3 for Macintosh. He set to work creating an environment that, while not quite austere, would seem almost Japanese in its simplicity. The upstairs walls would be painted white to serve as a gallery for rotating collections of Ansel Adams photographs and Japanese woodcuts and Mexican masks. The flooring had to be redone because the workmen didn't join the boards properly. As with everything Steve put his name on, it had to be perfect.

The lawsuit made engineering work impossible, since they couldn't start designing until they knew what was an Apple secret and what wasn't. They didn't know what microprocessor to use or what operating system it should run. But they could do market research, so the six of them hit the road, trying to figure out what their customers wanted. They visited most of the leading computer-science schools—Stanford, Berkeley, Michigan, Carnegie-Mellon, MIT—and talked to students and professors to find out what kind of machine they wanted. They'd fly into Pittsburgh or Boston and all pile into a rented car together while Steve's assistant—another defector from Apple—stayed home and answered the phone. Susan's mother told her they were like a PT-boat patrol in World War II.

The basic guidelines for the product they wanted to create had been set forth in a paper, published by Carnegie-Mellon in 1979, that described what had come to be known as "the 3M machine"—a million bytes of memory, a million dots of screen resolution, and a processing speed of a million instructions per second. Such a machine would be a powerful and graphically sophisticated computer similar to the work stations made by Sun Microsystems, which sold for $20,000 and up. Yet the buyers' association that Carnegie-Mellon had organized, the Inter-University Consortium for Educational Computing, wanted a product that could be bought for less than $10,000. A number of companies, including IBM, AT&T, Digital Equipment, and Apple, had already been given the specs and asked to produce one.

By definition, a 3M machine would be in a different class from any version of Macintosh that was on the market; it would be more on the order of the Big Mac Rich Page had built at Apple. In their travels, however, they found that most academics wanted a machine that would run UNIX, the powerful operating system that over the past few years had become the standard for university research, and they wanted to buy it for as little as $3,000. Since what Steve and his people had done with Macintosh was find great technology and pull it down to a price point that was affordable to large numbers of people, this seemed like an appropriate challenge to undertake. They began to think of what they would build as a "scholar's work-station" that could be used for both research and instruction. Imbued with artificial intelligence, it could be used to simulate not just scientific laboratories but entire social environments—for instance, the court of Louis XIV, which some programmers at Stanford had already done in a crude way on a Macintosh. By developing an easy-to-learn computer language that could enable professors to write their own software, Next could make that kind of interactive learning environment far simpler to build. They could start a revolution in the way people learn in college. And they were doing it, as they sometimes liked to remind themselves, not to make a buck but out of a zeal to make that revolution happen.

■ ■ ■

The depositions began in mid-November. The first witness was Peter Ashkin, Rich Page's former manager in the engineering lab, who'd been called by Balabanian to address the trade-secrets issue. The proceedings took place in McCutchen, Doyle's sleekly appointed offices on the twenty-eighth floor of one of Embarcadero Center's triple towers. Though the glass-and-leather suite had stunning views of the financial district and the Bay Bridge, Ashkin and the Apple attorneys were ushered into a windowless conference room and seated at a table that could have handled twenty comfortably. Steve and Rich were there, along with a raft of lawyers and two video cameramen on hand to tape the events—one for McCutchen, Doyle, one for Apple. The questioning had barely begun when Brown raised an objection: Apple couldn't permit any discussion of trade secrets while Jobs and Page were in the room.

This struck Balabanian as a curious twist—Apple banishing the defendants from the deposition room lest they learn the secrets they'd been accused of stealing. And since he considered Apple's revised list of trade secrets to be no less all-encompassing than the first, it practically meant they'd be banned from the proceedings. So the lawyers got on the phone to Judge Phelps, who listened to their arguments from the comfort of his office in downtown Palo Alto and made a ruling over the phone. Phelps decided that Apple could expel Jobs and Page whenever trade secrets came up, unless the questioning concerned documents they'd written or received themselves. So whenever Jobs or Page had to leave the room, McCutchen's cameraman made a show of following them out the door and down the hall, as if to demonstrate that they didn't have the information they were allegedly threatening to misappropriate.

During the phone conversation with Judge Phelps, Balabanian had suggested they all get together to work up some ground rules for future discussions. He wanted to get Phelps involved; there'd be more disagreements no matter what kind of rules they set, and he wanted to resolve the case as quickly as possible. Plaintiffs in cases like this were often happy to keep the defendants tied up in legal limbo indefinitely, spending their energies in the deposition room instead of the lab while the spark behind their start-up died out. By involving their rent-a-judge directly, they might be able to move things along. So they drove down to Palo Alto one day to meet with him, and during the meeting they suggested that he might like to come to the depositions himself. The case was front-page news; who wouldn't like to hear the story behind it? Judge Phelps accepted.

From that point on, discovery became less the standard pretrial grind and more like a trial itself. When the judge wasn't there, the depositions plodded along as they normally do, with hours spent marking documents (Was this Ashkin's memo? Was that Job's signature?) and asking questions in a random and often exploratory fashion, trying to pin down the witness, testing lines of questioning that might or might not prove fruitful. When the judge showed up, however, they suddenly pulled themselves together and started conducting themselves as if they were in a courtroom. The result was almost as if they'd started trying the case piecemeal, a few days at a time. They spent the better part of a week on Ashkin. The next week they spent two days grilling Sculley. After Thanksgiving, Brown and his team spent four days on Jobs at Brown & Bain's offices in Palo Alto, and the week after that they spent a couple of days on Page. Then there was a lull while Balabanian got ready for the second round, which was due to begin with Mike Markkula.

Talk of a settlement never entirely ended. The lawyers would make comments to each other in the hall outside the deposition room; Steve and Al would spend a few minutes talking. Then, on the day they were finishing up with Jobs, Judge Phelps said that he would be willing to hear Brown's motion for a preliminary injunction himself rather than sending it back to Judge Stone. After summing up the facts of the case to date in a way that conceded a clear advantage to neither side, he suggested that this particular lawsuit wasn't serving any useful purpose and ought to be resolved. Shortly afterwards, the conversations between the two sides became more serious. One day as Page was being deposed in Palo Alto, Brown invited Balabanian into his office and made a proposal. It wasn't something Balabanian could live with, but it did suggest movement—in particular, a willingness to believe that Next wasn't planning simply to market Big Mac or some other advanced Macintosh clone. Talks continued intensively after that, in meetings and in telephone conferences, with Steve and Al actively involved; by January they were faxing drafts of a settlement back and forth between Embarcadero Center and Palo Alto.

The basic terms of the agreement strongly resembled the terms they'd discussed in September, before the suit was filed. Steve agreed not to use any of Apple's trade secrets—the Macintosh firmware, the Macintosh disk-drive interface, several custom chips. Any computer Next built would have to have certain minimum performance standards to avoid competing with Apple products—a provision Steve and his colleagues thought would make a great marketing document, since it stated that Next couldn't build a computer that didn't perform significantly better than Apple's. Apple would have the right to inspect Next's prototype machine to make sure he was abiding by the agreement. There would be a restriction on his freedom to hire other people away from Apple. One of the last issues to be settled was whether Apple would drop the suit. Steve insisted that it be dropped; finally they agreed to have it dismissed without prejudice, leaving Apple free to file again if Next failed to live up to the bargain. Apple's board approved the terms, and the signing was set for Balabanian's office in the late afternoon on Friday, January 17, 1986—by coincidence, the final day of the AppleWorld Conference in San Francisco. And so, a couple of hours after John got onstage at the new symphony hall to set forth his ideas about the art of corporate self-actualization, Steve rode the elevator to the top floor of 3 Embarcadero Center to sign the slip of paper that would free him from the enterprise he'd fathered.

■ ■ ■

The others were waiting by the radio. They had a little transistor tuned to an all-news station so they'd hear the instant it got out on the wire services. The phone had already rung with the news. Bud had gone out for champagne. Susan was coming in from L.A. on a 6:30 flight. Andy Cunningham was on the phone to reporters, giving them the news. They'd all gathered on the second floor of Next's new offices, around Steve's desk. The first floor was still a construction zone, but the upstairs office cubicles were nearly finished—that is, the carpet was laid and the walls were up and painted white. The modular Herman Miller office systems that were supposed to divide their work areas hadn't arrived yet, so the second floor was still one big bullpen. The windows looked out across palomino hills studded with live oaks and horses and the million-dollar ranch homes of Los

Altos Hills. Across the road, the Stars and Stripes and the Bear Flag of the California Republic flew above a low-slung Hewlett-Packard office building nestled into the hillside. It was dusk.

Steve swooped in off 280 and into a parking space by the front door. He bounded past the piles of two-by-fours and sheetrock and up the steps to the bullpen just as Bud was popping the cork. They all cheered and guzzled champagne and jumped up and down. Someone got on the phone and ordered dinner from Fuki Sushi, the little Japanese place on El Camino. They all pulled their chairs around Steve's desk and started talking about press strategy. Apple was trying to play the news as "Next Settles"; they preferred to describe it as "Apple Drops Suit." But whatever the message, they were prepared to celebrate.

It would have been better, of course, if the lawsuit had never happened. It would have been better if lots of things had never happened: the bungled exit, the Siberian exile, the break with John, the China ploy, the failure—but you could keep adding to that list for a long time. Something had been torn out of them, just as they'd been torn out of Apple. Neither one was better off for it.

At least with Next they had a way of reliving the Macintosh experience. The bond that had developed on Bandley Drive, the sense that they were a tiny band bent on achieving their absolute best, guided by a charismatic leader who'd chosen *them* to realize his dream—that yielded a high few people in the conventional world of freeways and office parks and pinstripes seemed to know. That was why they'd joined Steve in September, why they'd stepped off the cliff—for the chance to do it again, to crash and burn perhaps, but also to change the world.

As for Steve—well, if the new Apple was like Hewlett-Packard, a place where you turned a crank and the products came out, that meant it just stood for mediocrity. When was the last time an insanely great product had come out of Hewlett-Packard? He'd wanted Apple to be a place where somebody who wanted to do something great in the world could do it, but nobody there seemed to talk about doing anything great anymore. Mediocrity was fine, as long as it was on schedule. It made for such an unsatisfying end to what had once been such a wonderful story—his own. But he tried to tell himself it was okay. Life goes on; you start over and build something new.

Steve's desk, like all the others in the bullpen, was a handsome piece of burled maple, hand-crafted by a Redwood City cabinet maker. They'd decided on desks here at Next, not work tables as they'd had at Apple, not to be formal or stuffy but because they wanted to be able to sit on them. The desks were large—six feet long—and blond and sleek. Like the art photographs on the walls and the innovative health-insurance plan, the desks were one ingredient in the making of the perfect enterprise. Even in the swirl of laughter and excitement that accompanied their triumph, however, it was hard not to notice something missing.

It was a small thing, really, just a shadow on Steve's Macintosh. At the lower-left-hand corner of the machine, where the rainbow-hued Apple logo should have been, was a small, jagged hole. In a fit of fury and despair the logo had been gouged out, like a heart that wouldn't stop beating. An angry scar had been left in the beige plastic case, and nothing could ever make it perfect again.

AUTHOR'S NOTE

The idea for this book originated with Amanda Vaill, my editor at Viking, who rang me up in September 1985, when Steve Jobs was in the news for his stormy exit from Apple to form Next. From the beginning, what intrigued me most about Apple was not the business or the technology but the fact that it seemed to constitute a social movement. After a few months of research, I decided it would be most revealing to focus on the period from January 1983 to January 1986—that is, from a few months before John Sculley's arrival at Apple to a few months after Steve Jobs's departure. It was already clear that the new Apple was quite different from the old; my job was to document the transition. And my ambition was not just to describe the soap-opera aspects of what had happened but to put it in social and historical context—in short, to make sense of it, to divine the pattern beneath the seeming randomness of events.

I began work in December 1985, shortly after most of the events in the book took place. The only incident I witnessed directly was the January 1986 AppleWorld Conference—the subject of the prologue. The rest of my account is based primarily on taped interviews with more than a hundred people, including current and former executives of Apple and IBM; Apple engineers and marketing people; employees and executives at such allied enterprises as Chiat/Day, Regis McKenna, and Lotus Development; alumni of Xerox PARC and of SRI's Augmentation Research Center; early associates of Steven Jobs and Stephen Wozniak; Wall Street analysts; and a number of reporters, lawyers, consultants, and other individuals whose paths crossed Apple's at critical moments. Both Sculley and Jobs eventually agreed to be interviewed, as did Steve Wozniak. Of the three founders, only Mike Markkula declined to cooperate.

Apple itself, after a few months of friendly hesitation, decided that its energies would better be directed at other projects, such as Sculley's autobiography, which was then in progress. This had the twin effect of denying me corporate assistance and of sparing me a public-relations attempt. Since most of the key people in the story had already left Apple, and many still there were willing to help me regardless, I had no lack of sources. Among those I interviewed were most of the executive staff members named in the book, most of Jobs's staff members in the Macintosh division, most of the central figures in the Apple II division, and the founders of Next. Many responded to detailed questioning in repeated sessions that lasted from one to four hours each; several used personal journals and appointment calendars to refresh their memories. Some made available other materials—interoffice memos, sales forecasts, marketing plans, product introduction plans, promotional brochures, video-tapes, and the like—which corroborated and expanded upon their recollections.

I lived in Silicon Valley from January through October 1986. During that period, as I drove the freeways and back roads from San Rafael to Santa Cruz, going to office parks, modest ranch-style homes, hillside estates, theme bars, and more-or-less excellent restaurants, I was struck by the number of people who told me that working at Apple had been the high point of their lives—not their careers, but their lives. The zeal they felt for Apple seemed to spill over into their dealings with me. They'd been present for something special, and they wanted it remembered. Because much of the material is sensitive and the web of personal relationships and conflicting loyalties is so complex, most did not wish their names to be used. I'll have to thank them all collectively: Without their help, this book could never have been written.

After returning to New York I began the time-consuming effort of transforming the information I'd accumulated into a coherent narrative. Because human memory is so inexact, and because my own imaginative capacities are not infallible, I thought it best to avoid the appearance of dialogue. Anything that appears in quotes was either recorded on the spot or (in the case of certain brief outbursts) reliably recalled by witnesses. While my sources had radically differing opinions about the people and events in the story, in most cases they managed to concur on the facts. In the rare instances when they didn't, I was forced to choose the version that seemed most likely, based on corroborating accounts when available and on my own knowledge of the personalities involved. Like any other non-fiction work, then, this book is necessarily an asymptotic approximation of what actually happened.

Apple Computer and the people who built it have been chronicled extensively over the past ten years, and this account benefits from those that preceded it. Steven Levy's *Hackers* offers a particularly vivid and insightful portrait of the hobbyist milieu from which Apple emerged. *Fire in the Valley,* by Paul Freiberger and Michael Swaine, focuses on the Homebrew Computer Club members who created the personal-computer industry. Howard Rheingold's *Tools for Thought* offers a fascinating look at the researchers who pursued the ARPA dream. *The Little Kingdom,* by Michael Moritz, carries the Apple story to approximately the point at which my narrative starts. Doug Garr's *Woz* and Jeffrey Young's *Steve Jobs* focus on the co-founders of Apple. *Odyssey,* by John Sculley with John Byrne, details Sculley's early life and describes events at Apple from his perspective, while *The Other Guy Blinked,* by Roger Enrico and Jesse Kornbluth, offers an inside look at life at PepsiCo by the man who succeeded him there. And in *The Third Apple,* Jean-Louis Gassée offers his own meditation on the personal-computer revolution.

It would be difficult to write about entrepreneurship in the 1980s without reference to *The Spirit of Enterprise,* the gospel according to George Gilder. In a more practical vein there is *In Search of Excellence,* the famed management guide by Thomas Peters and Robert Waterman, Jr. Rober Lacey's *Ford* retells the story of an earlier visionary entrepreneur whose life has long fascinated Jobs. David Halberstam's *The Powers That Be* is a most informative guide to the American media establishment. I also consulted several books about other companies in the information industry: *The Computer Establishment,* by Katherine Fishman; *IBM,* by Robert Sobel; *The IBM Way,* by Buck Rodgers; *The Biggest Company on Earth,* by Sonny Kleinfeld; and *Three Degrees Above Zero,* by Jeremy Bernstein. And I benefitted as well from Joel Shurkin's *Engines of the Mind,* a history of the computer, and from *Turing's Man,* by the classicist J. David Bolter, which offers the most profound analysis I've yet encountered of the computer's role in human society.

As a source both of inspiration and of factual material, *Americans and the California Dream* and *Inventing the Dream,* the first two volumes of a projected three-volume history of California by Kevin Starr, were invaluable to me. Charles Wollenberg's *Golden Gate Metropolis* tells much about the development of the San Francisco Bay Area; *The WPA Guide to California* presents it as it was fifty years ago. Dirk Hansen's *The New Alchemists* and Gene Bylinsky's lavishly illustrated *High Tech* show Silicon Valley and how it got that way; *The Big Score,* by Michael Malone, and *Silicon Valley Fever,* by Everett Rogers and Judith Larsen, are full of insights about the people who make it hum. Two Stanford University publications, *The Founders & the Architects* and *Stanford from the Beginning,* provide many details about Leland Stanford and the university he founded. *Cupertino Chronicle* and *Historias,* both published by the California History Center at De Anza College, offer fascinating accounts of the early years of Cupertino and the Santa Clara Valley. I'm particularly indebted to James Williams and the staff of the California History Center for helping me get a picture of life in the Valley before the electronics industry.

Personal computers in general and Apple in particular have been extensively covered in the news media, and I've made use of a wealth of newspaper and magazine articles to augment my own reporting. Among the publications I consulted were *The New York Times, The Wall Street Journal,* the *San Jose Mercury-News,* the *San Francisco Chronicle,* the *San Francisco Examiner,* the *Los Angeles Times, The Washington Post,* and *The Boston Globe; Newsweek, Time, Esquire, Rolling Stone, Playboy,* and *Ms.; Business Week, Forbes, Fortune,* and *Inc.; Byte, Datamation, InfoWorld, MacWorld, Personal Computing, Popular Computing,* and *Softalk;* the trade journals *Electronics News, Computer Retail News, Computer + Software News, MIS Week, MicroMarket World,* and *Advertising Age;* and the industry newsletters *RELease 1.0, Technologic Computer Letter,* and *California Technology Stock Letter.* Two Harvard Business School case studies, "Donna Dubinsky and Apple Computer, Inc." and "Debi Coleman and Apple Computer, Inc.," shed light on the distribution issue that became a major point of contention in early 1985. Fred Danzig of *Advertising Age* quite generously made its library available to me. Many other journalists gave freely of their time and suggestions, among them Pete Carey, Katherine Hafner, John Markoff, Michael Murphy, Randall Rothenberg, Richard Shaffer, and Deborah Wise. I'm particularly indebted to Steven Levy, who shared with me the transcript of his early 1984 interview with Steve Jobs; together with my own unpublished interview with Steve Wozniak from the same period, it provided a window that would otherwise have been unavailable.

Aside from my editor, a great many other people at Viking have worked to ensure that this would be a well-published book, among them Cynthia Achar, Kate Griggs, Victoria Meyer, Neil Stuart, Anne Tergesen, and Katharine Walker. My agent, Mary Evans of the Virginia Barber Agency, provided regular support and advice; like Ginger Barber herself, she went out of her way to aid a project she believed in. Bonnie Stall helped in innumerable ways, as did Peter Passell; I'm deeply grateful to both. Sean Corcoran, David Hirshey, Steve and Marian Holtzman, Leonard Koren, Allan Lundell, Lynda and Area Maderas, Joan Peters, Everett Phiele, Ellen Rashbaum, John Wallace, and Margaret Young all made important contributions at crucial moments. And Beth Rashbaum had the faith to see a long project through; without her, I wouldn't have been able to go on.

New York, N.Y.
September 1988

INDEX